P9-CSG-937

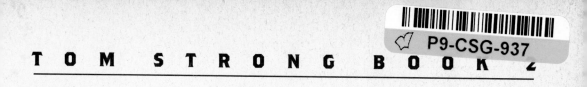

CHRIS SPROUSE &
JOSE VILLARRUBIA

JIM LEE
Editorial Director

JOHN NEE
VP and General Manager

SCOTT DUNBIER
Group Editor

ERIC DESANTIS
JEFF MARIOTTE
Assistant Editors

TOM STRONG BOOK 2: Published by America's Best Comics, LLC. Cover, design pages and compilation © 2002 America's Best Comics, LLC. Tom Strong and all related characters and elements are trademarks of America's Best Comics. All Rights Reserved. Originally published in single magazine form as TOM STRONG, #8-14. Copyright © 2000, 2001 America's Best Comics, LLC. Editorial Offices: 888 Prospect St., Suite 240, La Jolla, CA 92037. Any similarities to persons living or dead is purely coincidental. PRINTED IN CANADA. FIRST PRINTING. ISBN 1-56389874-8

TOM STRONG

COLLECTED EDITION
BOOK 2

ALAN MOORE
writer

CHRIS SPROUSE
penciller

ALAN GORDON
inker

ADDITIONAL ART BY

ALAN WEISS   **PAUL CHADWICK**   **GARY GIANNI**   **RUSS HEATH**

KYLE BAKER   **PETE POPLASKI**   **HILARY BARTA**

MATT HOLLINGSWORTH
MIKE GARCIA
WILDSTORM FX
DAVID BARON
coloring

TODD KLEIN
lettering, logos and design

TOM STRONG created by
Alan Moore & Chris Sprouse

AMERICA'S BEST COMICS

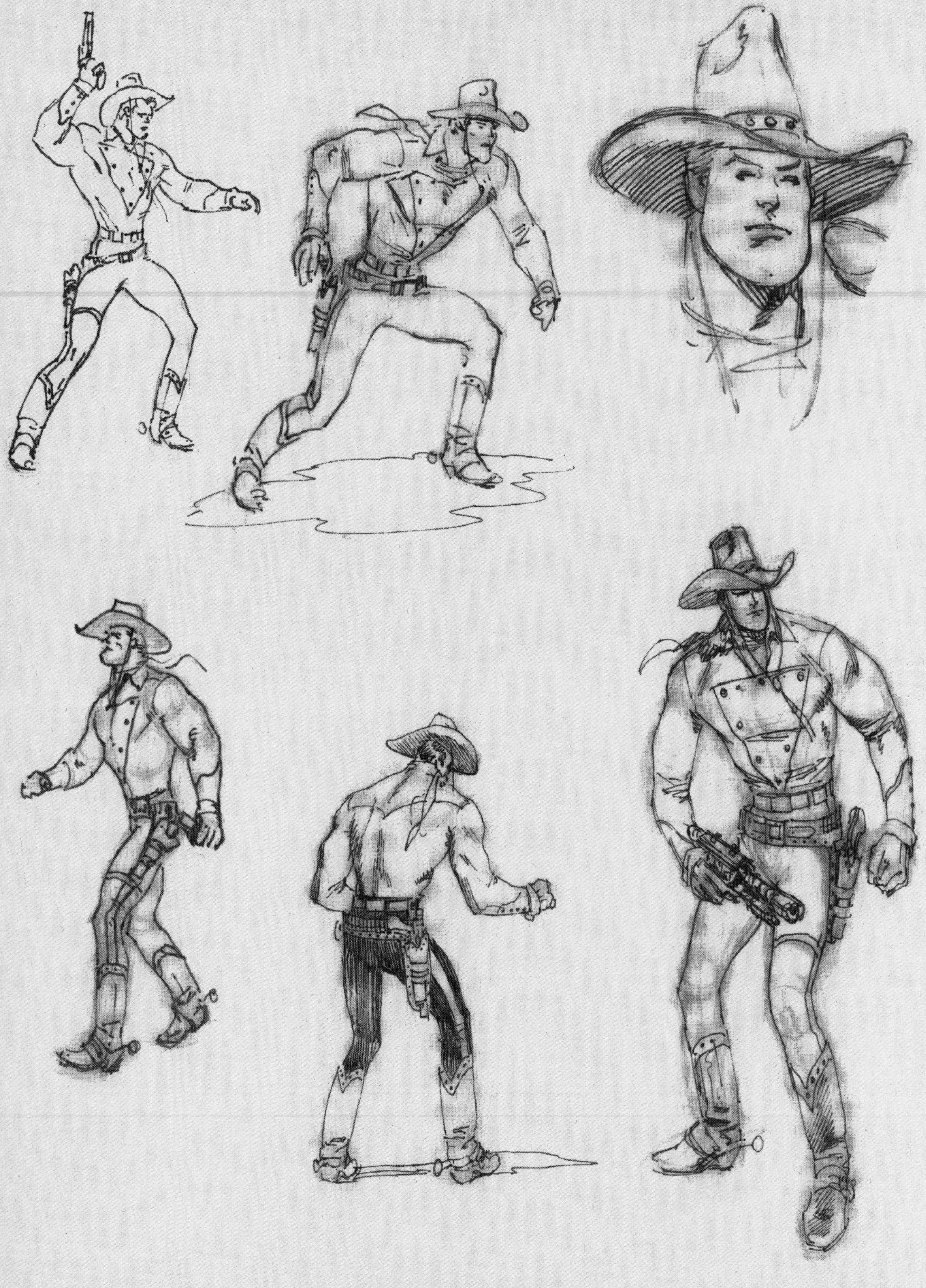

Character sketches
by ALAN WEISS

CHAPTER ONE

In which Tom and Solomon ride into trouble,
Timmy Turbo learns lessons the hard way,
and Tesla ventures too close to the fire.

Cover art:
Alan Weiss

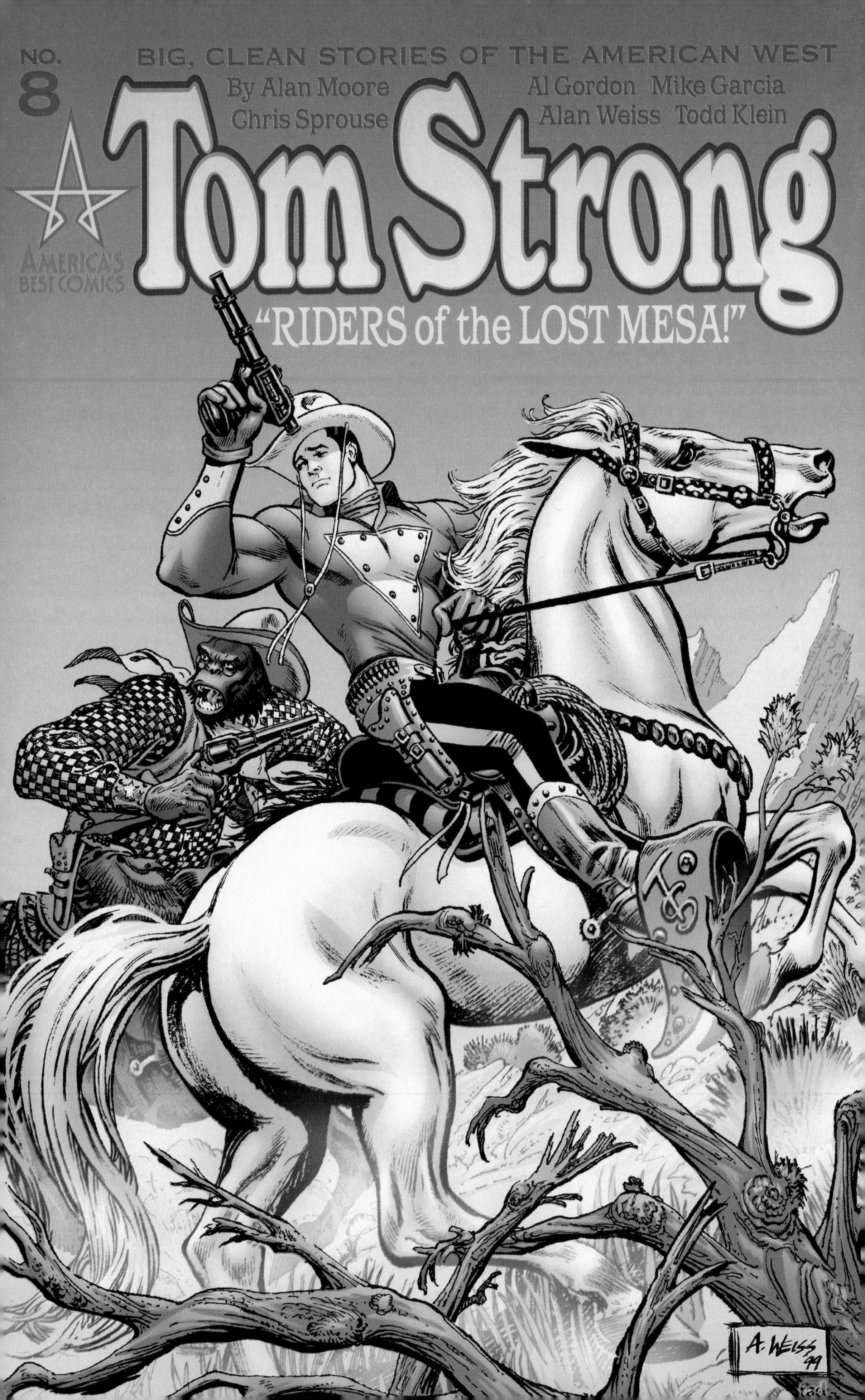

NO. 8
BIG, CLEAN STORIES OF THE AMERICAN WEST
By Alan Moore
Chris Sprouse
Al Gordon
Mike Garcia
Alan Weiss
Todd Klein
Tom Strong
AMERICA'S BEST COMICS
"RIDERS of the LOST MESA!"
A. WEISS 99

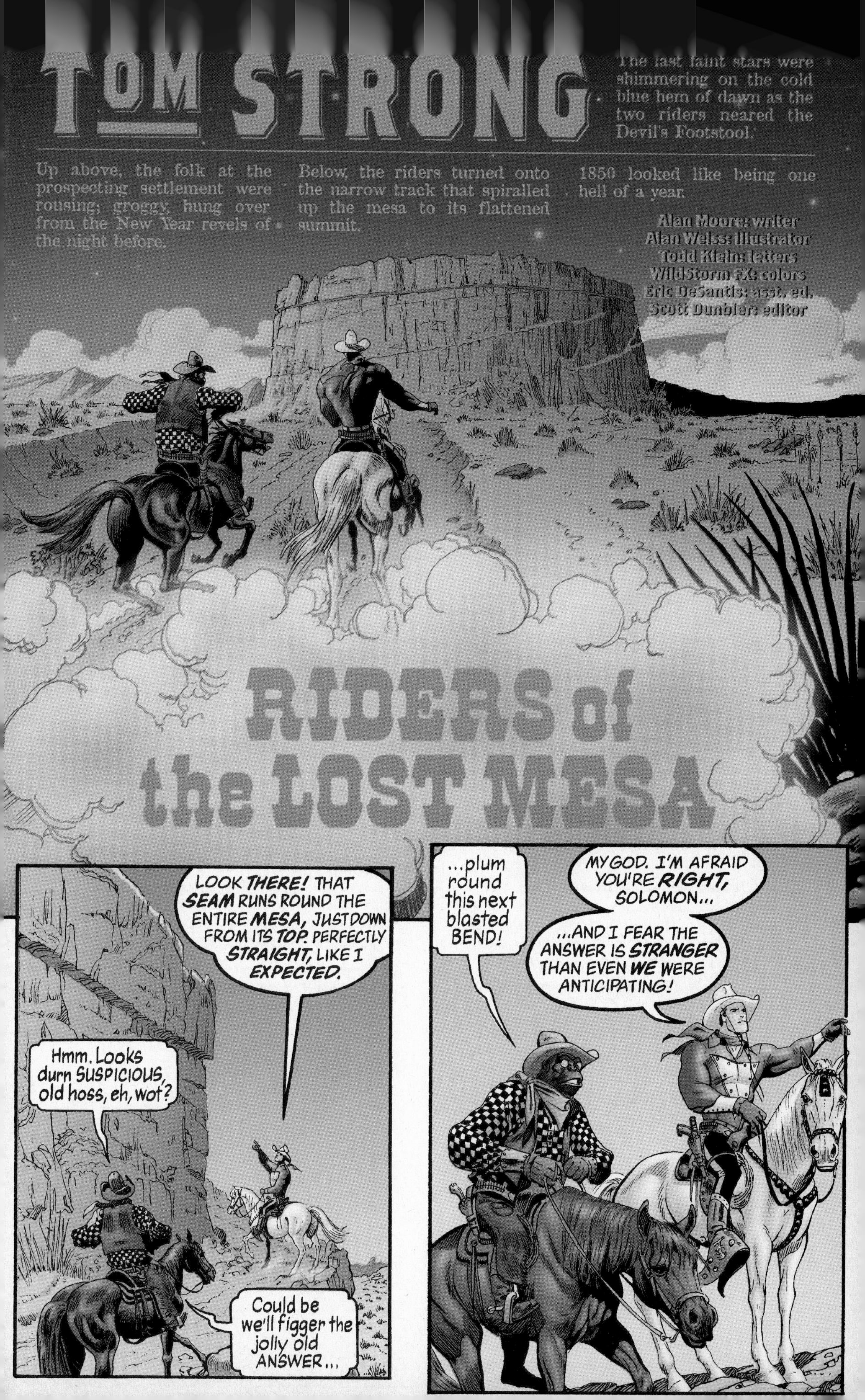
TOM STRONG
The last faint stars were shimmering on the cold blue hem of dawn as the two riders neared the Devil's Footstool.
Up above, the folk at the prospecting settlement were rousing; groggy, hung over from the New Year revels of the night before.
Below, the riders turned onto the narrow track that spiralled up the mesa to its flattened summit.
1850 looked like being one hell of a year.
Alan Moore: writer
Alan Weiss: illustrator
Todd Klein: letters
WildStorm FX: colors
Eric DeSantis: asst. ed.
Scott Dunbier: editor
RIDERS of the LOST MESA
LOOK THERE! THAT SEAM RUNS ROUND THE ENTIRE MESA, JUST DOWN FROM ITS TOP. PERFECTLY STRAIGHT, LIKE I EXPECTED.
Hmm. Looks durn SUSPICIOUS, old hoss, eh, wot?
Could be we'll figger the jolly old ANSWER...
...plum round this next blasted BEND!
MY GOD. I'M AFRAID YOU'RE RIGHT, SOLOMON...
...AND I FEAR THE ANSWER IS STRANGER THAN EVEN WE WERE ANTICIPATING!

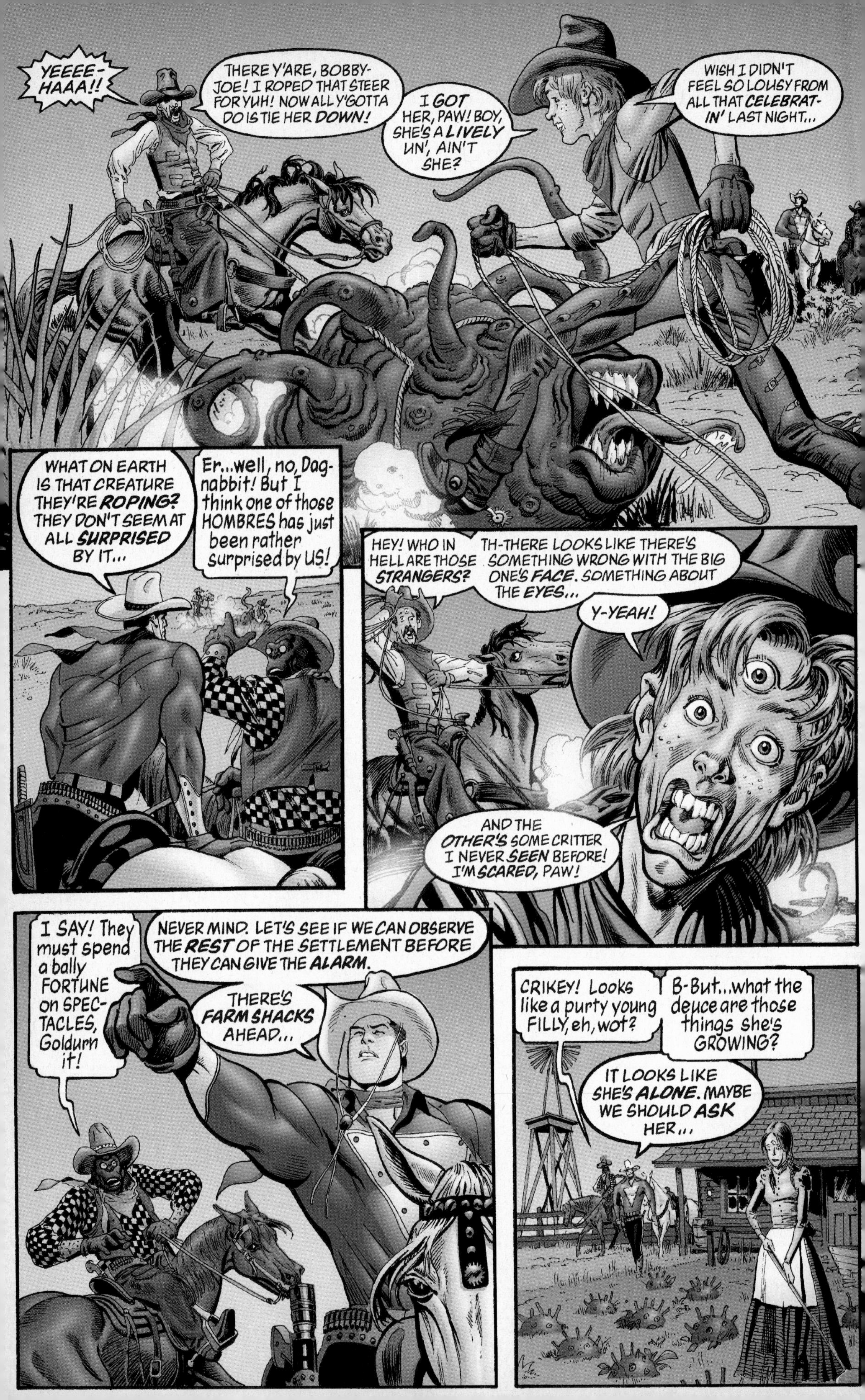
YEEEE-HAAA!!
THERE Y'ARE, BOBBY-JOE! I ROPED THAT STEER FOR YUH! NOW ALL Y'GOTTA DO IS TIE HER DOWN!
I GOT HER, PAW! BOY, SHE'S A LIVELY UN', AIN'T SHE?
WISH I DIDN'T FEEL SO LOUSY FROM ALL THAT CELEBRAT-IN' LAST NIGHT...
WHAT ON EARTH IS THAT CREATURE THEY'RE ROPING? THEY DON'T SEEM AT ALL SURPRISED BY IT...
Er...well, no, Dag-nabbit! But I think one of those HOMBRES has just been rather surprised by US!
HEY! WHO IN HELL ARE THOSE STRANGERS?
TH-THERE LOOKS LIKE THERE'S SOMETHING WRONG WITH THE BIG ONE'S FACE. SOMETHING ABOUT THE EYES...
Y-YEAH!
AND THE OTHER'S SOME CRITTER I NEVER SEEN BEFORE! I'M SCARED, PAW!
I SAY! They must spend a bally FORTUNE on SPEC-TACLES, Goldurn it!
NEVER MIND. LET'S SEE IF WE CAN OBSERVE THE REST OF THE SETTLEMENT BEFORE THEY CAN GIVE THE ALARM.
THERE'S FARM SHACKS AHEAD...
CRIKEY! Looks like a purty young FILLY, eh, wot?
B-But...what the deuce are those things she's GROWING?
IT LOOKS LIKE SHE'S ALONE. MAYBE WE SHOULD ASK HER...

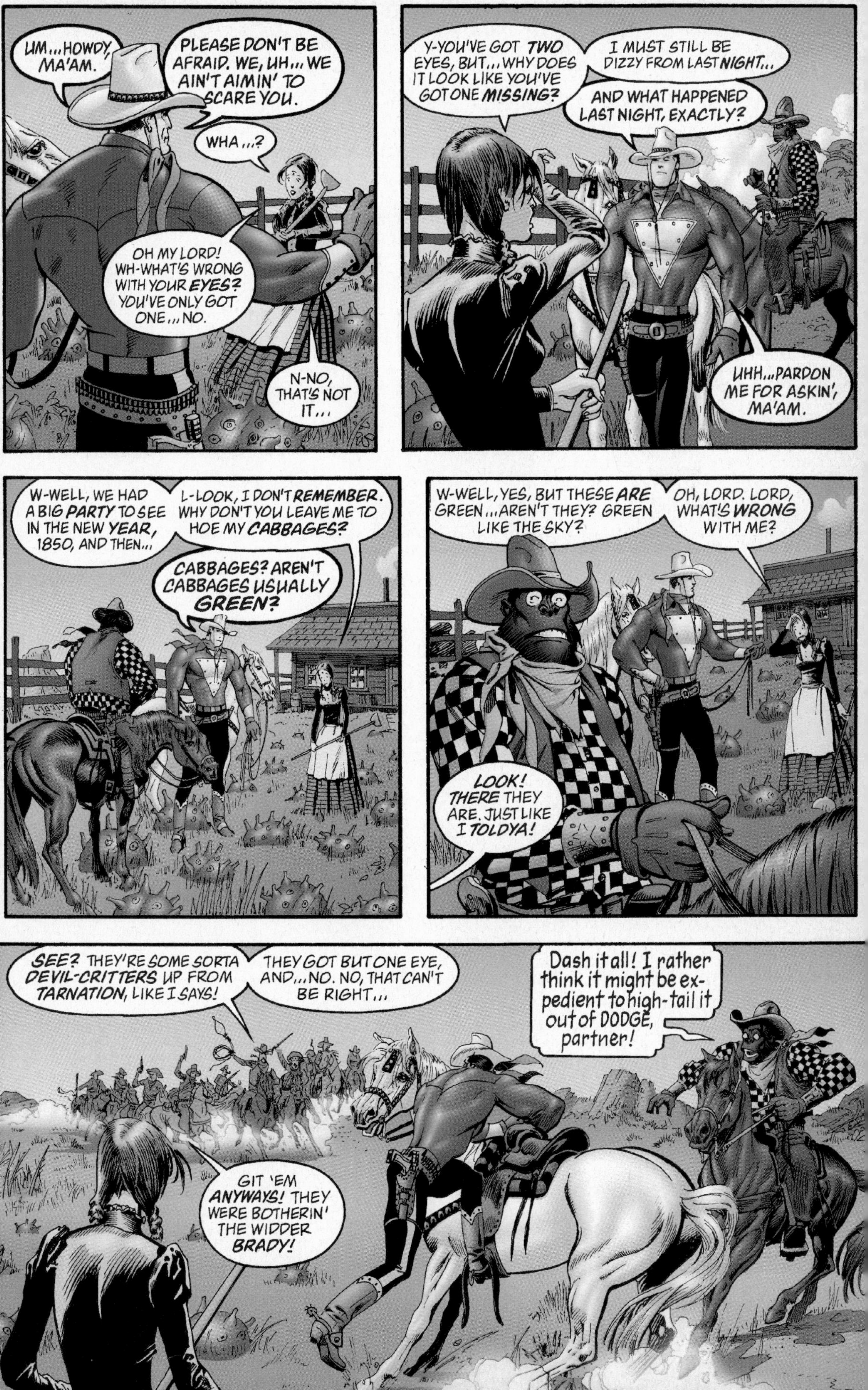
UM... HOWDY, MA'AM.
PLEASE DON'T BE AFRAID. WE, UH... WE AIN'T AIMIN' TO SCARE YOU.
WHA...?
OH MY LORD! WH-WHAT'S WRONG WITH YOUR EYES? YOU'VE ONLY GOT ONE... NO.
N-NO, THAT'S NOT IT...
Y-YOU'VE GOT TWO EYES, BUT... WHY DOES IT LOOK LIKE YOU'VE GOT ONE MISSING?
I MUST STILL BE DIZZY FROM LAST NIGHT...
AND WHAT HAPPENED LAST NIGHT, EXACTLY?
UHH... PARDON ME FOR ASKIN', MA'AM.
W-WELL, WE HAD A BIG PARTY TO SEE IN THE NEW YEAR, 1850, AND THEN...
L-LOOK, I DON'T REMEMBER. WHY DON'T YOU LEAVE ME TO HOE MY CABBAGES?
CABBAGES? AREN'T CABBAGES USUALLY GREEN?
W-WELL, YES, BUT THESE ARE GREEN... AREN'T THEY? GREEN LIKE THE SKY?
OH, LORD. LORD, WHAT'S WRONG WITH ME?
LOOK! THERE THEY ARE. JUST LIKE I TOLDYA!
SEE? THEY'RE SOME SORTA DEVIL-CRITTERS UP FROM TARNATION, LIKE I SAYS!
THEY GOT BUT ONE EYE, AND... NO. NO, THAT CAN'T BE RIGHT...
Dash it all! I rather think it might be expedient to high-tail it out of DODGE, partner!
GIT 'EM ANYWAYS! THEY WERE BOTHERIN' THE WIDDER BRADY!

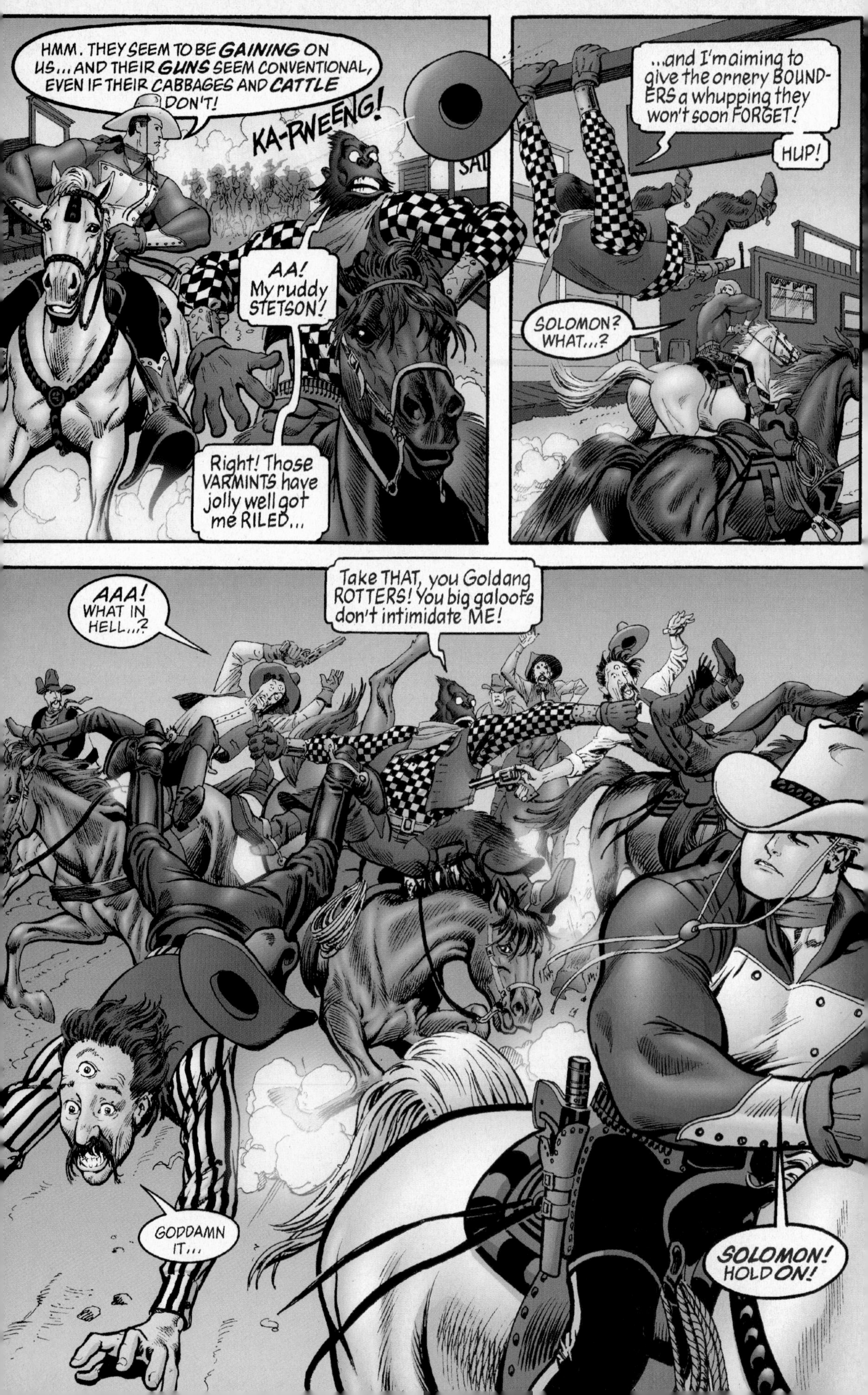
HMM. THEY SEEM TO BE GAINING ON US... AND THEIR GUNS SEEM CONVENTIONAL, EVEN IF THEIR CABBAGES AND CATTLE DON'T!
KA-RWEENG!
AA! My ruddy STETSON!
Right! Those VARMINTS have jolly well got me RILED...
...and I'm aiming to give the ornery BOUNDERS a whupping they won't soon FORGET!
HUP!
SOLOMON? WHAT...?
AAA! WHAT IN HELL...?
Take THAT, you Goldang ROTTERS! You big galoofs don't intimidate ME!
GODDAMN IT...
SOLOMON! HOLD ON!

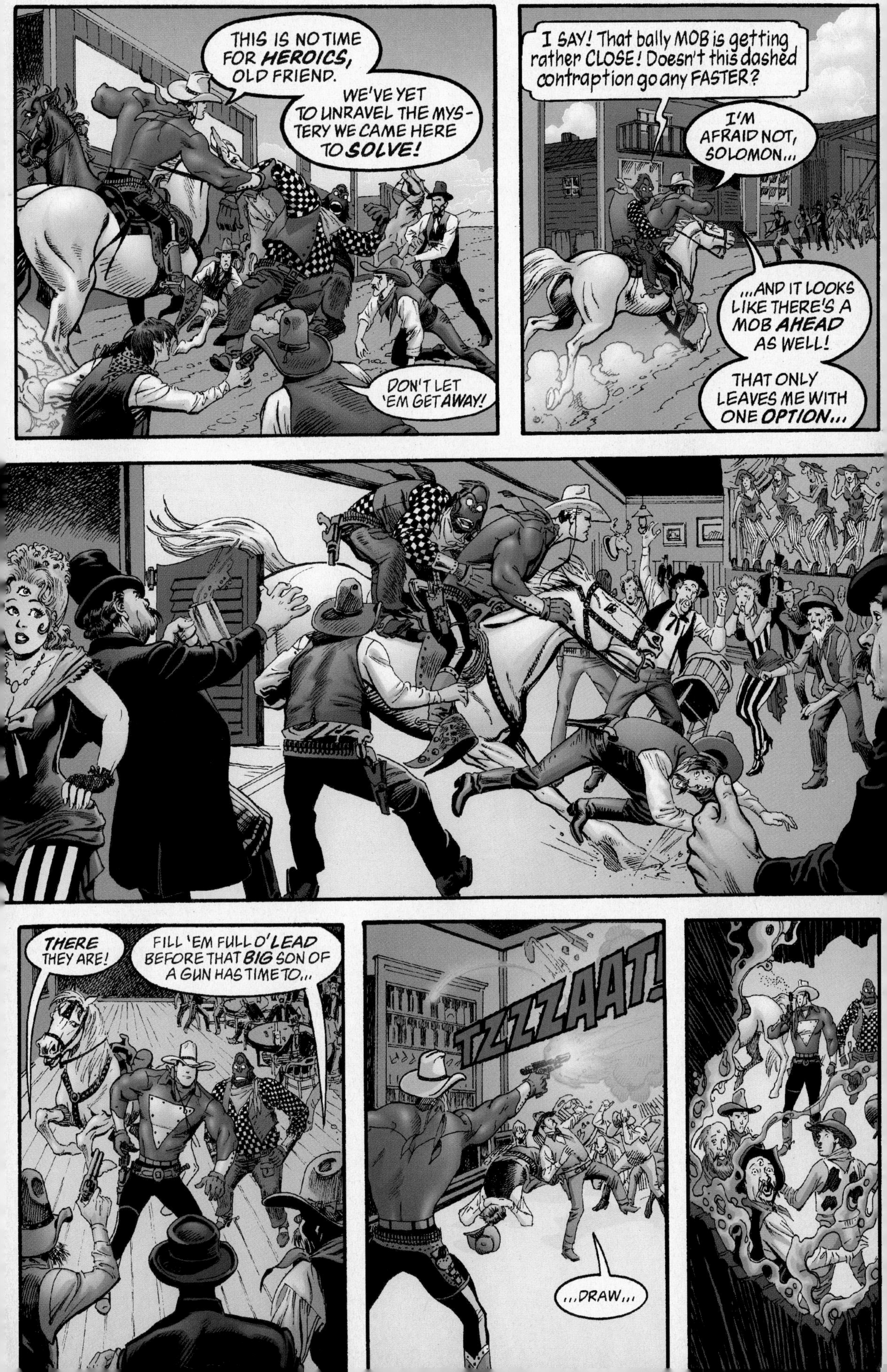

THIS IS NO TIME FOR HEROICS, OLD FRIEND.
WE'VE YET TO UNRAVEL THE MYSTERY WE CAME HERE TO SOLVE!
DON'T LET 'EM GET AWAY!
I SAY! That bally MOB is getting rather CLOSE! Doesn't this dashed contraption go any FASTER?
I'M AFRAID NOT, SOLOMON...
...AND IT LOOKS LIKE THERE'S A MOB AHEAD AS WELL!
THAT ONLY LEAVES ME WITH ONE OPTION...
THERE THEY ARE!
FILL 'EM FULL O' LEAD BEFORE THAT BIG SON OF A GUN HAS TIME TO...
TZZZAAT!
...DRAW...

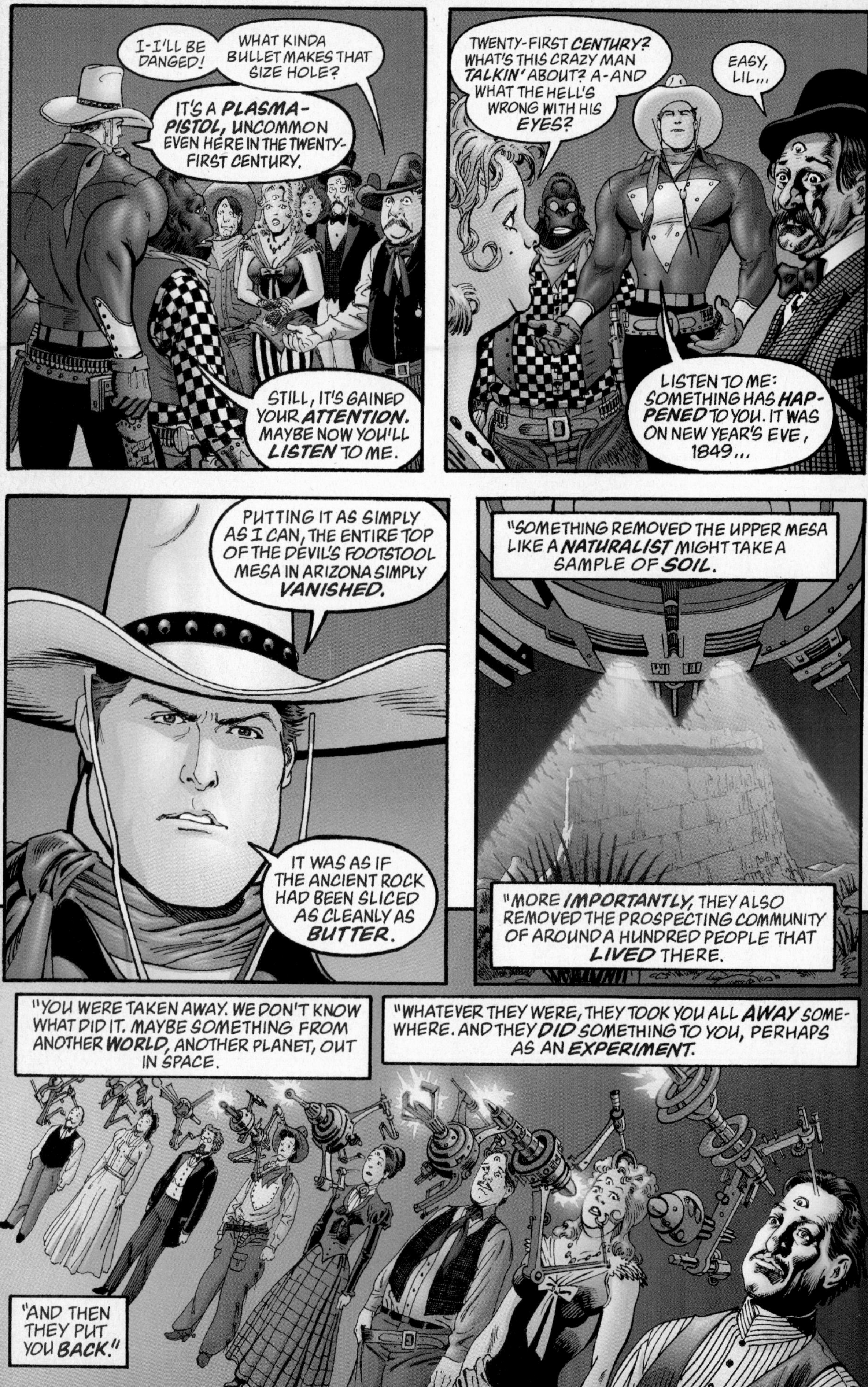
I-I'LL BE DANGED!
WHAT KINDA BULLET MAKES THAT SIZE HOLE?
IT'S A PLASMA-PISTOL, UNCOMMON EVEN HERE IN THE TWENTY-FIRST CENTURY.
STILL, IT'S GAINED YOUR ATTENTION. MAYBE NOW YOU'LL LISTEN TO ME.
TWENTY-FIRST CENTURY? WHAT'S THIS CRAZY MAN TALKIN' ABOUT? A-AND WHAT THE HELL'S WRONG WITH HIS EYES?
EASY, LIL...
LISTEN TO ME: SOMETHING HAS HAPPENED TO YOU. IT WAS ON NEW YEAR'S EVE, 1849...
PUTTING IT AS SIMPLY AS I CAN, THE ENTIRE TOP OF THE DEVIL'S FOOTSTOOL MESA IN ARIZONA SIMPLY VANISHED.
IT WAS AS IF THE ANCIENT ROCK HAD BEEN SLICED AS CLEANLY AS BUTTER.
"SOMETHING REMOVED THE UPPER MESA LIKE A NATURALIST MIGHT TAKE A SAMPLE OF SOIL.
"MORE IMPORTANTLY, THEY ALSO REMOVED THE PROSPECTING COMMUNITY OF AROUND A HUNDRED PEOPLE THAT LIVED THERE.
"YOU WERE TAKEN AWAY. WE DON'T KNOW WHAT DID IT. MAYBE SOMETHING FROM ANOTHER WORLD, ANOTHER PLANET, OUT IN SPACE.
"WHATEVER THEY WERE, THEY TOOK YOU ALL AWAY SOMEWHERE. AND THEY DID SOMETHING TO YOU, PERHAPS AS AN EXPERIMENT.
"AND THEN THEY PUT YOU BACK."

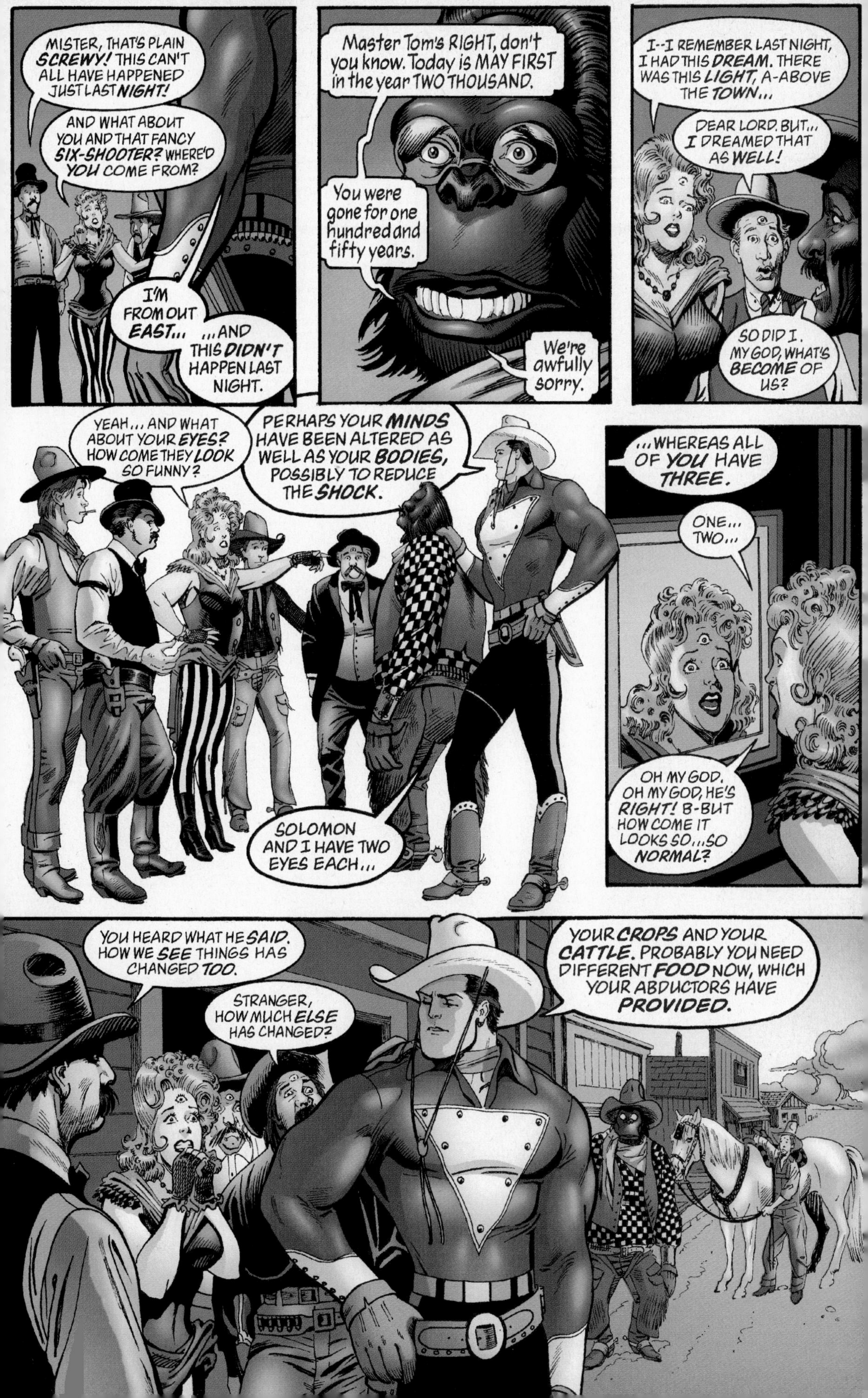

MISTER, THAT'S PLAIN SCREWY! THIS CAN'T ALL HAVE HAPPENED JUST LAST NIGHT!
AND WHAT ABOUT YOU AND THAT FANCY SIX-SHOOTER? WHERE'D YOU COME FROM?
I'M FROM OUT EAST...
...AND THIS DIDN'T HAPPEN LAST NIGHT.
Master Tom's RIGHT, don't you know. Today is MAY FIRST in the year TWO THOUSAND.
You were gone for one hundred and fifty years.
We're awfully sorry.
I--I REMEMBER LAST NIGHT, I HAD THIS DREAM. THERE WAS THIS LIGHT, A-ABOVE THE TOWN...
DEAR LORD. BUT... I DREAMED THAT AS WELL!
SO DID I. MY GOD, WHAT'S BECOME OF US?
YEAH... AND WHAT ABOUT YOUR EYES? HOW COME THEY LOOK SO FUNNY?
PERHAPS YOUR MINDS HAVE BEEN ALTERED AS WELL AS YOUR BODIES, POSSIBLY TO REDUCE THE SHOCK.
SOLOMON AND I HAVE TWO EYES EACH...
...WHEREAS ALL OF YOU HAVE THREE.
ONE... TWO...
OH MY GOD. OH MY GOD, HE'S RIGHT! B-BUT HOW COME IT LOOKS SO... SO NORMAL?
YOU HEARD WHAT HE SAID. HOW WE SEE THINGS HAS CHANGED TOO.
STRANGER, HOW MUCH ELSE HAS CHANGED?
YOUR CROPS AND YOUR CATTLE. PROBABLY YOU NEED DIFFERENT FOOD NOW, WHICH YOUR ABDUCTORS HAVE PROVIDED.

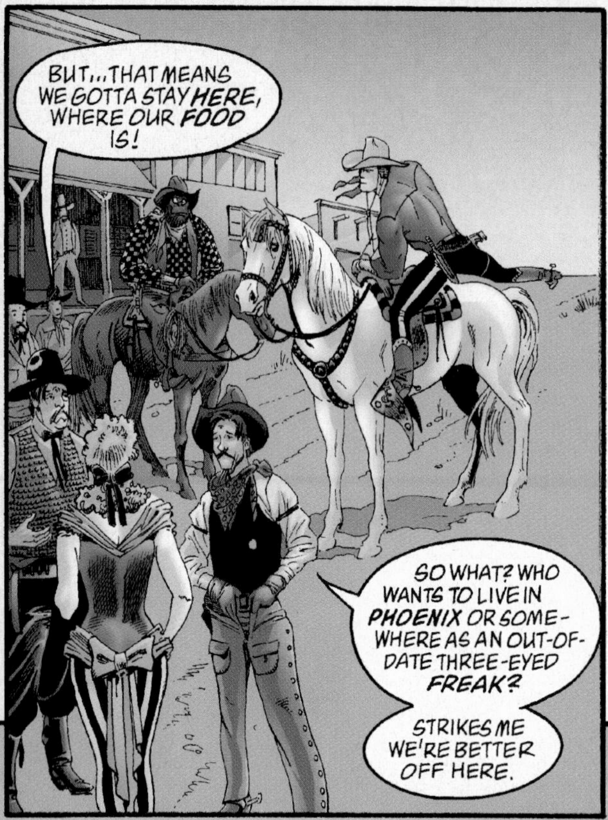
BUT... THAT MEANS WE GOTTA STAY HERE, WHERE OUR FOOD IS!
SO WHAT? WHO WANTS TO LIVE IN PHOENIX OR SOMEWHERE AS AN OUT-OF-DATE THREE-EYED FREAK?
STRIKES ME WE'RE BETTER OFF HERE.

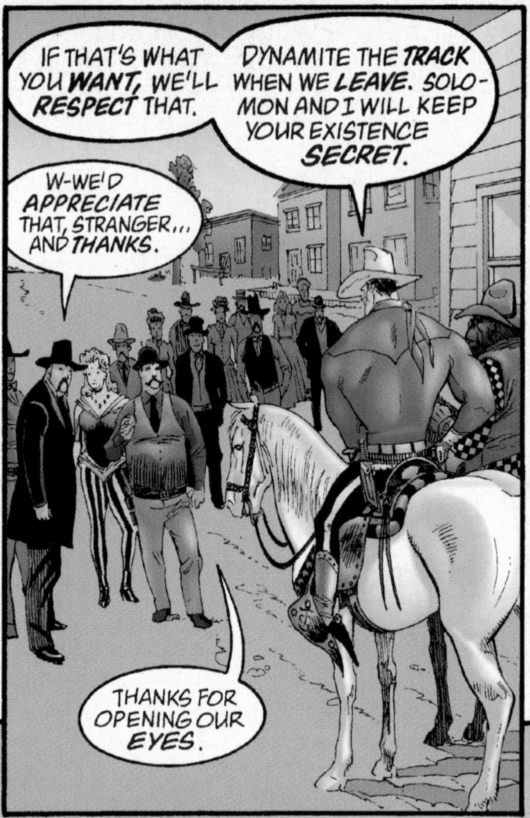
IF THAT'S WHAT YOU WANT, WE'LL RESPECT THAT.
DYNAMITE THE TRACK WHEN WE LEAVE. SOLOMON AND I WILL KEEP YOUR EXISTENCE SECRET.
W-WE'D APPRECIATE THAT, STRANGER... AND THANKS.
THANKS FOR OPENING OUR EYES.

The sun was at its highest point, on the top rung of the celestial mud-chute leading down to afternoon and night.

The dull boom of the dynamite behind them echoed off towards the far rim of the sky's inverted blue glass bowl.

Above, the townsfolk talked, then shrugged, then got on with their labors.

There was work that needed to be done. In their planted rows the crops writhed, squealing, in need of attention.

1850 looked like being one hell of a year.

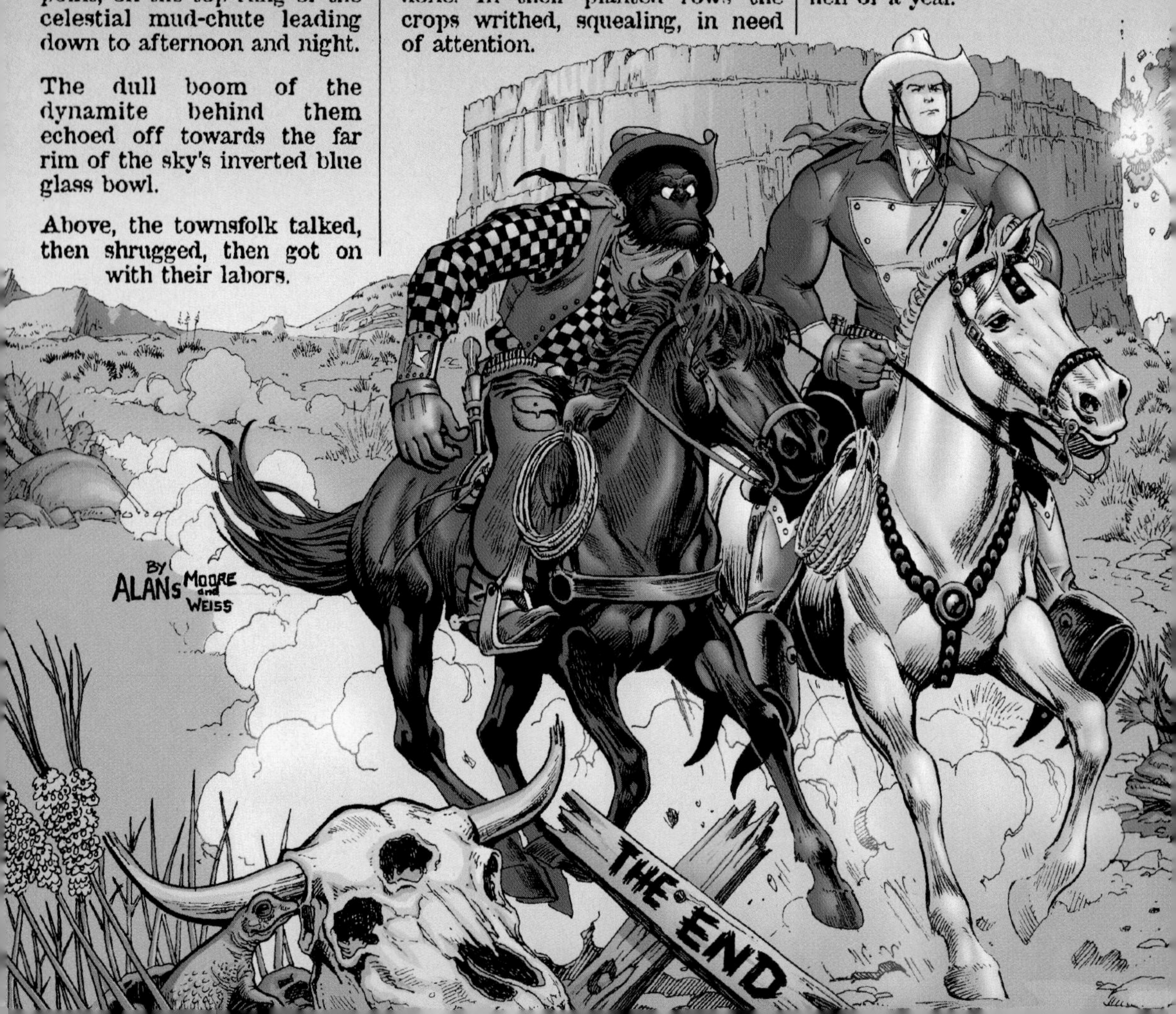
BY ALANs MOORE and WEISS
THE END

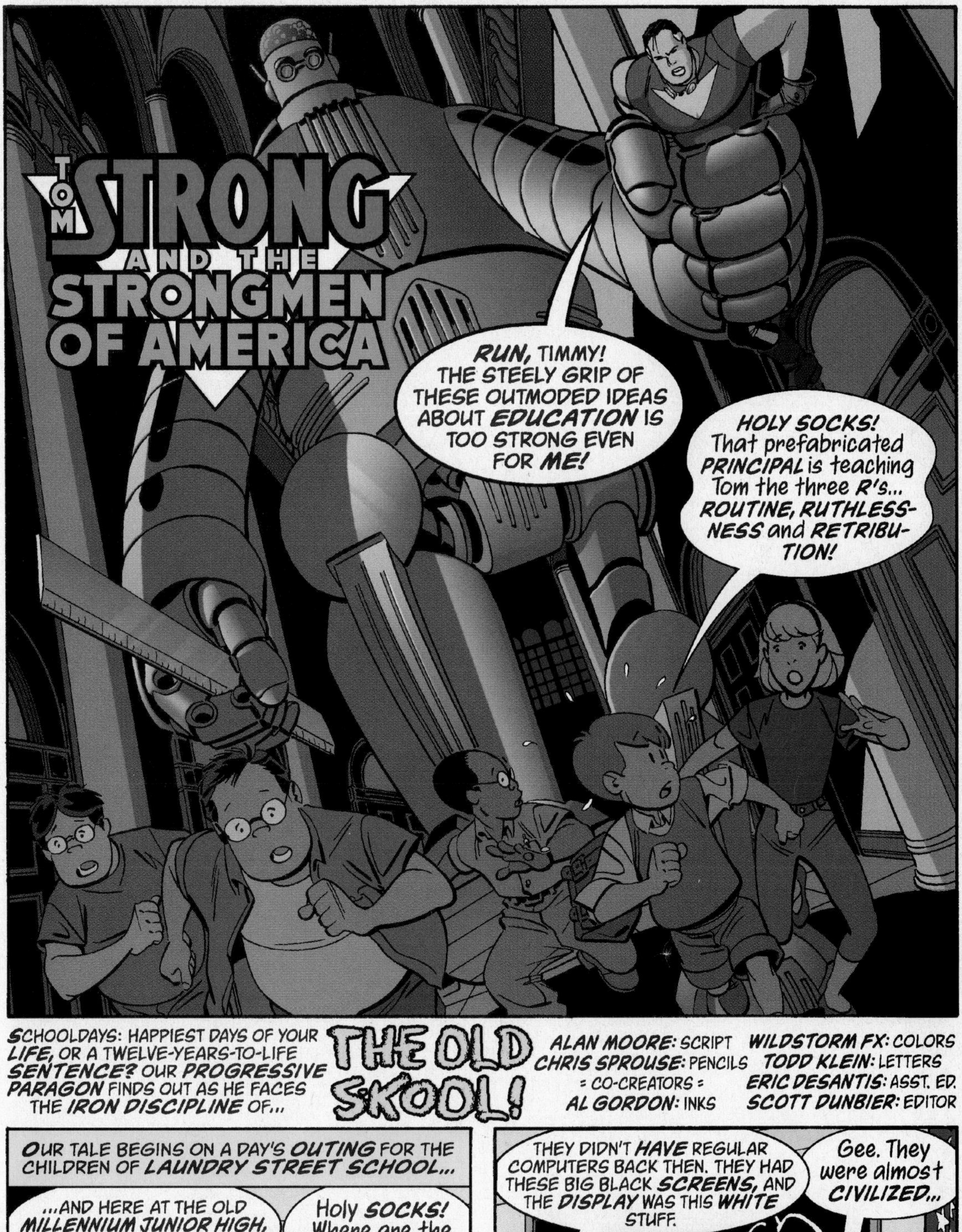
TOM STRONG AND THE STRONGMEN OF AMERICA
RUN, TIMMY! THE STEELY GRIP OF THESE OUTMODED IDEAS ABOUT EDUCATION IS TOO STRONG EVEN FOR ME!
HOLY SOCKS! That prefabricated PRINCIPAL is teaching Tom the three R's... ROUTINE, RUTHLESS-NESS and RETRIBU-TION!

SCHOOLDAYS: HAPPIEST DAYS OF YOUR LIFE, OR A TWELVE-YEARS-TO-LIFE SENTENCE? OUR PROGRESSIVE PARAGON FINDS OUT AS HE FACES THE IRON DISCIPLINE OF...

THE OLD SKOOL!

ALAN MOORE: SCRIPT
CHRIS SPROUSE: PENCILS
= CO-CREATORS =
AL GORDON: INKS
WILDSTORM FX: COLORS
TODD KLEIN: LETTERS
ERIC DESANTIS: ASST. ED.
SCOTT DUNBIER: EDITOR

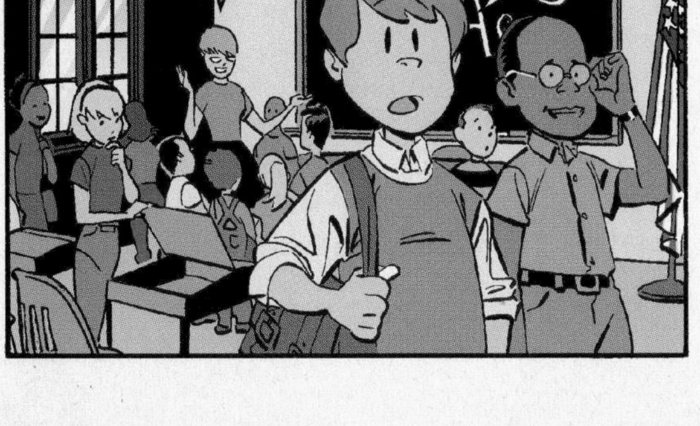
OUR TALE BEGINS ON A DAY'S OUTING FOR THE CHILDREN OF LAUNDRY STREET SCHOOL...
...AND HERE AT THE OLD MILLENNIUM JUNIOR HIGH, YOU SEE HOW SCHOOLS USED TO BE!
Holy SOCKS! Where are the COMPUTERS?

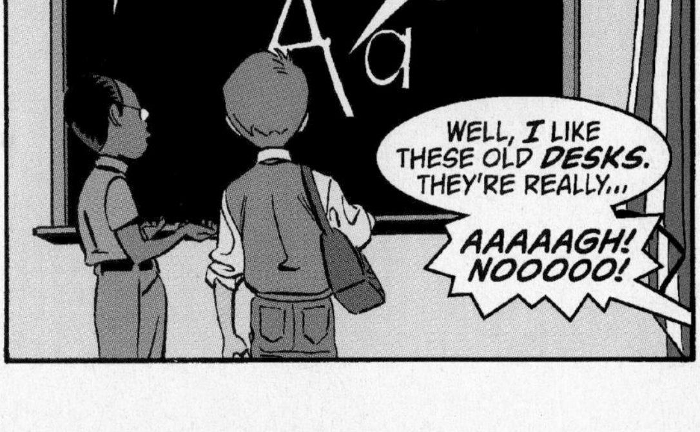
THEY DIDN'T HAVE REGULAR COMPUTERS BACK THEN. THEY HAD THESE BIG BLACK SCREENS, AND THE DISPLAY WAS THIS WHITE STUFF.
Gee. They were almost CIVILIZED...
apple
A a
WELL, I LIKE THESE OLD DESKS. THEY'RE REALLY...
AAAAAGH! NOOOOO!

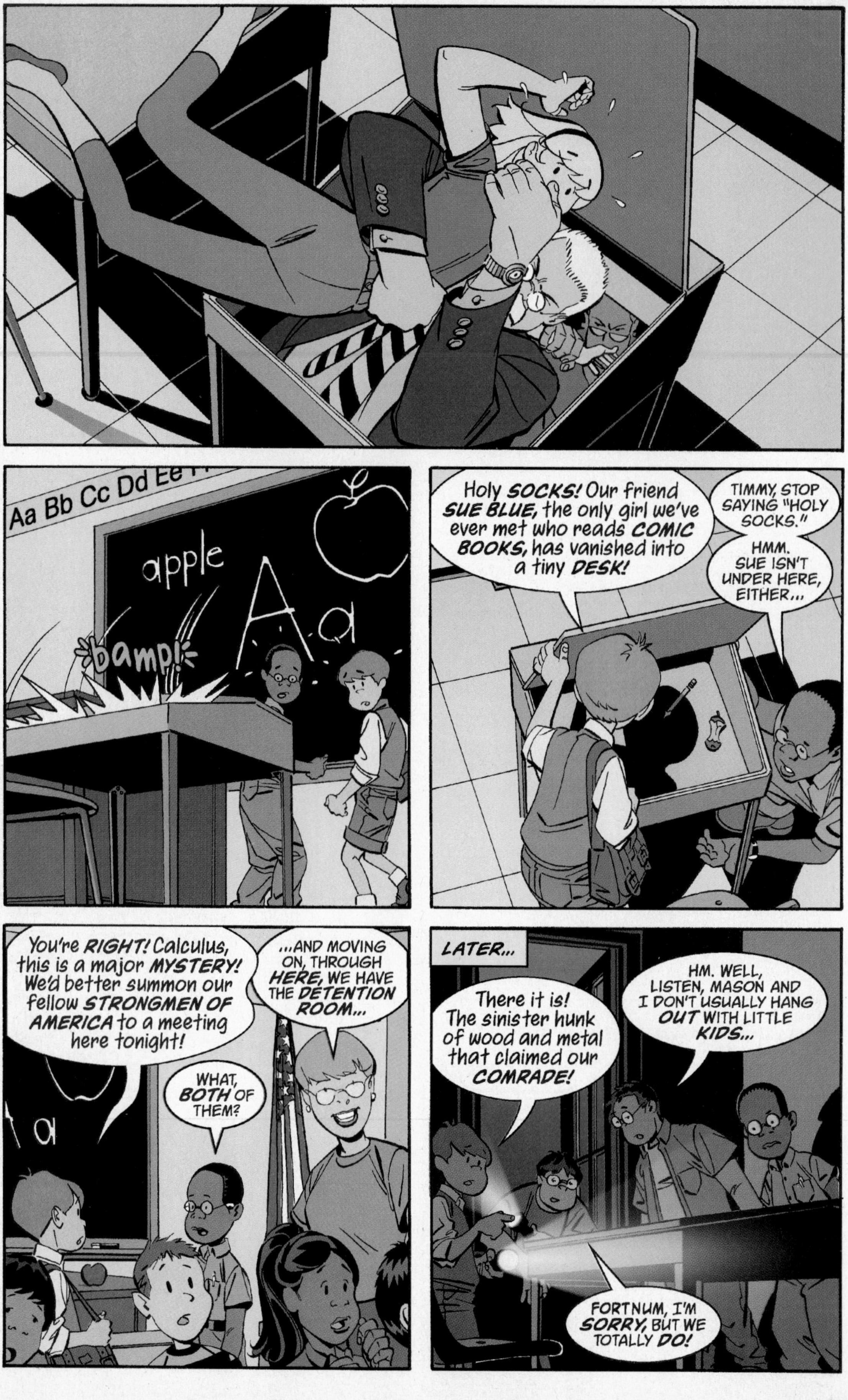
Aa Bb Cc Dd Ee
apple
A a
bamp!
Holy SOCKS! Our friend SUE BLUE, the only girl we've ever met who reads COMIC BOOKS, has vanished into a tiny DESK!
TIMMY, STOP SAYING "HOLY SOCKS."
HMM. SUE ISN'T UNDER HERE, EITHER...
You're RIGHT! Calculus, this is a major MYSTERY! We'd better summon our fellow STRONGMEN OF AMERICA to a meeting here tonight!
...AND MOVING ON, THROUGH HERE, WE HAVE THE DETENTION ROOM...
WHAT, BOTH OF THEM?
LATER...
There it is! The sinister hunk of wood and metal that claimed our COMRADE!
HM. WELL, LISTEN, MASON AND I DON'T USUALLY HANG OUT WITH LITTLE KIDS...
FORTNUM, I'M SORRY, BUT WE TOTALLY DO!

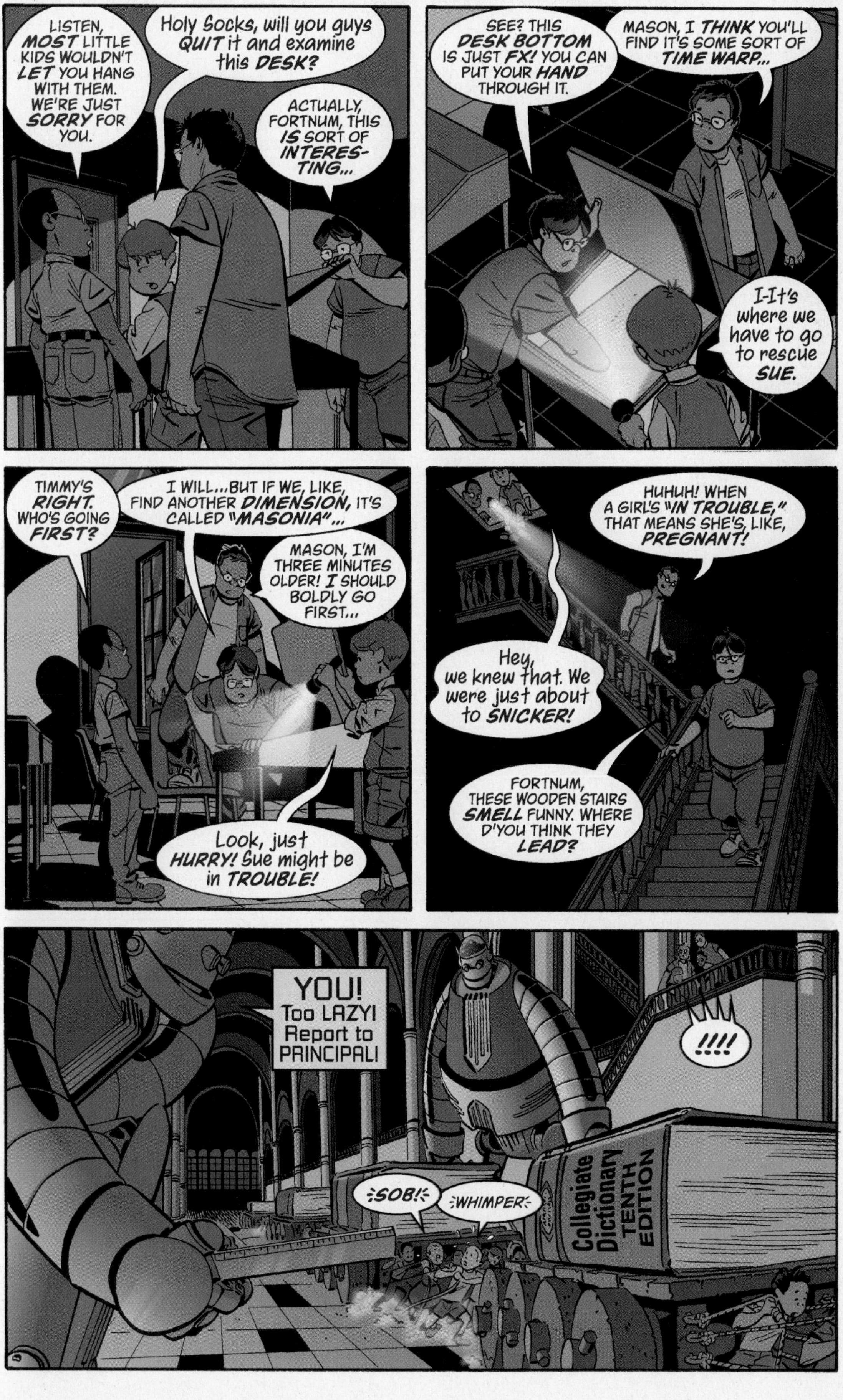
LISTEN, MOST LITTLE KIDS WOULDN'T LET YOU HANG WITH THEM. WE'RE JUST SORRY FOR YOU.
Holy Socks, will you guys QUIT it and examine this DESK?
ACTUALLY, FORTNUM, THIS IS SORT OF INTERES-TING...
SEE? THIS DESK BOTTOM IS JUST FX! YOU CAN PUT YOUR HAND THROUGH IT.
MASON, I THINK YOU'LL FIND IT'S SOME SORT OF TIME WARP...
I-It's where we have to go to rescue SUE.
TIMMY'S RIGHT. WHO'S GOING FIRST?
I WILL...BUT IF WE, LIKE, FIND ANOTHER DIMENSION, IT'S CALLED "MASONIA"...
MASON, I'M THREE MINUTES OLDER! I SHOULD BOLDLY GO FIRST...
Look, just HURRY! Sue might be in TROUBLE!
HUHUH! WHEN A GIRL'S "IN TROUBLE," THAT MEANS SHE'S, LIKE, PREGNANT!
Hey, we knew that. We were just about to SNICKER!
FORTNUM, THESE WOODEN STAIRS SMELL FUNNY. WHERE D'YOU THINK THEY LEAD?
YOU! Too LAZY! Report to PRINCIPAL!
!!!!
Collegiate Dictionary TENTH EDITION
-SOB!-
-WHIMPER-

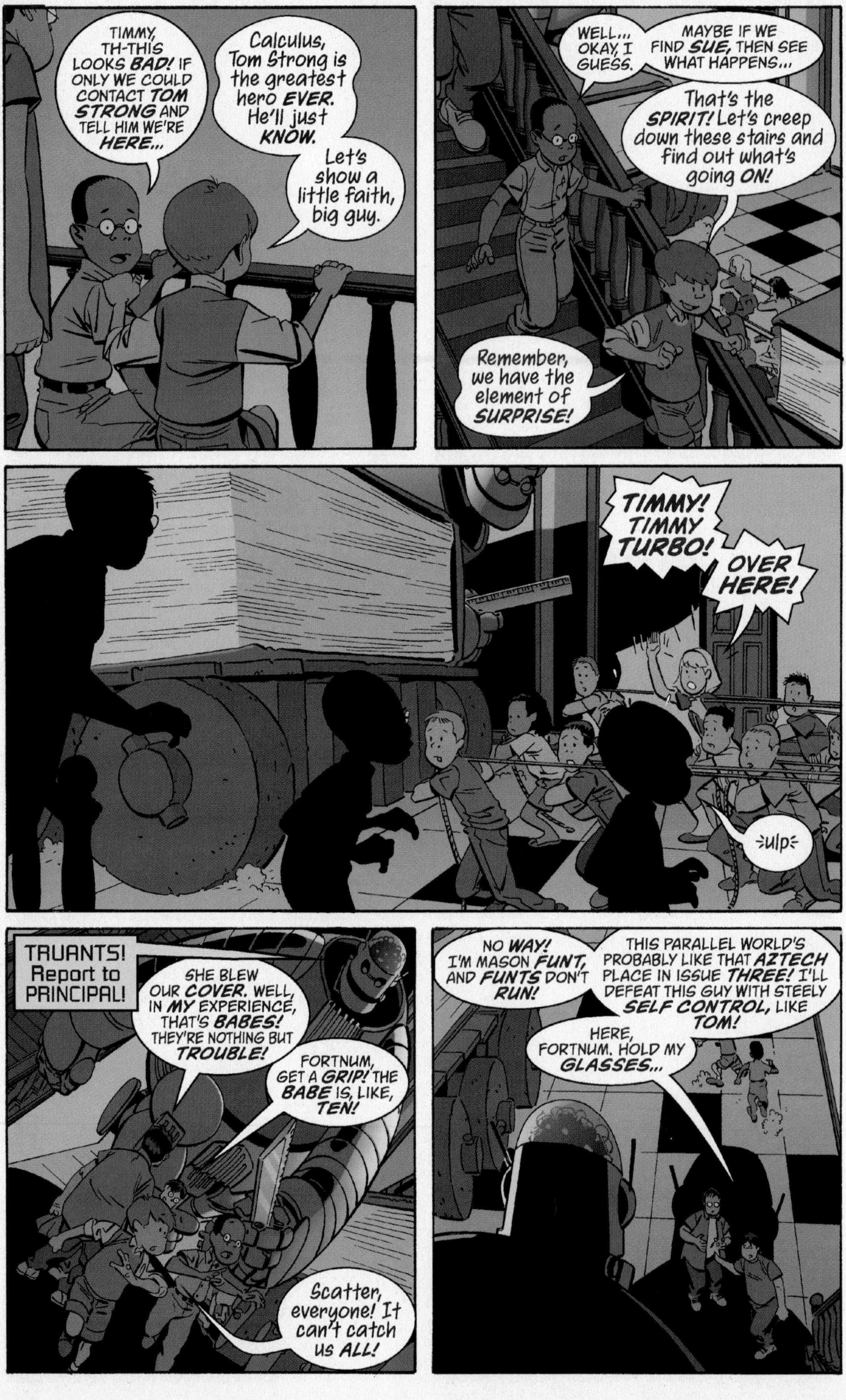
TIMMY, TH-THIS LOOKS BAD! IF ONLY WE COULD CONTACT TOM STRONG AND TELL HIM WE'RE HERE...
Calculus, Tom Strong is the greatest hero EVER. He'll just KNOW.
Let's show a little faith, big guy.
WELL... OKAY, I GUESS.
MAYBE IF WE FIND SUE, THEN SEE WHAT HAPPENS...
That's the SPIRIT! Let's creep down these stairs and find out what's going ON!
Remember, we have the element of SURPRISE!
TIMMY! TIMMY TURBO!
OVER HERE!
ulp
TRUANTS! Report to PRINCIPAL!
SHE BLEW OUR COVER. WELL, IN MY EXPERIENCE, THAT'S BABES! THEY'RE NOTHING BUT TROUBLE!
FORTNUM, GET A GRIP! THE BABE IS, LIKE, TEN!
Scatter, everyone! It can't catch us ALL!
NO WAY! I'M MASON FUNT, AND FUNTS DON'T RUN!
THIS PARALLEL WORLD'S PROBABLY LIKE THAT AZTECH PLACE IN ISSUE THREE! I'LL DEFEAT THIS GUY WITH STEELY SELF CONTROL, LIKE TOM!
HERE, FORTNUM. HOLD MY GLASSES...

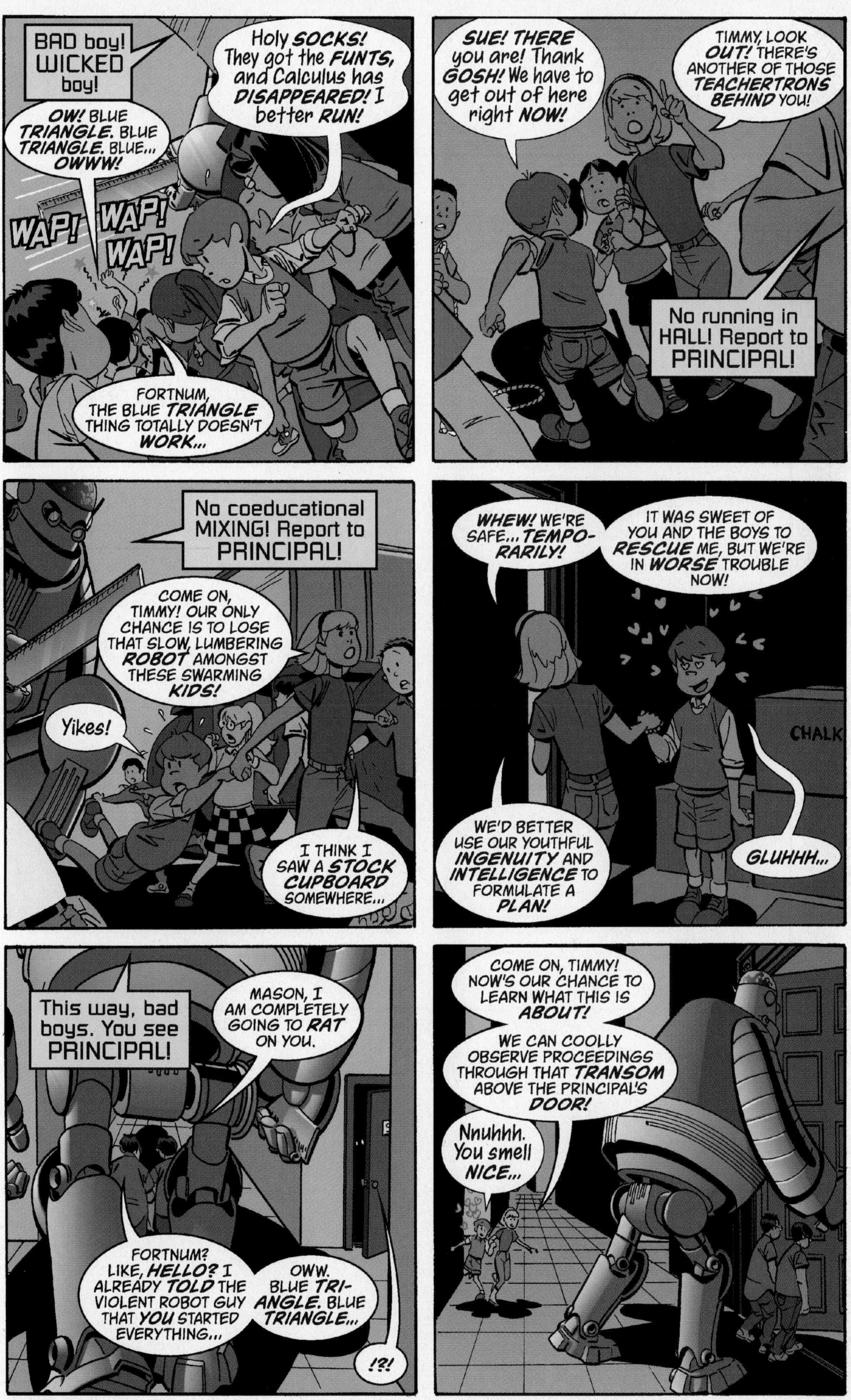
BAD boy! WICKED boy!
Holy SOCKS! They got the FUNTS, and Calculus has DISAPPEARED! I better RUN!
OW! BLUE TRIANGLE. BLUE TRIANGLE. BLUE... OWWW!
WAP! WAP! WAP!
FORTNUM, THE BLUE TRIANGLE THING TOTALLY DOESN'T WORK...
SUE! THERE you are! Thank GOSH! We have to get out of here right NOW!
TIMMY, LOOK OUT! THERE'S ANOTHER OF THOSE TEACHERTRONS BEHIND YOU!
No running in HALL! Report to PRINCIPAL!
No coeducational MIXING! Report to PRINCIPAL!
COME ON, TIMMY! OUR ONLY CHANCE IS TO LOSE THAT SLOW, LUMBERING ROBOT AMONGST THESE SWARMING KIDS!
Yikes!
I THINK I SAW A STOCK CUPBOARD SOMEWHERE...
WHEW! WE'RE SAFE... TEMPO-RARILY!
IT WAS SWEET OF YOU AND THE BOYS TO RESCUE ME, BUT WE'RE IN WORSE TROUBLE NOW!
CHALK
WE'D BETTER USE OUR YOUTHFUL INGENUITY AND INTELLIGENCE TO FORMULATE A PLAN!
GLUHHH...
This way, bad boys. You see PRINCIPAL!
MASON, I AM COMPLETELY GOING TO RAT ON YOU.
FORTNUM? LIKE, HELLO? I ALREADY TOLD THE VIOLENT ROBOT GUY THAT YOU STARTED EVERYTHING...
OWW. BLUE TRI-ANGLE. BLUE TRIANGLE...
!?!
COME ON, TIMMY! NOW'S OUR CHANCE TO LEARN WHAT THIS IS ABOUT!
WE CAN COOLLY OBSERVE PROCEEDINGS THROUGH THAT TRANSOM ABOVE THE PRINCIPAL'S DOOR!
Nnuhhh. You smell NICE...

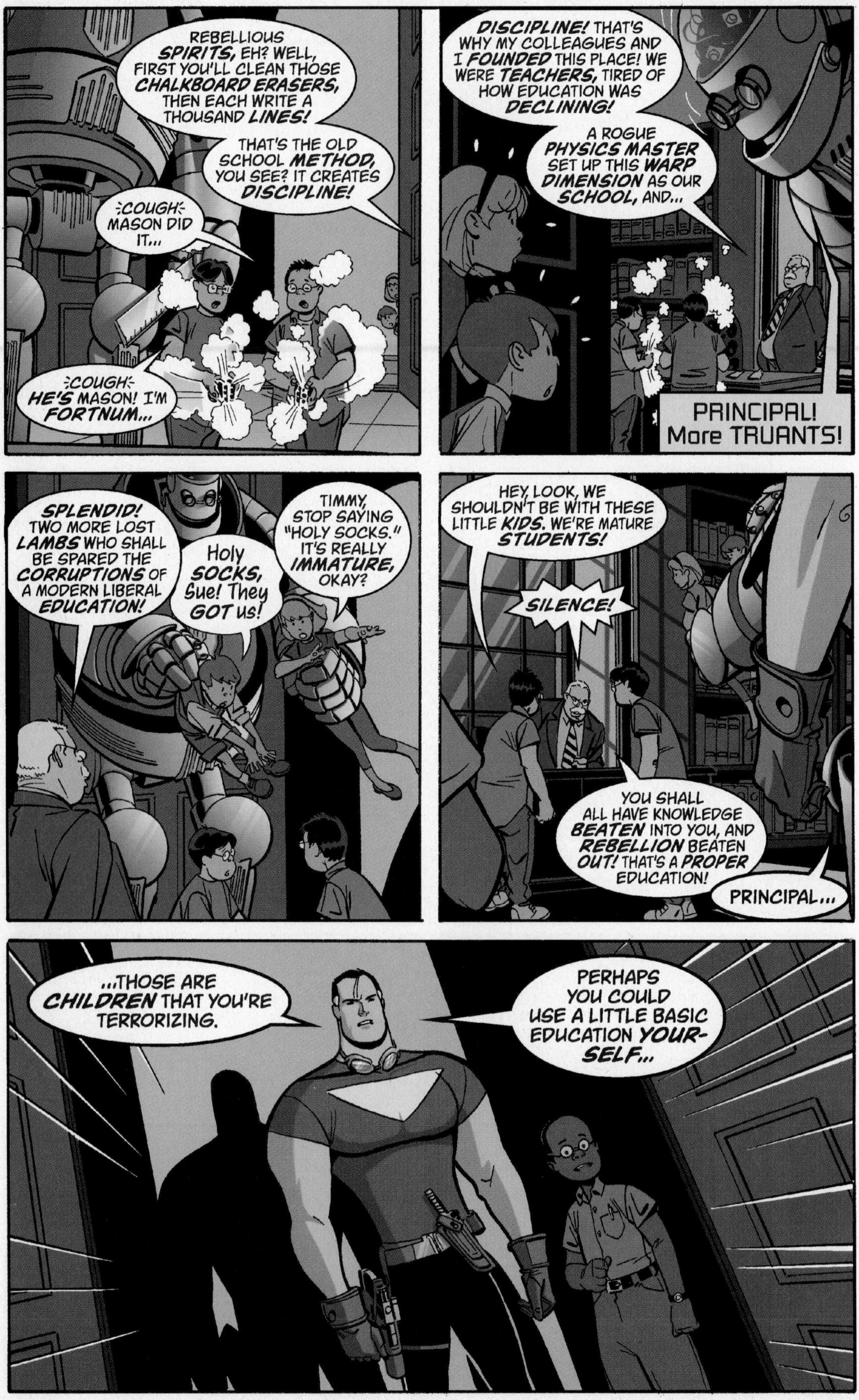

REBELLIOUS SPIRITS, EH? WELL, FIRST YOU'LL CLEAN THOSE CHALKBOARD ERASERS, THEN EACH WRITE A THOUSAND LINES!
THAT'S THE OLD SCHOOL METHOD, YOU SEE? IT CREATES DISCIPLINE!
COUGH MASON DID IT...
COUGH HE'S MASON! I'M FORTNUM...
DISCIPLINE! THAT'S WHY MY COLLEAGUES AND I FOUNDED THIS PLACE! WE WERE TEACHERS, TIRED OF HOW EDUCATION WAS DECLINING!
A ROGUE PHYSICS MASTER SET UP THIS WARP DIMENSION AS OUR SCHOOL, AND...
PRINCIPAL! More TRUANTS!
SPLENDID! TWO MORE LOST LAMBS WHO SHALL BE SPARED THE CORRUPTIONS OF A MODERN LIBERAL EDUCATION!
Holy SOCKS, Sue! They GOT us!
TIMMY, STOP SAYING "HOLY SOCKS." IT'S REALLY IMMATURE, OKAY?
HEY, LOOK, WE SHOULDN'T BE WITH THESE LITTLE KIDS. WE'RE MATURE STUDENTS!
SILENCE!
YOU SHALL ALL HAVE KNOWLEDGE BEATEN INTO YOU, AND REBELLION BEATEN OUT! THAT'S A PROPER EDUCATION!
PRINCIPAL...
...THOSE ARE CHILDREN THAT YOU'RE TERRORIZING.
PERHAPS YOU COULD USE A LITTLE BASIC EDUCATION YOUR-SELF...

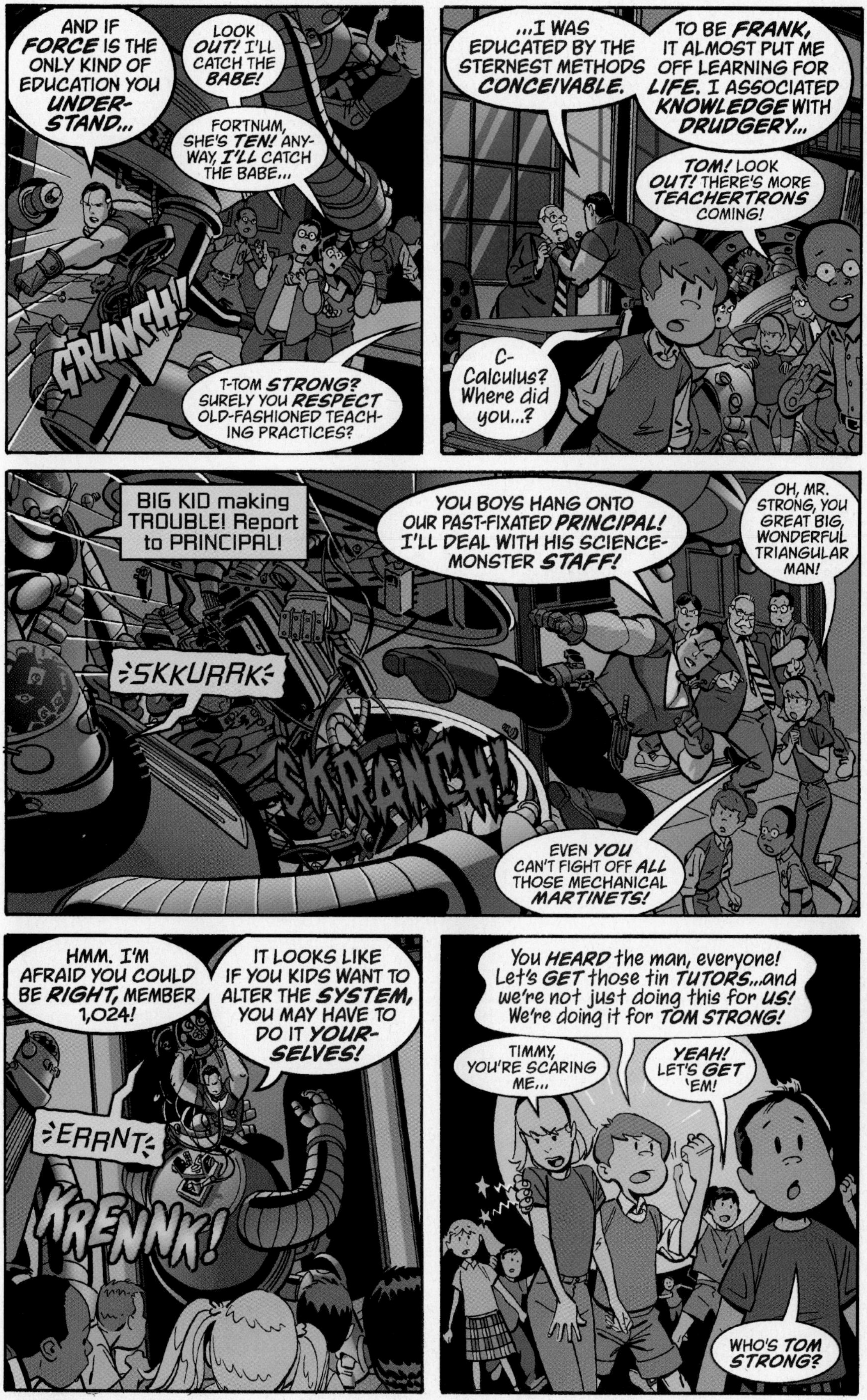
AND IF FORCE IS THE ONLY KIND OF EDUCATION YOU UNDER-STAND...
LOOK OUT! I'LL CATCH THE BABE!
FORTNUM, SHE'S TEN! ANY-WAY, I'LL CATCH THE BABE...
GRUNCH!
T-TOM STRONG? SURELY YOU RESPECT OLD-FASHIONED TEACH-ING PRACTICES?
...I WAS EDUCATED BY THE STERNEST METHODS CONCEIVABLE.
TO BE FRANK, IT ALMOST PUT ME OFF LEARNING FOR LIFE. I ASSOCIATED KNOWLEDGE WITH DRUDGERY...
TOM! LOOK OUT! THERE'S MORE TEACHERTRONS COMING!
C-Calculus? Where did you...?
BIG KID making TROUBLE! Report to PRINCIPAL!
YOU BOYS HANG ONTO OUR PAST-FIXATED PRINCIPAL! I'LL DEAL WITH HIS SCIENCE-MONSTER STAFF!
OH, MR. STRONG, YOU GREAT BIG, WONDERFUL TRIANGULAR MAN!
SKKURRK
SKRANCH!
EVEN YOU CAN'T FIGHT OFF ALL THOSE MECHANICAL MARTINETS!
HMM. I'M AFRAID YOU COULD BE RIGHT, MEMBER 1,024!
IT LOOKS LIKE IF YOU KIDS WANT TO ALTER THE SYSTEM, YOU MAY HAVE TO DO IT YOUR-SELVES!
ERRNT
KRENNK!
You HEARD the man, everyone! Let's GET those tin TUTORS...and we're not just doing this for US! We're doing it for TOM STRONG!
TIMMY, YOU'RE SCARING ME...
YEAH! LET'S GET 'EM!
WHO'S TOM STRONG?

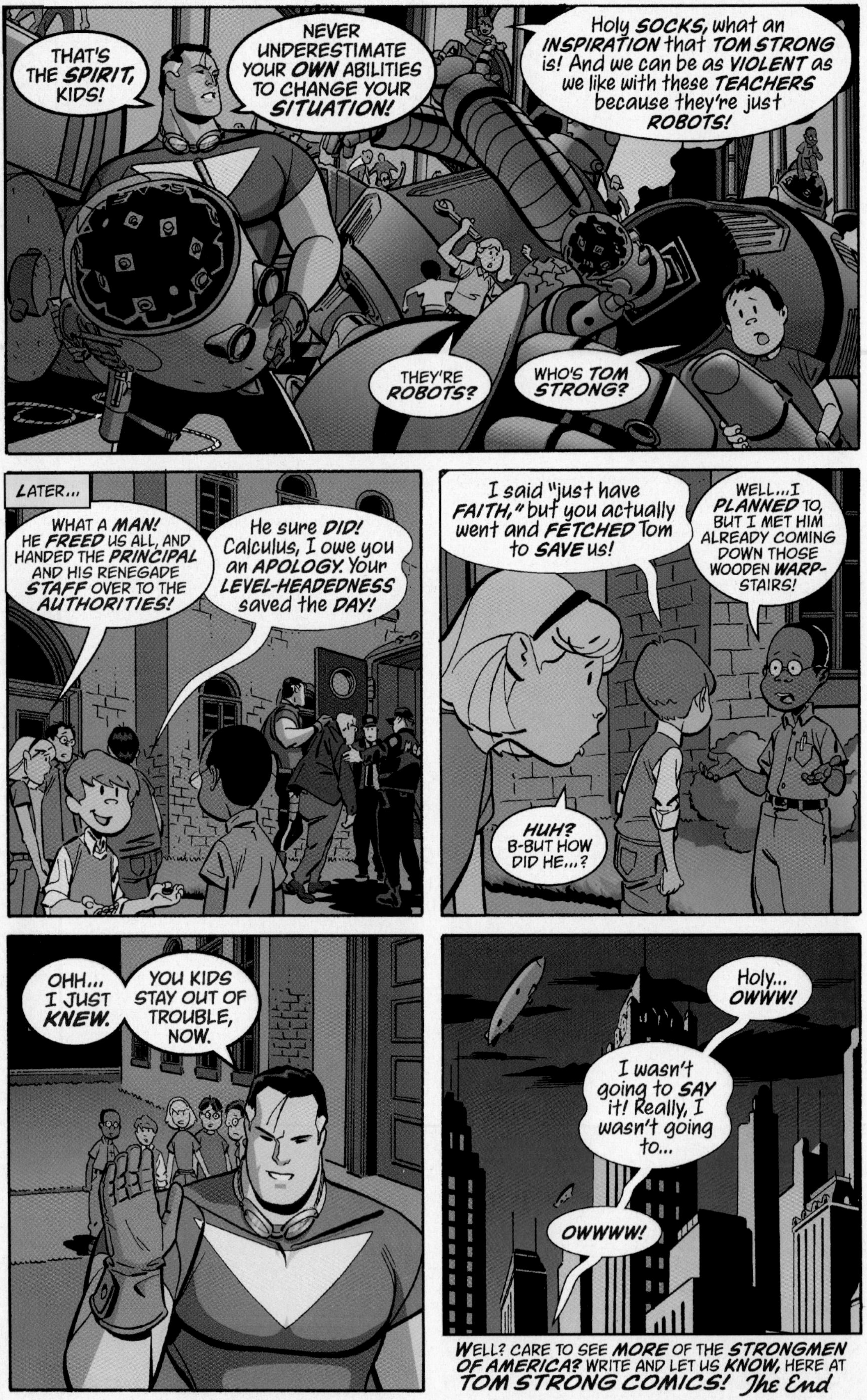
THAT'S THE SPIRIT, KIDS!
NEVER UNDERESTIMATE YOUR OWN ABILITIES TO CHANGE YOUR SITUATION!
Holy SOCKS, what an INSPIRATION that TOM STRONG is! And we can be as VIOLENT as we like with these TEACHERS because they're just ROBOTS!
THEY'RE ROBOTS?
WHO'S TOM STRONG?
LATER...
WHAT A MAN! HE FREED US ALL, AND HANDED THE PRINCIPAL AND HIS RENEGADE STAFF OVER TO THE AUTHORITIES!
He sure DID! Calculus, I owe you an APOLOGY. Your LEVEL-HEADEDNESS saved the DAY!
I said "just have FAITH," but you actually went and FETCHED Tom to SAVE us!
WELL...I PLANNED TO, BUT I MET HIM ALREADY COMING DOWN THOSE WOODEN WARP-STAIRS!
HUH? B-BUT HOW DID HE...?
OHH... I JUST KNEW.
YOU KIDS STAY OUT OF TROUBLE, NOW.
Holy... OWWW!
I wasn't going to SAY it! Really, I wasn't going to...
OWWWW!
WELL? CARE TO SEE MORE OF THE STRONGMEN OF AMERICA? WRITE AND LET US KNOW, HERE AT TOM STRONG COMICS! The End

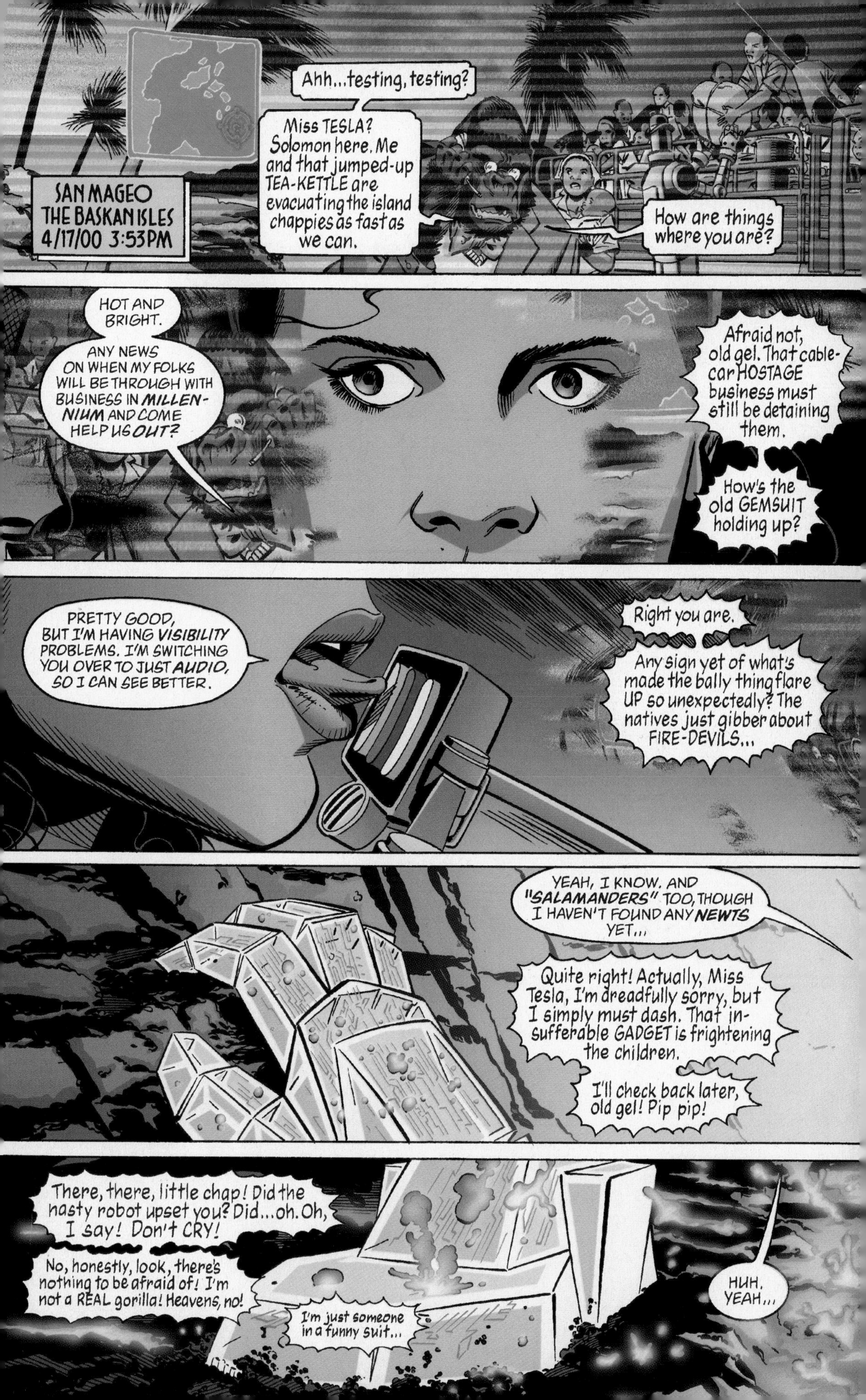
SAN MAGEO
THE BASKAN ISLES
4/17/00 3:53PM
Ahh...testing, testing?
Miss TESLA? Solomon here. Me and that jumped-up TEA-KETTLE are evacuating the island chappies as fast as we can.
How are things where you are?
HOT AND BRIGHT.
ANY NEWS ON WHEN MY FOLKS WILL BE THROUGH WITH BUSINESS IN MILLENNIUM AND COME HELP US OUT?
Afraid not, old gel. That cable-car HOSTAGE business must still be detaining them.
How's the old GEMSUIT holding up?
PRETTY GOOD, BUT I'M HAVING VISIBILITY PROBLEMS. I'M SWITCHING YOU OVER TO JUST AUDIO, SO I CAN SEE BETTER.
Right you are.
Any sign yet of what's made the bally thing flare UP so unexpectedly? The natives just gibber about FIRE-DEVILS...
YEAH, I KNOW. AND "SALAMANDERS" TOO, THOUGH I HAVEN'T FOUND ANY NEWTS YET...
Quite right! Actually, Miss Tesla, I'm dreadfully sorry, but I simply must dash. That insufferable GADGET is frightening the children.
I'll check back later, old gel! Pip pip!
There, there, little chap! Did the nasty robot upset you? Did...oh. Oh, I say! Don't CRY!
No, honestly, look, there's nothing to be afraid of! I'm not a REAL gorilla! Heavens, no!
I'm just someone in a funny suit...
HUH. YEAH...

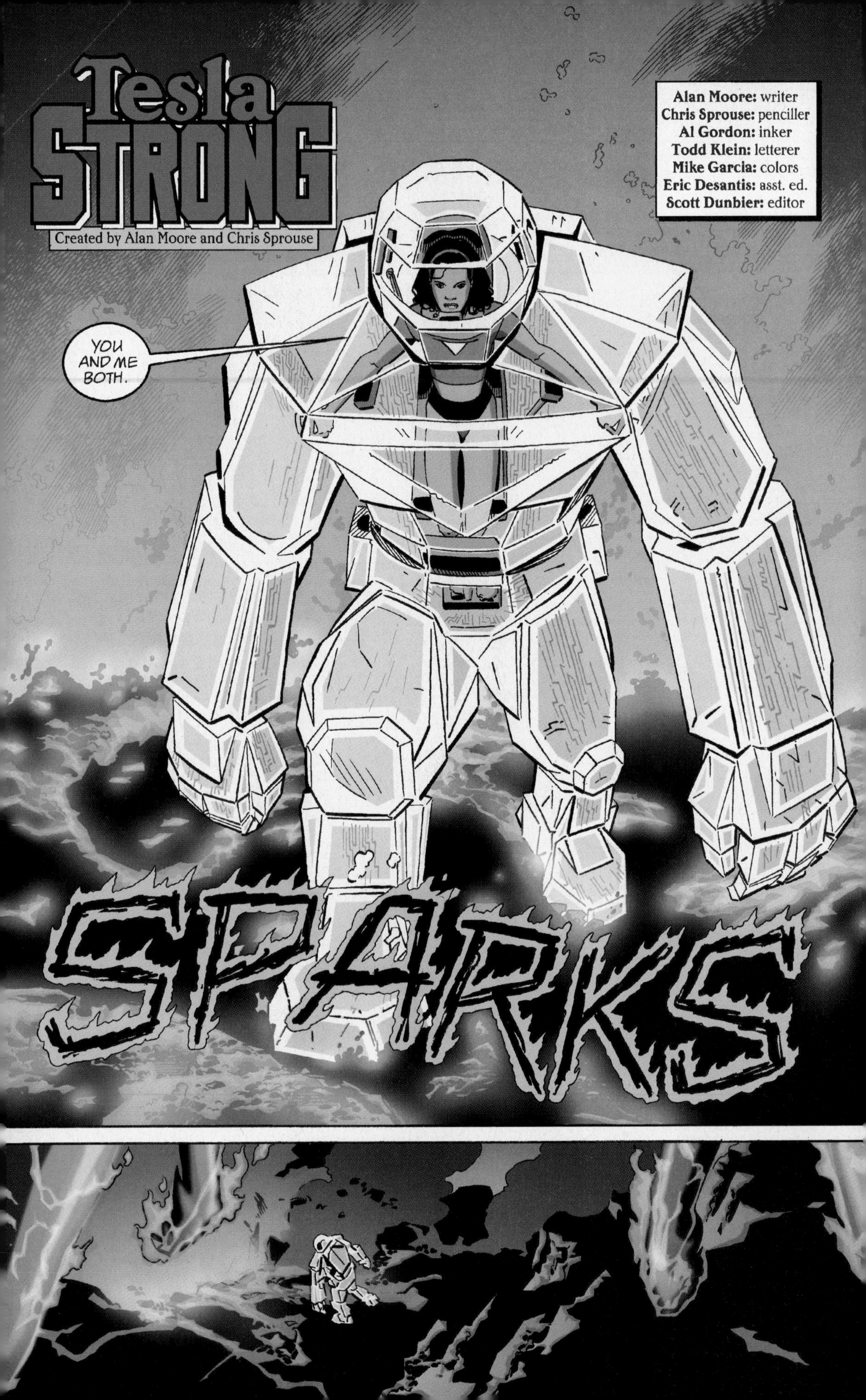
Tesla STRONG
Created by Alan Moore and Chris Sprouse
Alan Moore: writer
Chris Sprouse: penciller
Al Gordon: inker
Todd Klein: letterer
Mike Garcia: colors
Eric Desantis: asst. ed.
Scott Dunbier: editor
YOU AND ME BOTH.
SPARKS

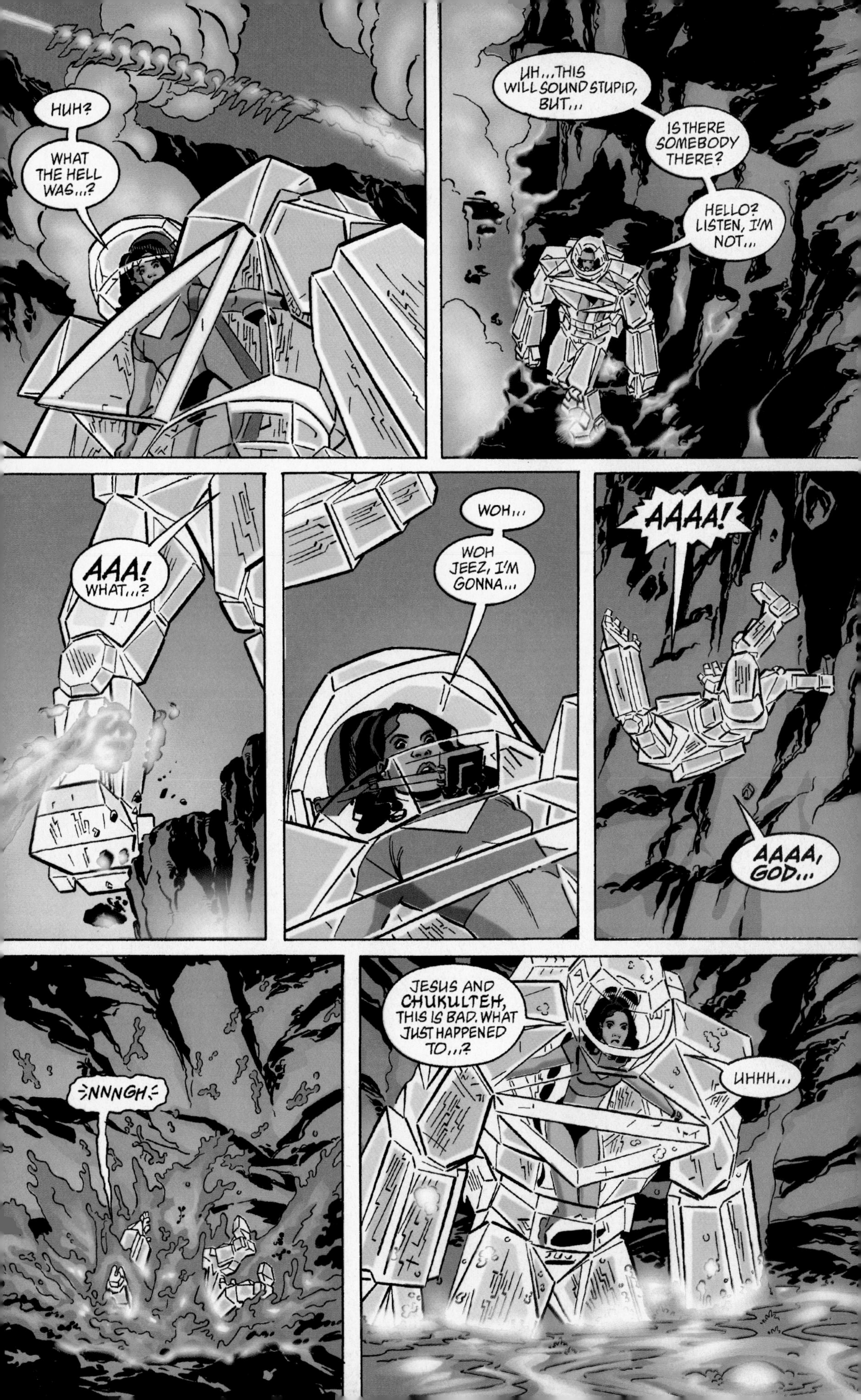
HUH?
WHAT THE HELL WAS...?
UH... THIS WILL SOUND STUPID, BUT...
IS THERE SOMEBODY THERE?
HELLO? LISTEN, I'M NOT...
AAA! WHAT...?
WOH...
WOH JEEZ, I'M GONNA...
AAAA!
AAAA, GOD...
NNNGH
JESUS AND CHUKULTEH, THIS IS BAD. WHAT JUST HAPPENED TO...?
UHHH...

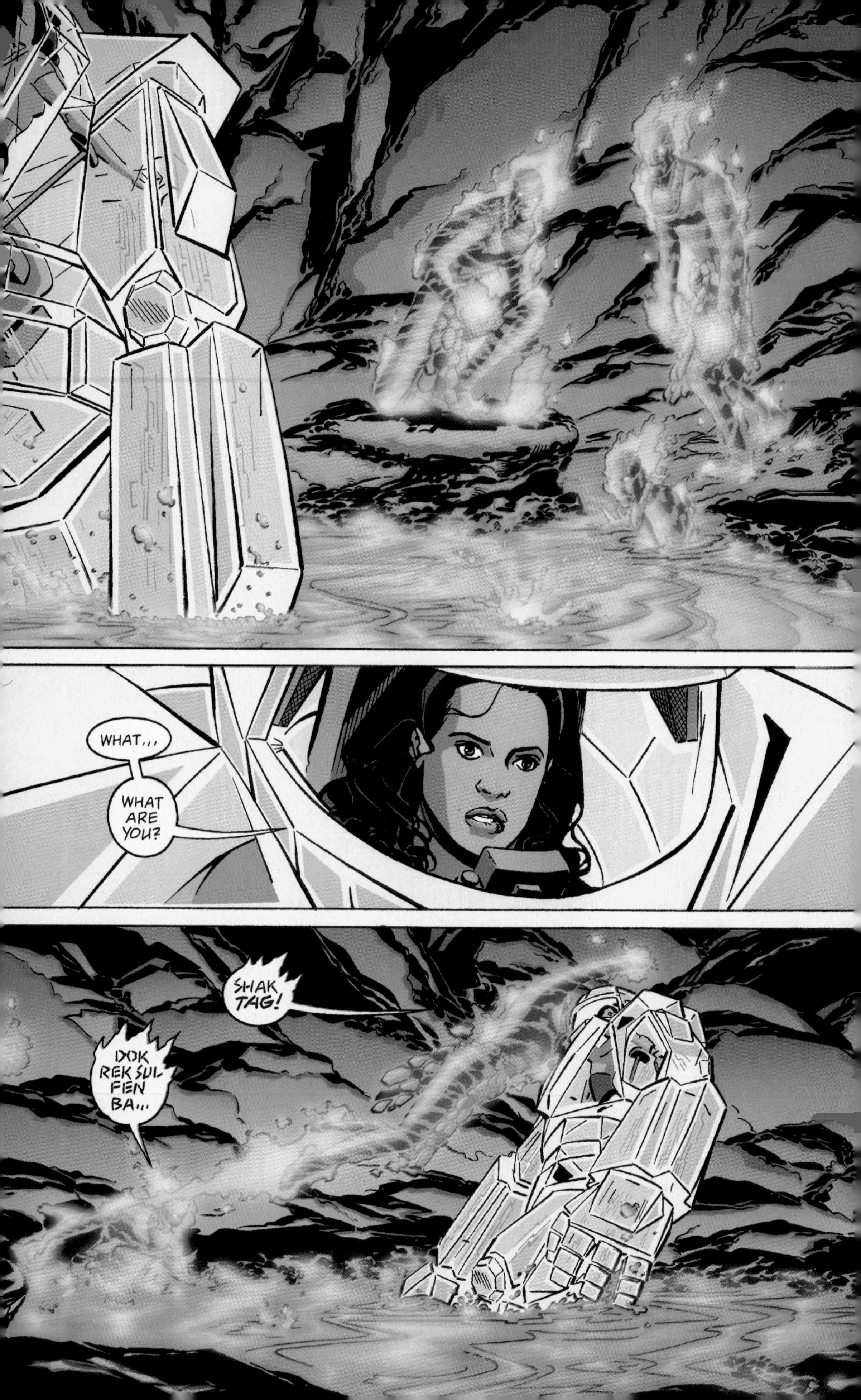
WHAT...
WHAT ARE YOU?
SHAK TAG!
IXOK REK SUL FEN BA...

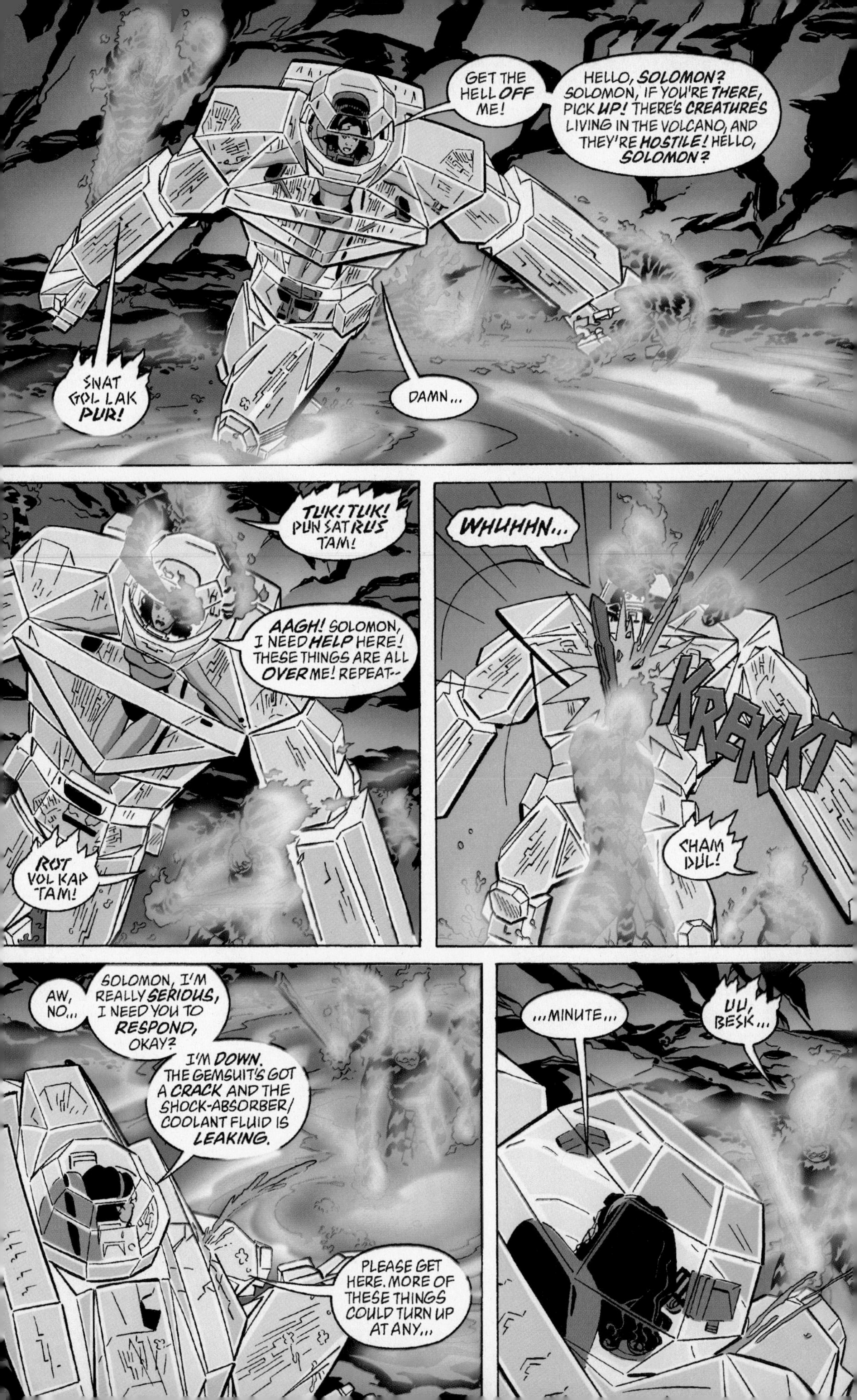
GET THE HELL OFF ME!
HELLO, SOLOMON? SOLOMON, IF YOU'RE THERE, PICK UP! THERE'S CREATURES LIVING IN THE VOLCANO, AND THEY'RE HOSTILE! HELLO, SOLOMON?
SNAT GOL LAK PUR!
DAMN...
TUK! TUK! PUN SAT RUS TAM!
AAGH! SOLOMON, I NEED HELP HERE! THESE THINGS ARE ALL OVER ME! REPEAT--
ROT VOL KAP TAM!
WHUHHN...
KRAKKT
CHAM DUL!
AW, NO...
SOLOMON, I'M REALLY SERIOUS, I NEED YOU TO RESPOND, OKAY?
I'M DOWN. THE GEMSUIT'S GOT A CRACK AND THE SHOCK-ABSORBER/ COOLANT FLUID IS LEAKING.
PLEASE GET HERE. MORE OF THESE THINGS COULD TURN UP AT ANY...
...MINUTE...
UU, BESK...

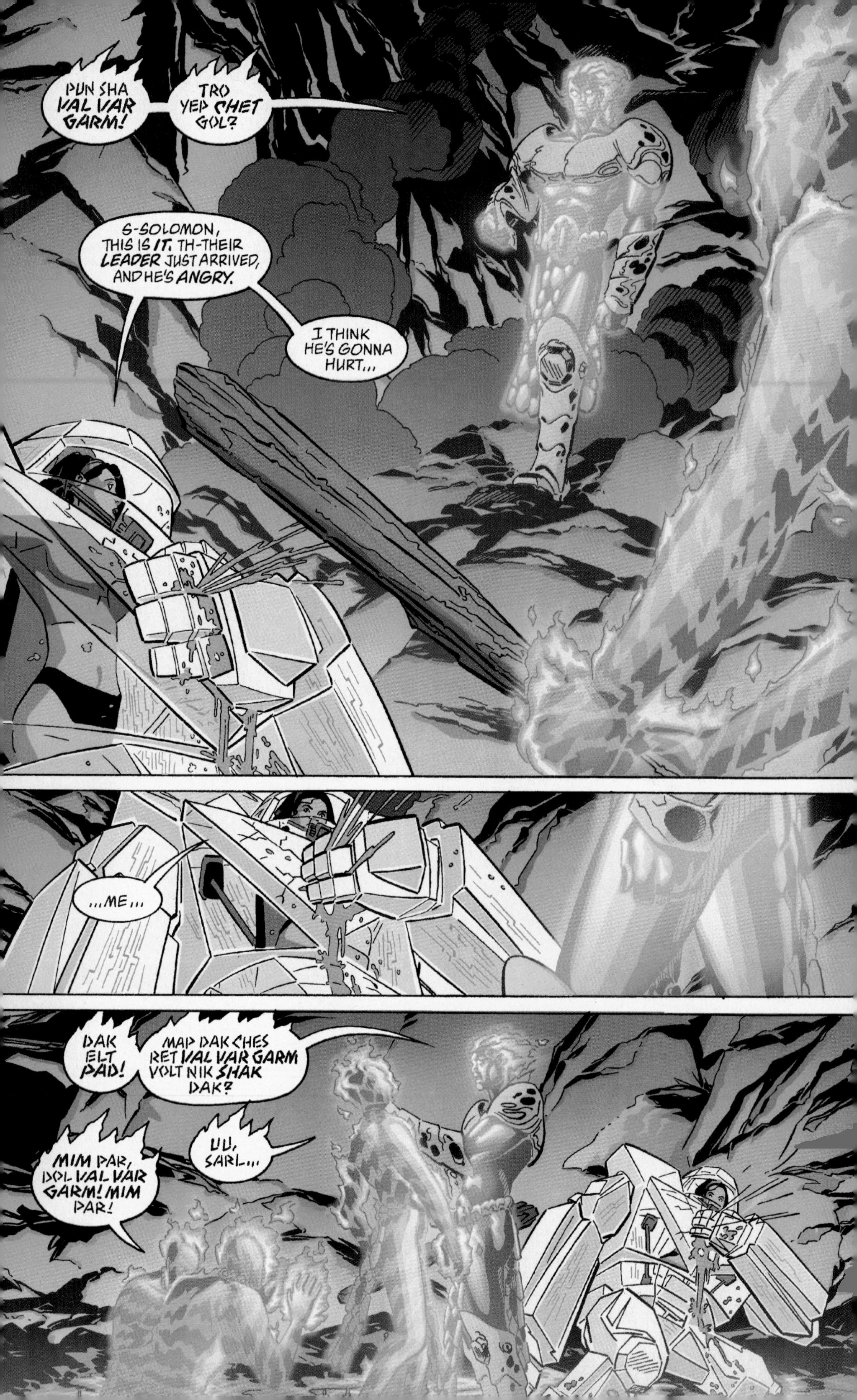
PUN SHA VAL VAR GARM!
TRO YEP CHET GOL?
S-SOLOMON, THIS IS IT. TH-THEIR LEADER JUST ARRIVED, AND HE'S ANGRY.
I THINK HE'S GONNA HURT...
...ME...
DAK ELT PAD!
MAP DAK CHES RET VAL VAR GARM VOLT NIK SHAK DAK?
MIM PAR, DOL VAL VAR GARM! MIM PAR!
UU, SARL...

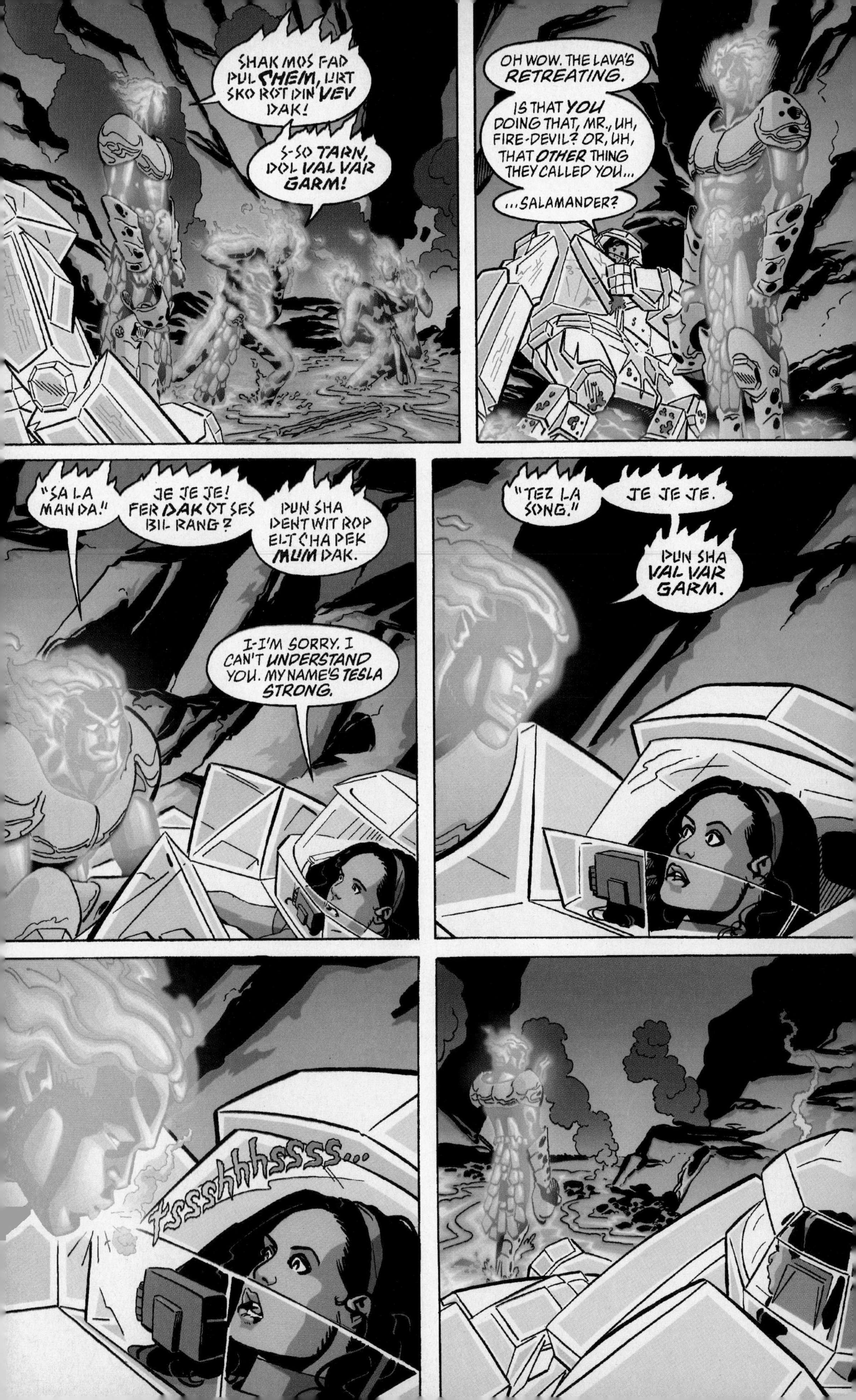
SHAK MOS FAD PUL CHEM, URT SKO ROT DIN VEV DAK!
S-SO TARN, DOL VAL VAR GARM!
OH WOW. THE LAVA'S RETREATING.
IS THAT YOU DOING THAT, MR., UH, FIRE-DEVIL? OR, UH, THAT OTHER THING THEY CALLED YOU...
...SALAMANDER?
"SA LA MAN DA."
JE JE JE! FER DAK OT SES BIL RANG?
DUN SHA DENT WIT ROP ELT CHA PEK MUM DAK.
I-I'M SORRY. I CAN'T UNDERSTAND YOU. MY NAME'S TESLA STRONG.
"TEZ LA SONG."
JE JE JE.
DUN SHA VAL VAR GARM.
tssshhhsssss...

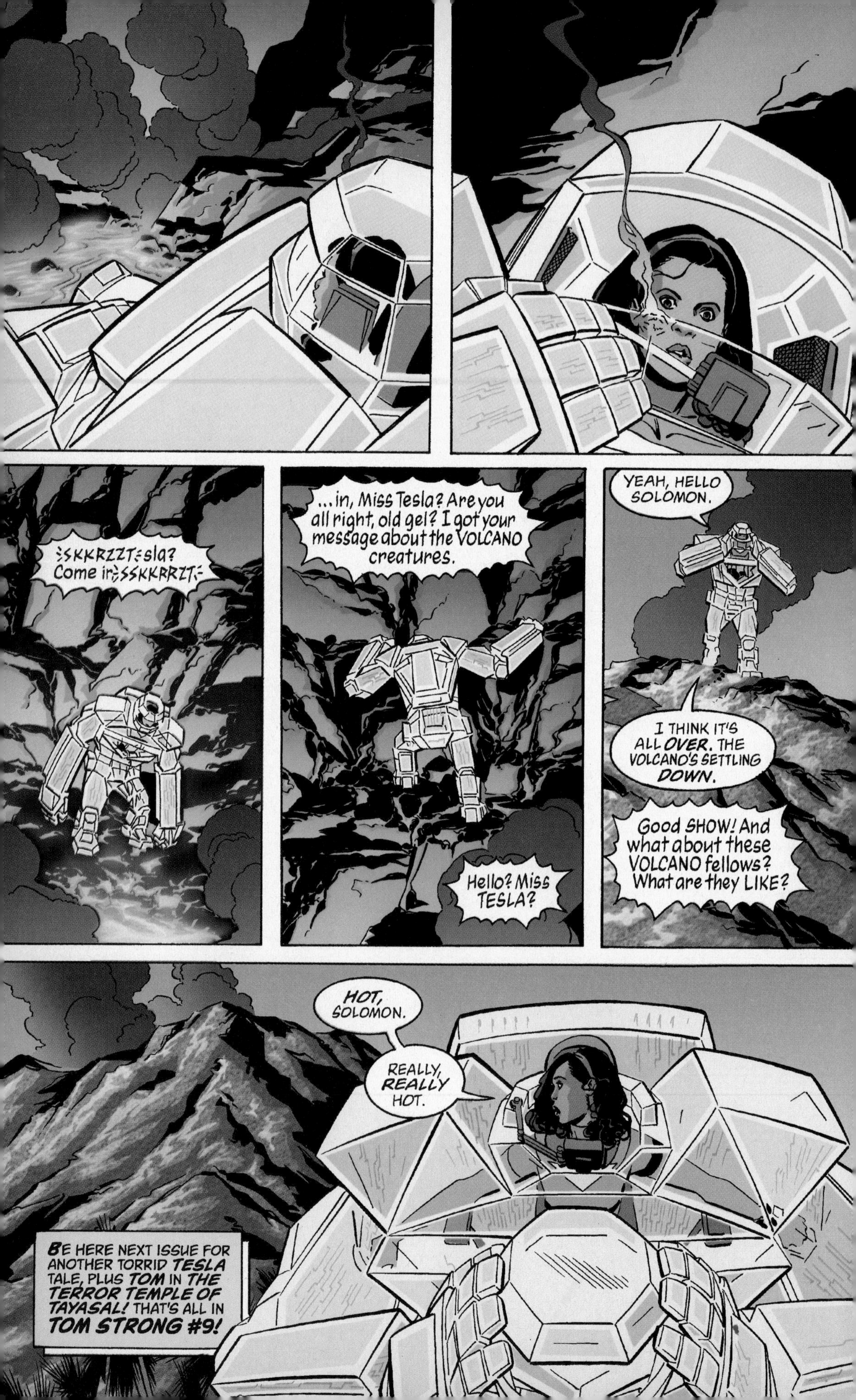
SSKKRZZT sla? Come in SSKKRRZT
...in, Miss Tesla? Are you all right, old gel? I got your message about the VOLCANO creatures.
Hello? Miss TESLA?
YEAH, HELLO SOLOMON.
I THINK IT'S ALL OVER. THE VOLCANO'S SETTLING DOWN.
Good SHOW! And what about these VOLCANO fellows? What are they LIKE?
HOT, SOLOMON.
REALLY, REALLY HOT.
BE HERE NEXT ISSUE FOR ANOTHER TORRID TESLA TALE, PLUS TOM IN THE TERROR TEMPLE OF TAYASAL! THAT'S ALL IN TOM STRONG #9!

CHAPTER TWO

In which Tom delves deep into the jungle,
Dhalua dreams darkly in the spirit world,
and Tesla deals with a new angle.

Cover art:
Paul Chadwick

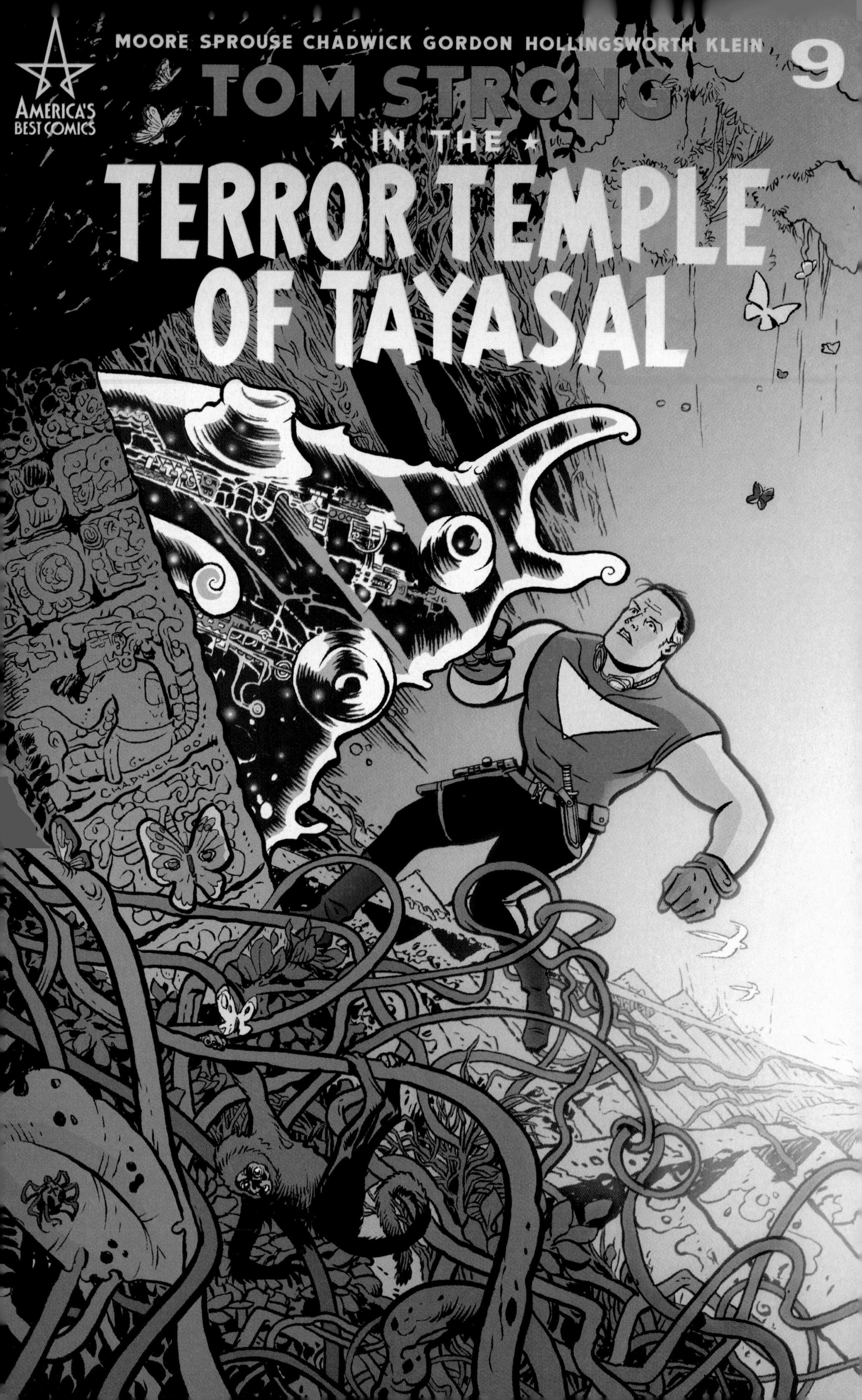
AMERICA'S BEST COMICS
MOORE SPROUSE CHADWICK GORDON HOLLINGSWORTH KLEIN
9
TOM STRONG
IN THE
TERROR TEMPLE OF TAYASAL

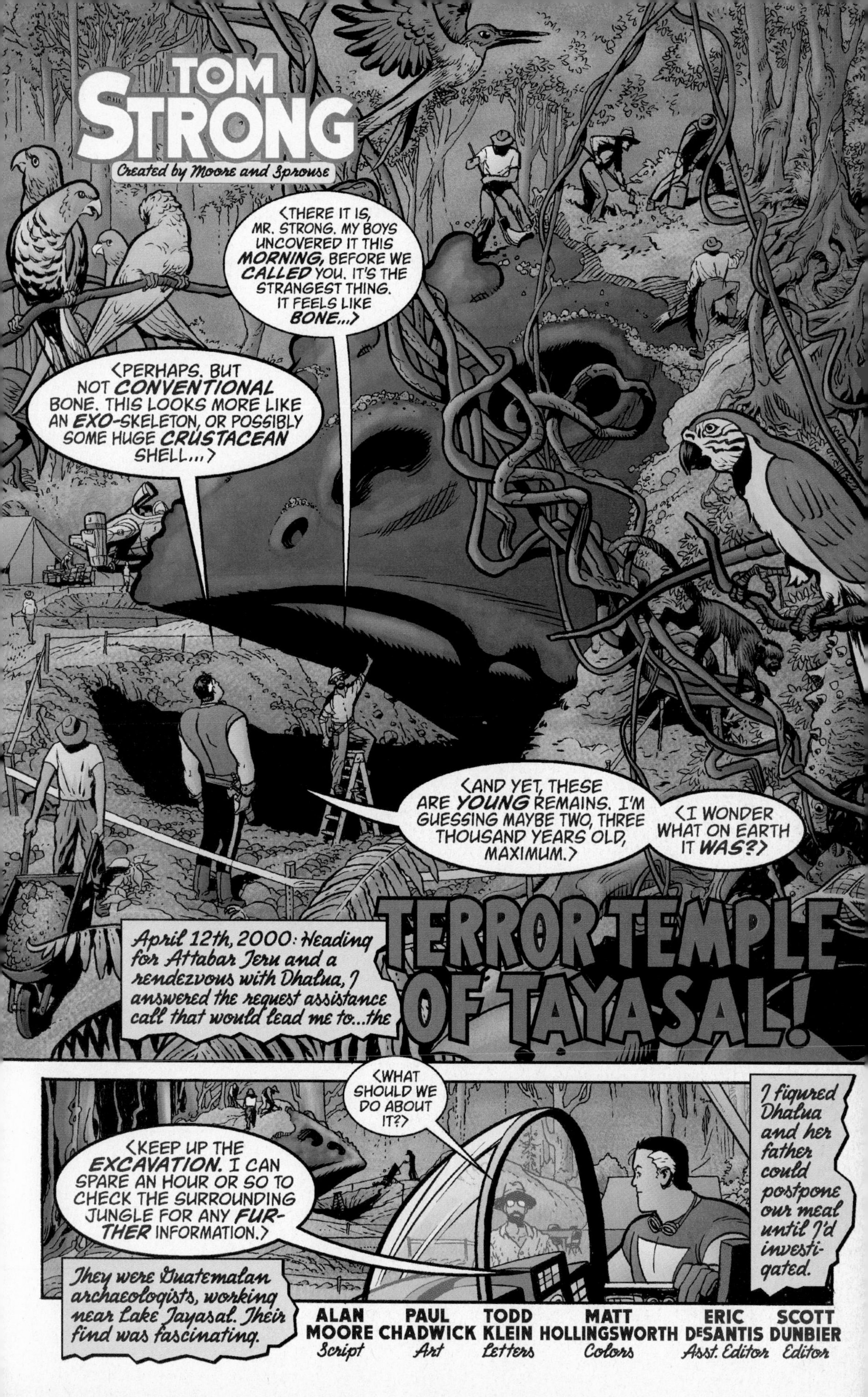
TOM STRONG
Created by Moore and Sprouse
<THERE IT IS, MR. STRONG. MY BOYS UNCOVERED IT THIS MORNING, BEFORE WE CALLED YOU. IT'S THE STRANGEST THING. IT FEELS LIKE BONE...>
<PERHAPS. BUT NOT CONVENTIONAL BONE. THIS LOOKS MORE LIKE AN EXO-SKELETON, OR POSSIBLY SOME HUGE CRUSTACEAN SHELL...>
<AND YET, THESE ARE YOUNG REMAINS. I'M GUESSING MAYBE TWO, THREE THOUSAND YEARS OLD, MAXIMUM.>
<I WONDER WHAT ON EARTH IT WAS?>
April 12th, 2000: Heading for Attabar Teru and a rendezvous with Dhalua, I answered the request assistance call that would lead me to...the
TERROR TEMPLE OF TAYASAL!
<WHAT SHOULD WE DO ABOUT IT?>
<KEEP UP THE EXCAVATION. I CAN SPARE AN HOUR OR SO TO CHECK THE SURROUNDING JUNGLE FOR ANY FURTHER INFORMATION.>
I figured Dhalua and her father could postpone our meal until I'd investigated.
They were Guatemalan archaeologists, working near Lake Tayasal. Their find was fascinating.
ALAN MOORE Script
PAUL CHADWICK Art
TODD KLEIN Letters
MATT HOLLINGSWORTH Colors
ERIC DeSANTIS Asst. Editor
SCOTT DUNBIER Editor

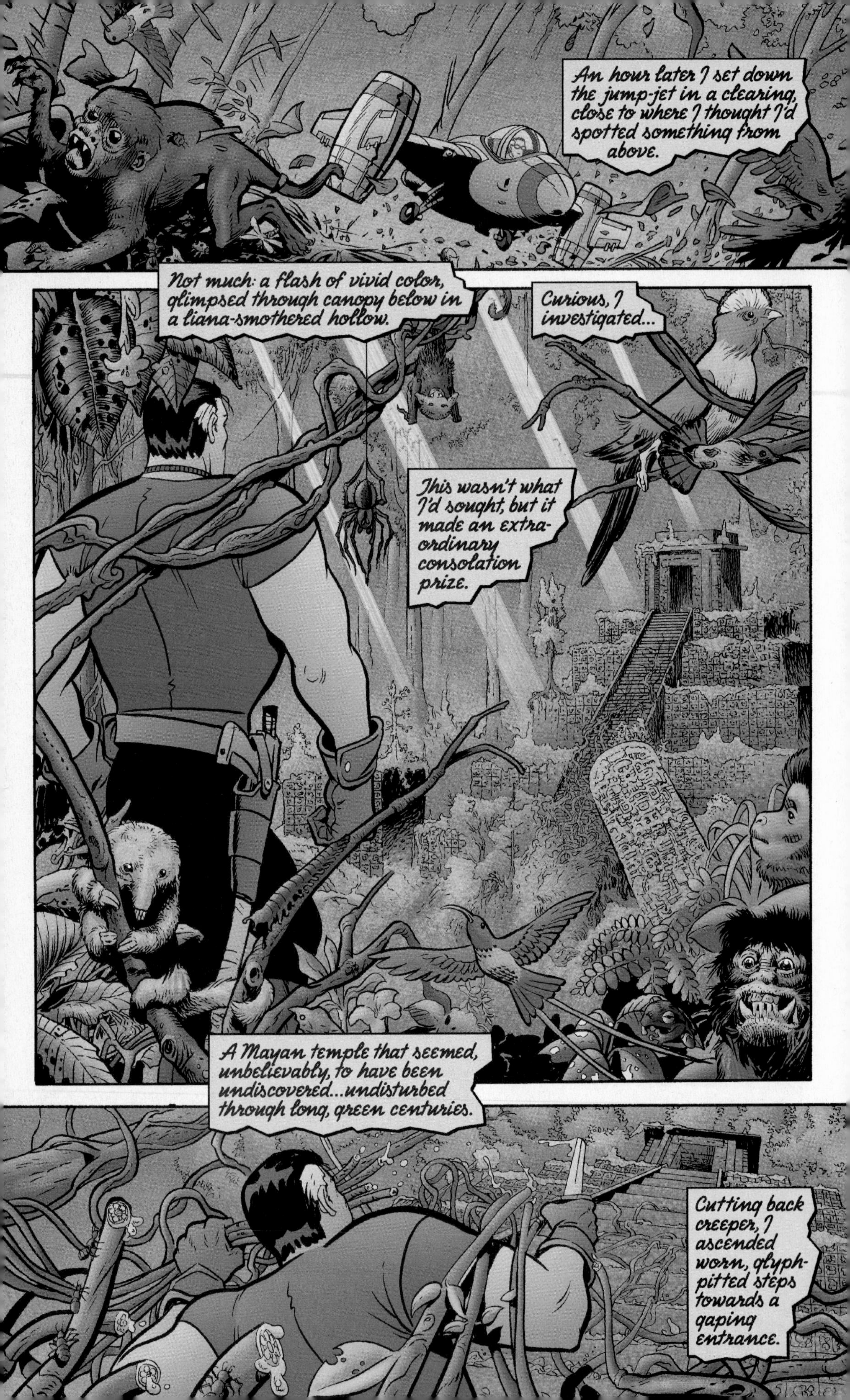
An hour later I set down the jump-jet in a clearing, close to where I thought I'd spotted something from above.
Not much: a flash of vivid color, glimpsed through canopy below in a liana-smothered hollow.
Curious, I investigated...
This wasn't what I'd sought, but it made an extra-ordinary consolation prize.
A Mayan temple that seemed, unbelievably, to have been undiscovered...undisturbed through long, green centuries.
Cutting back creeper, I ascended worn, glyph-pitted steps towards a gaping entrance.

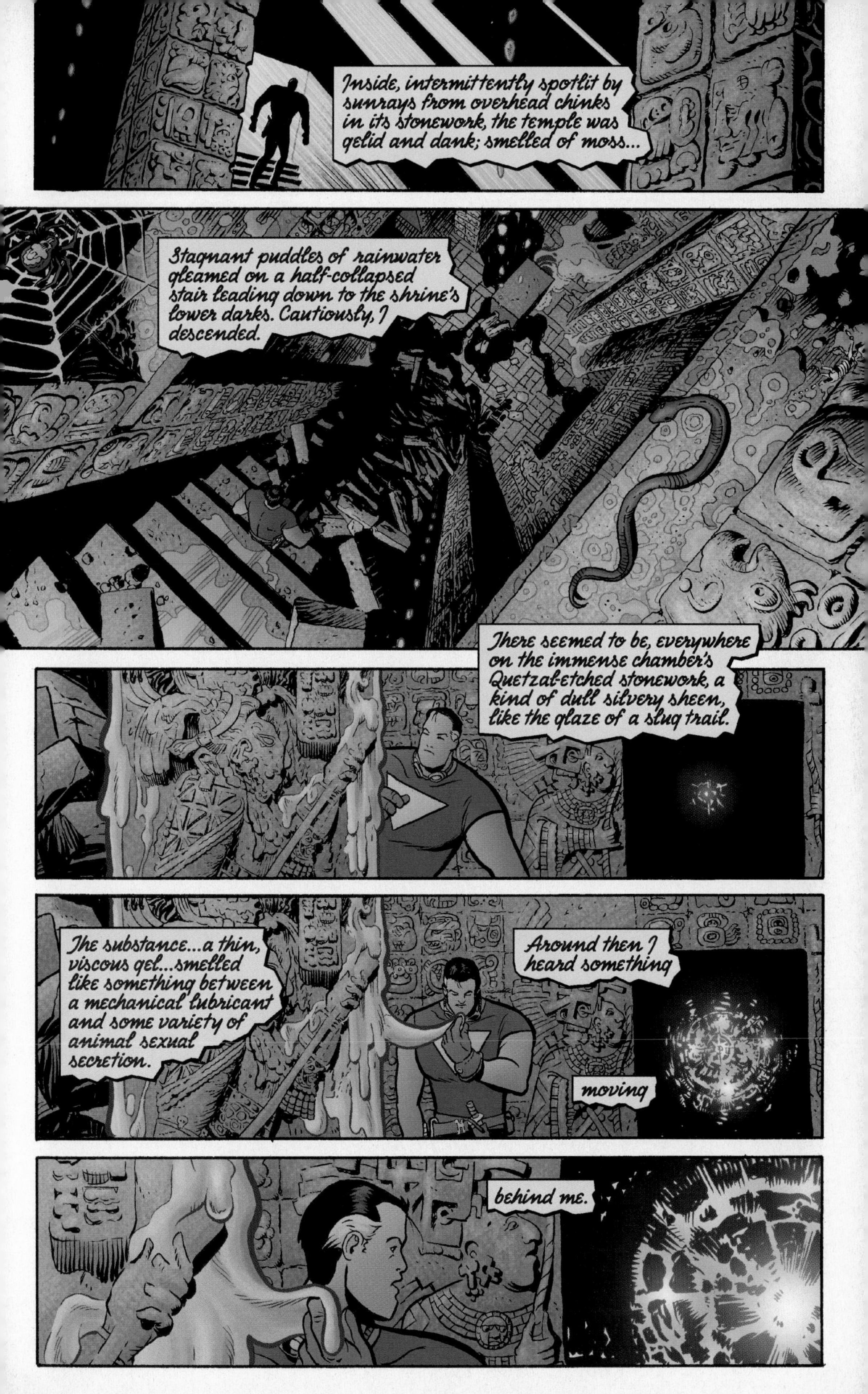
Inside, intermittently spotlit by sunrays from overhead chinks in its stonework, the temple was gelid and dank; smelled of moss...
Stagnant puddles of rainwater gleamed on a half-collapsed stair leading down to the shrine's lower darks. Cautiously, I descended.
There seemed to be, everywhere on the immense chamber's Quetzal-etched stonework, a kind of dull silvery sheen, like the glaze of a slug trail.
The substance...a thin, viscous gel...smelled like something between a mechanical lubricant and some variety of animal sexual secretion.
Around then I heard something
moving
behind me.

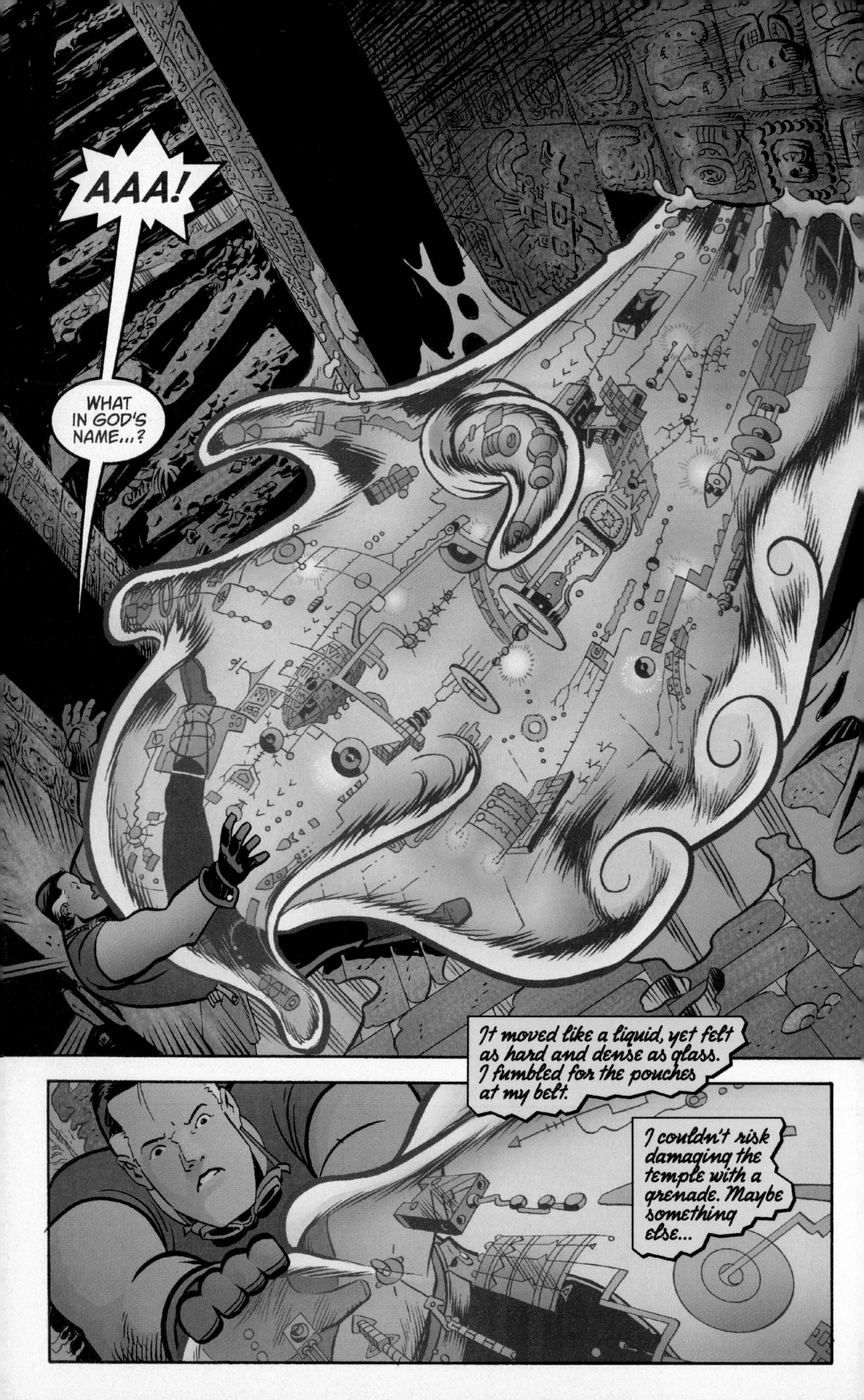
AAA!
WHAT IN GOD'S NAME...?
It moved like a liquid, yet felt as hard and dense as glass. I fumbled for the pouches at my belt.
I couldn't risk damaging the temple with a grenade. Maybe something else...

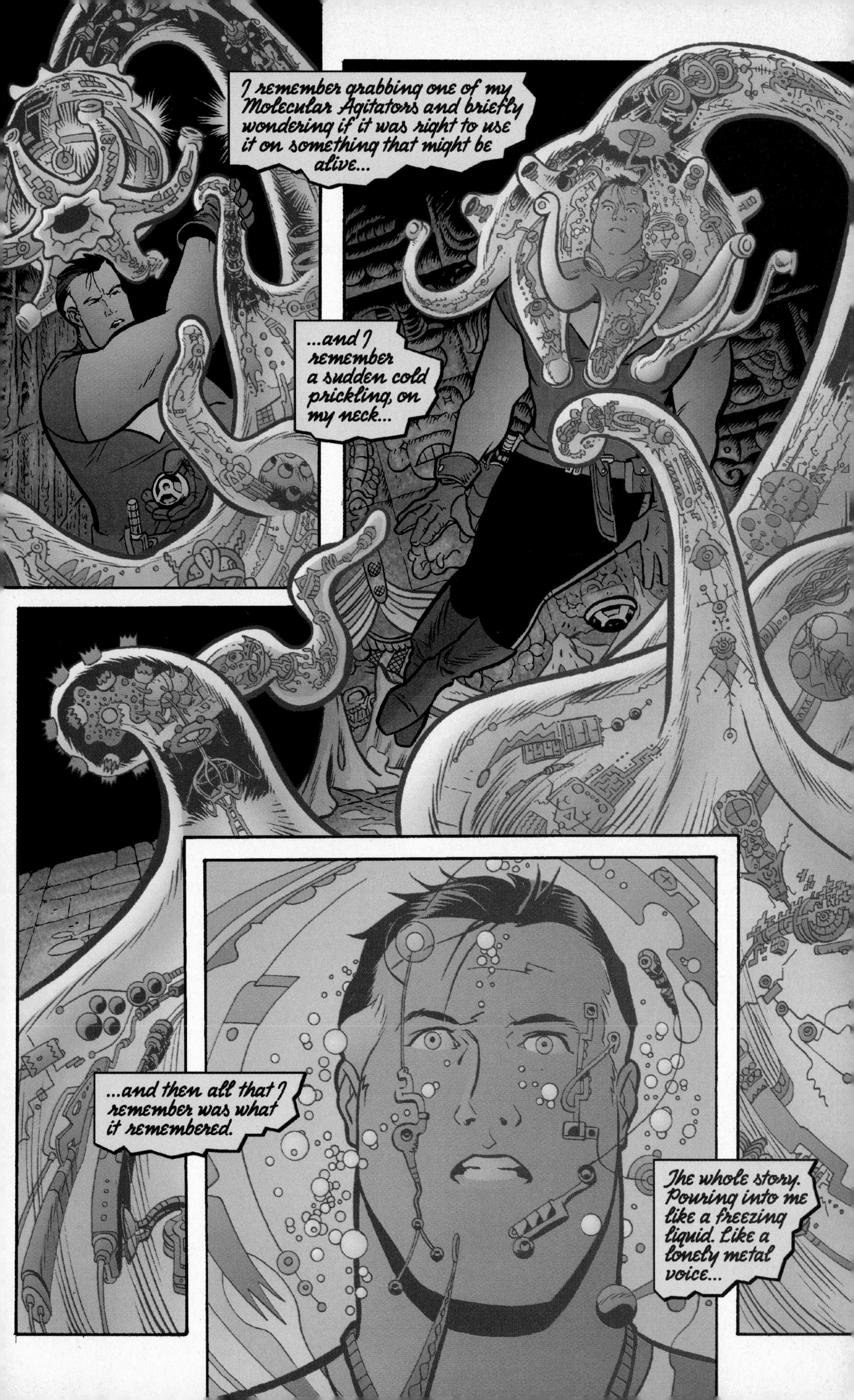
I remember grabbing one of my Molecular Agitators and briefly wondering if it was right to use it on something that might be alive...
...and I remember a sudden cold prickling, on my neck...
...and then all that I remember was what it remembered.
The whole story. Pouring into me like a freezing liquid. Like a lonely metal voice...

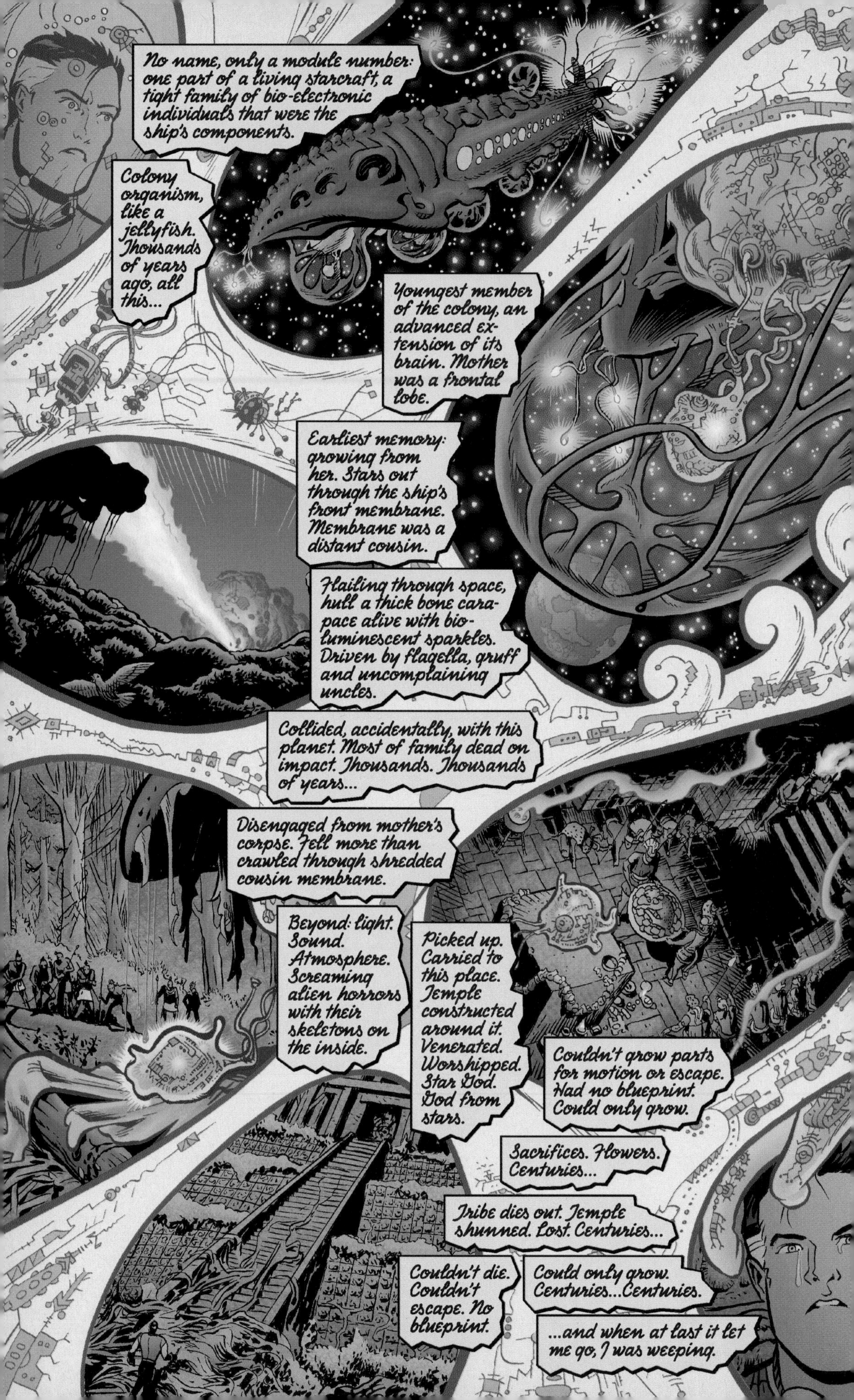
No name, only a module number: one part of a living starcraft, a tight family of bio-electronic individuals that were the ship's components.
Colony organism, like a jellyfish. Thousands of years ago, all this...
Youngest member of the colony, an advanced extension of its brain. Mother was a frontal lobe.
Earliest memory: growing from her. Stars out through the ship's front membrane. Membrane was a distant cousin.
Flailing through space, hull a thick bone carapace alive with bioluminescent sparkles. Driven by flagella, gruff and uncomplaining uncles.
Collided, accidentally, with this planet. Most of family dead on impact. Thousands. Thousands of years...
Disengaged from mother's corpse. Fell more than crawled through shredded cousin membrane.
Beyond: light. Sound. Atmosphere. Screaming alien horrors with their skeletons on the inside.
Picked up. Carried to this place. Temple constructed around it. Venerated. Worshipped. Star God. God from stars.
Couldn't grow parts for motion or escape. Had no blueprint. Could only grow.
Sacrifices. Flowers. Centuries...
Tribe dies out. Temple shunned. Lost. Centuries...
Couldn't die. Couldn't escape. No blueprint.
Could only grow. Centuries...Centuries.
...and when at last it let me go, I was weeping.

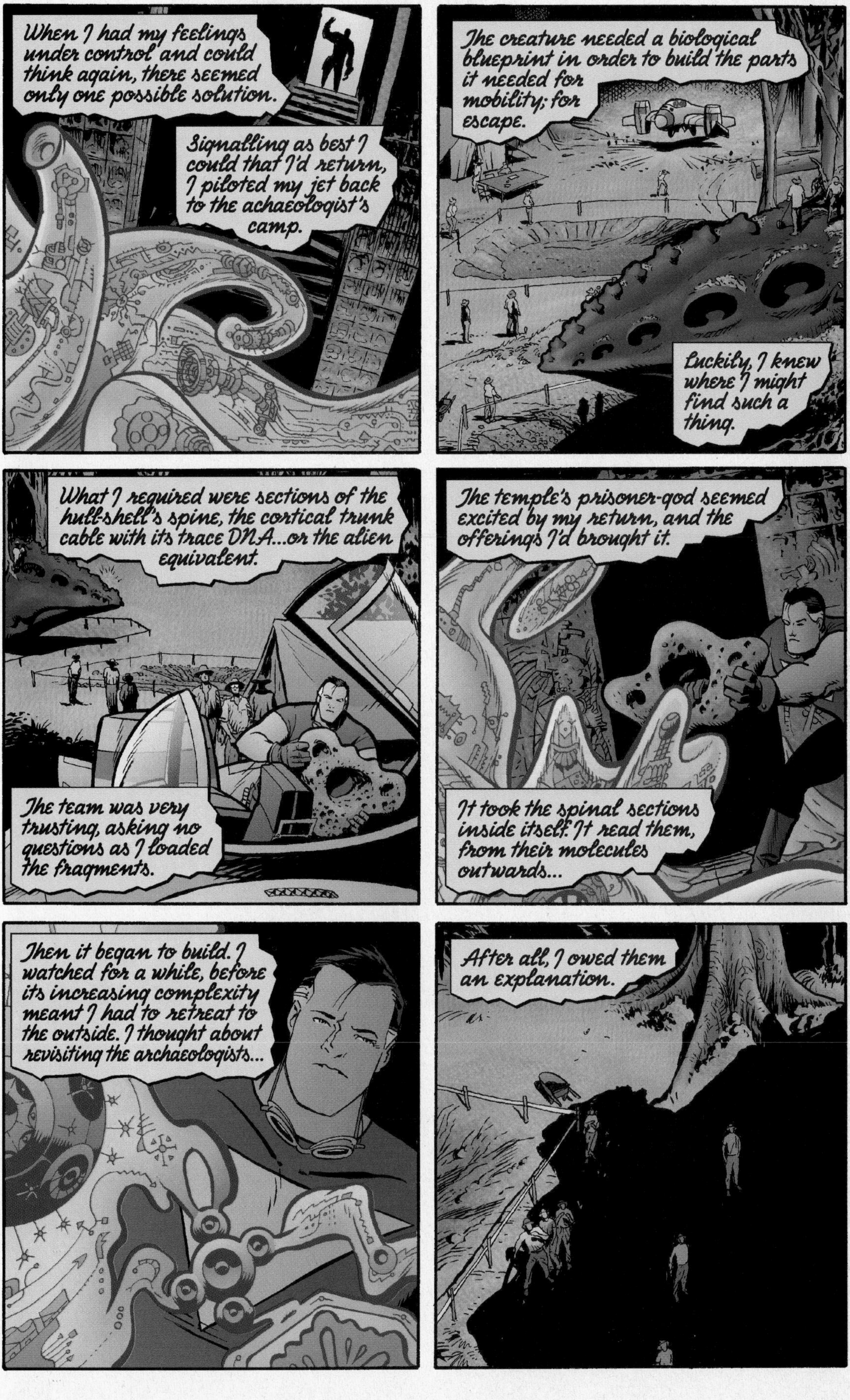
When I had my feelings under control and could think again, there seemed only one possible solution.
Signalling as best I could that I'd return, I piloted my jet back to the achaeologist's camp.
The creature needed a biological blueprint in order to build the parts it needed for mobility; for escape.
Luckily, I knew where I might find such a thing.
What I required were sections of the hull-shell's spine, the cortical trunk cable with its trace DNA...or the alien equivalent.
The team was very trusting, asking no questions as I loaded the fragments.
The temple's prisoner-god seemed excited by my return, and the offerings I'd brought it.
It took the spinal sections inside itself. It read them, from their molecules outwards...
Then it began to build. I watched for a while, before its increasing complexity meant I had to retreat to the outside. I thought about revisiting the archaeologists...
After all, I owed them an explanation.

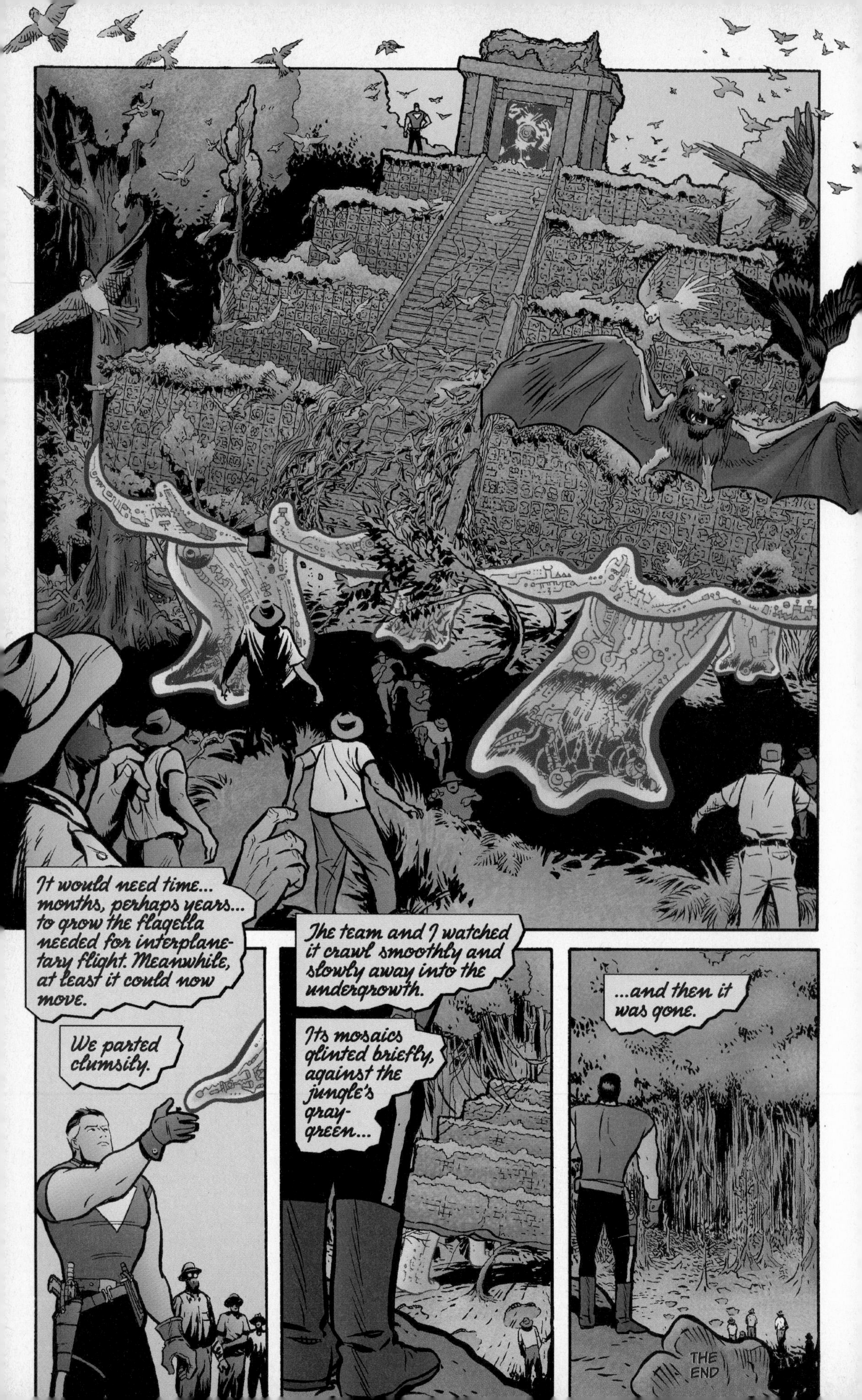
It would need time... months, perhaps years... to grow the flagella needed for interplanetary flight. Meanwhile, at least it could now move.
We parted clumsily.
The team and I watched it crawl smoothly and slowly away into the undergrowth.
Its mosaics glinted briefly, against the jungle's gray-green...
...and then it was gone.
THE END

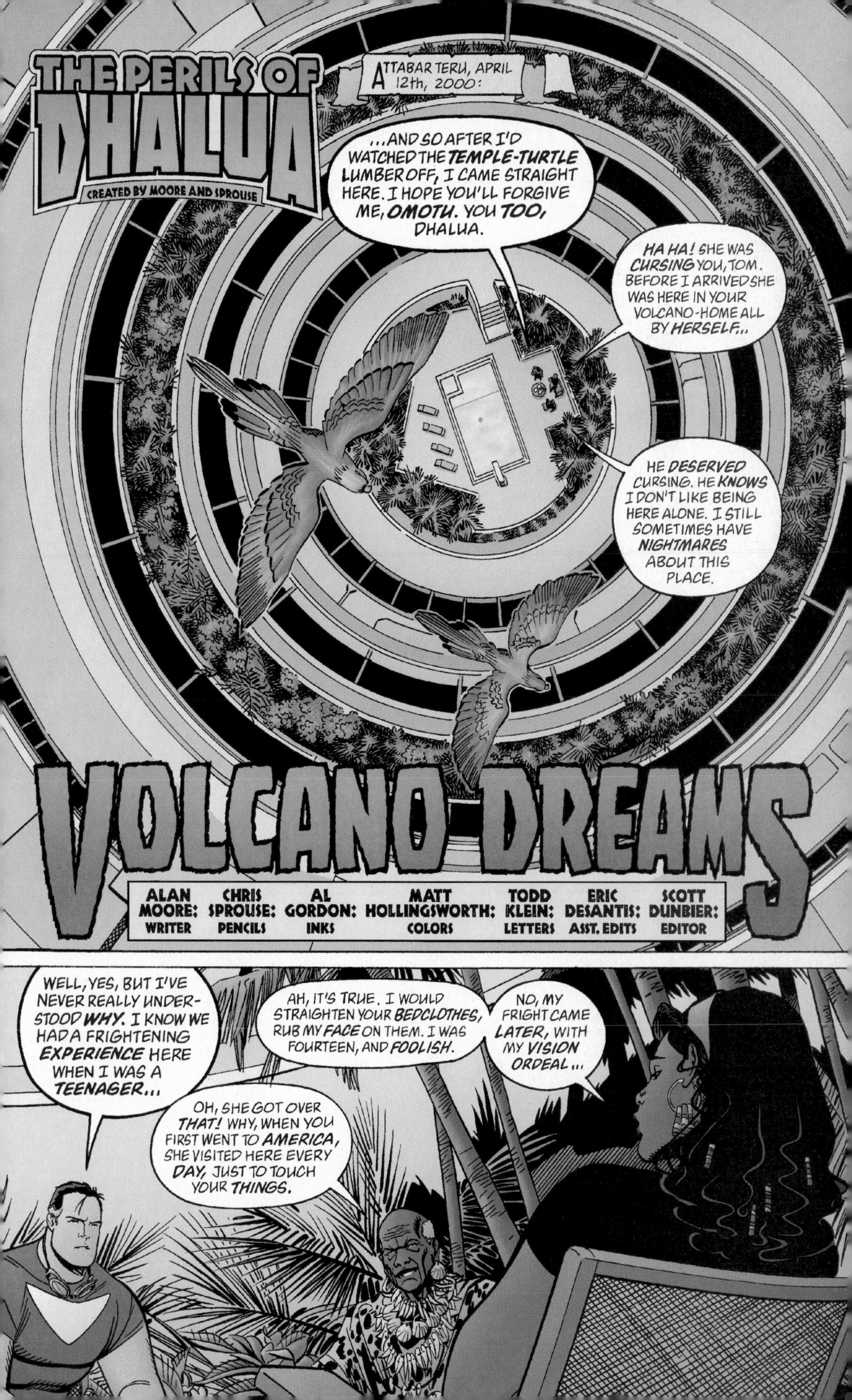
THE PERILS OF DHALUA
CREATED BY MOORE AND SPROUSE
ATTABAR TERU, APRIL 12th, 2000:
...AND SO AFTER I'D WATCHED THE TEMPLE-TURTLE LUMBER OFF, I CAME STRAIGHT HERE. I HOPE YOU'LL FORGIVE ME, OMOTU. YOU TOO, DHALUA.
HA HA! SHE WAS CURSING YOU, TOM. BEFORE I ARRIVED SHE WAS HERE IN YOUR VOLCANO-HOME ALL BY HERSELF...
HE DESERVED CURSING. HE KNOWS I DON'T LIKE BEING HERE ALONE. I STILL SOMETIMES HAVE NIGHTMARES ABOUT THIS PLACE.
VOLCANO DREAMS
ALAN MOORE: WRITER
CHRIS SPROUSE: PENCILS
AL GORDON: INKS
MATT HOLLINGSWORTH: COLORS
TODD KLEIN: LETTERS
ERIC DESANTIS: ASST. EDITS
SCOTT DUNBIER: EDITOR
WELL, YES, BUT I'VE NEVER REALLY UNDERSTOOD WHY. I KNOW WE HAD A FRIGHTENING EXPERIENCE HERE WHEN I WAS A TEENAGER...
OH, SHE GOT OVER THAT! WHY, WHEN YOU FIRST WENT TO AMERICA, SHE VISITED HERE EVERY DAY, JUST TO TOUCH YOUR THINGS.
AH, IT'S TRUE. I WOULD STRAIGHTEN YOUR BEDCLOTHES, RUB MY FACE ON THEM. I WAS FOURTEEN, AND FOOLISH.
NO, MY FRIGHT CAME LATER, WITH MY VISION ORDEAL...

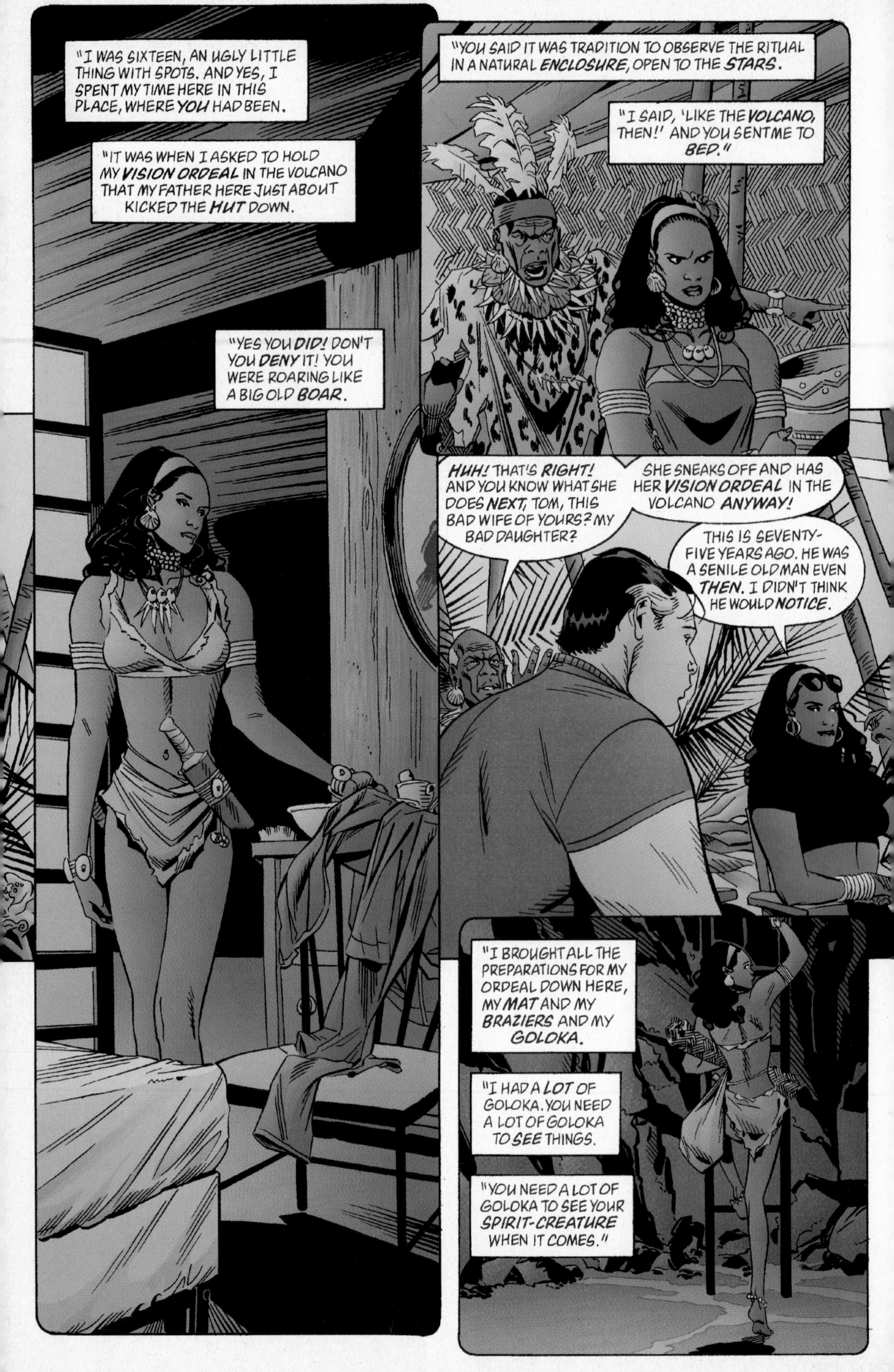

"I WAS SIXTEEN, AN UGLY LITTLE THING WITH SPOTS. AND YES, I SPENT MY TIME HERE IN THIS PLACE, WHERE YOU HAD BEEN.
"IT WAS WHEN I ASKED TO HOLD MY VISION ORDEAL IN THE VOLCANO THAT MY FATHER HERE JUST ABOUT KICKED THE HUT DOWN.
"YES YOU DID! DON'T YOU DENY IT! YOU WERE ROARING LIKE A BIG OLD BOAR.
"YOU SAID IT WAS TRADITION TO OBSERVE THE RITUAL IN A NATURAL ENCLOSURE, OPEN TO THE STARS.
"I SAID, 'LIKE THE VOLCANO, THEN!' AND YOU SENT ME TO BED."
HUH! THAT'S RIGHT! AND YOU KNOW WHAT SHE DOES NEXT, TOM, THIS BAD WIFE OF YOURS? MY BAD DAUGHTER?
SHE SNEAKS OFF AND HAS HER VISION ORDEAL IN THE VOLCANO ANYWAY!
THIS IS SEVENTY-FIVE YEARS AGO. HE WAS A SENILE OLD MAN EVEN THEN. I DIDN'T THINK HE WOULD NOTICE.
"I BROUGHT ALL THE PREPARATIONS FOR MY ORDEAL DOWN HERE, MY MAT AND MY BRAZIERS AND MY GOLOKA.
"I HAD A LOT OF GOLOKA. YOU NEED A LOT OF GOLOKA TO SEE THINGS.
"YOU NEED A LOT OF GOLOKA TO SEE YOUR SPIRIT-CREATURE WHEN IT COMES."

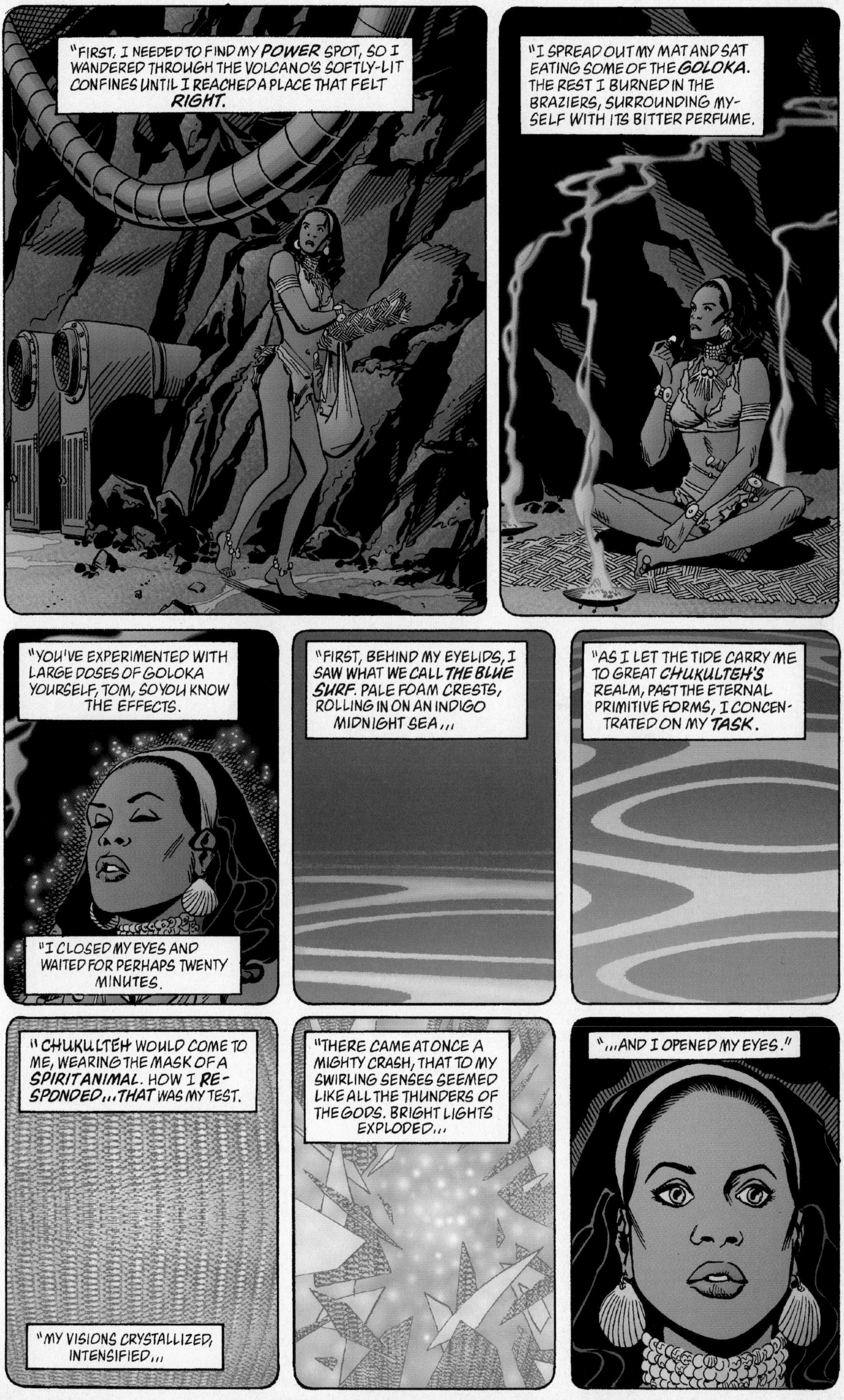
"FIRST, I NEEDED TO FIND MY POWER SPOT, SO I WANDERED THROUGH THE VOLCANO'S SOFTLY-LIT CONFINES UNTIL I REACHED A PLACE THAT FELT RIGHT.
"I SPREAD OUT MY MAT AND SAT EATING SOME OF THE GOLOKA. THE REST I BURNED IN THE BRAZIERS, SURROUNDING MY-SELF WITH ITS BITTER PERFUME.
"YOU'VE EXPERIMENTED WITH LARGE DOSES OF GOLOKA YOURSELF, TOM, SO YOU KNOW THE EFFECTS.
"I CLOSED MY EYES AND WAITED FOR PERHAPS TWENTY MINUTES.
"FIRST, BEHIND MY EYELIDS, I SAW WHAT WE CALL THE BLUE SURF. PALE FOAM CRESTS, ROLLING IN ON AN INDIGO MIDNIGHT SEA...
"AS I LET THE TIDE CARRY ME TO GREAT CHUKULTEH'S REALM, PAST THE ETERNAL PRIMITIVE FORMS, I CONCEN-TRATED ON MY TASK.
"CHUKULTEH WOULD COME TO ME, WEARING THE MASK OF A SPIRIT ANIMAL. HOW I RE-SPONDED...THAT WAS MY TEST.
"MY VISIONS CRYSTALLIZED, INTENSIFIED...
"THERE CAME AT ONCE A MIGHTY CRASH, THAT TO MY SWIRLING SENSES SEEMED LIKE ALL THE THUNDERS OF THE GODS. BRIGHT LIGHTS EXPLODED...
"...AND I OPENED MY EYES."

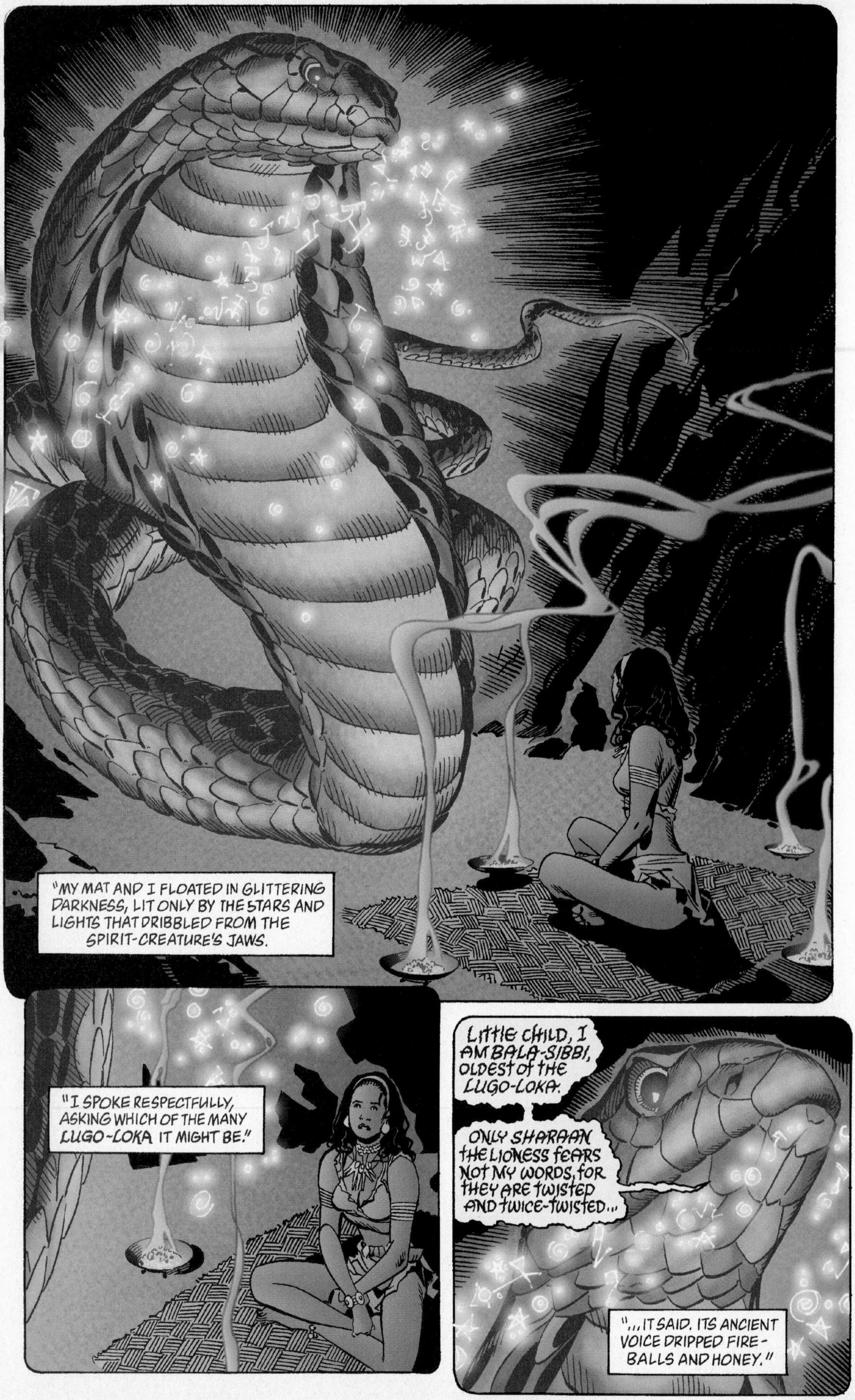
"MY MAT AND I FLOATED IN GLITTERING DARKNESS, LIT ONLY BY THE STARS AND LIGHTS THAT DRIBBLED FROM THE SPIRIT-CREATURE'S JAWS.
"I SPOKE RESPECTFULLY, ASKING WHICH OF THE MANY LUGO-LOKA IT MIGHT BE."
LITTLE CHILD, I AM BALA-SIBBI, OLDEST OF THE LUGO-LOKA.
ONLY SHARAAN THE LIONESS FEARS NOT MY WORDS, FOR THEY ARE TWISTED AND TWICE-TWISTED...
"...IT SAID. ITS ANCIENT VOICE DRIPPED FIRE-BALLS AND HONEY."

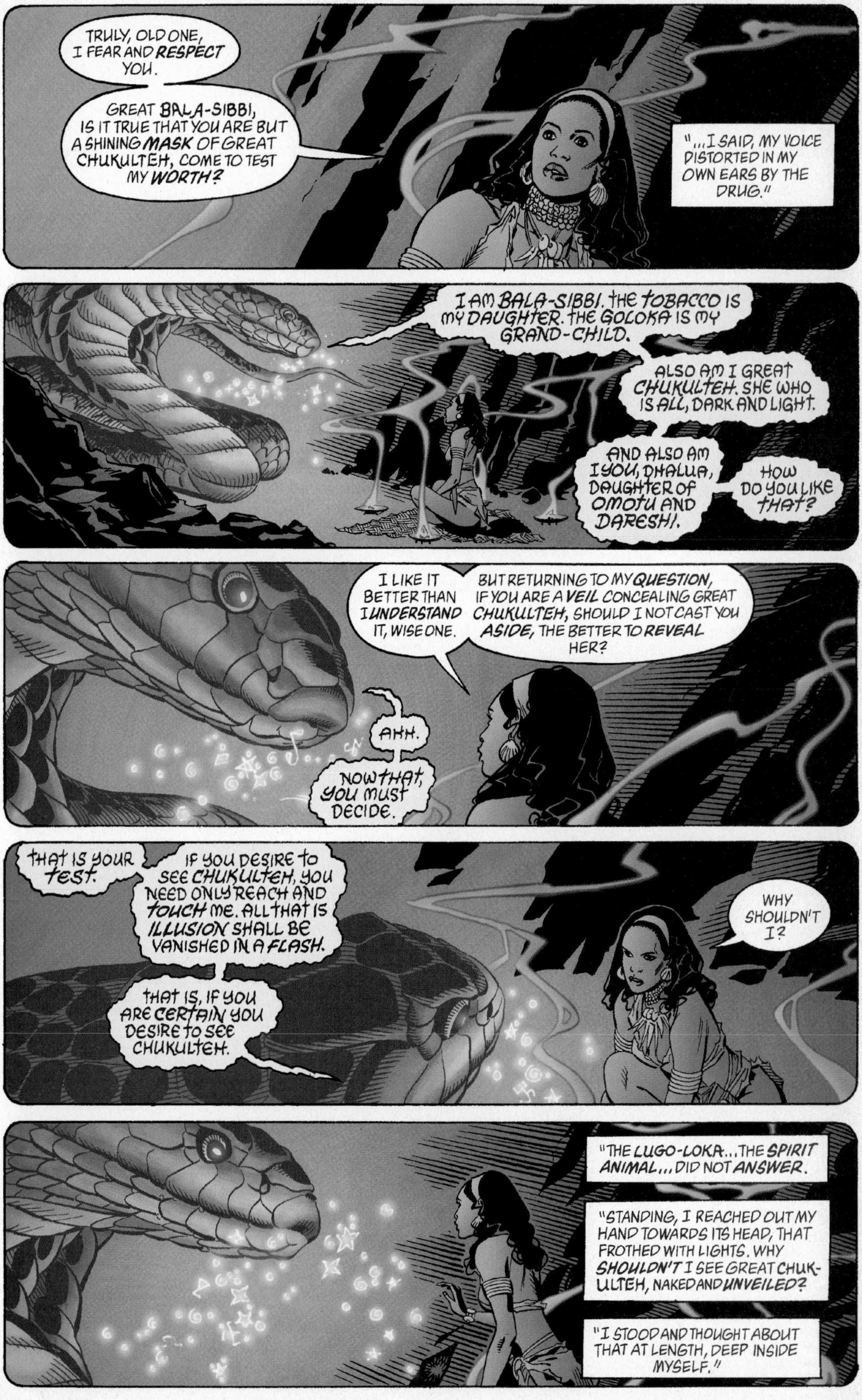
TRULY, OLD ONE, I FEAR AND RESPECT YOU.
GREAT BALA-SIBBI, IS IT TRUE THAT YOU ARE BUT A SHINING MASK OF GREAT CHUKULTEH, COME TO TEST MY WORTH?
"...I SAID, MY VOICE DISTORTED IN MY OWN EARS BY THE DRUG."
I AM BALA-SIBBI. THE TOBACCO IS MY DAUGHTER. THE GOLOKA IS MY GRAND-CHILD.
ALSO AM I GREAT CHUKULTEH. SHE WHO IS ALL, DARK AND LIGHT.
AND ALSO AM I YOU, DHALUA, DAUGHTER OF OMOTU AND DARESHI.
HOW DO YOU LIKE THAT?
I LIKE IT BETTER THAN I UNDERSTAND IT, WISE ONE.
BUT RETURNING TO MY QUESTION, IF YOU ARE A VEIL CONCEALING GREAT CHUKULTEH, SHOULD I NOT CAST YOU ASIDE, THE BETTER TO REVEAL HER?
AHH.
NOW THAT, YOU MUST DECIDE.
THAT IS YOUR TEST.
IF YOU DESIRE TO SEE CHUKULTEH, YOU NEED ONLY REACH AND TOUCH ME. ALL THAT IS ILLUSION SHALL BE VANISHED IN A FLASH.
THAT IS, IF YOU ARE CERTAIN YOU DESIRE TO SEE CHUKULTEH.
WHY SHOULDN'T I?
"THE LUGO-LOKA... THE SPIRIT ANIMAL... DID NOT ANSWER.
"STANDING, I REACHED OUT MY HAND TOWARDS ITS HEAD, THAT FROTHED WITH LIGHTS. WHY SHOULDN'T I SEE GREAT CHUK-ULTEH, NAKED AND UNVEILED?
"I STOOD AND THOUGHT ABOUT THAT AT LENGTH, DEEP INSIDE MYSELF."

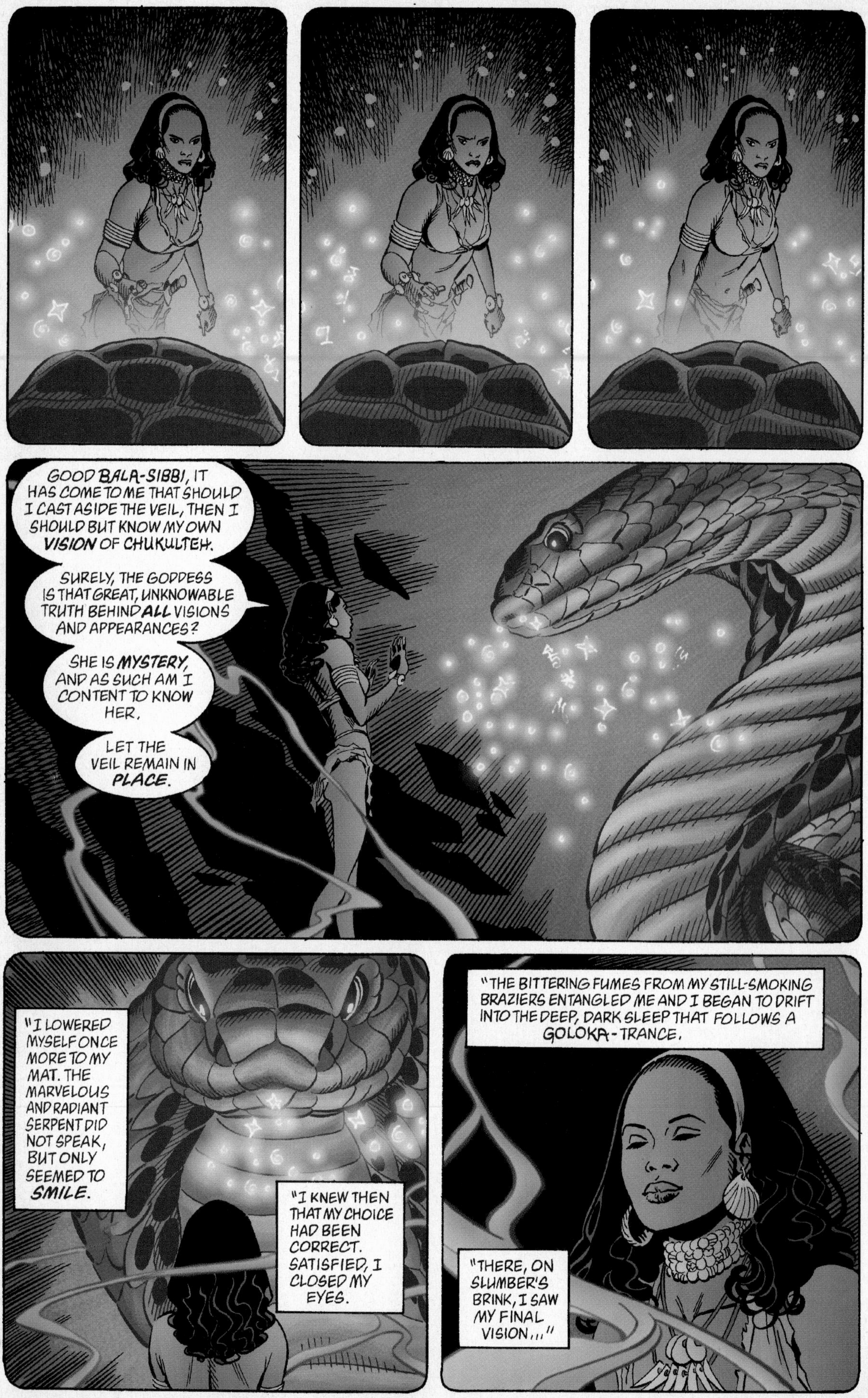
GOOD BALA-SIBBI, IT HAS COME TO ME THAT SHOULD I CAST ASIDE THE VEIL, THEN I SHOULD BUT KNOW MY OWN VISION OF CHUKULTEH.
SURELY, THE GODDESS IS THAT GREAT, UNKNOWABLE TRUTH BEHIND ALL VISIONS AND APPEARANCES?
SHE IS MYSTERY, AND AS SUCH AM I CONTENT TO KNOW HER.
LET THE VEIL REMAIN IN PLACE.
"I LOWERED MYSELF ONCE MORE TO MY MAT. THE MARVELOUS AND RADIANT SERPENT DID NOT SPEAK, BUT ONLY SEEMED TO SMILE.
"I KNEW THEN THAT MY CHOICE HAD BEEN CORRECT. SATISFIED, I CLOSED MY EYES.
"THE BITTERING FUMES FROM MY STILL-SMOKING BRAZIERS ENTANGLED ME AND I BEGAN TO DRIFT INTO THE DEEP, DARK SLEEP THAT FOLLOWS A GOLOKA-TRANCE.
"THERE, ON SLUMBER'S BRINK, I SAW MY FINAL VISION..."

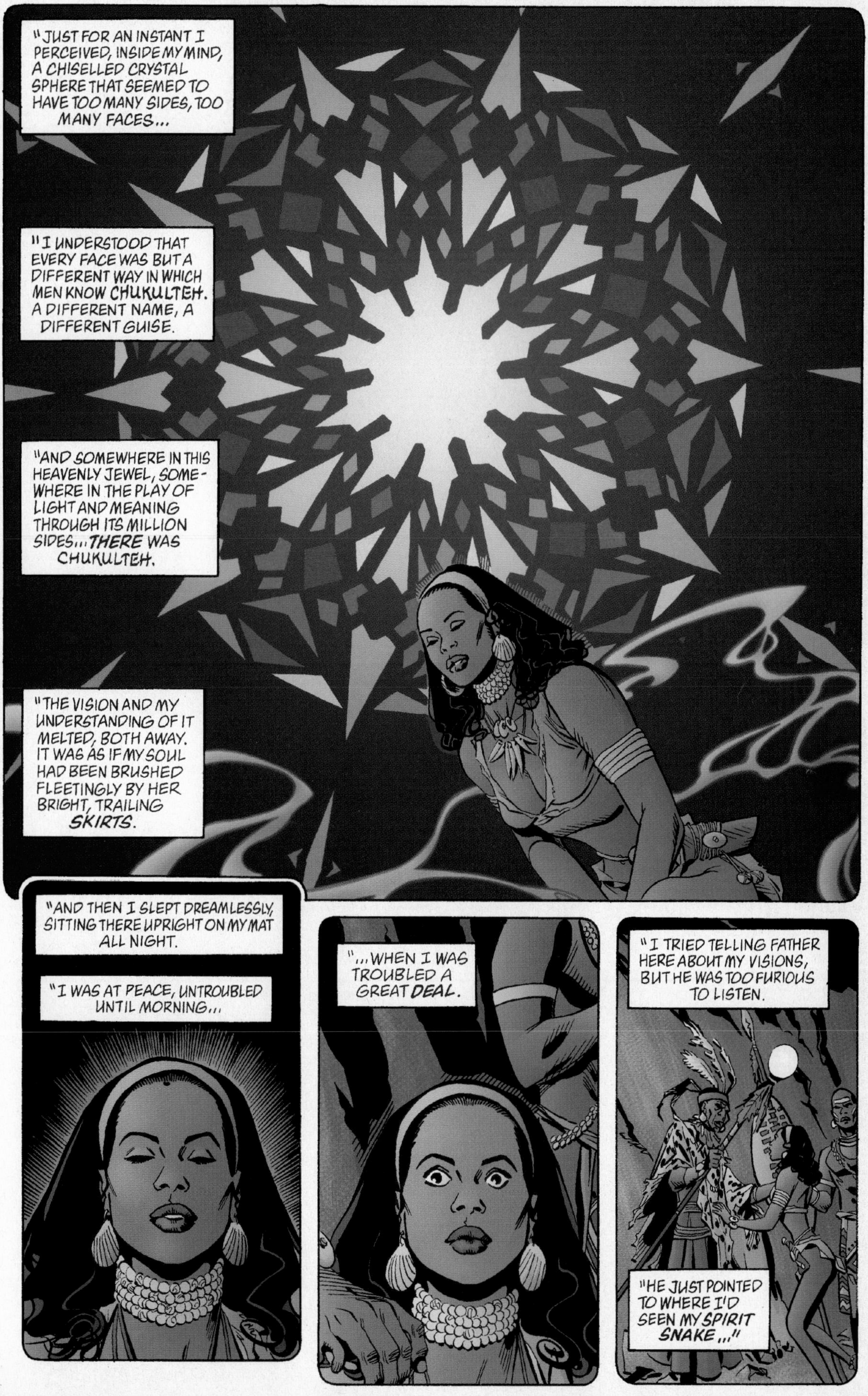
"JUST FOR AN INSTANT I PERCEIVED, INSIDE MY MIND, A CHISELLED CRYSTAL SPHERE THAT SEEMED TO HAVE TOO MANY SIDES, TOO MANY FACES...
"I UNDERSTOOD THAT EVERY FACE WAS BUT A DIFFERENT WAY IN WHICH MEN KNOW CHUKULTEH. A DIFFERENT NAME, A DIFFERENT GUISE.
"AND SOMEWHERE IN THIS HEAVENLY JEWEL, SOME-WHERE IN THE PLAY OF LIGHT AND MEANING THROUGH ITS MILLION SIDES... THERE WAS CHUKULTEH.
"THE VISION AND MY UNDERSTANDING OF IT MELTED, BOTH AWAY. IT WAS AS IF MY SOUL HAD BEEN BRUSHED FLEETINGLY BY HER BRIGHT, TRAILING SKIRTS.
"AND THEN I SLEPT DREAMLESSLY, SITTING THERE UPRIGHT ON MY MAT ALL NIGHT.
"I WAS AT PEACE, UNTROUBLED UNTIL MORNING...
"...WHEN I WAS TROUBLED A GREAT DEAL.
"I TRIED TELLING FATHER HERE ABOUT MY VISIONS, BUT HE WAS TOO FURIOUS TO LISTEN.
"HE JUST POINTED TO WHERE I'D SEEN MY SPIRIT SNAKE..."

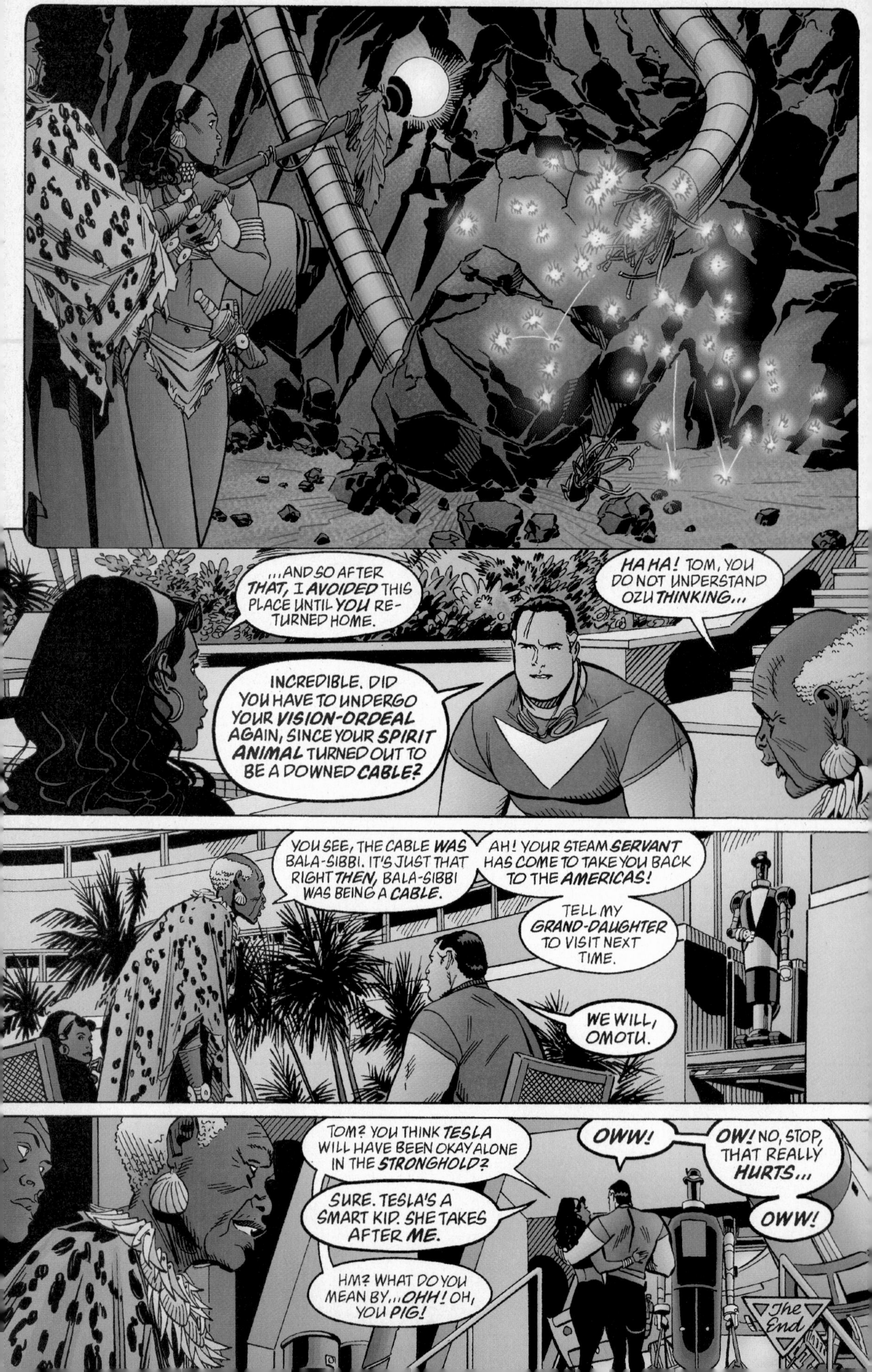

...AND SO AFTER THAT, I AVOIDED THIS PLACE UNTIL YOU RETURNED HOME.
HA HA! TOM, YOU DO NOT UNDERSTAND OZU THINKING...
INCREDIBLE. DID YOU HAVE TO UNDERGO YOUR VISION-ORDEAL AGAIN, SINCE YOUR SPIRIT ANIMAL TURNED OUT TO BE A DOWNED CABLE?
YOU SEE, THE CABLE WAS BALA-SIBBI. IT'S JUST THAT RIGHT THEN, BALA-SIBBI WAS BEING A CABLE.
AH! YOUR STEAM SERVANT HAS COME TO TAKE YOU BACK TO THE AMERICAS!
TELL MY GRAND-DAUGHTER TO VISIT NEXT TIME.
WE WILL, OMOTU.
TOM? YOU THINK TESLA WILL HAVE BEEN OKAY ALONE IN THE STRONGHOLD?
SURE. TESLA'S A SMART KID. SHE TAKES AFTER ME.
HM? WHAT DO YOU MEAN BY... OHH! OH, YOU PIG!
OWW!
OW! NO, STOP, THAT REALLY HURTS...
OWW!
The End

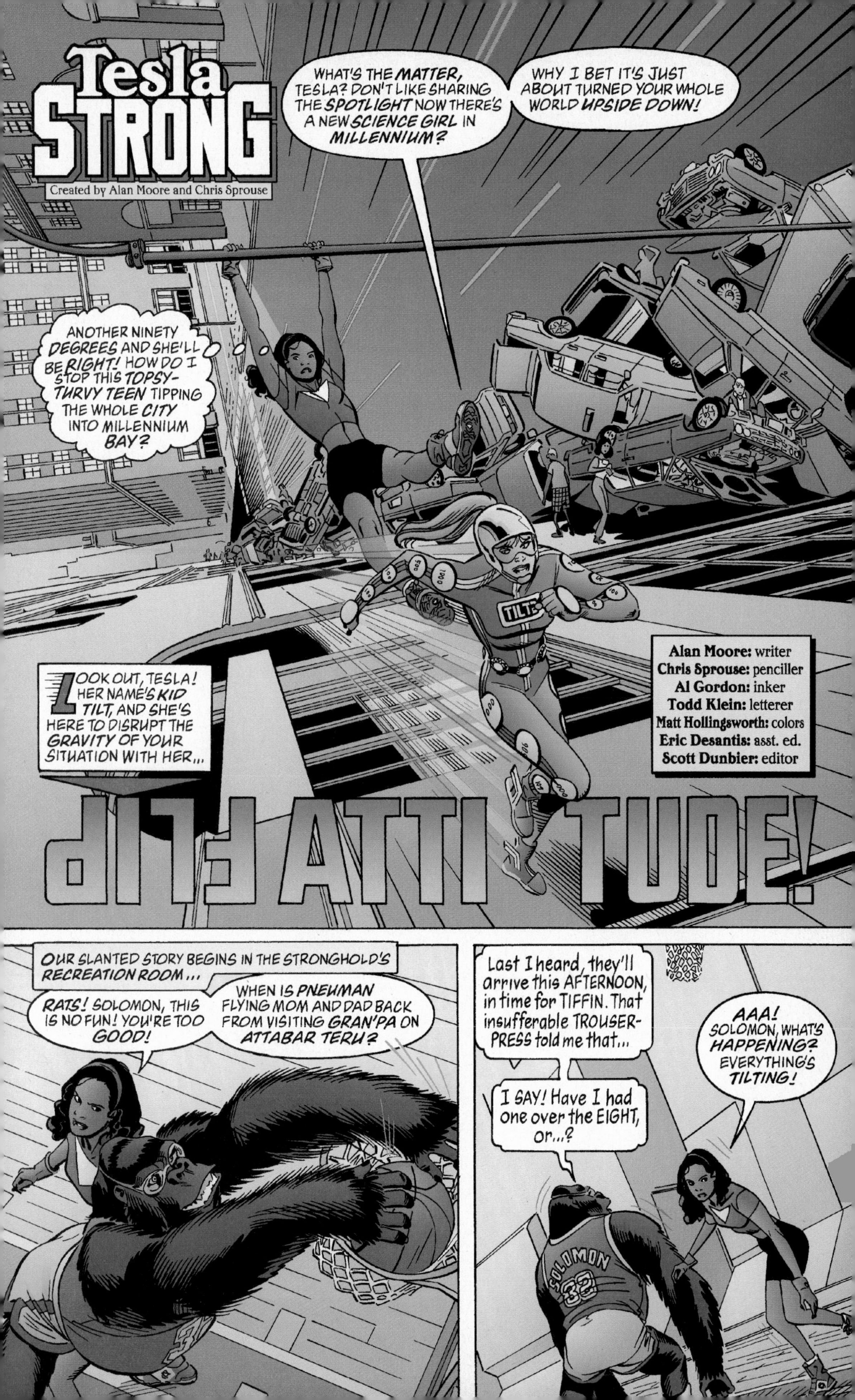
Tesla Strong
Created by Alan Moore and Chris Sprouse
WHAT'S THE MATTER, TESLA? DON'T LIKE SHARING THE SPOTLIGHT NOW THERE'S A NEW SCIENCE GIRL IN MILLENNIUM?
WHY I BET IT'S JUST ABOUT TURNED YOUR WHOLE WORLD UPSIDE DOWN!
ANOTHER NINETY DEGREES AND SHE'LL BE RIGHT! HOW DO I STOP THIS TOPSY-TURVY TEEN TIPPING THE WHOLE CITY INTO MILLENNIUM BAY?
TILT
LOOK OUT, TESLA! HER NAME'S KID TILT, AND SHE'S HERE TO DISRUPT THE GRAVITY OF YOUR SITUATION WITH HER...
Alan Moore: writer
Chris Sprouse: penciller
Al Gordon: inker
Todd Klein: letterer
Matt Hollingsworth: colors
Eric Desantis: asst. ed.
Scott Dunbier: editor
FLIP ATTITUDE!
OUR SLANTED STORY BEGINS IN THE STRONGHOLD'S RECREATION ROOM...
RATS! SOLOMON, THIS IS NO FUN! YOU'RE TOO GOOD!
WHEN IS PNEUMAN FLYING MOM AND DAD BACK FROM VISITING GRAN'PA ON ATTABAR TERU?
Last I heard, they'll arrive this AFTERNOON, in time for TIFFIN. That insufferable TROUSER-PRESS told me that...
I SAY! Have I had one over the EIGHT, or...?
AAA! SOLOMON, WHAT'S HAPPENING? EVERYTHING'S TILTING!
SOLOMON
33

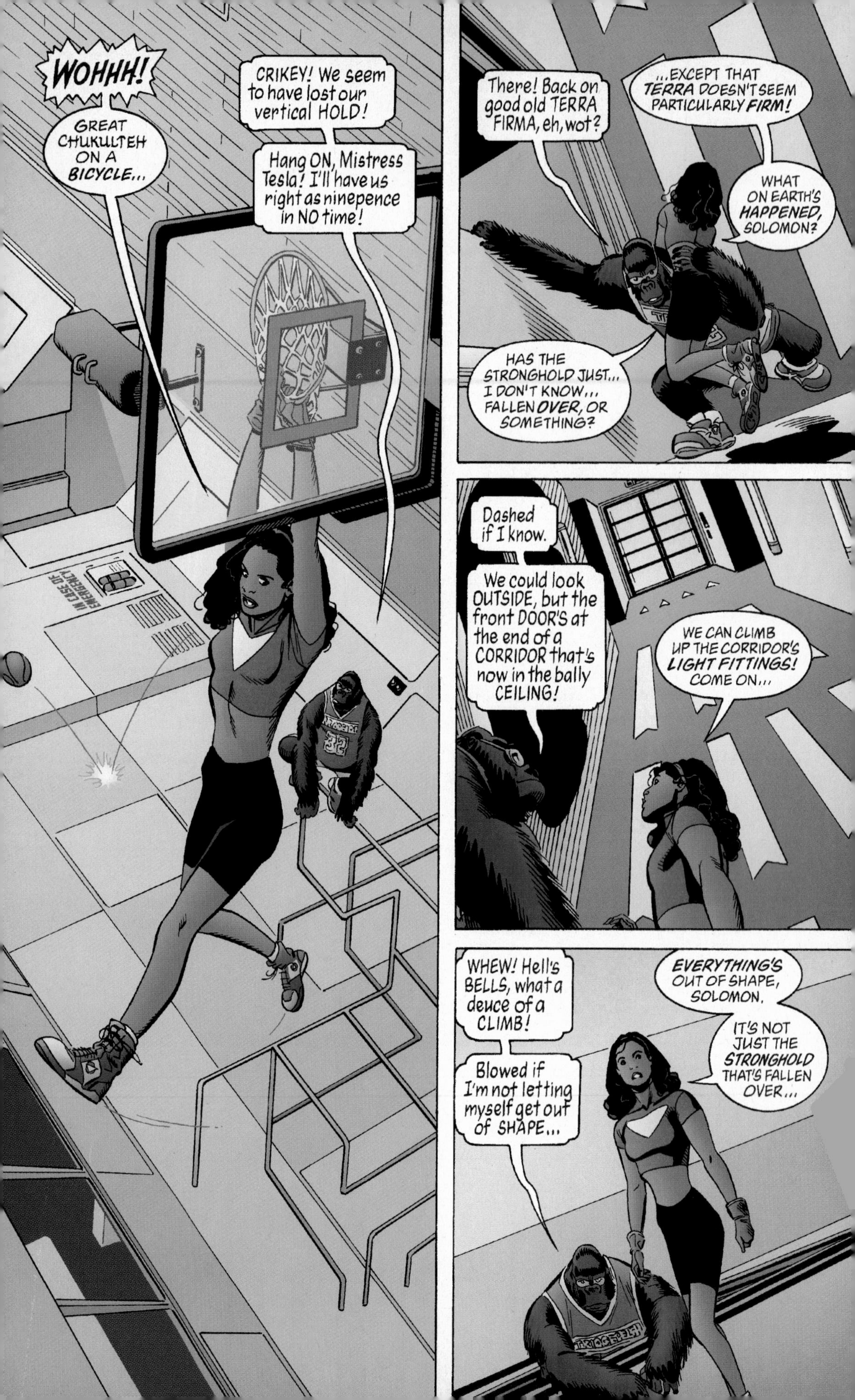
WOHHH!
GREAT CHUKULTEH ON A BICYCLE...
CRIKEY! We seem to have lost our vertical HOLD!
Hang ON, Mistress Tesla! I'll have us right as ninepence in NO time!
IN CASE OF EMERGENCY
There! Back on good old TERRA FIRMA, eh, wot?
...EXCEPT THAT TERRA DOESN'T SEEM PARTICULARLY FIRM!
WHAT ON EARTH'S HAPPENED, SOLOMON?
HAS THE STRONGHOLD JUST... I DON'T KNOW... FALLEN OVER, OR SOMETHING?
Dashed if I know.
We could look OUTSIDE, but the front DOOR'S at the end of a CORRIDOR that's now in the bally CEILING!
WE CAN CLIMB UP THE CORRIDOR'S LIGHT FITTINGS! COME ON...
WHEW! Hell's BELLS, what a deuce of a CLIMB!
Blowed if I'm not letting myself get out of SHAPE...
EVERYTHING'S OUT OF SHAPE, SOLOMON.
IT'S NOT JUST THE STRONGHOLD THAT'S FALLEN OVER...

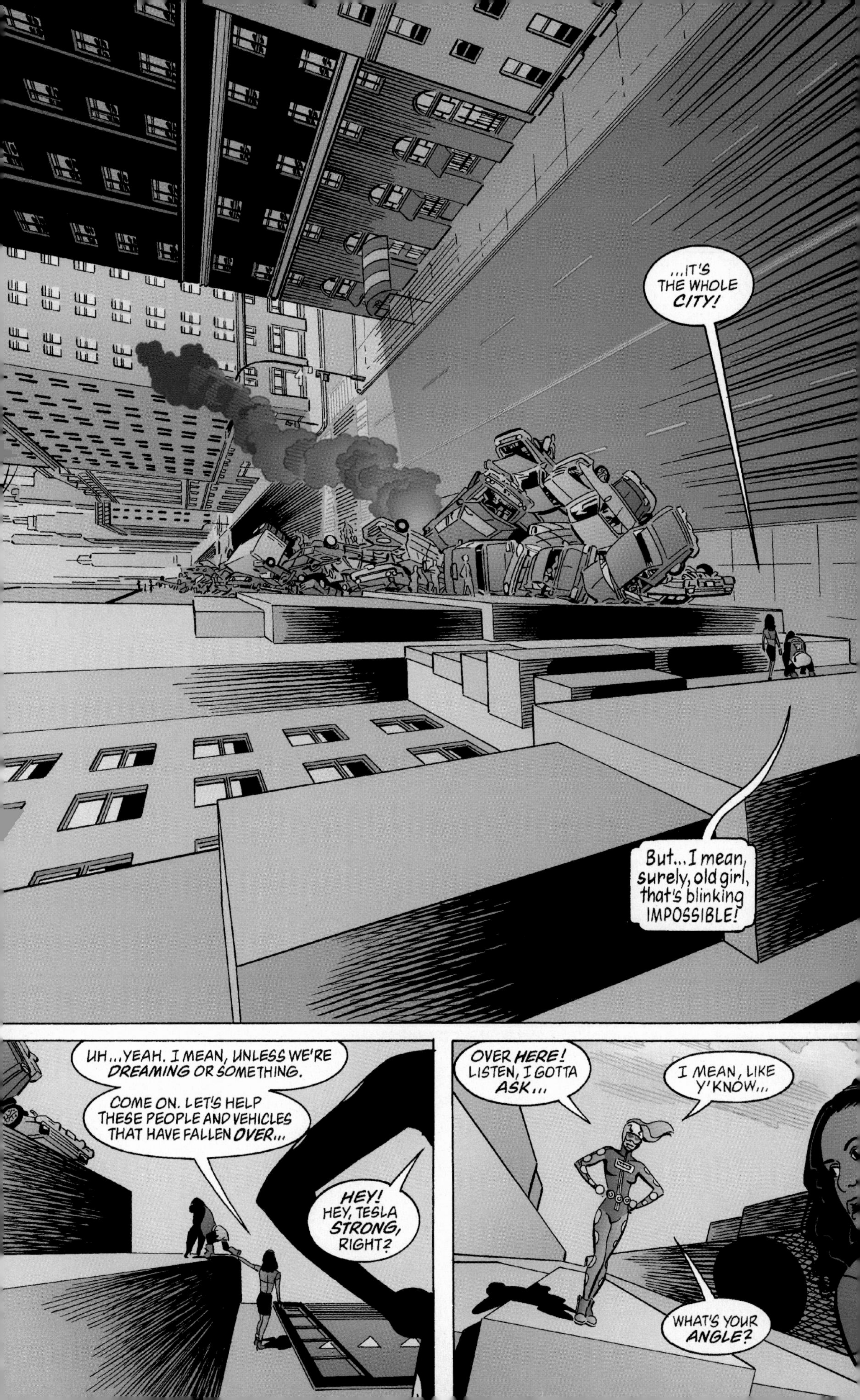
...IT'S THE WHOLE CITY!
But... I mean, surely, old girl, that's blinking IMPOSSIBLE!
UH...YEAH. I MEAN, UNLESS WE'RE DREAMING OR SOMETHING.
COME ON. LET'S HELP THESE PEOPLE AND VEHICLES THAT HAVE FALLEN OVER...
HEY! HEY, TESLA STRONG, RIGHT?
OVER HERE! LISTEN, I GOTTA ASK...
I MEAN, LIKE Y'KNOW...
WHAT'S YOUR ANGLE?

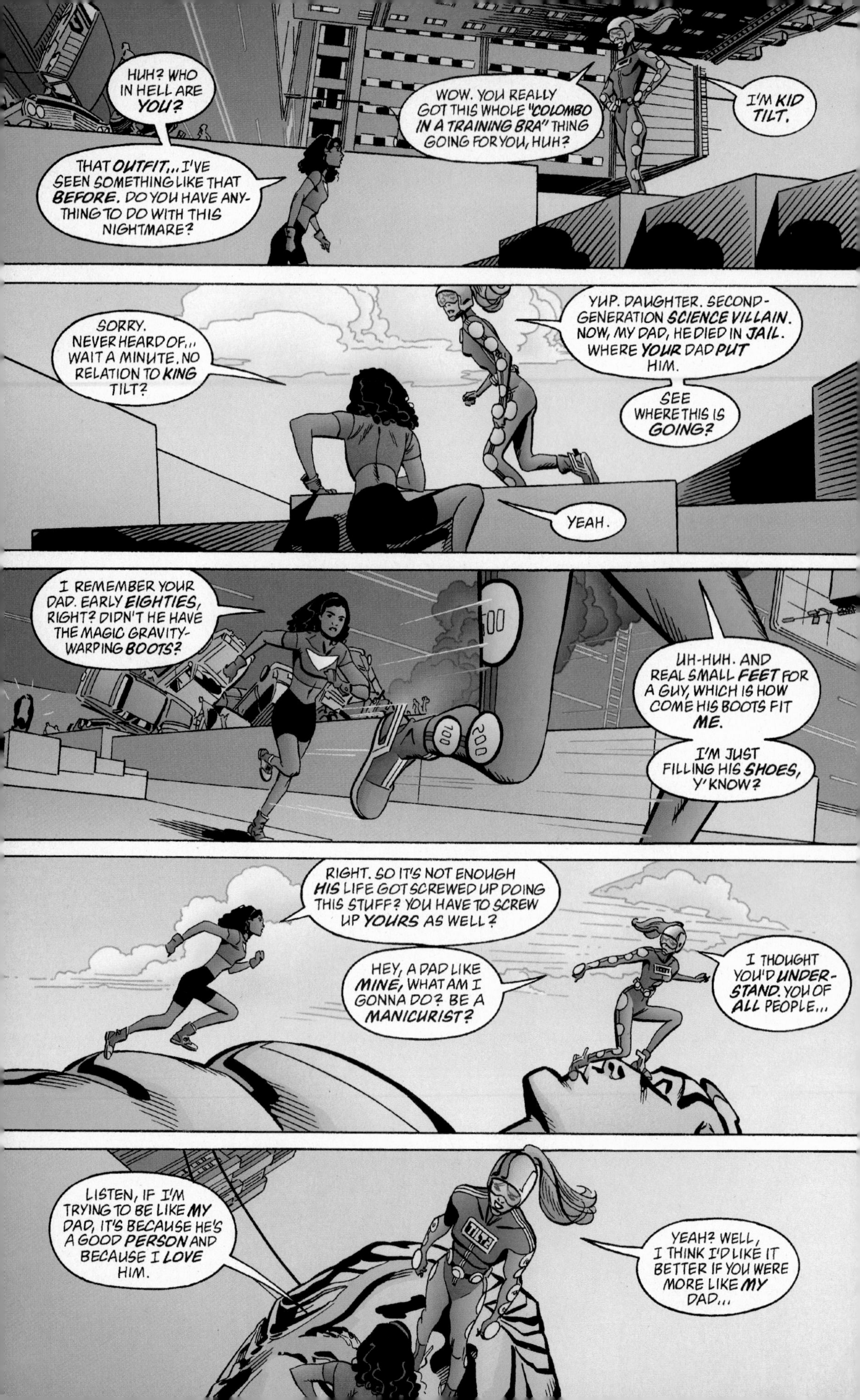
HUH? WHO IN HELL ARE YOU?
THAT OUTFIT... I'VE SEEN SOMETHING LIKE THAT BEFORE. DO YOU HAVE ANY-THING TO DO WITH THIS NIGHTMARE?
WOW. YOU REALLY GOT THIS WHOLE "COLOMBO IN A TRAINING BRA" THING GOING FOR YOU, HUH?
I'M KID TILT.
SORRY. NEVER HEARD OF... WAIT A MINUTE. NO RELATION TO KING TILT?
YUP. DAUGHTER. SECOND-GENERATION SCIENCE VILLAIN. NOW, MY DAD, HE DIED IN JAIL. WHERE YOUR DAD PUT HIM.
SEE WHERE THIS IS GOING?
YEAH.
I REMEMBER YOUR DAD. EARLY EIGHTIES, RIGHT? DIDN'T HE HAVE THE MAGIC GRAVITY-WARPING BOOTS?
UH-HUH. AND REAL SMALL FEET FOR A GUY, WHICH IS HOW COME HIS BOOTS FIT ME.
I'M JUST FILLING HIS SHOES, Y'KNOW?
RIGHT. SO IT'S NOT ENOUGH HIS LIFE GOT SCREWED UP DOING THIS STUFF? YOU HAVE TO SCREW UP YOURS AS WELL?
HEY, A DAD LIKE MINE, WHAT AM I GONNA DO? BE A MANICURIST?
I THOUGHT YOU'D UNDER-STAND. YOU OF ALL PEOPLE...
LISTEN, IF I'M TRYING TO BE LIKE MY DAD, IT'S BECAUSE HE'S A GOOD PERSON AND BECAUSE I LOVE HIM.
YEAH? WELL, I THINK I'D LIKE IT BETTER IF YOU WERE MORE LIKE MY DAD...

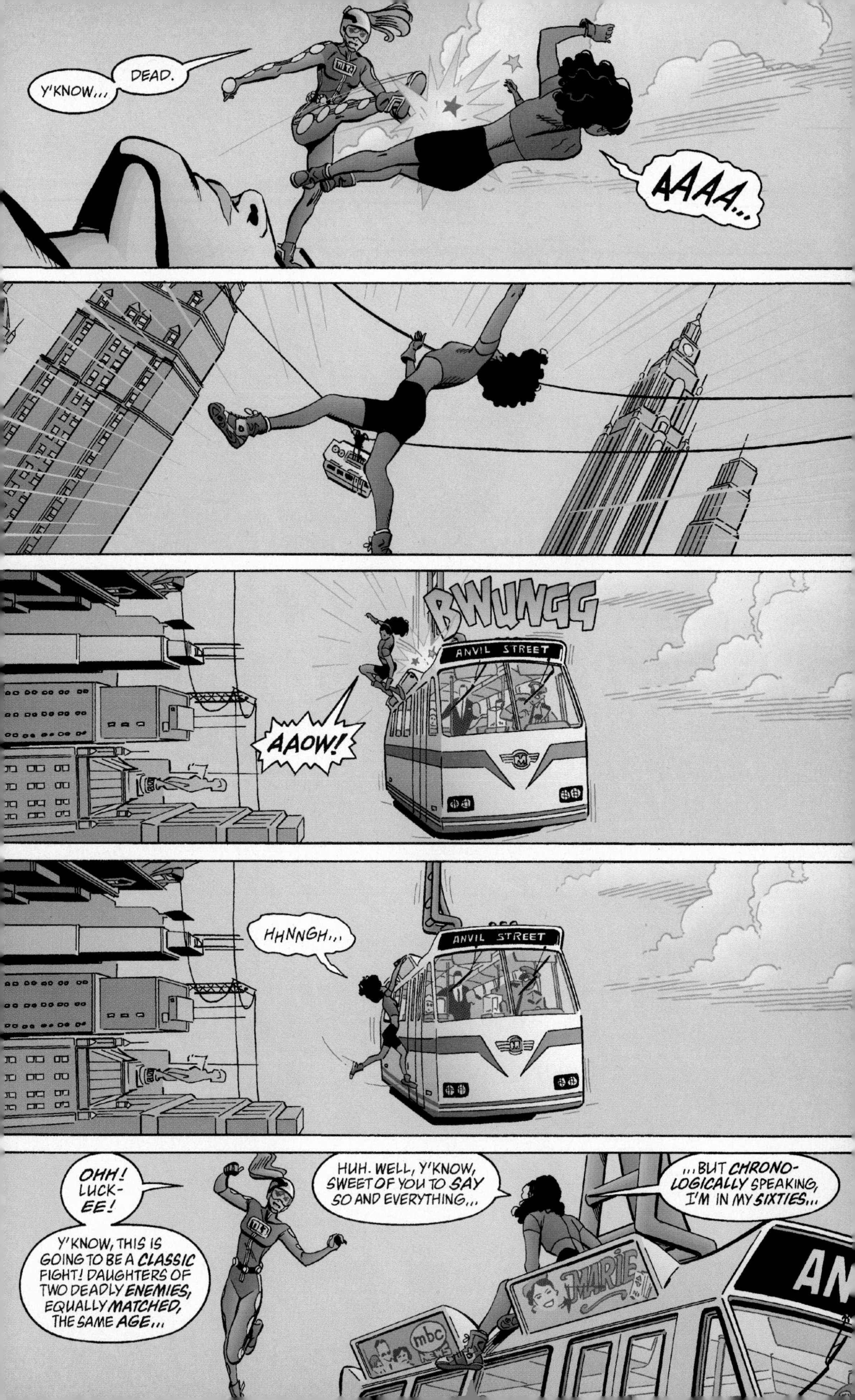
Y'KNOW...
DEAD.
AAAA...
BWUNGG
ANVIL STREET
AAOW!
HHNNGH...
ANVIL STREET
OHH! LUCK-EE!
Y'KNOW, THIS IS GOING TO BE A CLASSIC FIGHT! DAUGHTERS OF TWO DEADLY ENEMIES, EQUALLY MATCHED, THE SAME AGE...
HUH. WELL, Y'KNOW, SWEET OF YOU TO SAY SO AND EVERYTHING...
...BUT CHRONO-LOGICALLY SPEAKING, I'M IN MY SIXTIES...
MARIE

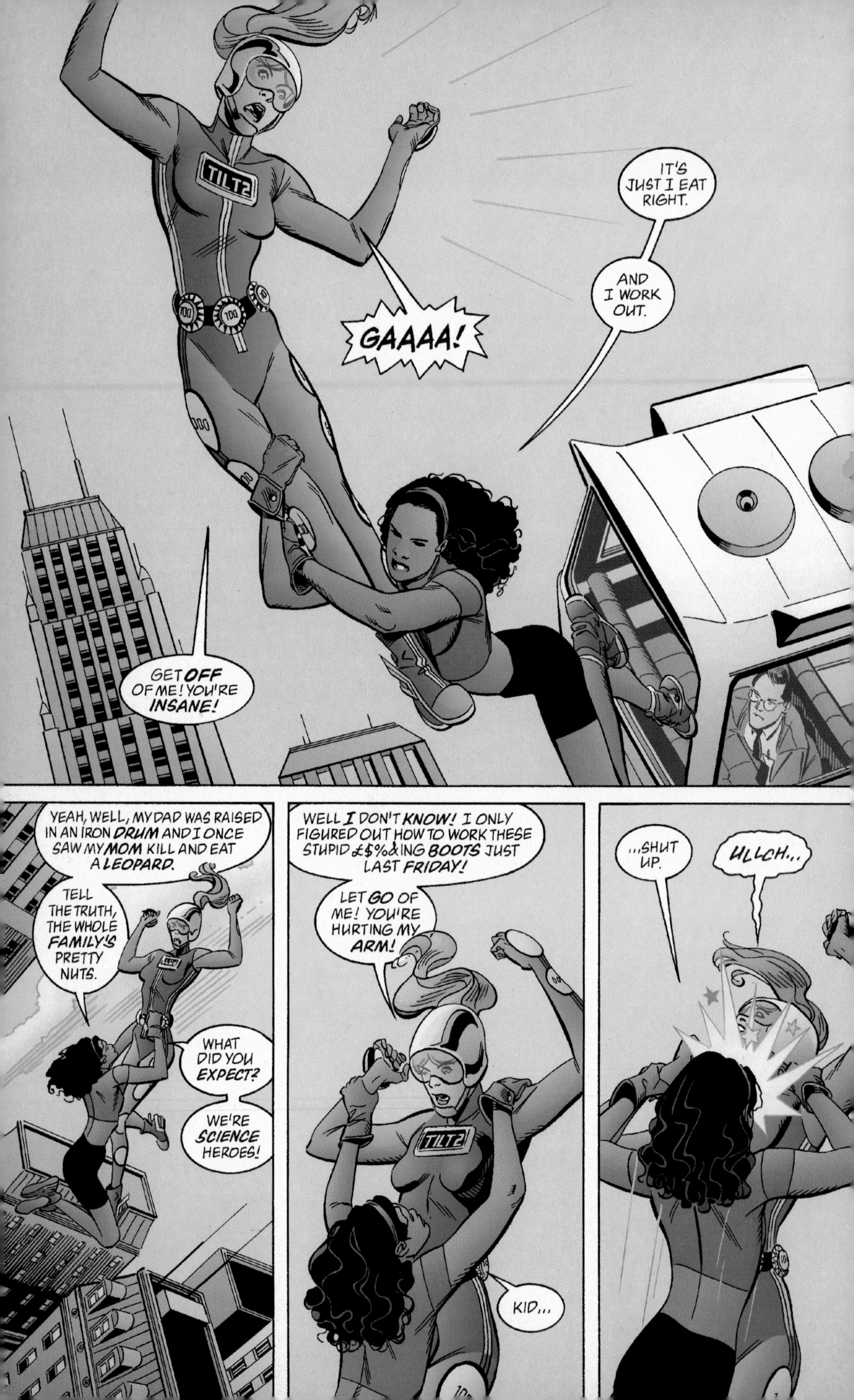
GAAAA!
IT'S JUST I EAT RIGHT.
AND I WORK OUT.
GET OFF OF ME! YOU'RE INSANE!
YEAH, WELL, MY DAD WAS RAISED IN AN IRON DRUM AND I ONCE SAW MY MOM KILL AND EAT A LEOPARD.
TELL THE TRUTH, THE WHOLE FAMILY'S PRETTY NUTS.
WHAT DID YOU EXPECT?
WE'RE SCIENCE HEROES!
WELL I DON'T KNOW! I ONLY FIGURED OUT HOW TO WORK THESE STUPID £$%&ING BOOTS JUST LAST FRIDAY!
LET GO OF ME! YOU'RE HURTING MY ARM!
KID...
...SHUT UP.
ULLCH...

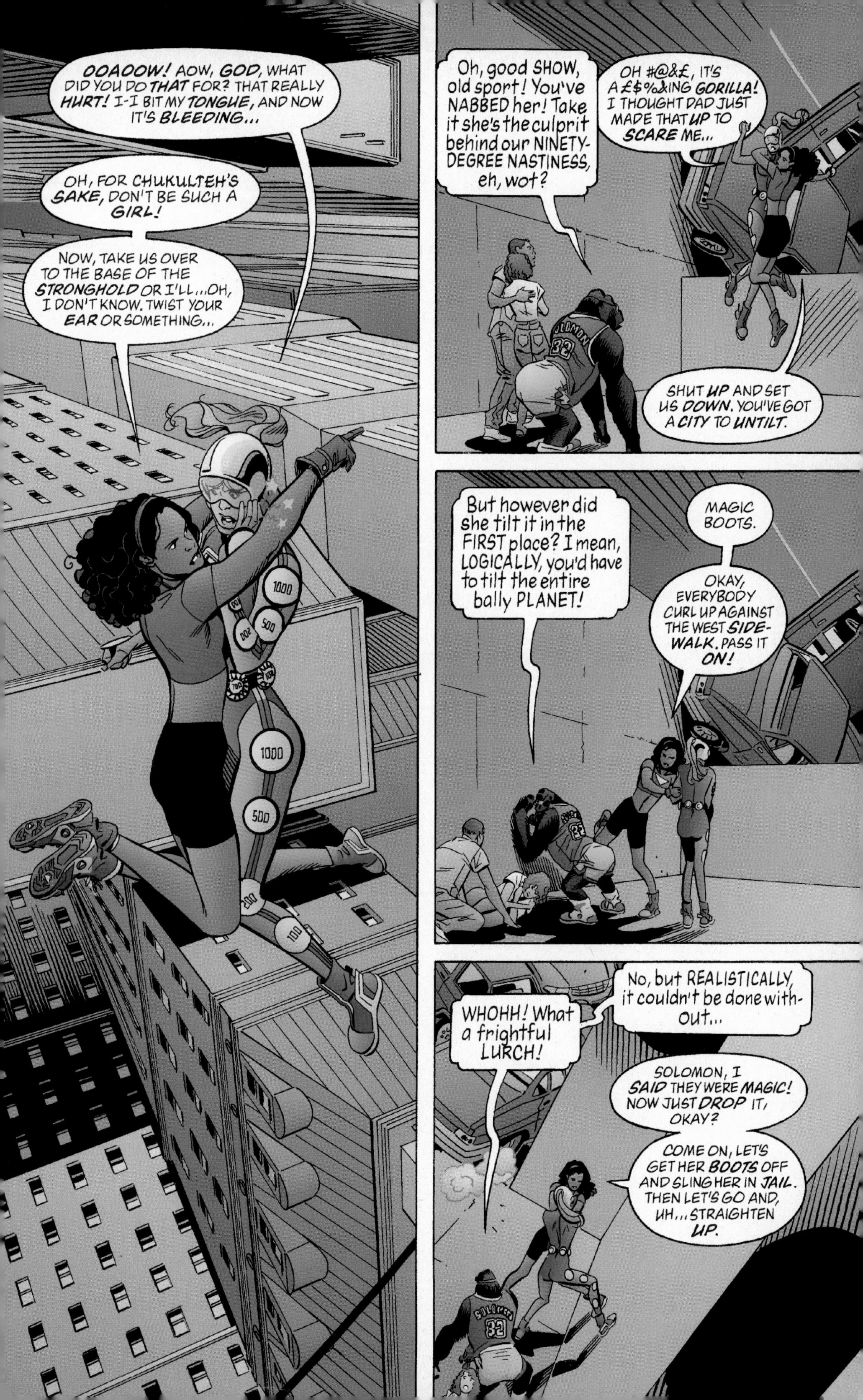

OOAOOW! AOW, GOD, WHAT DID YOU DO THAT FOR? THAT REALLY HURT! I-I BIT MY TONGUE, AND NOW IT'S BLEEDING...
OH, FOR CHUKULTEH'S SAKE, DON'T BE SUCH A GIRL!
NOW, TAKE US OVER TO THE BASE OF THE STRONGHOLD OR I'LL...OH, I DON'T KNOW. TWIST YOUR EAR OR SOMETHING...
1000
500
200
1000
500
200
100
Oh, good SHOW, old sport! You've NABBED her! Take it she's the culprit behind our NINETY-DEGREE NASTINESS, eh, wot?
OH #@&£, IT'S A £$%&ING GORILLA! I THOUGHT DAD JUST MADE THAT UP TO SCARE ME...
SOLOMON
32
SHUT UP AND SET US DOWN. YOU'VE GOT A CITY TO UNTILT.
But however did she tilt it in the FIRST place? I mean, LOGICALLY, you'd have to tilt the entire bally PLANET!
MAGIC BOOTS.
OKAY, EVERYBODY CURL UP AGAINST THE WEST SIDE-WALK. PASS IT ON!
WHOHH! What a frightful LURCH!
No, but REALISTICALLY, it couldn't be done with-out...
SOLOMON, I SAID THEY WERE MAGIC! NOW JUST DROP IT, OKAY?
COME ON, LET'S GET HER BOOTS OFF AND SLING HER IN JAIL. THEN LET'S GO AND, UH... STRAIGHTEN UP.

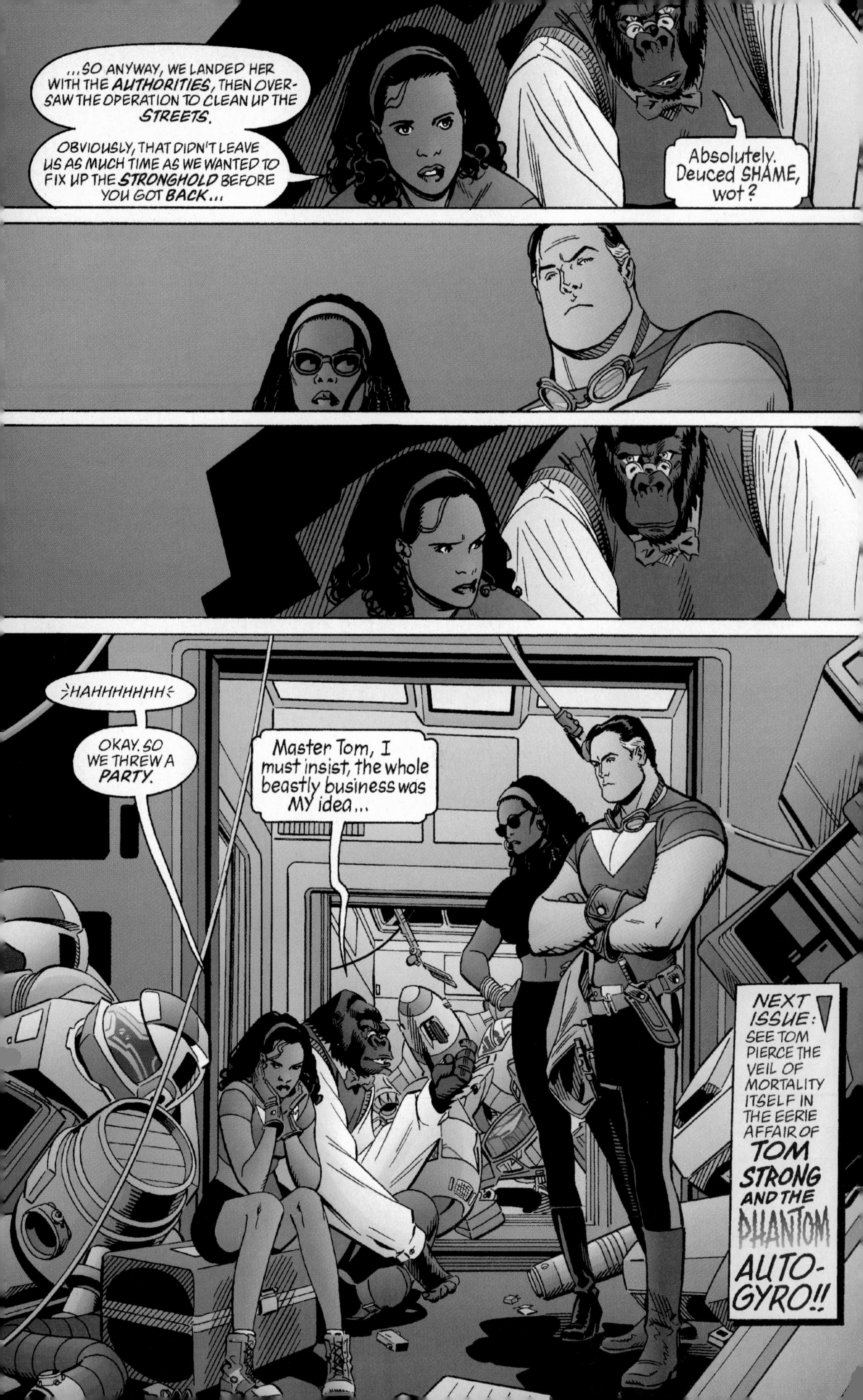
...SO ANYWAY, WE LANDED HER WITH THE AUTHORITIES, THEN OVER-SAW THE OPERATION TO CLEAN UP THE STREETS.
OBVIOUSLY, THAT DIDN'T LEAVE US AS MUCH TIME AS WE WANTED TO FIX UP THE STRONGHOLD BEFORE YOU GOT BACK...
Absolutely. Deuced SHAME, wot?
HAHHHHHHH
OKAY. SO WE THREW A PARTY.
Master Tom, I must insist, the whole beastly business was MY idea...
NEXT ISSUE: SEE TOM PIERCE THE VEIL OF MORTALITY ITSELF IN THE EERIE AFFAIR OF TOM STRONG AND THE PHANTOM AUTO-GYRO!!

CHAPTER THREE

In which Tom travels back to family phantoms and slips into an oddly humorous situation, while Tesla has too much of a good thing.

Cover art:
Gary Gianni

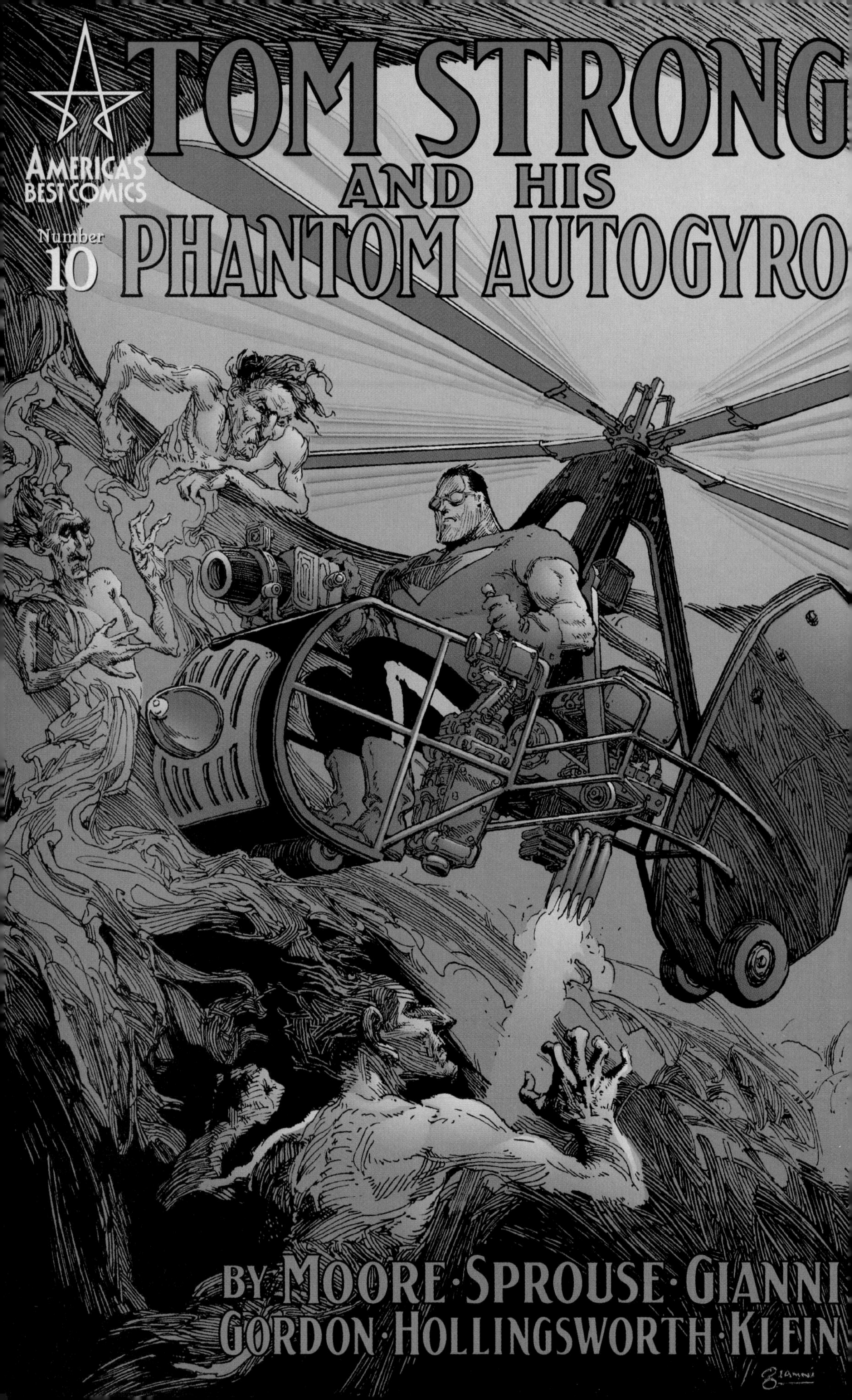
AMERICA'S BEST COMICS
Number 10
TOM STRONG
AND HIS
PHANTOM AUTOGYRO
BY MOORE·SPROUSE·GIANNI
GORDON·HOLLINGSWORTH·KLEIN

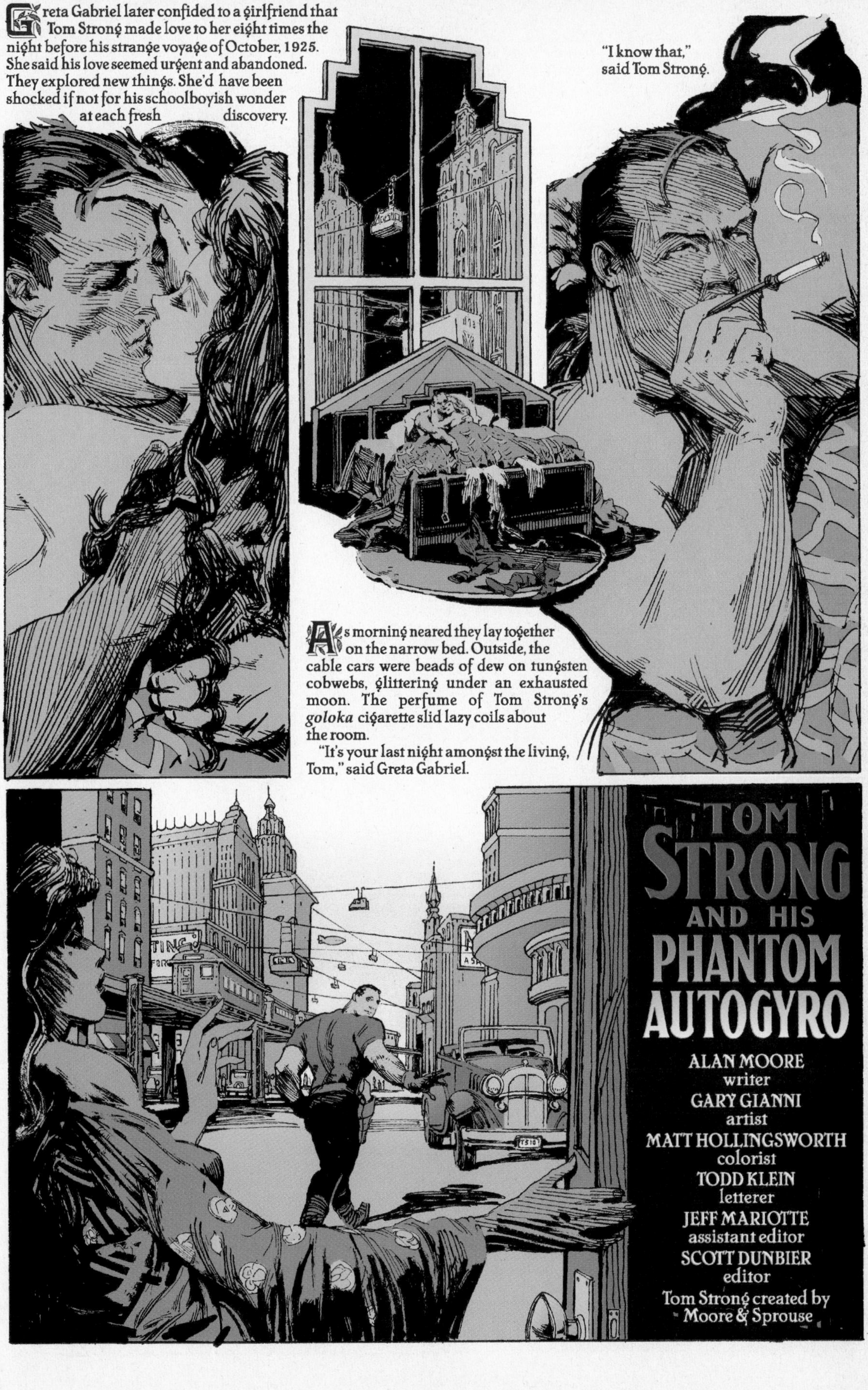
Greta Gabriel later confided to a girlfriend that Tom Strong made love to her eight times the night before his strange voyage of October, 1925. She said his love seemed urgent and abandoned. They explored new things. She'd have been shocked if not for his schoolboyish wonder at each fresh discovery.
"I know that," said Tom Strong.
As morning neared they lay together on the narrow bed. Outside, the cable cars were beads of dew on tungsten cobwebs, glittering under an exhausted moon. The perfume of Tom Strong's *goloka* cigarette slid lazy coils about the room.
"It's your last night amongst the living, Tom," said Greta Gabriel.
TOM STRONG AND HIS PHANTOM AUTOGYRO
ALAN MOORE writer
GARY GIANNI artist
MATT HOLLINGSWORTH colorist
TODD KLEIN letterer
JEFF MARIOTTE assistant editor
SCOTT DUNBIER editor
Tom Strong created by Moore & Sprouse

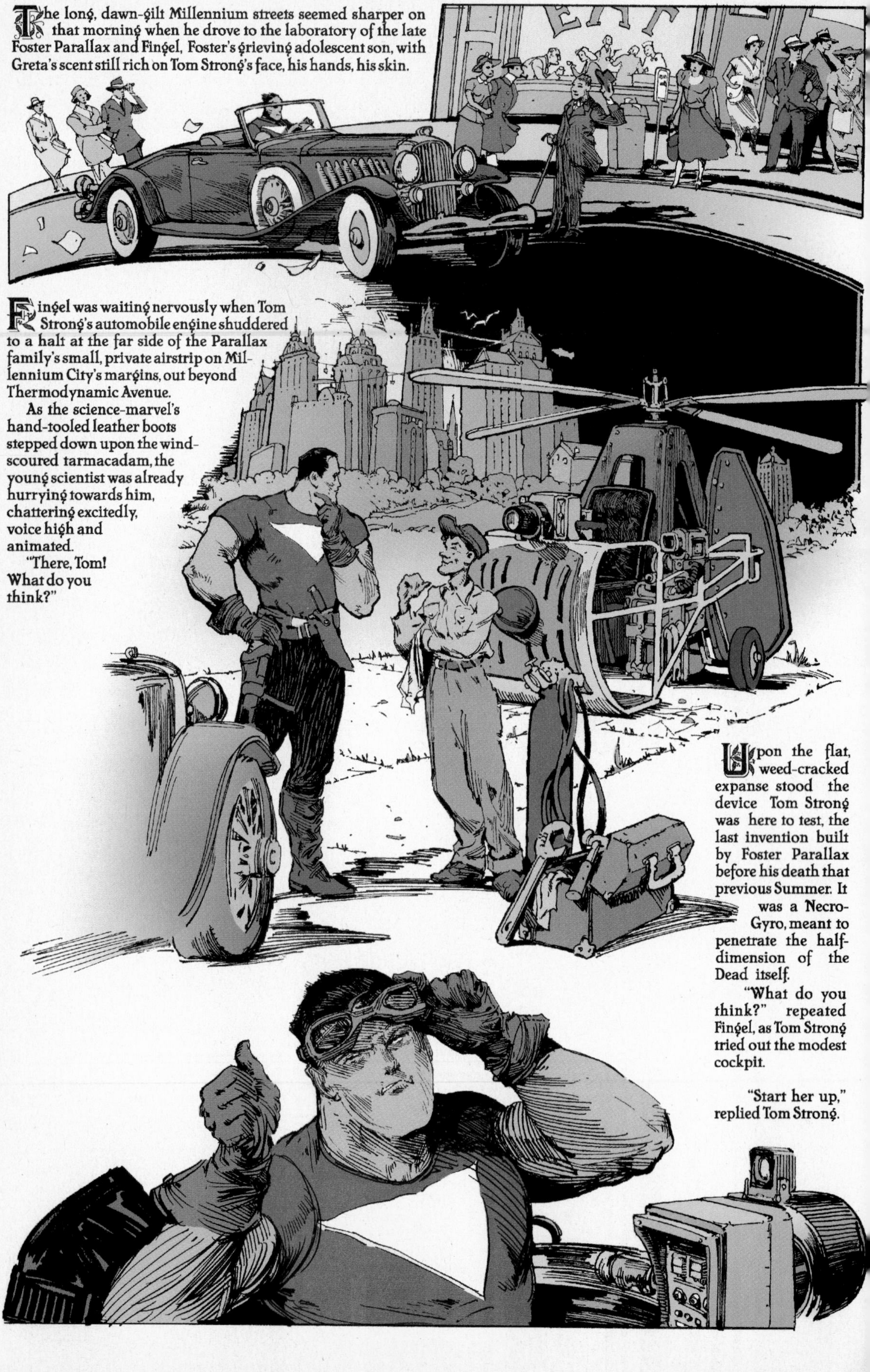

The long, dawn-gilt Millennium streets seemed sharper on that morning when he drove to the laboratory of the late Foster Parallax and Fingel, Foster's grieving adolescent son, with Greta's scent still rich on Tom Strong's face, his hands, his skin.

Fingel was waiting nervously when Tom Strong's automobile engine shuddered to a halt at the far side of the Parallax family's small, private airstrip on Millennium City's margins, out beyond Thermodynamic Avenue.

As the science-marvel's hand-tooled leather boots stepped down upon the wind-scoured tarmacadam, the young scientist was already hurrying towards him, chattering excitedly, voice high and animated.

"There, Tom! What do you think?"

Upon the flat, weed-cracked expanse stood the device Tom Strong was here to test, the last invention built by Foster Parallax before his death that previous Summer. It was a Necro-Gyro, meant to penetrate the half-dimension of the Dead itself.

"What do you think?" repeated Fingel, as Tom Strong tried out the modest cockpit.

"Start her up," replied Tom Strong.

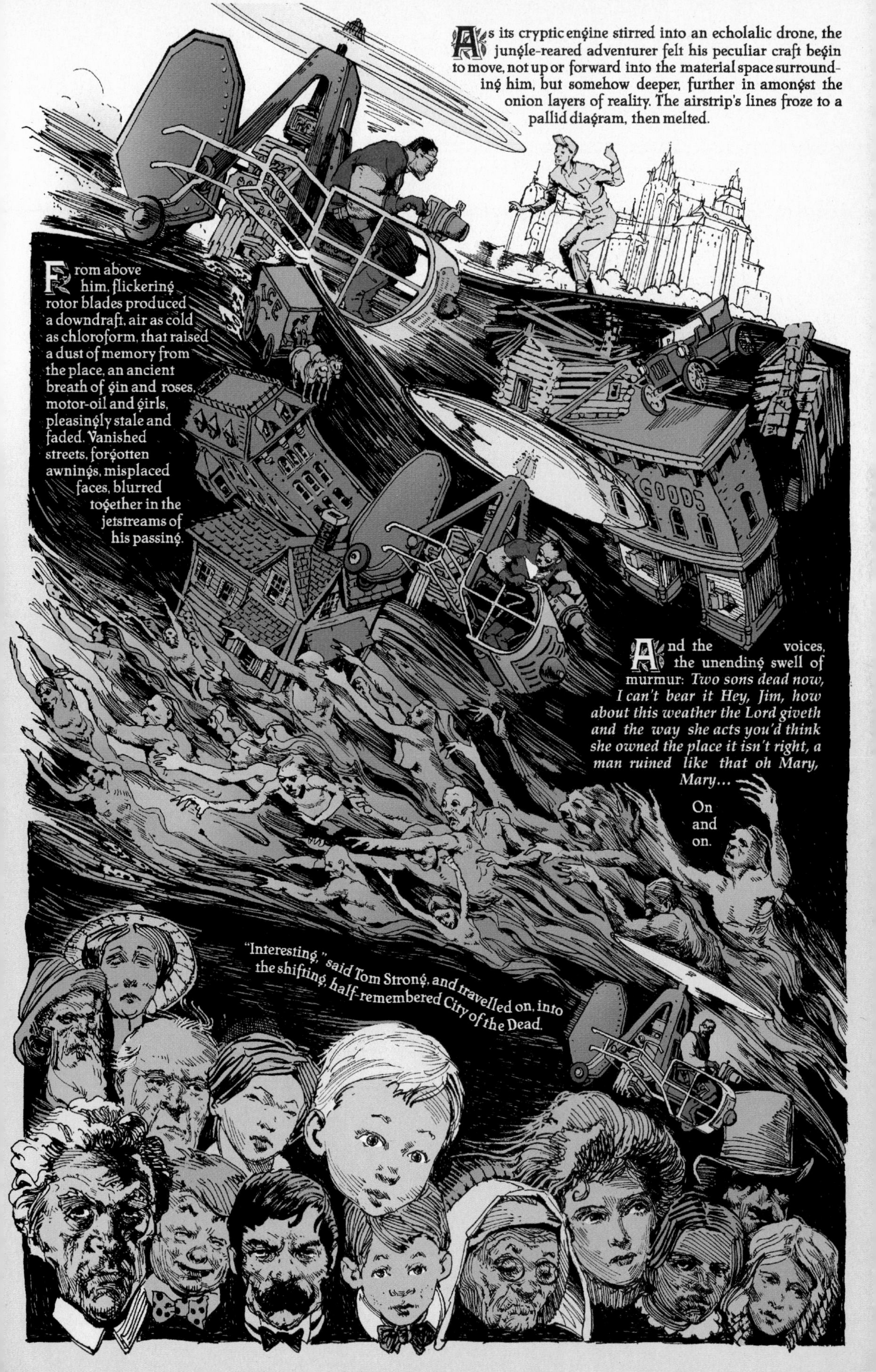
As its cryptic engine stirred into an echolalic drone, the jungle-reared adventurer felt his peculiar craft begin to move, not up or forward into the material space surrounding him, but somehow deeper, further in amongst the onion layers of reality. The airstrip's lines froze to a pallid diagram, then melted.
From above him, flickering rotor blades produced a downdraft, air as cold as chloroform, that raised a dust of memory from the place, an ancient breath of gin and roses, motor-oil and girls, pleasingly stale and faded. Vanished streets, forgotten awnings, misplaced faces, blurred together in the jetstreams of his passing.
ICE
GOODS
And the voices, the unending swell of murmur: *Two sons dead now, I can't bear it Hey, Jim, how about this weather the Lord giveth and the way she acts you'd think she owned the place it isn't right, a man ruined like that oh Mary, Mary…*
On and on.
"Interesting," said Tom Strong, and travelled on, into the shifting, half-remembered City of the Dead.

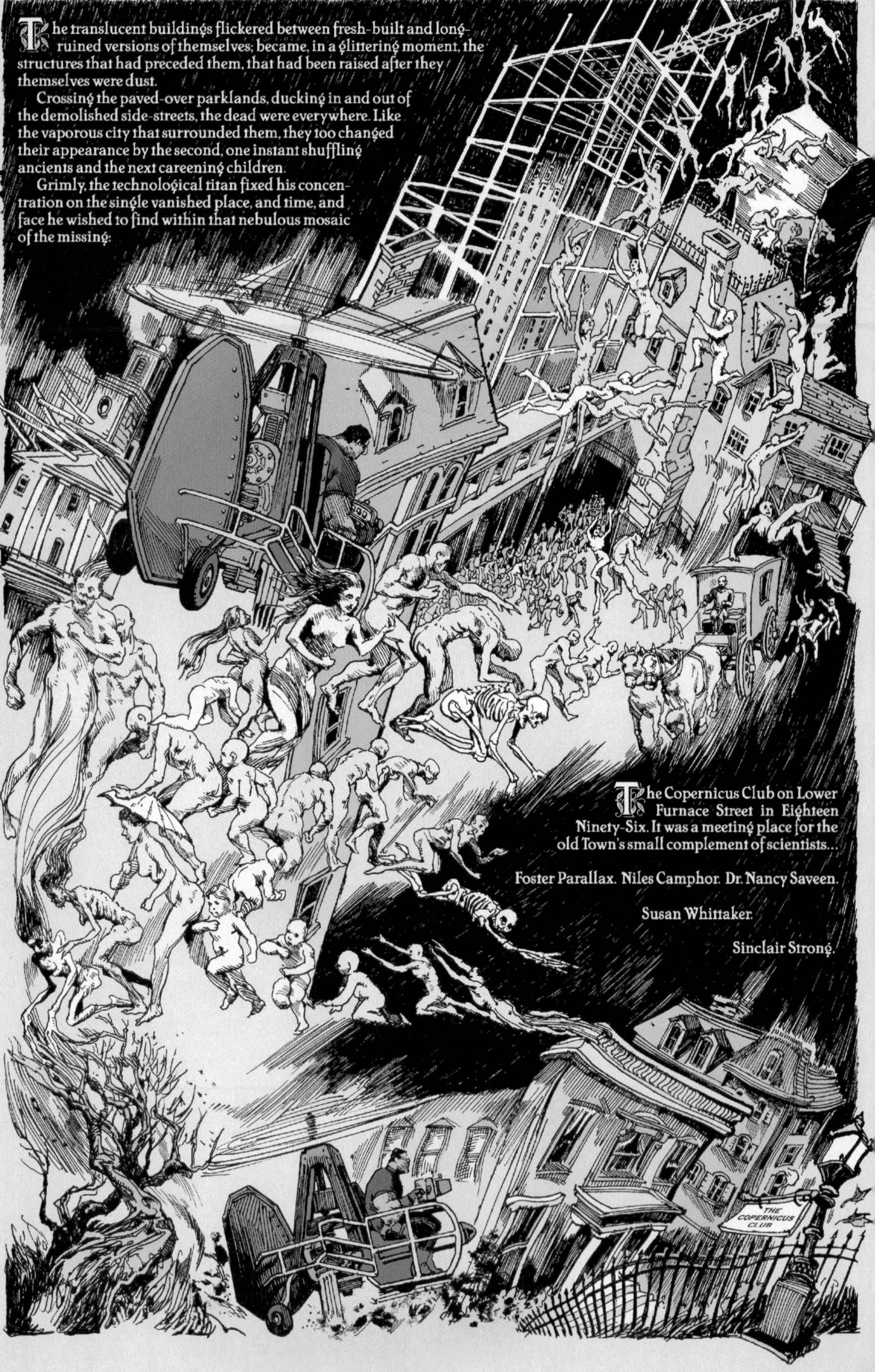
The translucent buildings flickered between fresh-built and long-ruined versions of themselves; became, in a glittering moment, the structures that had preceded them, that had been raised after they themselves were dust.
Crossing the paved-over parklands, ducking in and out of the demolished side-streets, the dead were everywhere. Like the vaporous city that surrounded them, they too changed their appearance by the second, one instant shuffling ancients and the next careening children.
Grimly, the technological titan fixed his concentration on the single vanished place, and time, and face he wished to find within that nebulous mosaic of the missing:
The Copernicus Club on Lower Furnace Street in Eighteen Ninety-Six. It was a meeting place for the old Town's small complement of scientists...
Foster Parallax. Niles Camphor. Dr. Nancy Saveen.
Susan Whittaker.
Sinclair Strong.
THE COPERNICUS CLUB

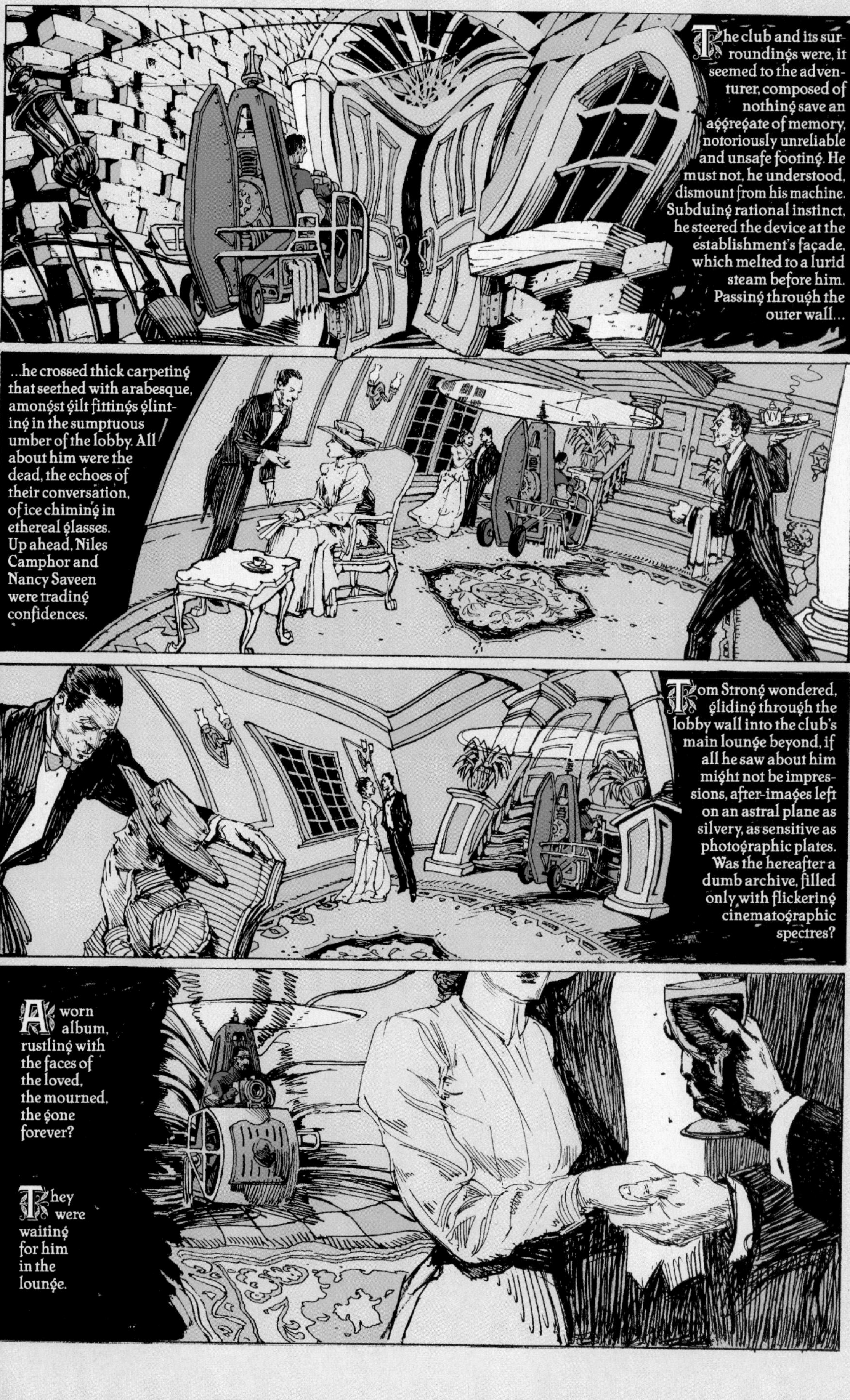
The club and its surroundings were, it seemed to the adventurer, composed of nothing save an aggregate of memory, notoriously unreliable and unsafe footing. He must not, he understood, dismount from his machine. Subduing rational instinct, he steered the device at the establishment's façade, which melted to a lurid steam before him. Passing through the outer wall…
…he crossed thick carpeting that seethed with arabesque, amongst gilt fittings glinting in the sumptuous umber of the lobby. All about him were the dead, the echoes of their conversation, of ice chiming in ethereal glasses. Up ahead, Niles Camphor and Nancy Saveen were trading confidences.
Tom Strong wondered, gliding through the lobby wall into the club's main lounge beyond, if all he saw about him might not be impressions, after-images left on an astral plane as silvery, as sensitive as photographic plates. Was the hereafter a dumb archive, filled only with flickering cinematographic spectres?
A worn album, rustling with the faces of the loved, the mourned, the gone forever?
They were waiting for him in the lounge.

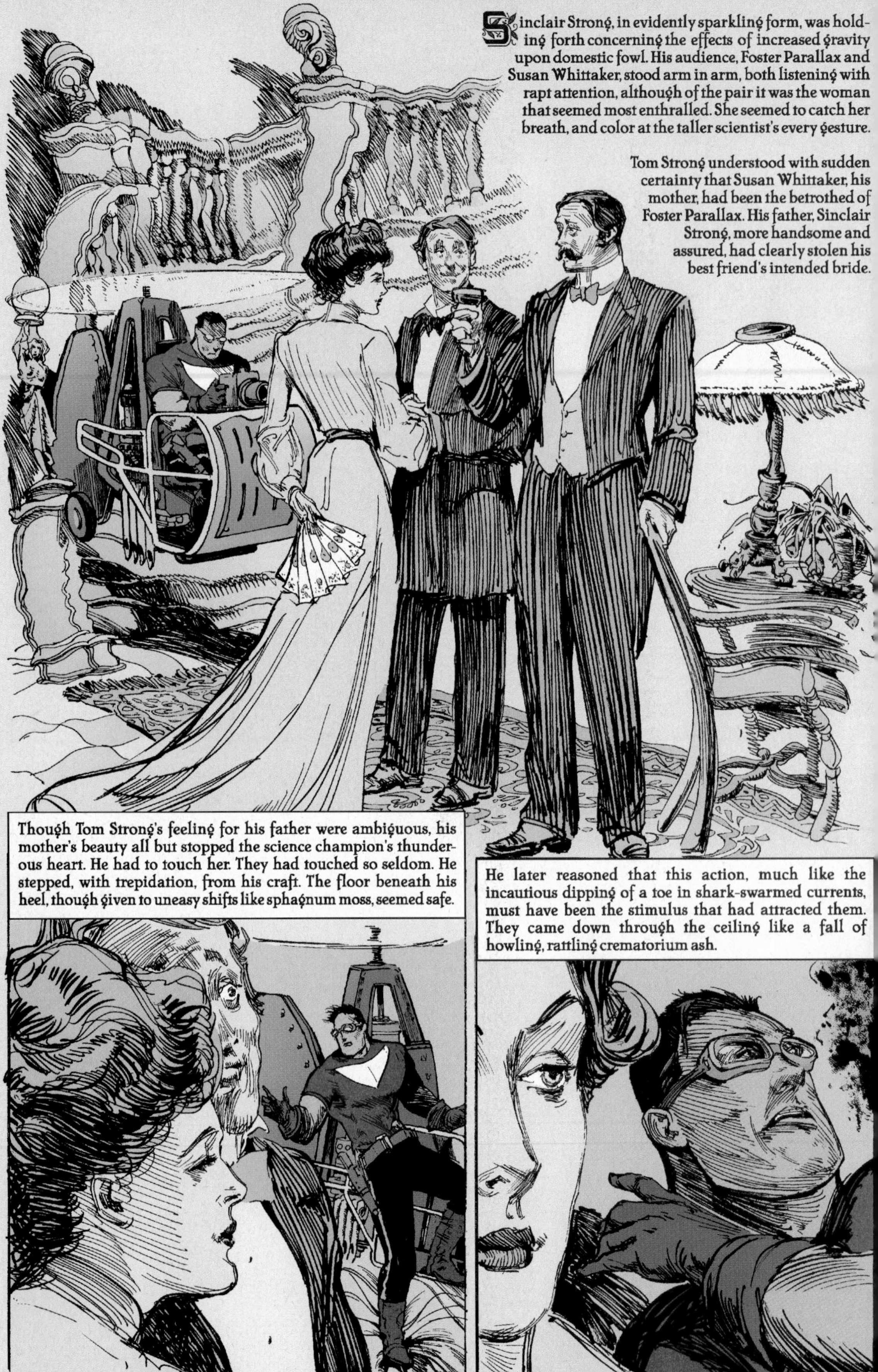
Sinclair Strong, in evidently sparkling form, was holding forth concerning the effects of increased gravity upon domestic fowl. His audience, Foster Parallax and Susan Whittaker, stood arm in arm, both listening with rapt attention, although of the pair it was the woman that seemed most enthralled. She seemed to catch her breath, and color at the taller scientist's every gesture.
Tom Strong understood with sudden certainty that Susan Whittaker, his mother, had been the betrothed of Foster Parallax. His father, Sinclair Strong, more handsome and assured, had clearly stolen his best friend's intended bride.
Though Tom Strong's feeling for his father were ambiguous, his mother's beauty all but stopped the science champion's thunderous heart. He had to touch her. They had touched so seldom. He stepped, with trepidation, from his craft. The floor beneath his heel, though given to uneasy shifts like sphagnum moss, seemed safe.
He later reasoned that this action, much like the incautious dipping of a toe in shark-swarmed currents, must have been the stimulus that had attracted them. They came down through the ceiling like a fall of howling, rattling crematorium ash.

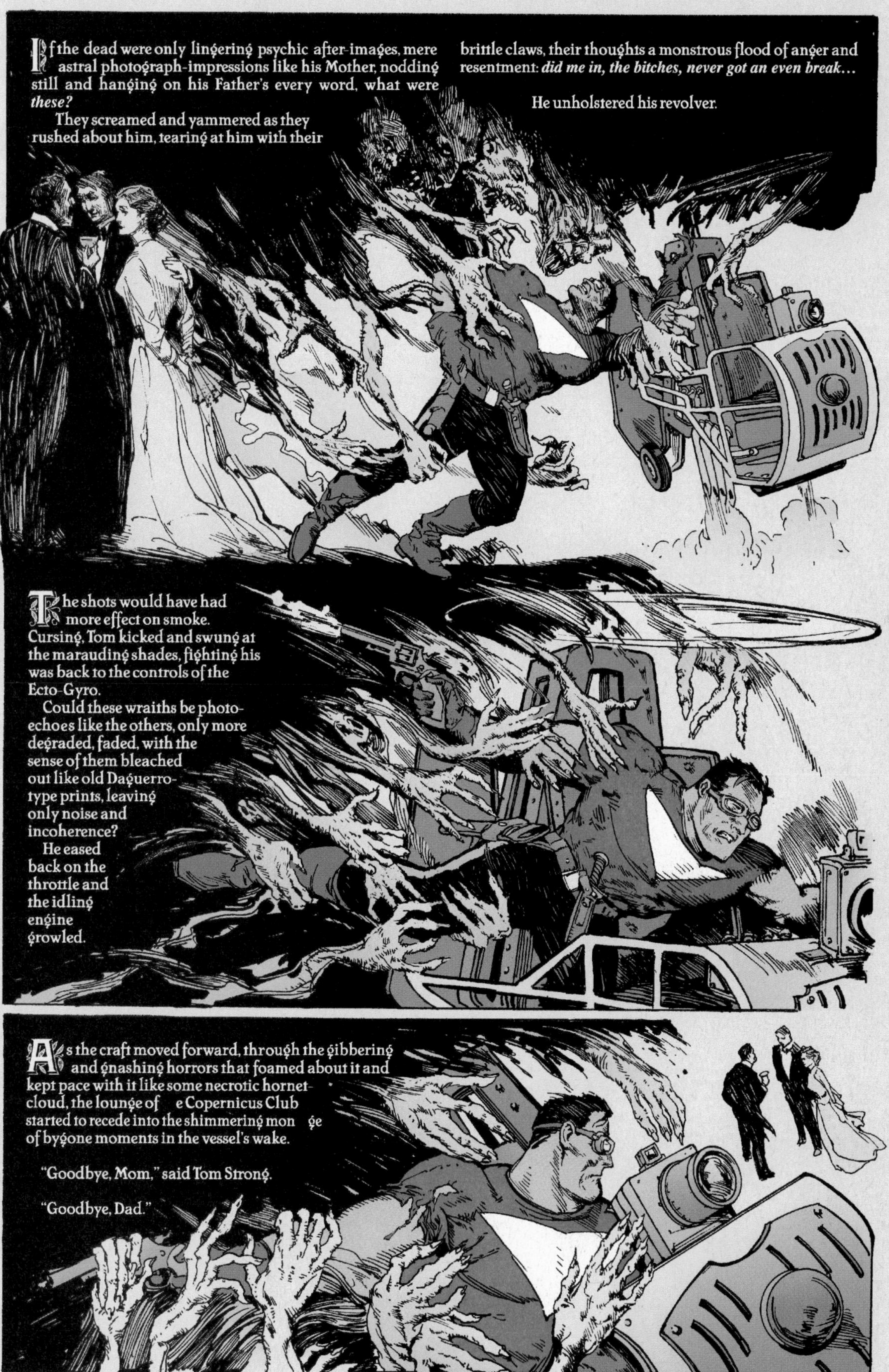
If the dead were only lingering psychic after-images, mere astral photograph-impressions like his Mother, nodding still and hanging on his Father's every word, what were *these?*
They screamed and yammered as they rushed about him, tearing at him with their brittle claws, their thoughts a monstrous flood of anger and resentment: *did me in, the bitches, never got an even break...*
He unholstered his revolver.
The shots would have had more effect on smoke. Cursing, Tom kicked and swung at the marauding shades, fighting his was back to the controls of the Ecto-Gyro.
Could these wraiths be photo-echoes like the others, only more degraded, faded, with the sense of them bleached out like old Daguerro-type prints, leaving only noise and incoherence?
He eased back on the throttle and the idling engine growled.
As the craft moved forward, through the gibbering and gnashing horrors that foamed about it and kept pace with it like some necrotic hornet-cloud, the lounge of e Copernicus Club started to recede into the shimmering mon ge of bygone moments in the vessel's wake.
"Goodbye, Mom," said Tom Strong.
"Goodbye, Dad."

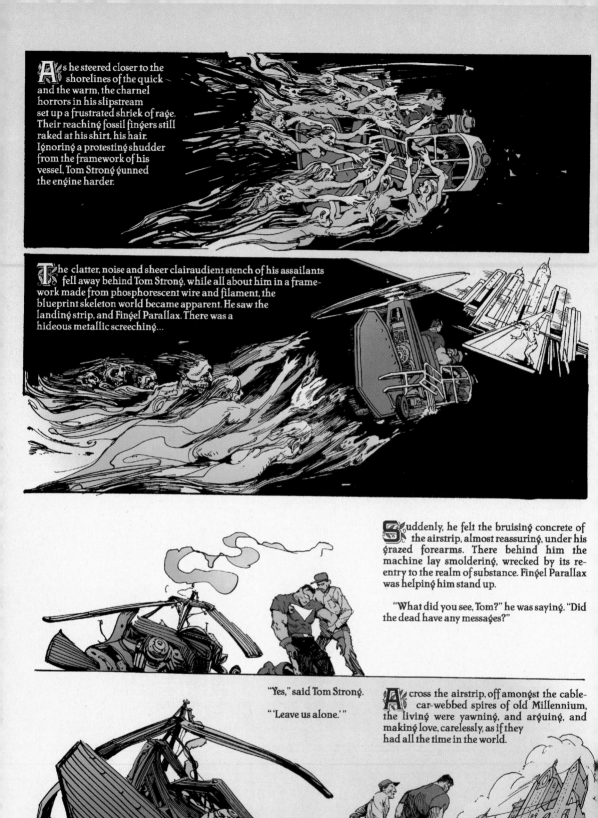

As he steered closer to the shorelines of the quick and the warm, the charnel horrors in his slipstream set up a frustrated shriek of rage. Their reaching fossil fingers still raked at his shirt, his hair. Ignoring a protesting shudder from the framework of his vessel, Tom Strong gunned the engine harder.

The clatter, noise and sheer clairaudient stench of his assailants fell away behind Tom Strong, while all about him in a framework made from phosphorescent wire and filament, the blueprint skeleton world became apparent. He saw the landing strip, and Fingel Parallax. There was a hideous metallic screeching...

Suddenly, he felt the bruising concrete of the airstrip, almost reassuring, under his grazed forearms. There behind him the machine lay smoldering, wrecked by its re-entry to the realm of substance. Fingel Parallax was helping him stand up.

"What did you see, Tom?" he was saying. "Did the dead have any messages?"

"Yes," said Tom Strong.

"'Leave us alone.'"

Across the airstrip, off amongst the cable-car-webbed spires of old Millennium, the living were yawning, and arguing, and making love, carelessly, as if they had all the time in the world.

END

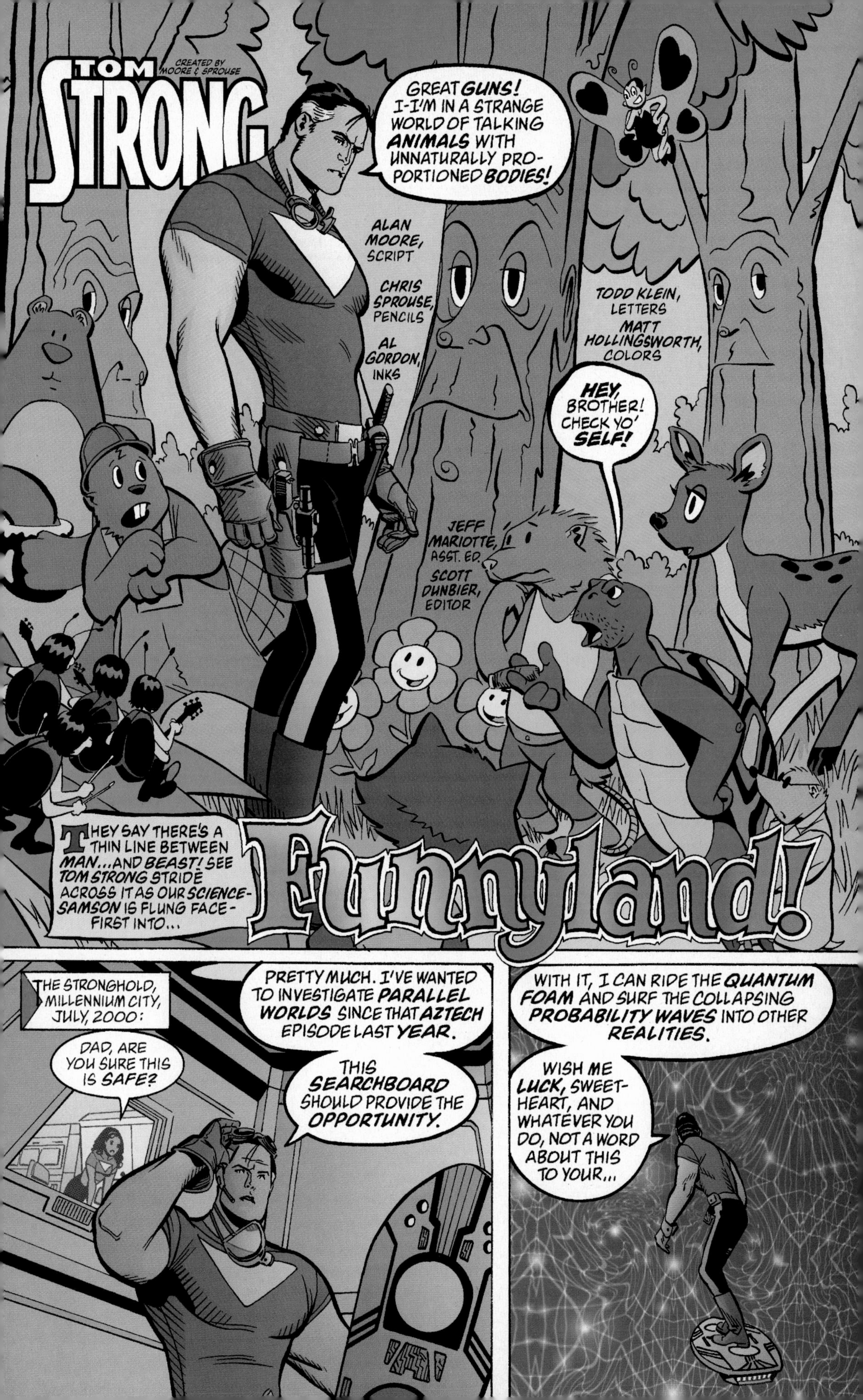
TOM STRONG
CREATED BY MOORE & SPROUSE
GREAT GUNS! I-I'M IN A STRANGE WORLD OF TALKING ANIMALS WITH UNNATURALLY PRO-PORTIONED BODIES!
ALAN MOORE, SCRIPT
CHRIS SPROUSE, PENCILS
AL GORDON, INKS
TODD KLEIN, LETTERS
MATT HOLLINGSWORTH, COLORS
HEY, BROTHER! CHECK YO' SELF!
JEFF MARIOTTE, ASST. ED.
SCOTT DUNBIER, EDITOR
THEY SAY THERE'S A THIN LINE BETWEEN MAN...AND BEAST! SEE TOM STRONG STRIDE ACROSS IT AS OUR SCIENCE-SAMSON IS FLUNG FACE-FIRST INTO...
Funnyland!
THE STRONGHOLD, MILLENNIUM CITY, JULY, 2000:
DAD, ARE YOU SURE THIS IS SAFE?
PRETTY MUCH. I'VE WANTED TO INVESTIGATE PARALLEL WORLDS SINCE THAT AZTECH EPISODE LAST YEAR.
THIS SEARCHBOARD SHOULD PROVIDE THE OPPORTUNITY.
WITH IT, I CAN RIDE THE QUANTUM FOAM AND SURF THE COLLAPSING PROBABILITY WAVES INTO OTHER REALITIES.
WISH ME LUCK, SWEET-HEART, AND WHATEVER YOU DO, NOT A WORD ABOUT THIS TO YOUR...

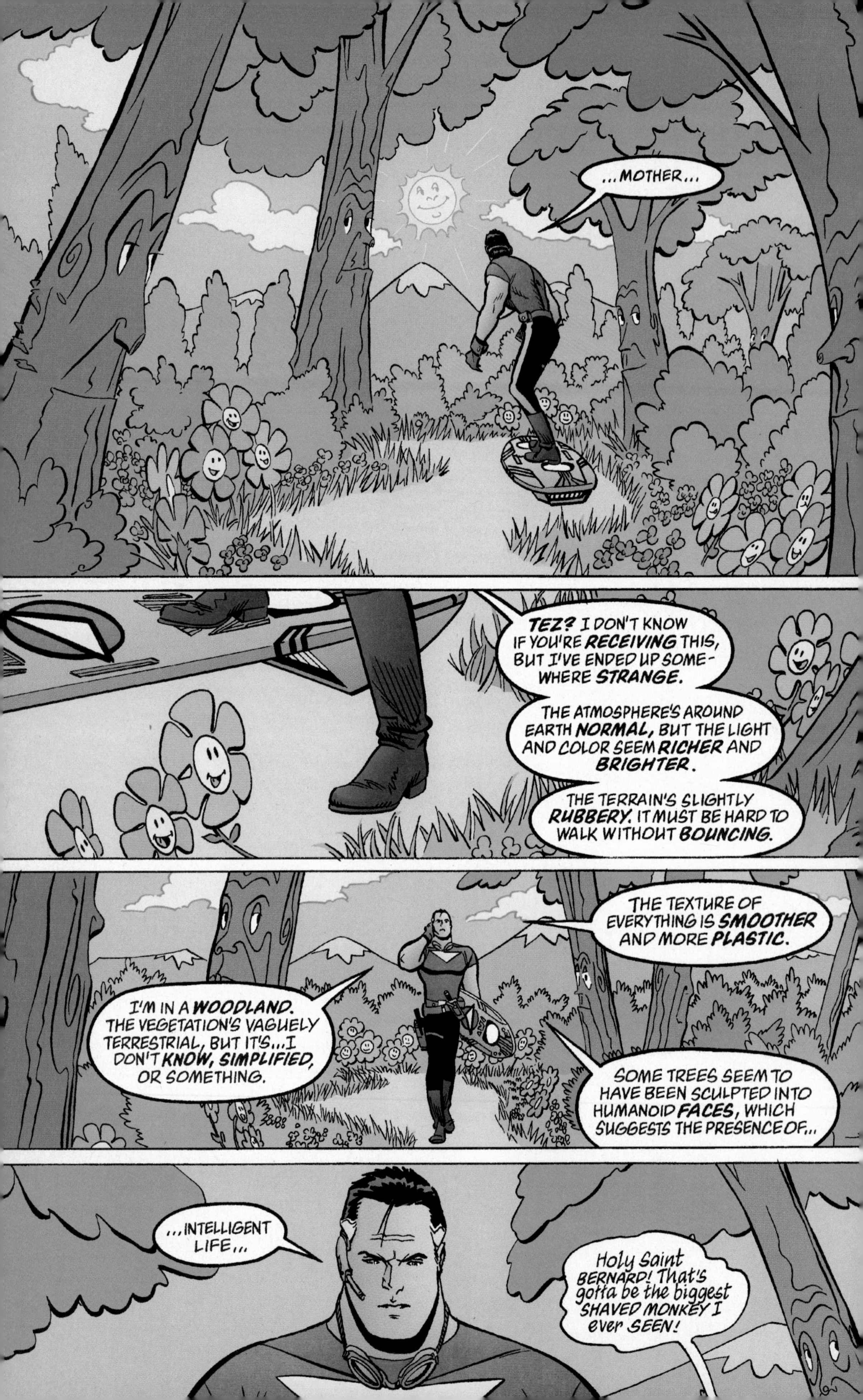
...MOTHER...
TEZ? I DON'T KNOW IF YOU'RE RECEIVING THIS, BUT I'VE ENDED UP SOME-WHERE STRANGE.
THE ATMOSPHERE'S AROUND EARTH NORMAL, BUT THE LIGHT AND COLOR SEEM RICHER AND BRIGHTER.
THE TERRAIN'S SLIGHTLY RUBBERY. IT MUST BE HARD TO WALK WITHOUT BOUNCING.
THE TEXTURE OF EVERYTHING IS SMOOTHER AND MORE PLASTIC.
I'M IN A WOODLAND. THE VEGETATION'S VAGUELY TERRESTRIAL, BUT IT'S...I DON'T KNOW, SIMPLIFIED, OR SOMETHING.
SOME TREES SEEM TO HAVE BEEN SCULPTED INTO HUMANOID FACES, WHICH SUGGESTS THE PRESENCE OF...
...INTELLIGENT LIFE...
Holy Saint BERNARD! That's gotta be the biggest SHAVED MONKEY I ever SEEN!

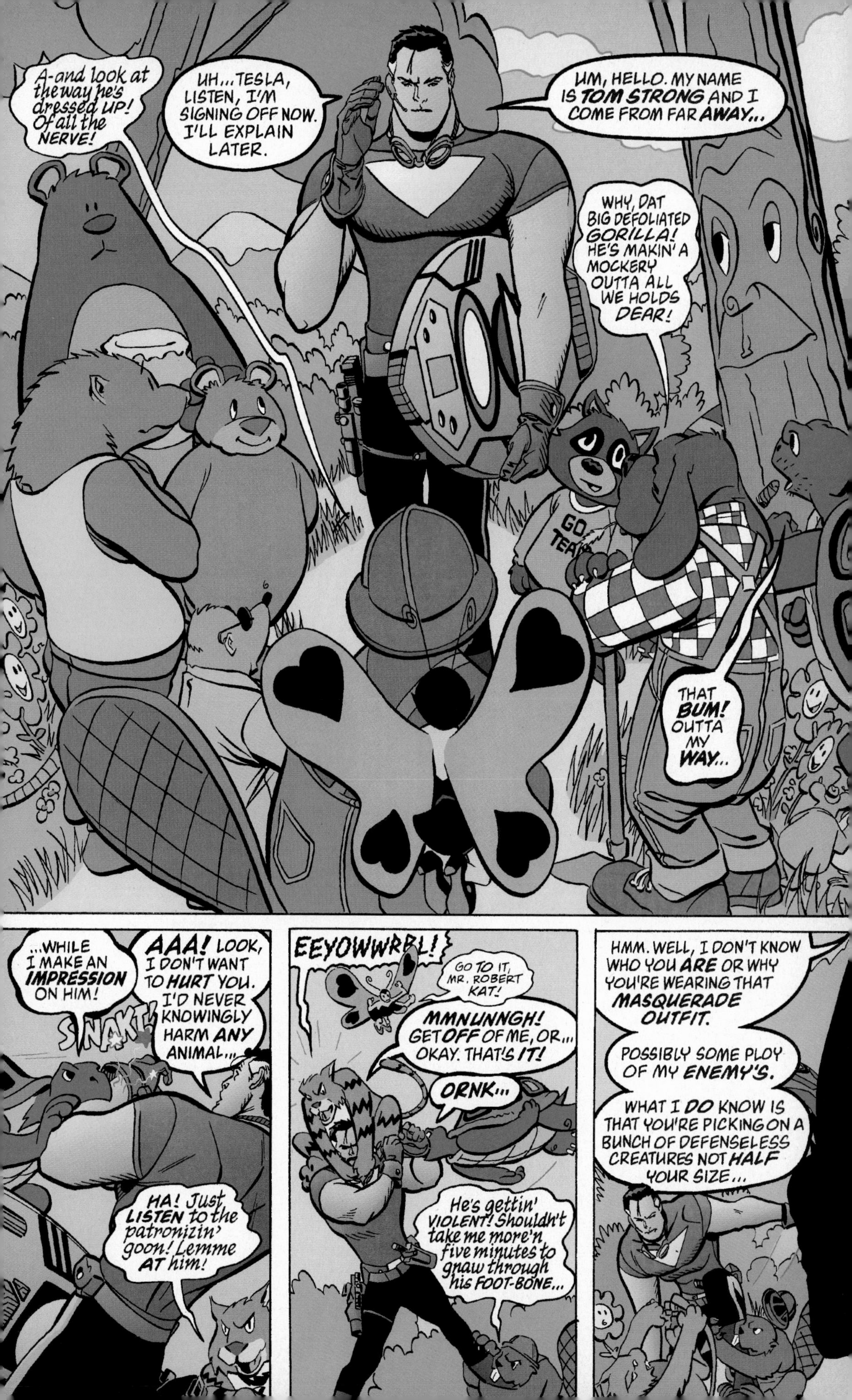
A-and look at the way he's dressed up! Of all the NERVE!
UH... TESLA, LISTEN, I'M SIGNING OFF NOW. I'LL EXPLAIN LATER.
UM, HELLO. MY NAME IS TOM STRONG AND I COME FROM FAR AWAY...
WHY, DAT BIG DEFOLIATED GORILLA! HE'S MAKIN' A MOCKERY OUTTA ALL WE HOLDS DEAR!
GO TEAM
THAT BUM! OUTTA MY WAY...
...WHILE I MAKE AN IMPRESSION ON HIM!
AAA! LOOK, I DON'T WANT TO HURT YOU. I'D NEVER KNOWINGLY HARM ANY ANIMAL...
SNAKT!
HA! Just LISTEN to the patronizin' goon! Lemme AT him!
EEYOWWRBL!
GO TO IT, MR. ROBERT KAT!
MMNUNNGH! GET OFF OF ME, OR... OKAY. THAT'S IT!
ORNK...
He's gettin' VIOLENT! Shouldn't take me more'n five minutes to gnaw through his FOOT-BONE...
HMM. WELL, I DON'T KNOW WHO YOU ARE OR WHY YOU'RE WEARING THAT MASQUERADE OUTFIT.
POSSIBLY SOME PLOY OF MY ENEMY'S.
WHAT I DO KNOW IS THAT YOU'RE PICKING ON A BUNCH OF DEFENSELESS CREATURES NOT HALF YOUR SIZE...

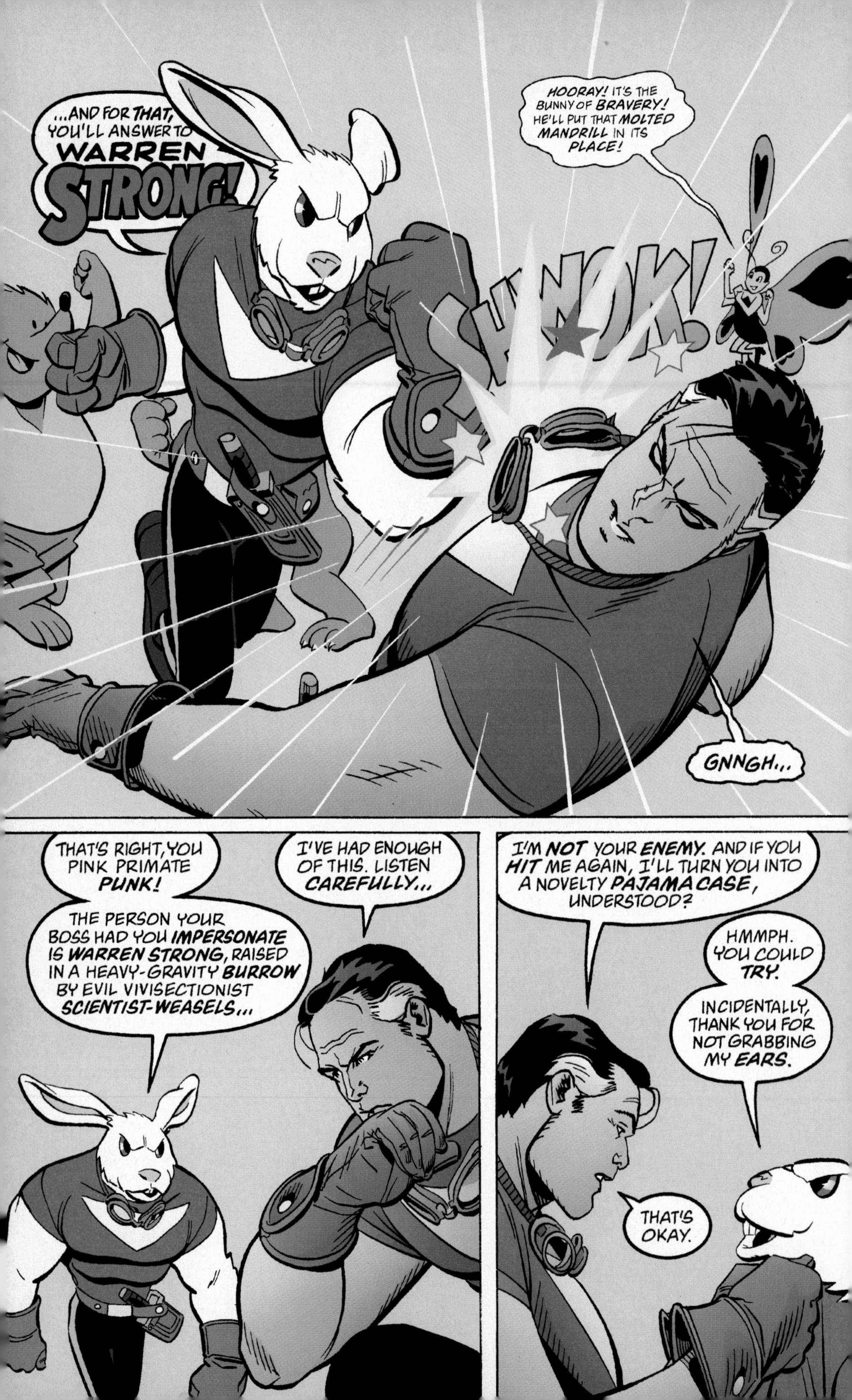
...AND FOR THAT, YOU'LL ANSWER TO WARREN STRONG!
HOORAY! IT'S THE BUNNY OF BRAVERY! HE'LL PUT THAT MOLTED MANDRILL IN ITS PLACE!
GNNGH...
THAT'S RIGHT, YOU PINK PRIMATE PUNK!
THE PERSON YOUR BOSS HAD YOU IMPERSONATE IS WARREN STRONG, RAISED IN A HEAVY-GRAVITY BURROW BY EVIL VIVISECTIONIST SCIENTIST-WEASELS...
I'VE HAD ENOUGH OF THIS. LISTEN CAREFULLY...
I'M NOT YOUR ENEMY. AND IF YOU HIT ME AGAIN, I'LL TURN YOU INTO A NOVELTY PAJAMA CASE, UNDERSTOOD?
HMMPH. YOU COULD TRY.
INCIDENTALLY, THANK YOU FOR NOT GRABBING MY EARS.
THAT'S OKAY.

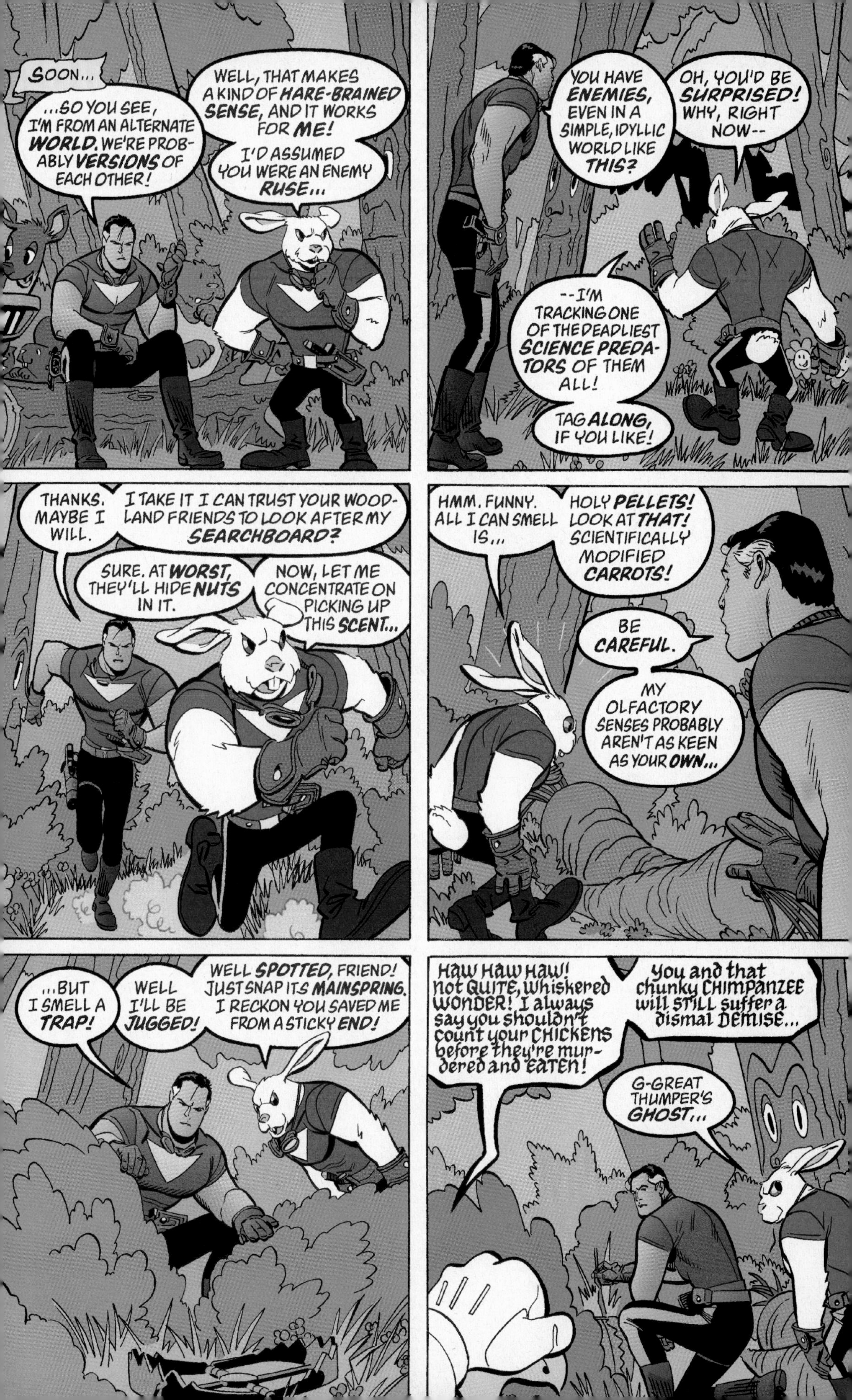
SOON...
...SO YOU SEE, I'M FROM AN ALTERNATE WORLD. WE'RE PROBABLY VERSIONS OF EACH OTHER!
WELL, THAT MAKES A KIND OF HARE-BRAINED SENSE, AND IT WORKS FOR ME!
I'D ASSUMED YOU WERE AN ENEMY RUSE...
YOU HAVE ENEMIES, EVEN IN A SIMPLE, IDYLLIC WORLD LIKE THIS?
OH, YOU'D BE SURPRISED! WHY, RIGHT NOW--
--I'M TRACKING ONE OF THE DEADLIEST SCIENCE PREDATORS OF THEM ALL!
TAG ALONG, IF YOU LIKE!
THANKS. MAYBE I WILL.
I TAKE IT I CAN TRUST YOUR WOODLAND FRIENDS TO LOOK AFTER MY SEARCHBOARD?
SURE. AT WORST, THEY'LL HIDE NUTS IN IT.
NOW, LET ME CONCENTRATE ON PICKING UP THIS SCENT...
HMM. FUNNY. ALL I CAN SMELL IS...
HOLY PELLETS! LOOK AT THAT! SCIENTIFICALLY MODIFIED CARROTS!
BE CAREFUL.
MY OLFACTORY SENSES PROBABLY AREN'T AS KEEN AS YOUR OWN...
...BUT I SMELL A TRAP!
WELL I'LL BE JUGGED!
WELL SPOTTED, FRIEND! JUST SNAP ITS MAINSPRING. I RECKON YOU SAVED ME FROM A STICKY END!
Haw Haw Haw! not QUITE, Whiskered WONDER! I always say you shouldn't count your CHICKENS before they're murdered and EATEN!
You and that chunky CHIMPANZEE will STILL suffer a dismal DEMISE...
G-GREAT THUMPER'S GHOST...

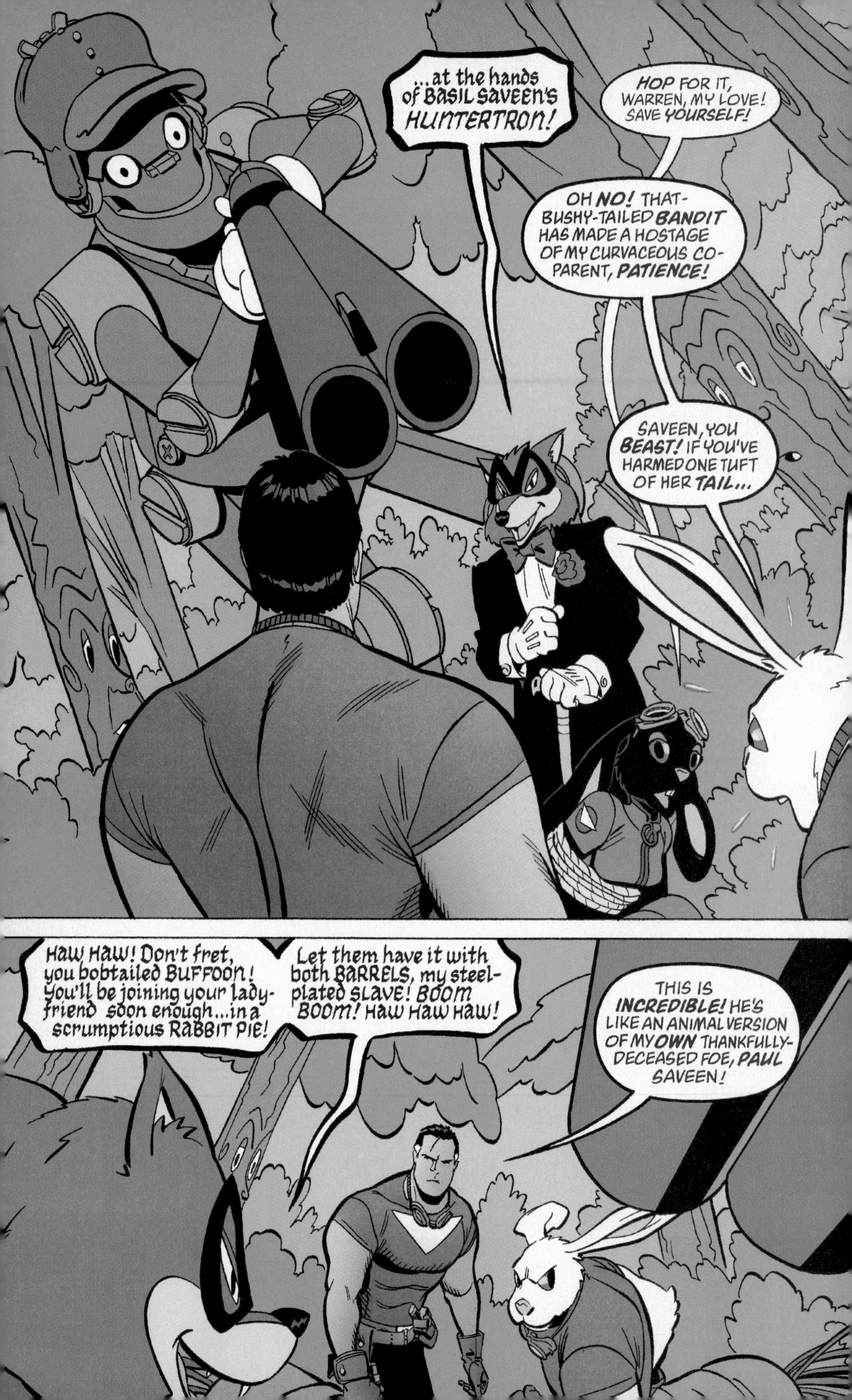
...at the hands of BASIL SAVEEN'S HUNTERTRON!
HOP FOR IT, WARREN, MY LOVE! SAVE YOURSELF!
OH NO! THAT-BUSHY-TAILED BANDIT HAS MADE A HOSTAGE OF MY CURVACEOUS CO-PARENT, PATIENCE!
SAVEEN, YOU BEAST! IF YOU'VE HARMED ONE TUFT OF HER TAIL...
HAW HAW! Don't fret, you bobtailed BUFFOON! You'll be joining your lady-friend soon enough...in a scrumptious RABBIT PIE!
Let them have it with both BARRELS, my steel-plated SLAVE! BOOM BOOM! HAW HAW HAW!
THIS IS INCREDIBLE! HE'S LIKE AN ANIMAL VERSION OF MY OWN THANKFULLY-DECEASED FOE, PAUL SAVEEN!

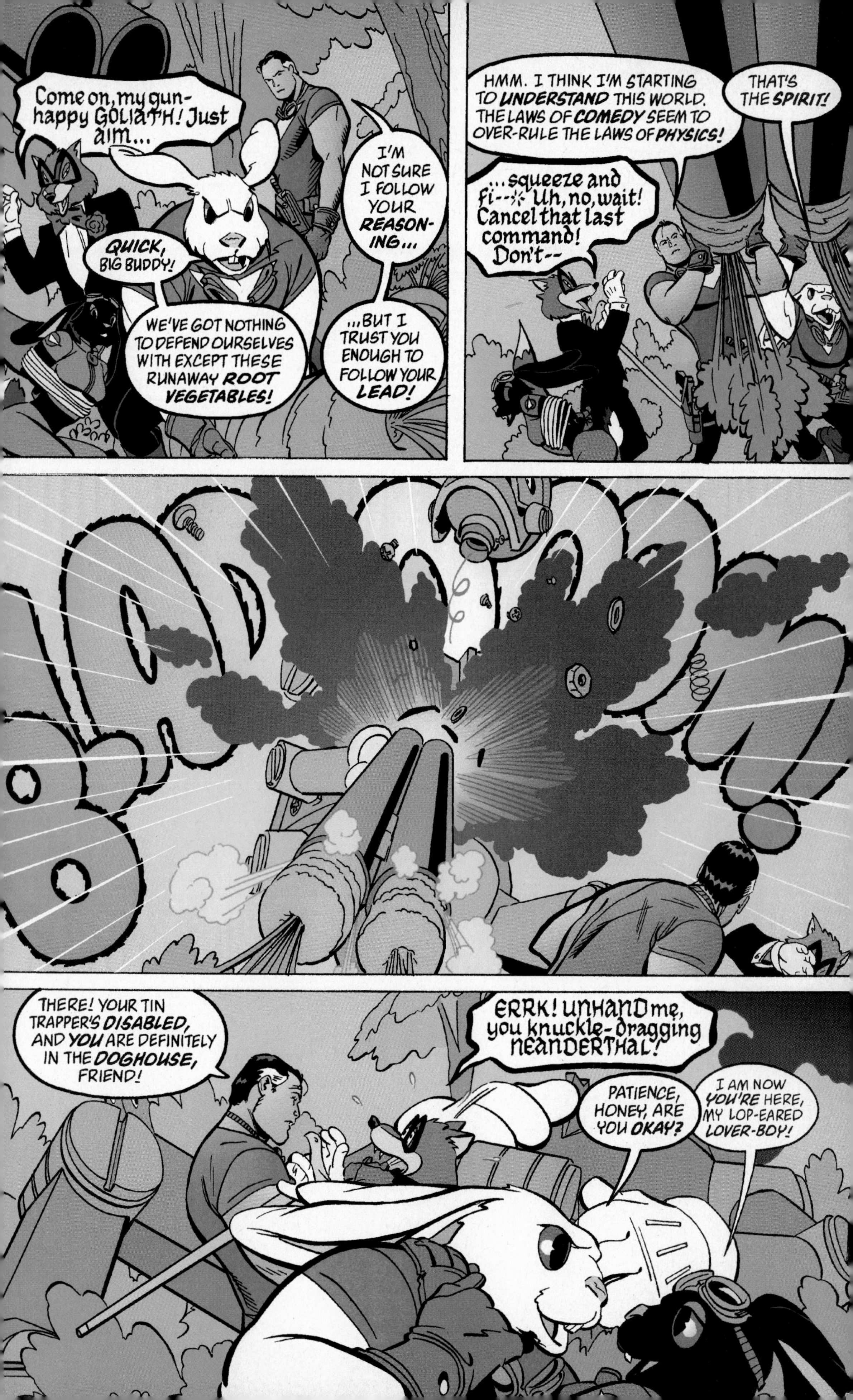
Come on, my gun-happy GOLIATH! Just aim...
QUICK, BIG BUDDY!
WE'VE GOT NOTHING TO DEFEND OURSELVES WITH EXCEPT THESE RUNAWAY ROOT VEGETABLES!
I'M NOT SURE I FOLLOW YOUR REASONING...
...BUT I TRUST YOU ENOUGH TO FOLLOW YOUR LEAD!
HMM. I THINK I'M STARTING TO UNDERSTAND THIS WORLD. THE LAWS OF COMEDY SEEM TO OVER-RULE THE LAWS OF PHYSICS!
THAT'S THE SPIRIT!
...squeeze and fi--* Uh, no, wait! Cancel that last command! Don't--
THERE! YOUR TIN TRAPPER'S DISABLED, AND YOU ARE DEFINITELY IN THE DOGHOUSE, FRIEND!
ERRK! UNHAND me, you knuckle-dragging NEANDERTHAL!
PATIENCE, HONEY, ARE YOU OKAY?
I AM NOW YOU'RE HERE, MY LOP-EARED LOVER-BOY!

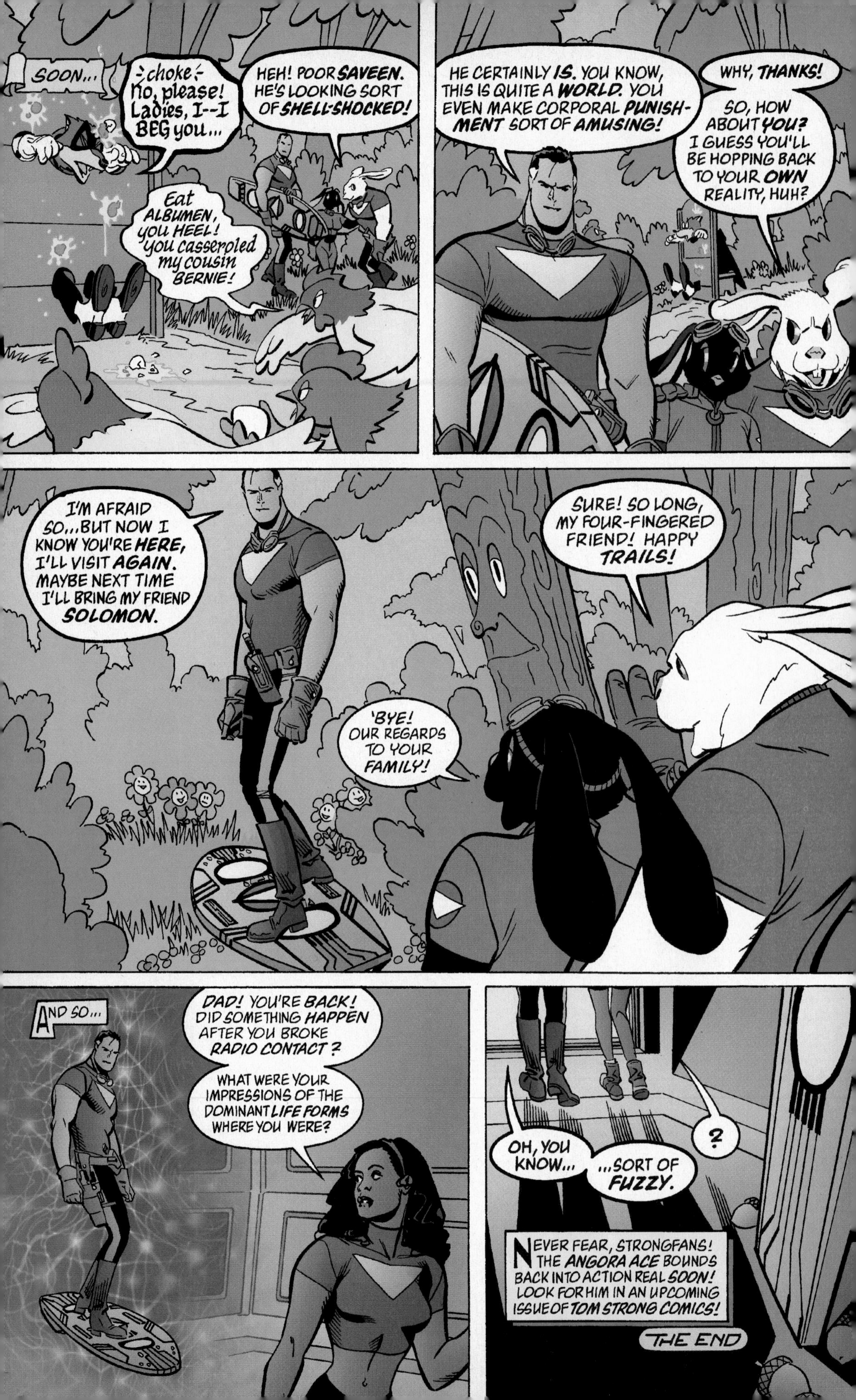
SOON...
-choke- No, please! Ladies, I--I BEG you...
HEH! POOR SAVEEN. HE'S LOOKING SORT OF SHELL-SHOCKED!
Eat ALBUMEN, you HEEL! you casseroled my cousin BERNIE!
HE CERTAINLY IS. YOU KNOW, THIS IS QUITE A WORLD. YOU EVEN MAKE CORPORAL PUNISHMENT SORT OF AMUSING!
WHY, THANKS!
SO, HOW ABOUT YOU? I GUESS YOU'LL BE HOPPING BACK TO YOUR OWN REALITY, HUH?
I'M AFRAID SO...BUT NOW I KNOW YOU'RE HERE, I'LL VISIT AGAIN. MAYBE NEXT TIME I'LL BRING MY FRIEND SOLOMON.
SURE! SO LONG, MY FOUR-FINGERED FRIEND! HAPPY TRAILS!
'BYE! OUR REGARDS TO YOUR FAMILY!
AND SO...
DAD! YOU'RE BACK! DID SOMETHING HAPPEN AFTER YOU BROKE RADIO CONTACT?
WHAT WERE YOUR IMPRESSIONS OF THE DOMINANT LIFE FORMS WHERE YOU WERE?
OH, YOU KNOW...
...SORT OF FUZZY.
?
NEVER FEAR, STRONGFANS! THE ANGORA ACE BOUNDS BACK INTO ACTION REAL SOON! LOOK FOR HIM IN AN UPCOMING ISSUE OF TOM STRONG COMICS!
THE END

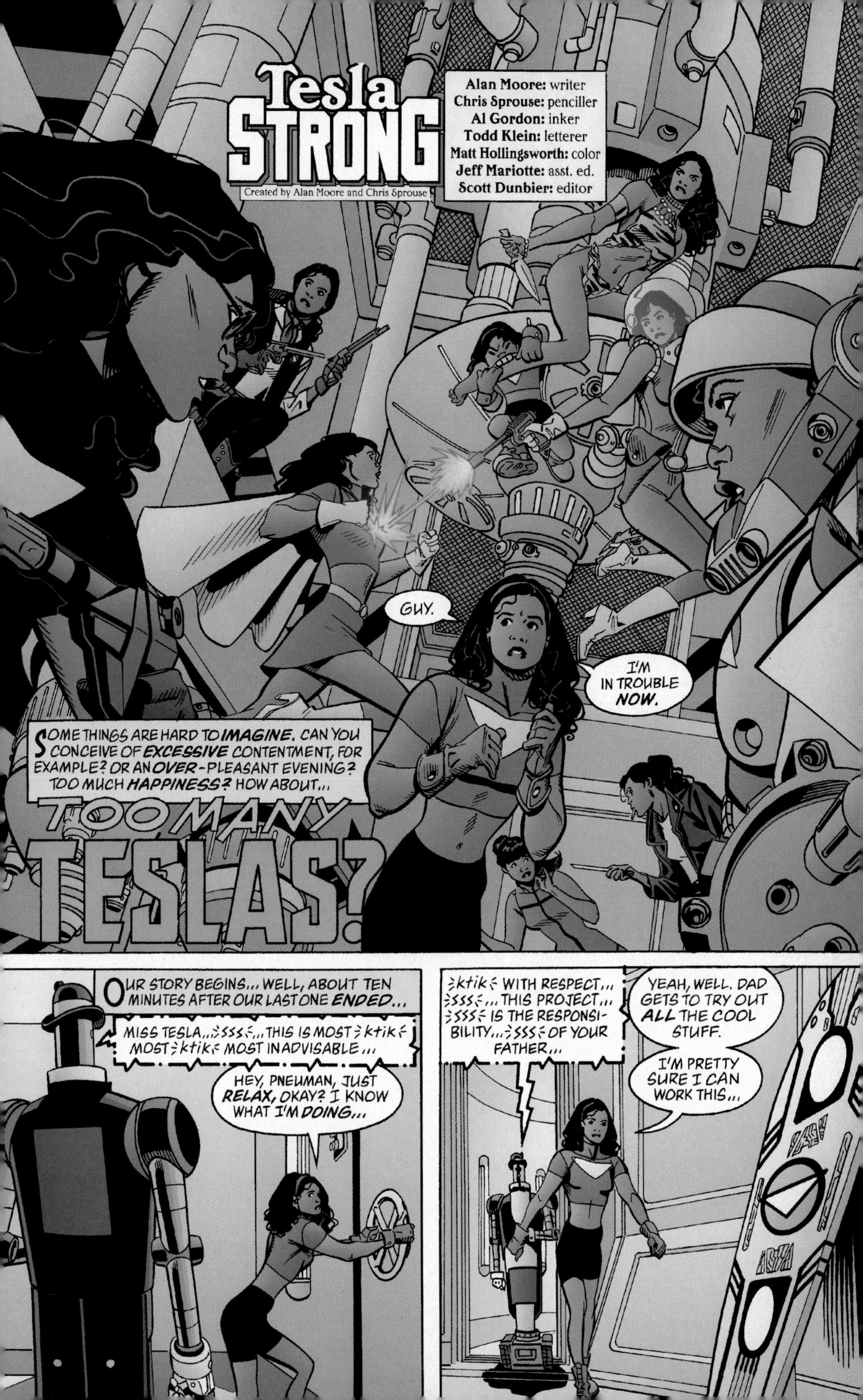
Tesla STRONG
Created by Alan Moore and Chris Sprouse
Alan Moore: writer
Chris Sprouse: penciller
Al Gordon: inker
Todd Klein: letterer
Matt Hollingsworth: color
Jeff Mariotte: asst. ed.
Scott Dunbier: editor
GUY.
I'M IN TROUBLE NOW.
SOME THINGS ARE HARD TO IMAGINE. CAN YOU CONCEIVE OF EXCESSIVE CONTENTMENT, FOR EXAMPLE? OR AN OVER-PLEASANT EVENING? TOO MUCH HAPPINESS? HOW ABOUT...
TOO MANY TESLAS?
OUR STORY BEGINS... WELL, ABOUT TEN MINUTES AFTER OUR LAST ONE ENDED...
MISS TESLA...sss... THIS IS MOST ktik MOST ktik MOST INADVISABLE...
HEY, PNEUMAN, JUST RELAX, OKAY? I KNOW WHAT I'M DOING...
ktik WITH RESPECT... sss... THIS PROJECT... sss IS THE RESPONSIBILITY... sss OF YOUR FATHER...
YEAH, WELL. DAD GETS TO TRY OUT ALL THE COOL STUFF.
I'M PRETTY SURE I CAN WORK THIS...

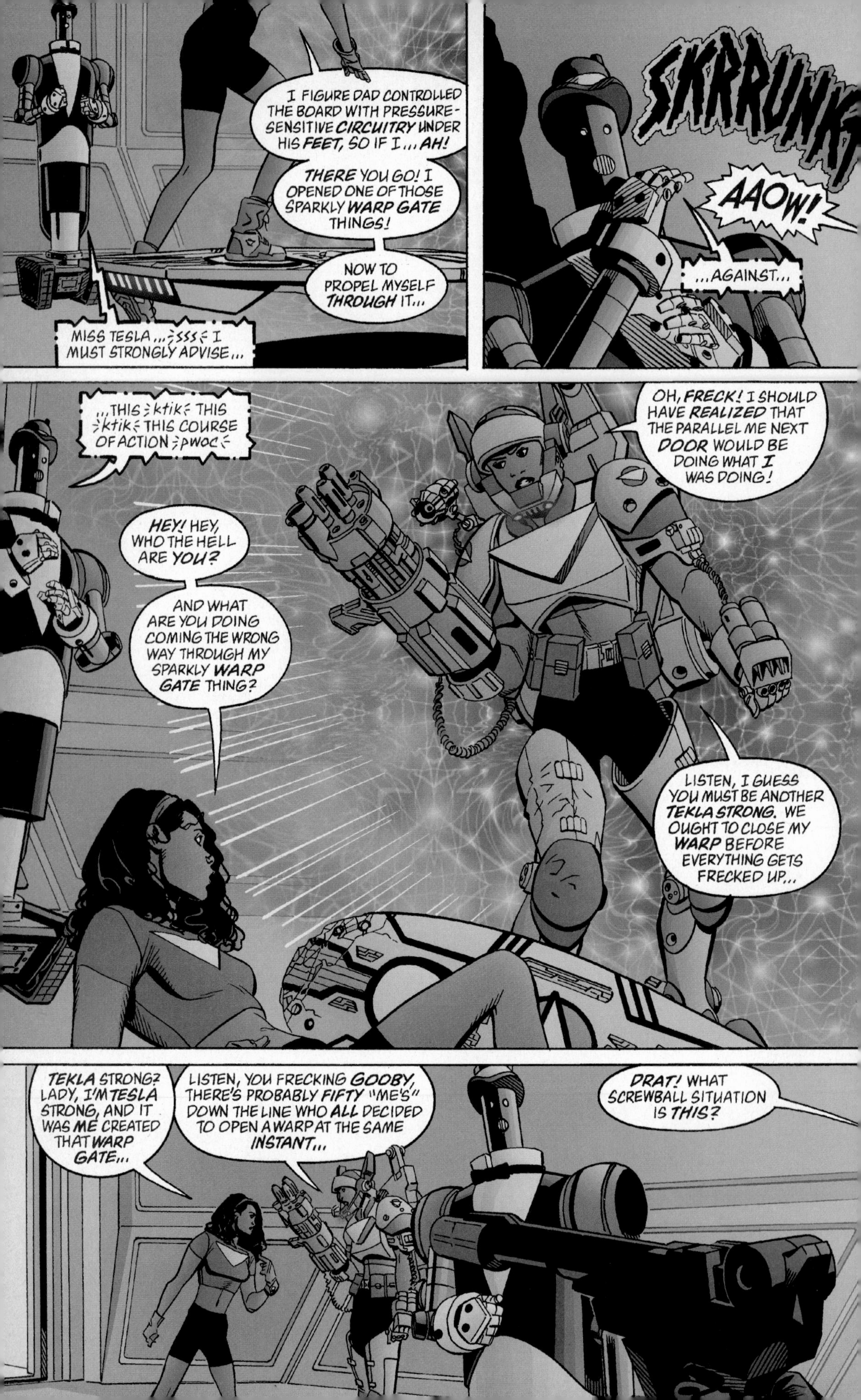
I FIGURE DAD CONTROLLED THE BOARD WITH PRESSURE-SENSITIVE CIRCUITRY UNDER HIS FEET, SO IF I... AH!
THERE YOU GO! I OPENED ONE OF THOSE SPARKLY WARP GATE THINGS!
NOW TO PROPEL MYSELF THROUGH IT...
MISS TESLA... sss I MUST STRONGLY ADVISE...
SKRRUNK!
AAOW!
...AGAINST...
...THIS ktik THIS ktik THIS COURSE OF ACTION pwoc
OH, FRECK! I SHOULD HAVE REALIZED THAT THE PARALLEL ME NEXT DOOR WOULD BE DOING WHAT I WAS DOING!
HEY! HEY, WHO THE HELL ARE YOU?
AND WHAT ARE YOU DOING COMING THE WRONG WAY THROUGH MY SPARKLY WARP GATE THING?
LISTEN, I GUESS YOU MUST BE ANOTHER TEKLA STRONG. WE OUGHT TO CLOSE MY WARP BEFORE EVERYTHING GETS FRECKED UP...
TEKLA STRONG? LADY, I'M TESLA STRONG, AND IT WAS ME CREATED THAT WARP GATE...
LISTEN, YOU FRECKING GOOBY, THERE'S PROBABLY FIFTY "ME'S" DOWN THE LINE WHO ALL DECIDED TO OPEN A WARP AT THE SAME INSTANT...
DRAT! WHAT SCREWBALL SITUATION IS THIS?

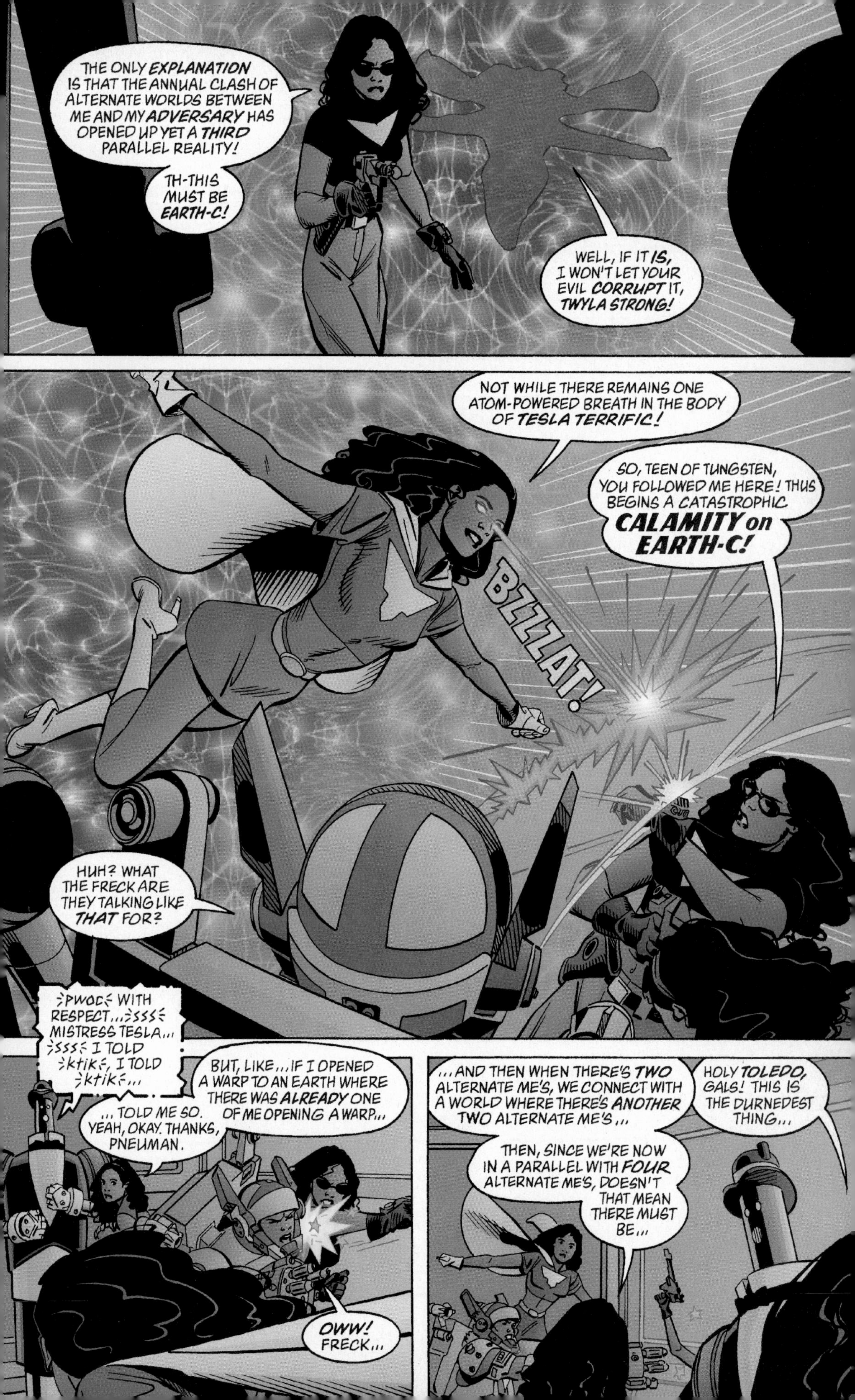
THE ONLY EXPLANATION IS THAT THE ANNUAL CLASH OF ALTERNATE WORLDS BETWEEN ME AND MY ADVERSARY HAS OPENED UP YET A THIRD PARALLEL REALITY!
TH-THIS MUST BE EARTH-C!
WELL, IF IT IS, I WON'T LET YOUR EVIL CORRUPT IT, TWYLA STRONG!
NOT WHILE THERE REMAINS ONE ATOM-POWERED BREATH IN THE BODY OF TESLA TERRIFIC!
SO, TEEN OF TUNGSTEN, YOU FOLLOWED ME HERE! THUS BEGINS A CATASTROPHIC CALAMITY on EARTH-C!
BZZZAT!
HUH? WHAT THE FRECK ARE THEY TALKING LIKE THAT FOR?
PWOC WITH RESPECT... SSS MISTRESS TESLA... SSS I TOLD ktik, I TOLD ktik...
... TOLD ME SO. YEAH, OKAY. THANKS, PNEUMAN.
BUT, LIKE... IF I OPENED A WARP TO AN EARTH WHERE THERE WAS ALREADY ONE OF ME OPENING A WARP...
OWW! FRECK...
... AND THEN WHEN THERE'S TWO ALTERNATE ME'S, WE CONNECT WITH A WORLD WHERE THERE'S ANOTHER TWO ALTERNATE ME'S...
HOLY TOLEDO, GALS! THIS IS THE DURNEDEST THING...
THEN, SINCE WE'RE NOW IN A PARALLEL WITH FOUR ALTERNATE ME'S, DOESN'T THAT MEAN THERE MUST BE...

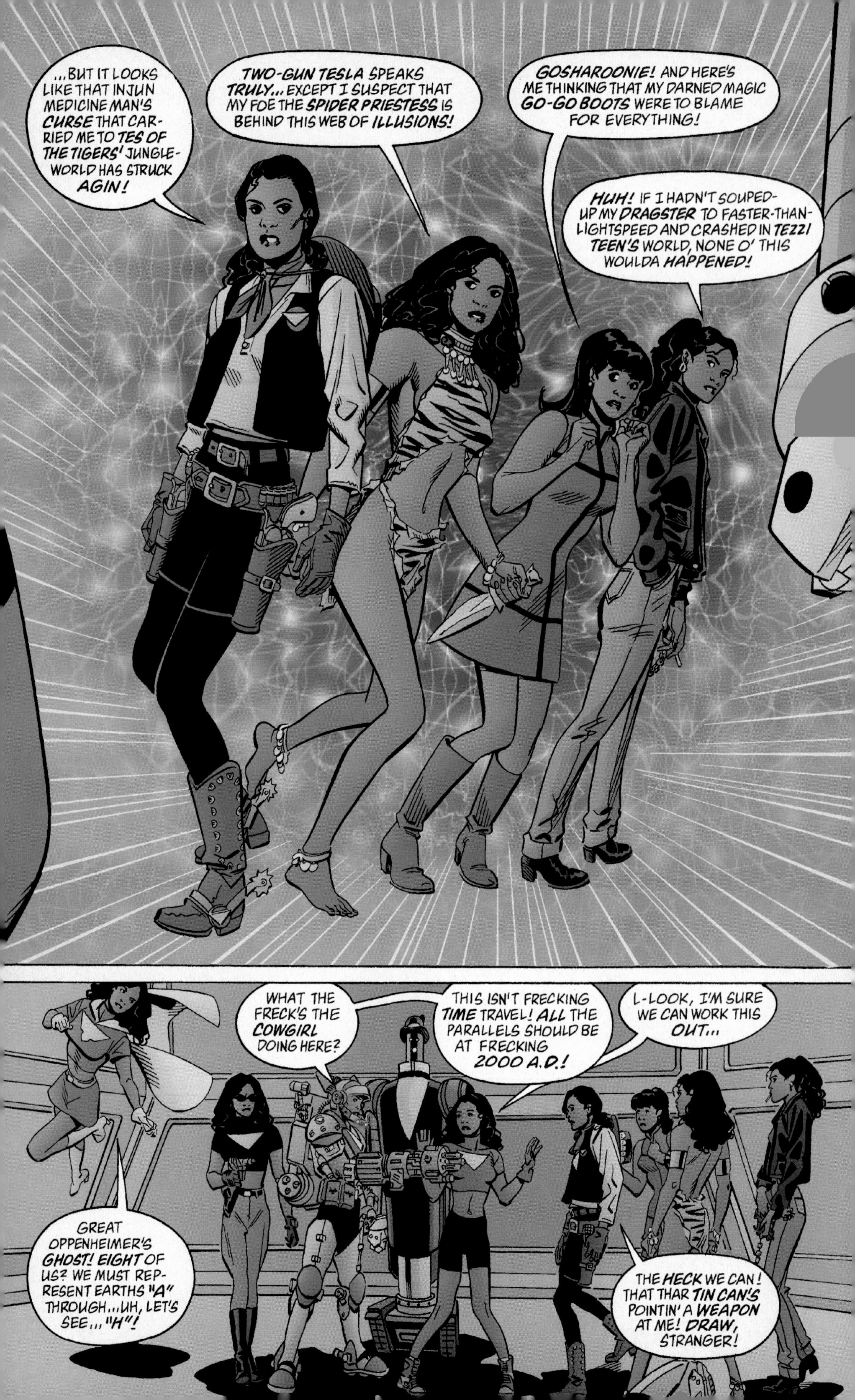
...BUT IT LOOKS LIKE THAT INJUN MEDICINE MAN'S CURSE THAT CARRIED ME TO TES OF THE TIGERS' JUNGLE-WORLD HAS STRUCK AGIN!
TWO-GUN TESLA SPEAKS TRULY... EXCEPT I SUSPECT THAT MY FOE THE SPIDER PRIESTESS IS BEHIND THIS WEB OF ILLUSIONS!
GOSHAROONIE! AND HERE'S ME THINKING THAT MY DARNED MAGIC GO-GO BOOTS WERE TO BLAME FOR EVERYTHING!
HUH! IF I HADN'T SOUPED-UP MY DRAGSTER TO FASTER-THAN-LIGHTSPEED AND CRASHED IN TEZZI TEEN'S WORLD, NONE O' THIS WOULDA HAPPENED!
WHAT THE FRECK'S THE COWGIRL DOING HERE?
THIS ISN'T FRECKING TIME TRAVEL! ALL THE PARALLELS SHOULD BE AT FRECKING 2000 A.D.!
L-LOOK, I'M SURE WE CAN WORK THIS OUT...
GREAT OPPENHEIMER'S GHOST! EIGHT OF US? WE MUST REPRESENT EARTHS "A" THROUGH...UH, LET'S SEE... "H"!
THE HECK WE CAN! THAT THAR TIN CAN'S POINTIN' A WEAPON AT ME! DRAW, STRANGER!

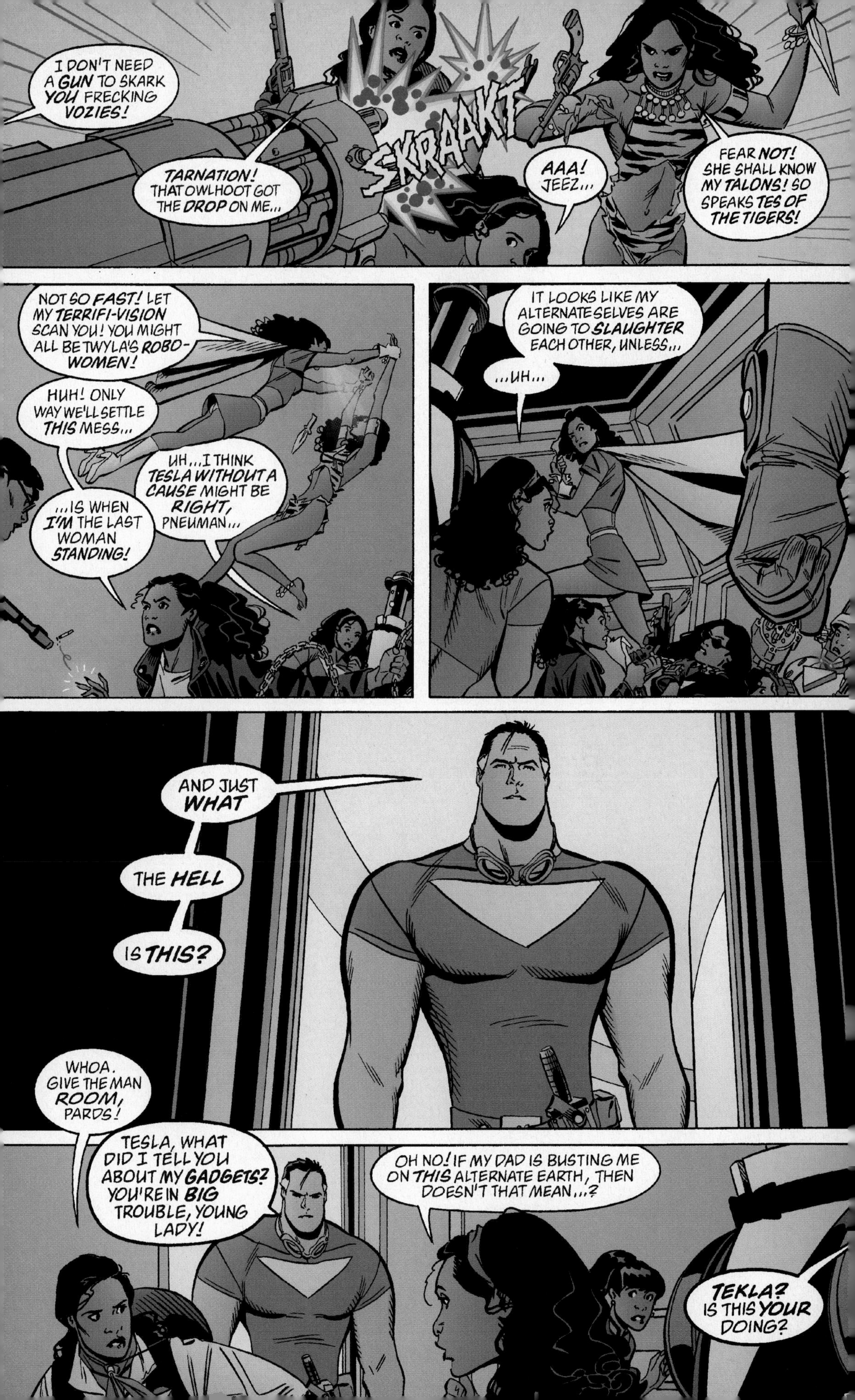
I DON'T NEED A GUN TO SKARK YOU FRECKING VOZIES!
TARNATION! THAT OWLHOOT GOT THE DROP ON ME...
SKRAAKT
AAA! JEEZ...
FEAR NOT! SHE SHALL KNOW MY TALONS! SO SPEAKS TES OF THE TIGERS!
NOT SO FAST! LET MY TERRIFI-VISION SCAN YOU! YOU MIGHT ALL BE TWYLA'S ROBO-WOMEN!
HUH! ONLY WAY WE'LL SETTLE THIS MESS...
...IS WHEN I'M THE LAST WOMAN STANDING!
UH...I THINK TESLA WITHOUT A CAUSE MIGHT BE RIGHT, PNEUMAN...
IT LOOKS LIKE MY ALTERNATE SELVES ARE GOING TO SLAUGHTER EACH OTHER, UNLESS...
...UH...
AND JUST WHAT
THE HELL
IS THIS?
WHOA. GIVE THE MAN ROOM, PARDS!
TESLA, WHAT DID I TELL YOU ABOUT MY GADGETS? YOU'RE IN BIG TROUBLE, YOUNG LADY!
OH NO! IF MY DAD IS BUSTING ME ON THIS ALTERNATE EARTH, THEN DOESN'T THAT MEAN...?
TEKLA? IS THIS YOUR DOING?

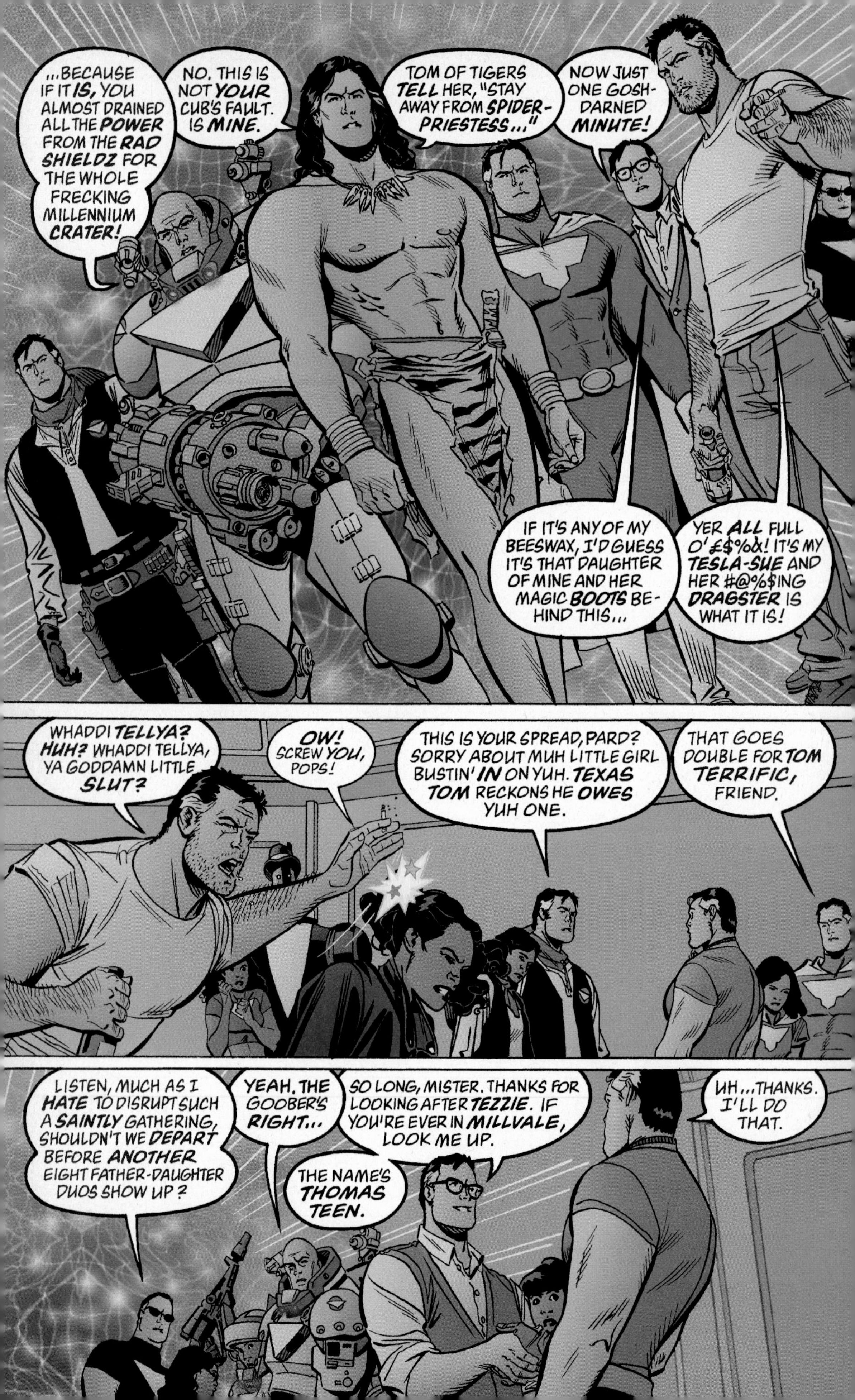
...BECAUSE IF IT IS, YOU ALMOST DRAINED ALL THE POWER FROM THE RAD SHIELDZ FOR THE WHOLE FRECKING MILLENNIUM CRATER!
NO. THIS IS NOT YOUR CUB'S FAULT. IS MINE.
TOM OF TIGERS TELL HER, "STAY AWAY FROM SPIDER-PRIESTESS..."
NOW JUST ONE GOSH-DARNED MINUTE!
IF IT'S ANY OF MY BEESWAX, I'D GUESS IT'S THAT DAUGHTER OF MINE AND HER MAGIC BOOTS BEHIND THIS...
YER ALL FULL O' £$%&! IT'S MY TESLA-SUE AND HER #@%$ING DRAGSTER IS WHAT IT IS!
WHADDI TELLYA? HUH? WHADDI TELLYA, YA GODDAMN LITTLE SLUT?
OW! SCREW YOU, POPS!
THIS IS YOUR SPREAD, PARD? SORRY ABOUT MUH LITTLE GIRL BUSTIN' IN ON YUH. TEXAS TOM RECKONS HE OWES YUH ONE.
THAT GOES DOUBLE FOR TOM TERRIFIC, FRIEND.
LISTEN, MUCH AS I HATE TO DISRUPT SUCH A SAINTLY GATHERING, SHOULDN'T WE DEPART BEFORE ANOTHER EIGHT FATHER-DAUGHTER DUOS SHOW UP?
YEAH. THE GOOBER'S RIGHT...
SO LONG, MISTER. THANKS FOR LOOKING AFTER TEZZIE. IF YOU'RE EVER IN MILLVALE, LOOK ME UP.
THE NAME'S THOMAS TEEN.
UH...THANKS. I'LL DO THAT.

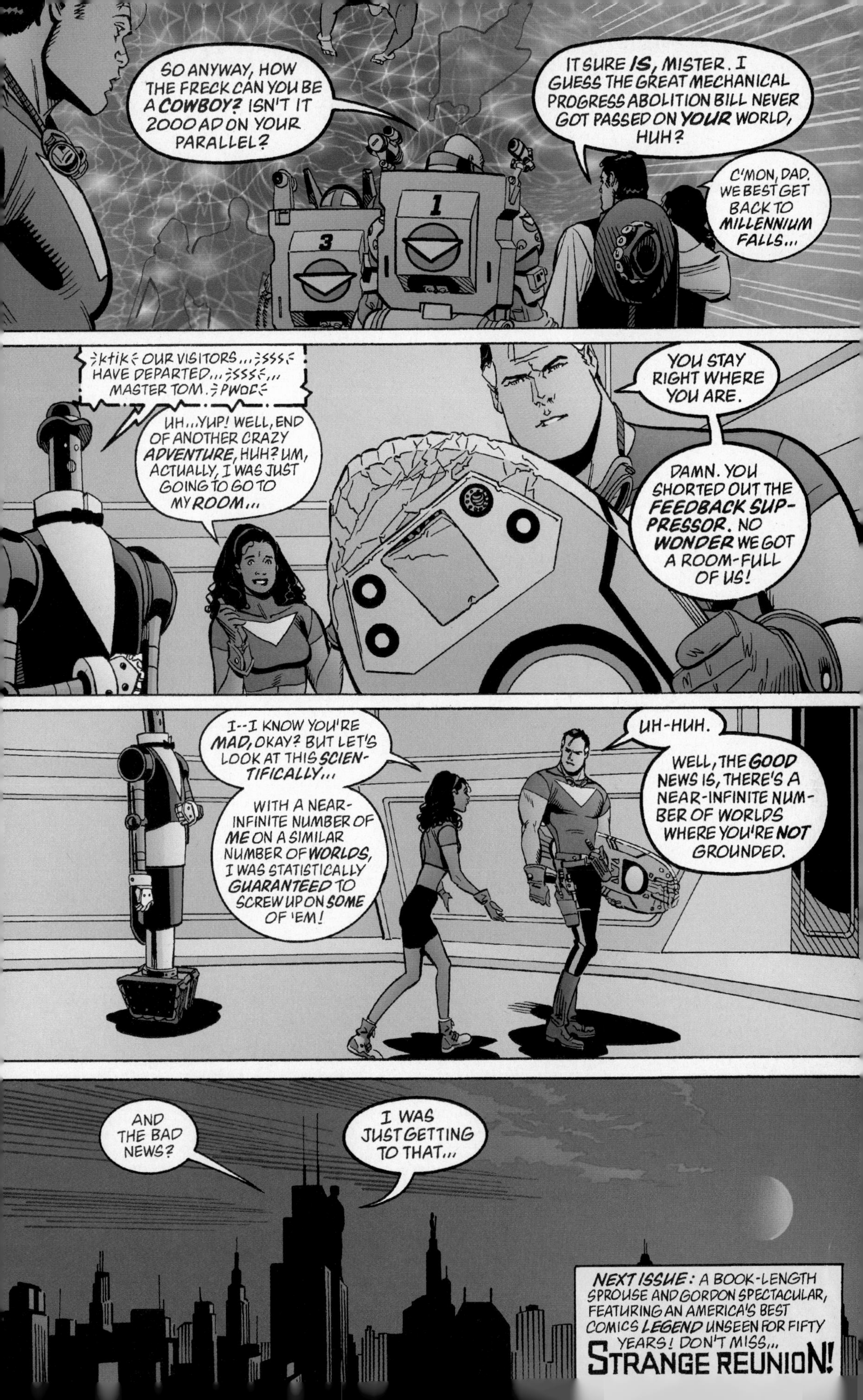
SO ANYWAY, HOW THE FRECK CAN YOU BE A COWBOY? ISN'T IT 2000 AD ON YOUR PARALLEL?
IT SURE IS, MISTER. I GUESS THE GREAT MECHANICAL PROGRESS ABOLITION BILL NEVER GOT PASSED ON YOUR WORLD, HUH?
C'MON, DAD. WE BEST GET BACK TO MILLENNIUM FALLS...
ktik OUR VISITORS... sss HAVE DEPARTED... sss... MASTER TOM. PWOC
UH...YUP! WELL, END OF ANOTHER CRAZY ADVENTURE, HUH? UM, ACTUALLY, I WAS JUST GOING TO GO TO MY ROOM...
YOU STAY RIGHT WHERE YOU ARE.
DAMN. YOU SHORTED OUT THE FEEDBACK SUPPRESSOR. NO WONDER WE GOT A ROOM-FULL OF US!
I--I KNOW YOU'RE MAD, OKAY? BUT LET'S LOOK AT THIS SCIENTIFICALLY...
WITH A NEAR-INFINITE NUMBER OF ME ON A SIMILAR NUMBER OF WORLDS, I WAS STATISTICALLY GUARANTEED TO SCREW UP ON SOME OF 'EM!
UH-HUH.
WELL, THE GOOD NEWS IS, THERE'S A NEAR-INFINITE NUMBER OF WORLDS WHERE YOU'RE NOT GROUNDED.
AND THE BAD NEWS?
I WAS JUST GETTING TO THAT...
NEXT ISSUE: A BOOK-LENGTH SPROUSE AND GORDON SPECTACULAR, FEATURING AN AMERICA'S BEST COMICS LEGEND UNSEEN FOR FIFTY YEARS! DON'T MISS...
STRANGE REUNION!

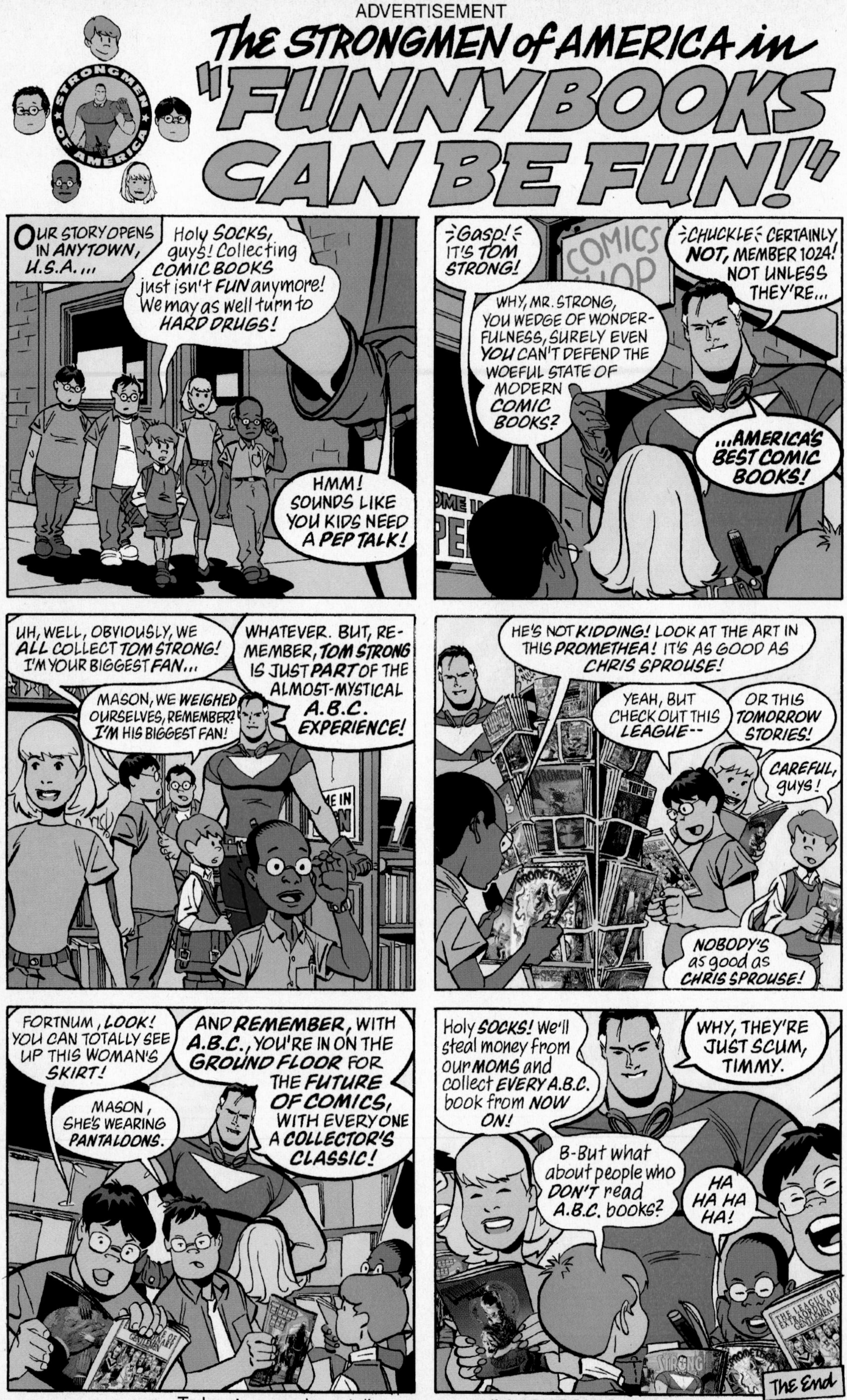

STRONGMEN OF AMERICA
The STRONGMEN of AMERICA in
"FUNNYBOOKS CAN BE FUN!"
OUR STORY OPENS IN ANYTOWN, U.S.A....
Holy SOCKS, guys! Collecting COMIC BOOKS just isn't FUN anymore! We may as well turn to HARD DRUGS!
HMM! SOUNDS LIKE YOU KIDS NEED A PEP TALK!
-Gasp!- IT'S TOM STRONG!
WHY, MR. STRONG, YOU WEDGE OF WONDERFULNESS, SURELY EVEN YOU CAN'T DEFEND THE WOEFUL STATE OF MODERN COMIC BOOKS?
-CHUCKLE- CERTAINLY NOT, MEMBER 1024! NOT UNLESS THEY'RE...
...AMERICA'S BEST COMIC BOOKS!
UH, WELL, OBVIOUSLY, WE ALL COLLECT TOM STRONG! I'M YOUR BIGGEST FAN...
MASON, WE WEIGHED OURSELVES, REMEMBER? I'M HIS BIGGEST FAN!
WHATEVER. BUT, REMEMBER, TOM STRONG IS JUST PART OF THE ALMOST-MYSTICAL A.B.C. EXPERIENCE!
HE'S NOT KIDDING! LOOK AT THE ART IN THIS PROMETHEA! IT'S AS GOOD AS CHRIS SPROUSE!
YEAH, BUT CHECK OUT THIS LEAGUE--
OR THIS TOMORROW STORIES!
CAREFUL, guys!
NOBODY'S as good as CHRIS SPROUSE!
FORTNUM, LOOK! YOU CAN TOTALLY SEE UP THIS WOMAN'S SKIRT!
MASON, SHE'S WEARING PANTALOONS.
AND REMEMBER, WITH A.B.C., YOU'RE IN ON THE GROUND FLOOR FOR THE FUTURE OF COMICS, WITH EVERY ONE A COLLECTOR'S CLASSIC!
Holy SOCKS! We'll steal money from our MOMS and collect EVERY A.B.C. book from NOW ON!
WHY, THEY'RE JUST SCUM, TIMMY.
B-But what about people who DON'T read A.B.C. books?
HA HA HA HA HA!
THE LEAGUE OF EXTRAORDINARY GENTLEMEN
THE End

CHAPTER FOUR

In which an obscure figure reemerges,
distant doomed battles are recounted,
and Tom journeys far to rescue friends.

Cover art:
Chris Sprouse & Al Gordon

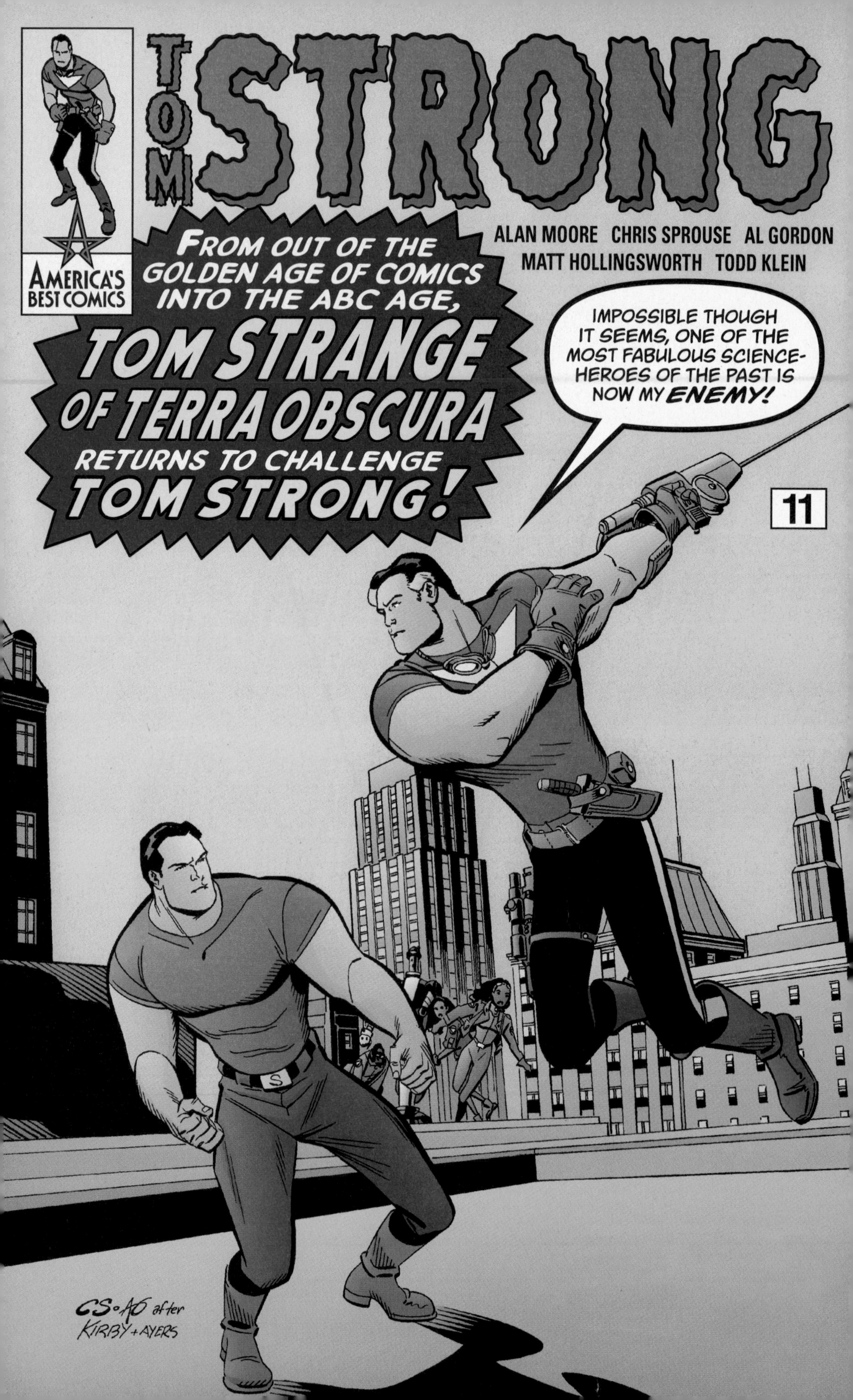
TOM STRONG
AMERICA'S BEST COMICS
ALAN MOORE CHRIS SPROUSE AL GORDON
MATT HOLLINGSWORTH TODD KLEIN
FROM OUT OF THE GOLDEN AGE OF COMICS INTO THE ABC AGE, TOM STRANGE OF TERRA OBSCURA RETURNS TO CHALLENGE TOM STRONG!
IMPOSSIBLE THOUGH IT SEEMS, ONE OF THE MOST FABULOUS SCIENCE-HEROES OF THE PAST IS NOW MY *ENEMY!*
11
CS•AG after KIRBY+AYERS

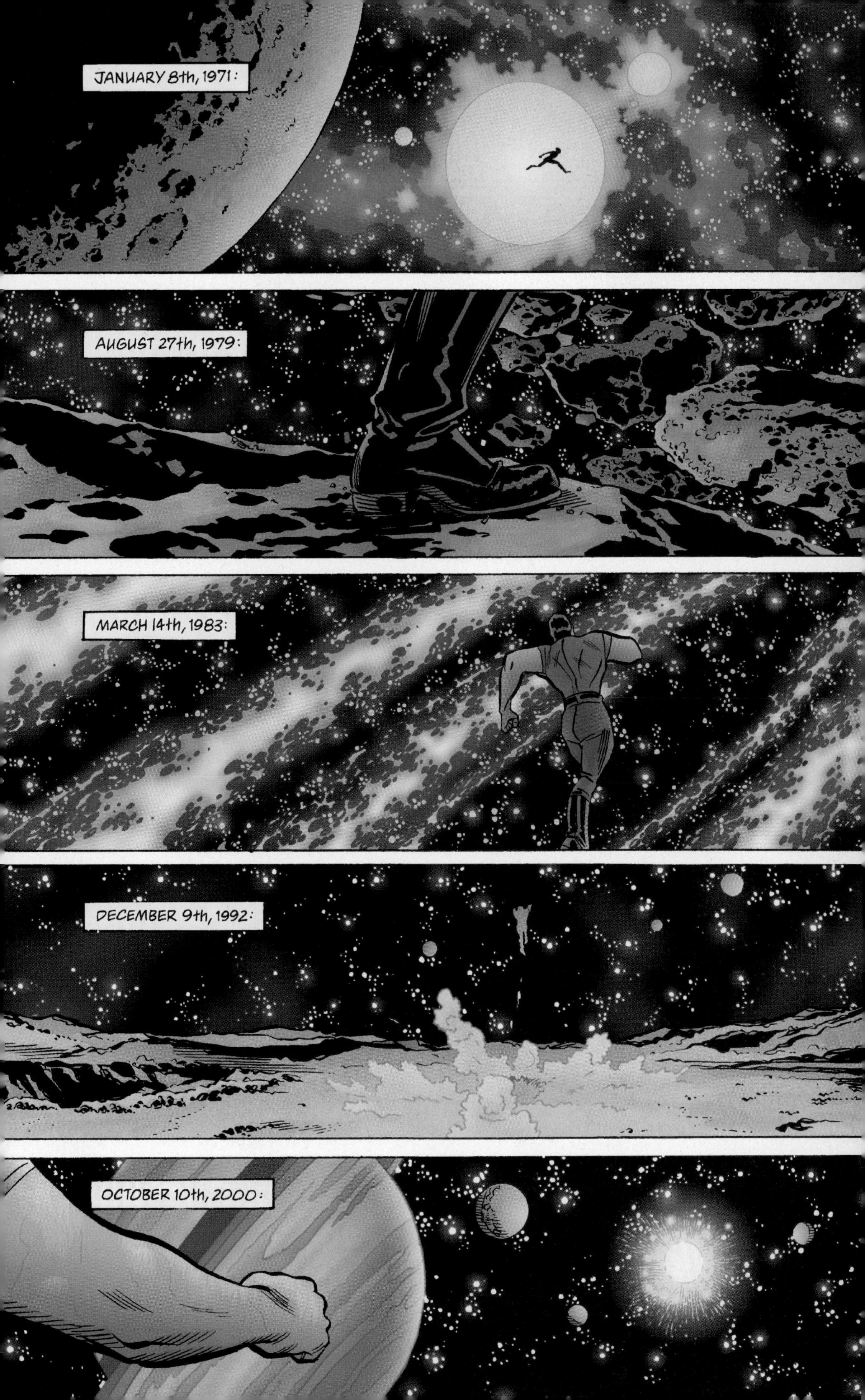
JANUARY 8th, 1971:
AUGUST 27th, 1979:
MARCH 14th, 1983:
DECEMBER 9th, 1992:
OCTOBER 10th, 2000:

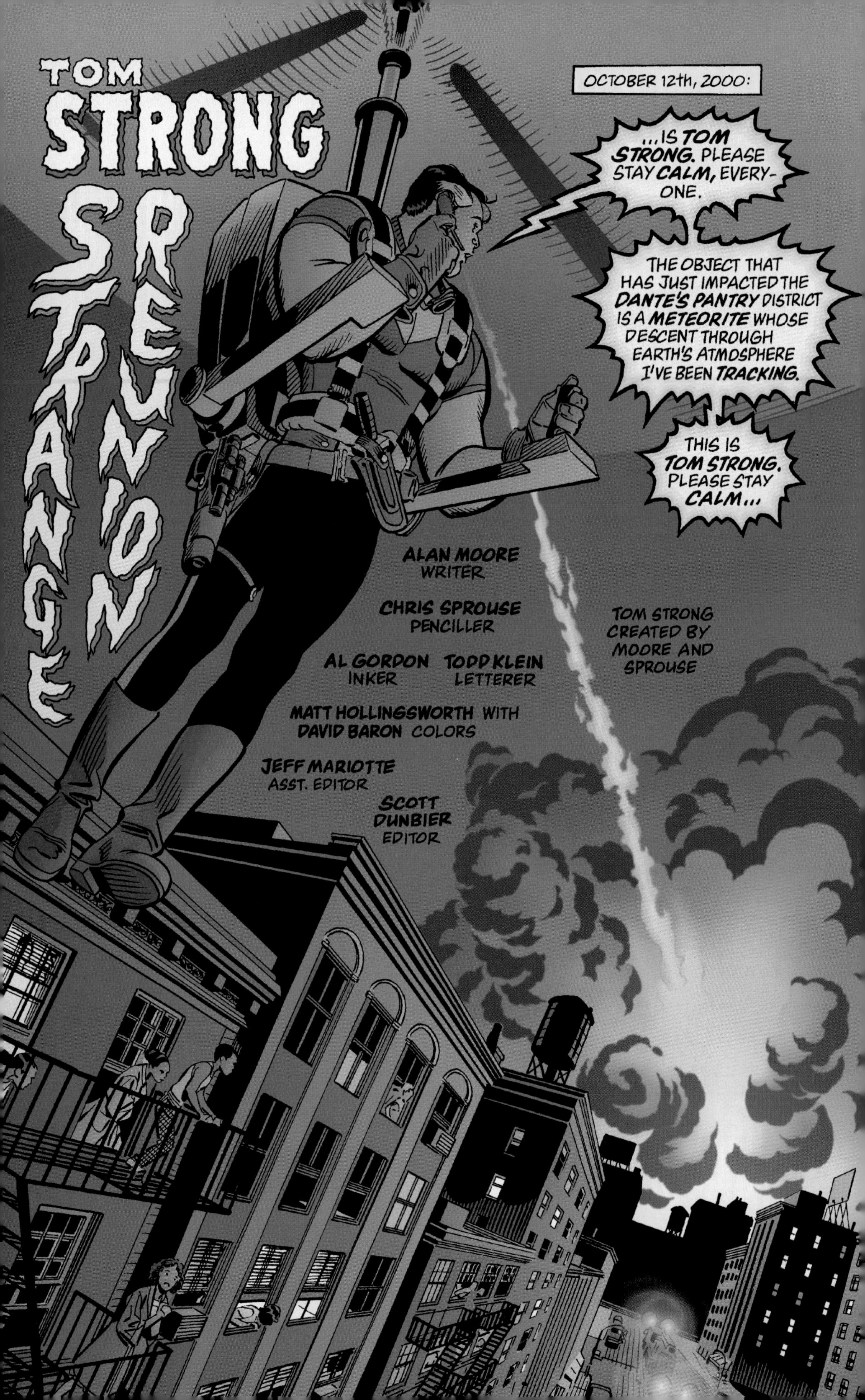
TOM STRONG
STRANGE REUNION
OCTOBER 12th, 2000:
...IS TOM STRONG. PLEASE STAY CALM, EVERY-ONE.
THE OBJECT THAT HAS JUST IMPACTED THE DANTE'S PANTRY DISTRICT IS A METEORITE WHOSE DESCENT THROUGH EARTH'S ATMOSPHERE I'VE BEEN TRACKING.
THIS IS TOM STRONG. PLEASE STAY CALM...
ALAN MOORE WRITER
CHRIS SPROUSE PENCILLER
AL GORDON INKER
TODD KLEIN LETTERER
MATT HOLLINGSWORTH WITH DAVID BARON COLORS
JEFF MARIOTTE ASST. EDITOR
SCOTT DUNBIER EDITOR
TOM STRONG CREATED BY MOORE AND SPROUSE

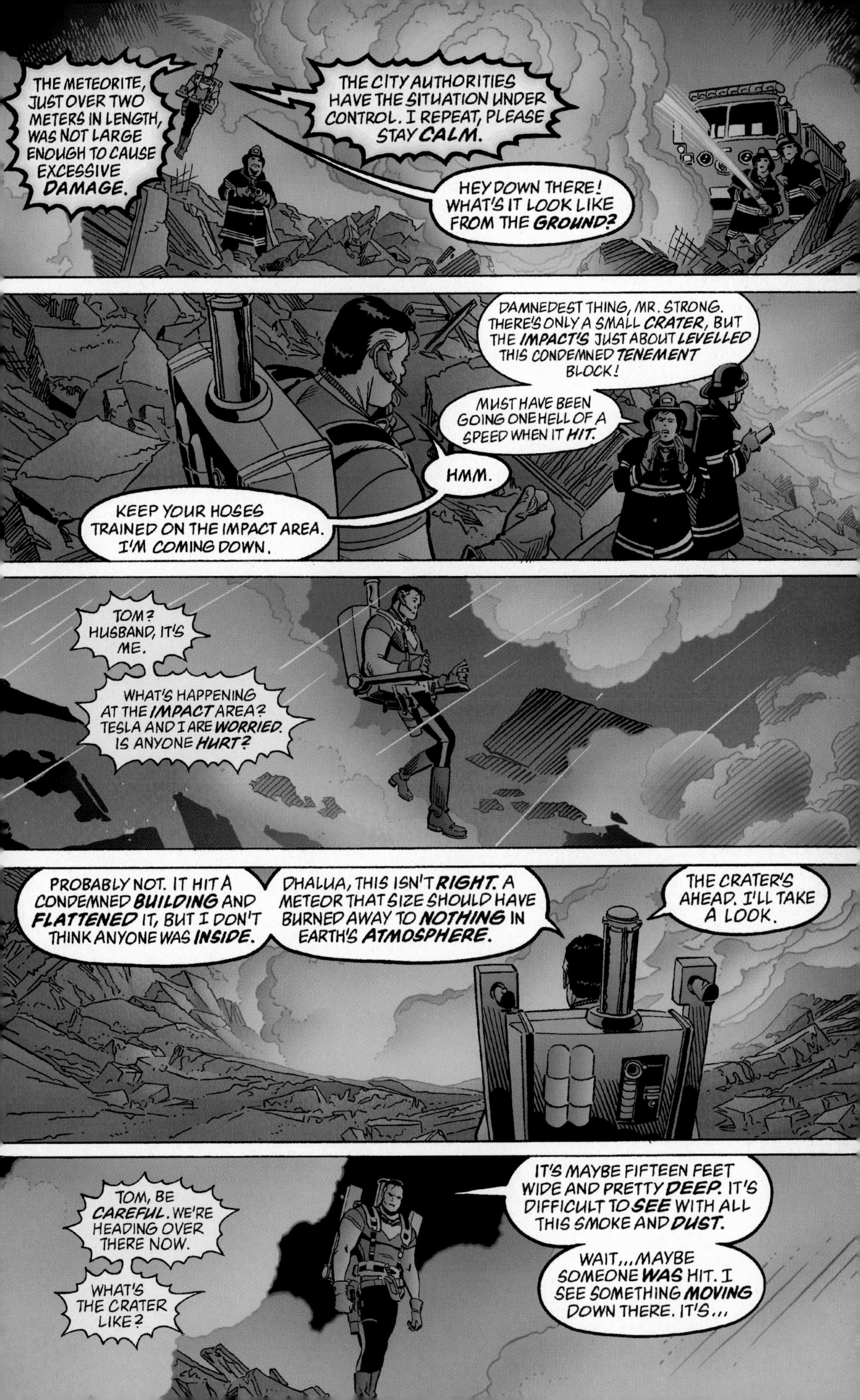
THE METEORITE, JUST OVER TWO METERS IN LENGTH, WAS NOT LARGE ENOUGH TO CAUSE EXCESSIVE DAMAGE.
THE CITY AUTHORITIES HAVE THE SITUATION UNDER CONTROL. I REPEAT, PLEASE STAY CALM.
HEY DOWN THERE! WHAT'S IT LOOK LIKE FROM THE GROUND?
DAMNEDEST THING, MR. STRONG. THERE'S ONLY A SMALL CRATER, BUT THE IMPACT'S JUST ABOUT LEVELLED THIS CONDEMNED TENEMENT BLOCK!
MUST HAVE BEEN GOING ONE HELL OF A SPEED WHEN IT HIT.
HMM.
KEEP YOUR HOSES TRAINED ON THE IMPACT AREA. I'M COMING DOWN.
TOM? HUSBAND, IT'S ME.
WHAT'S HAPPENING AT THE IMPACT AREA? TESLA AND I ARE WORRIED. IS ANYONE HURT?
PROBABLY NOT. IT HIT A CONDEMNED BUILDING AND FLATTENED IT, BUT I DON'T THINK ANYONE WAS INSIDE.
DHALUA, THIS ISN'T RIGHT. A METEOR THAT SIZE SHOULD HAVE BURNED AWAY TO NOTHING IN EARTH'S ATMOSPHERE.
THE CRATER'S AHEAD. I'LL TAKE A LOOK.
TOM, BE CAREFUL. WE'RE HEADING OVER THERE NOW.
WHAT'S THE CRATER LIKE?
IT'S MAYBE FIFTEEN FEET WIDE AND PRETTY DEEP. IT'S DIFFICULT TO SEE WITH ALL THIS SMOKE AND DUST.
WAIT,,, MAYBE SOMEONE WAS HIT. I SEE SOMETHING MOVING DOWN THERE. IT'S...

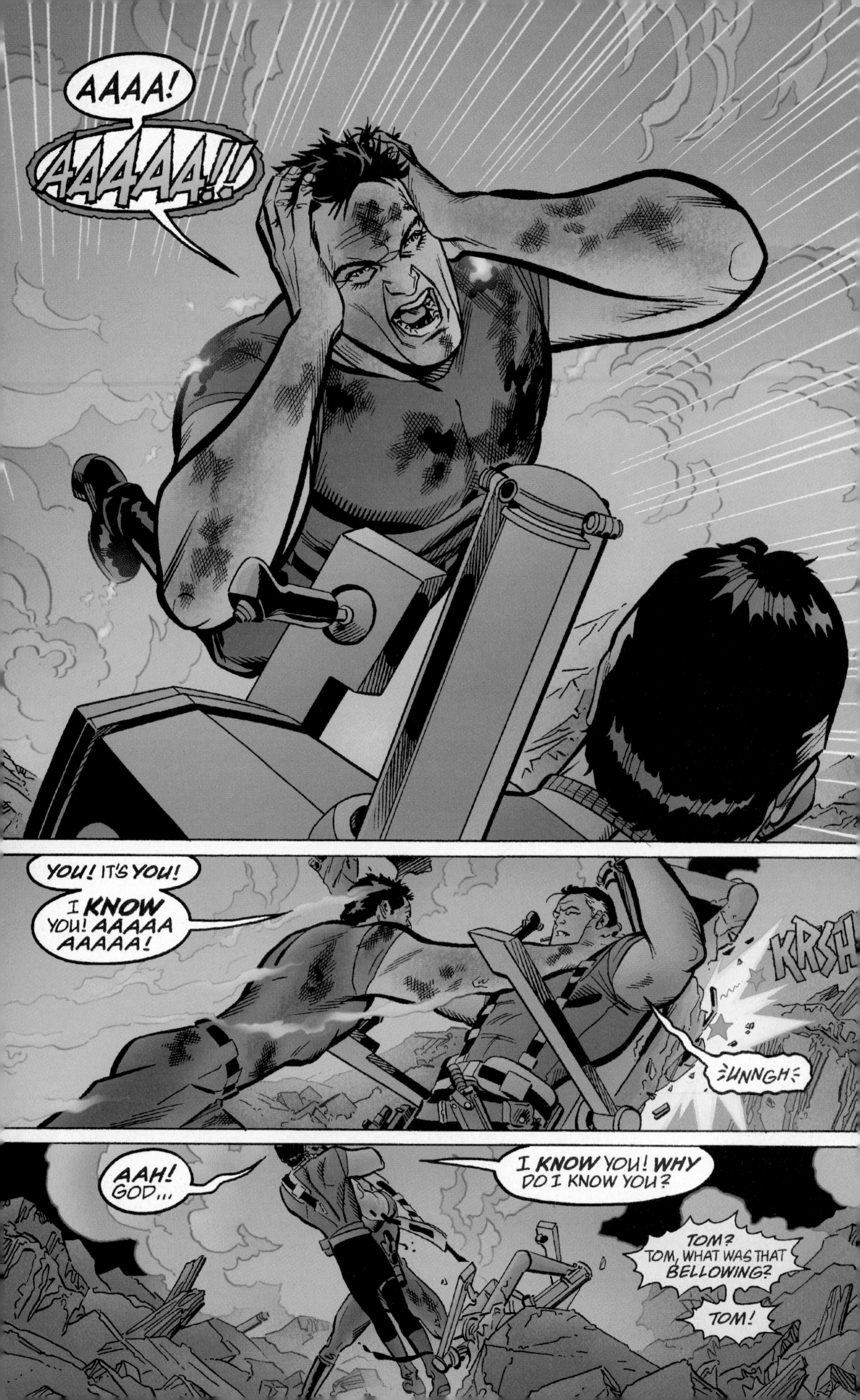
AAAA!
AAAAA!!
YOU! IT'S YOU! I KNOW YOU! AAAAA AAAAA!
KRSH
UNNGH
AAH! GOD...
I KNOW YOU! WHY DO I KNOW YOU?
TOM? TOM, WHAT WAS THAT BELLOWING?
TOM!

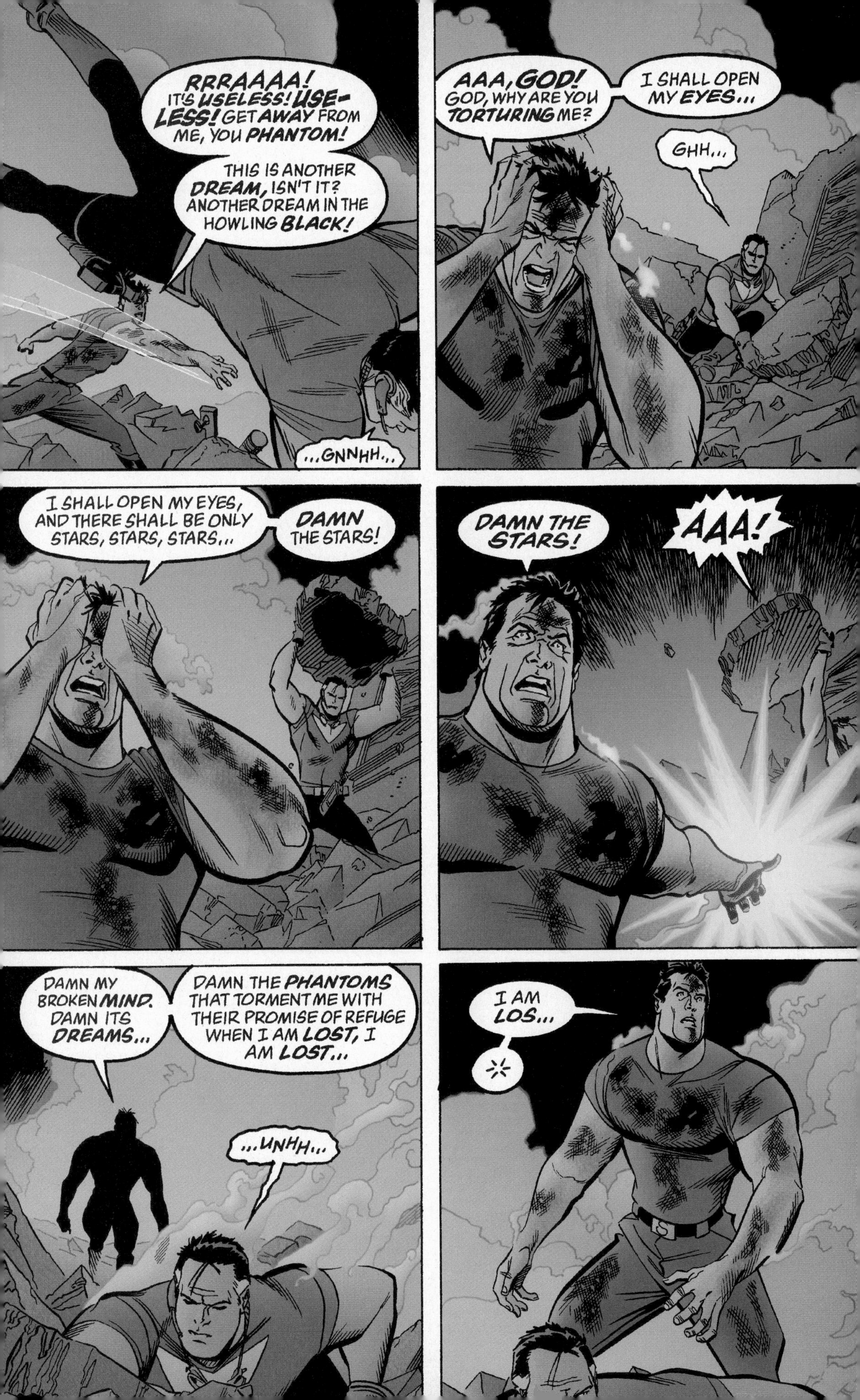
RRRAAAAA! IT'S USELESS! USE-LESS! GET AWAY FROM ME, YOU PHANTOM!
THIS IS ANOTHER DREAM, ISN'T IT? ANOTHER DREAM IN THE HOWLING BLACK!
...GNNHH...
AAA, GOD! GOD, WHY ARE YOU TORTURING ME?
I SHALL OPEN MY EYES...
GHH...
I SHALL OPEN MY EYES, AND THERE SHALL BE ONLY STARS, STARS, STARS...
DAMN THE STARS!
DAMN THE STARS!
AAA!
DAMN MY BROKEN MIND. DAMN ITS DREAMS...
DAMN THE PHANTOMS THAT TORMENT ME WITH THEIR PROMISE OF REFUGE WHEN I AM LOST, I AM LOST...
...UNHH...
I AM LOS...

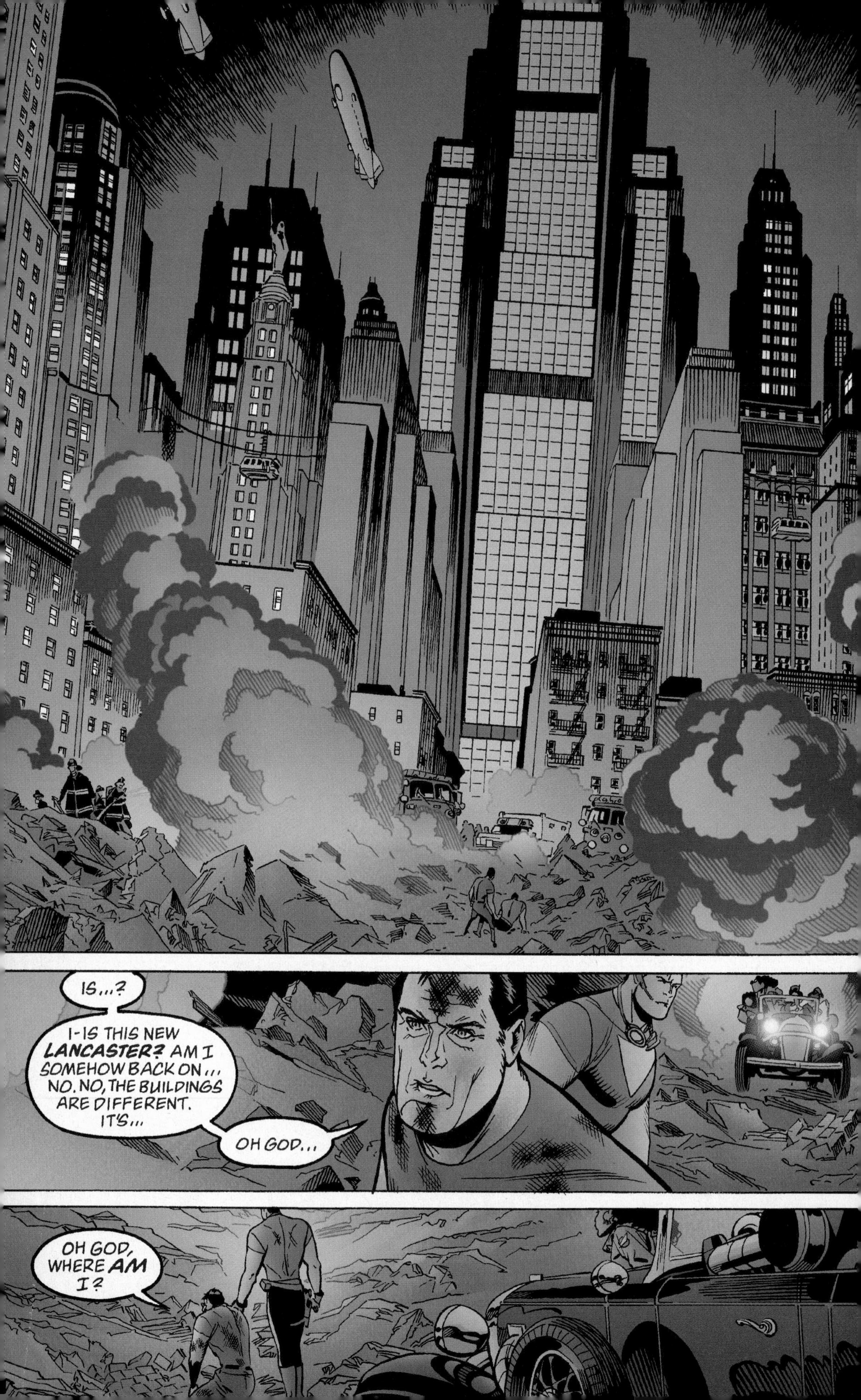
IS...?
I-IS THIS NEW LANCASTER? AM I SOMEHOW BACK ON... NO. NO, THE BUILDINGS ARE DIFFERENT. IT'S...
OH GOD...
OH GOD, WHERE AM I?

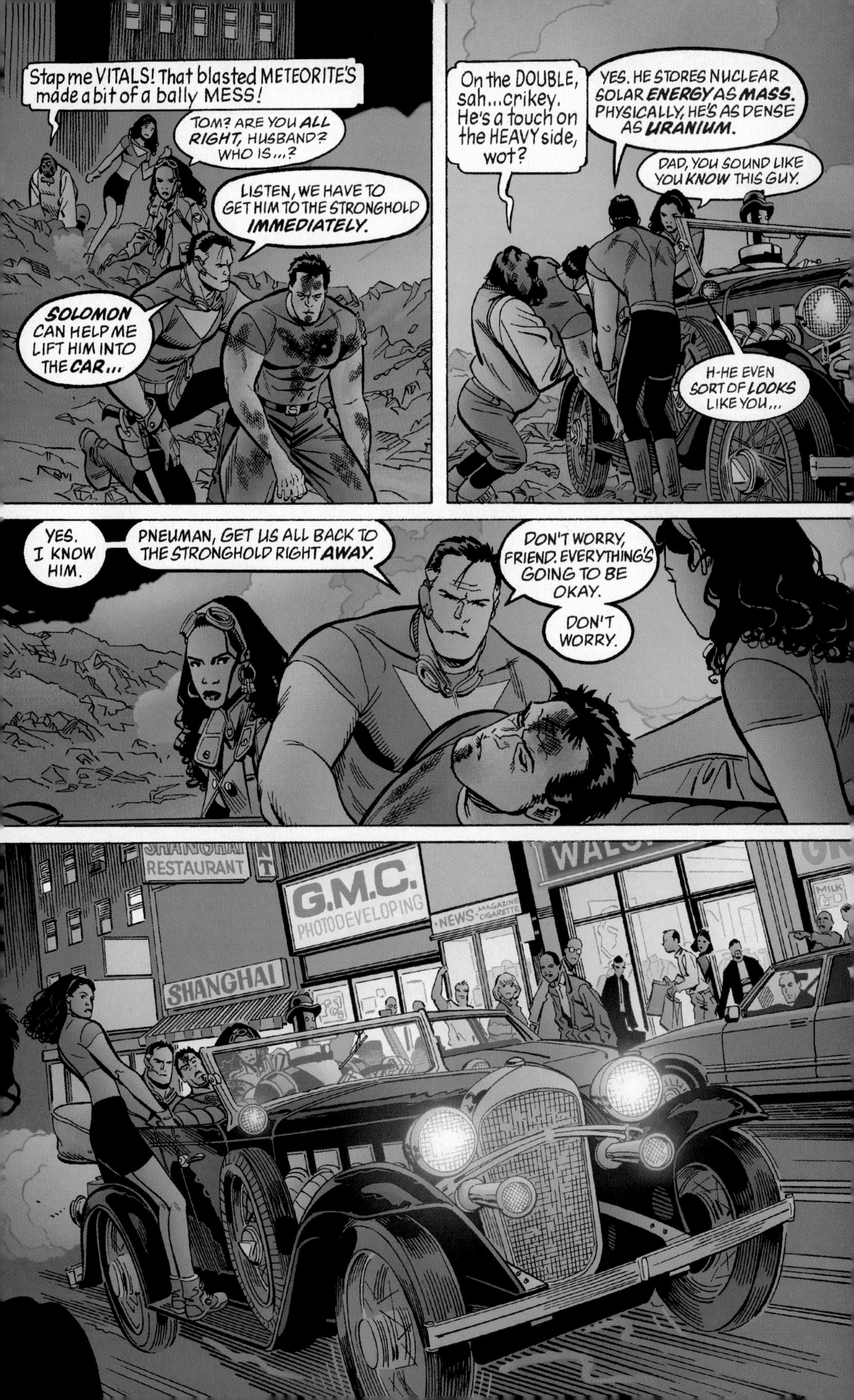
Stap me VITALS! That blasted METEORITE'S made a bit of a bally MESS!
TOM? ARE YOU ALL RIGHT, HUSBAND? WHO IS...?
LISTEN, WE HAVE TO GET HIM TO THE STRONGHOLD IMMEDIATELY.
SOLOMON CAN HELP ME LIFT HIM INTO THE CAR...
On the DOUBLE, sah...crikey. He's a touch on the HEAVY side, wot?
YES. HE STORES NUCLEAR SOLAR ENERGY AS MASS. PHYSICALLY, HE'S AS DENSE AS URANIUM.
DAD, YOU SOUND LIKE YOU KNOW THIS GUY.
H-HE EVEN SORT OF LOOKS LIKE YOU...
YES. I KNOW HIM.
PNEUMAN, GET US ALL BACK TO THE STRONGHOLD RIGHT AWAY.
DON'T WORRY, FRIEND. EVERYTHING'S GOING TO BE OKAY.
DON'T WORRY.
RESTAURANT
G.M.C.
PHOTODEVELOPING
NEWS
MAGAZINE
CIGARETTE
SHANGHAI
MILK

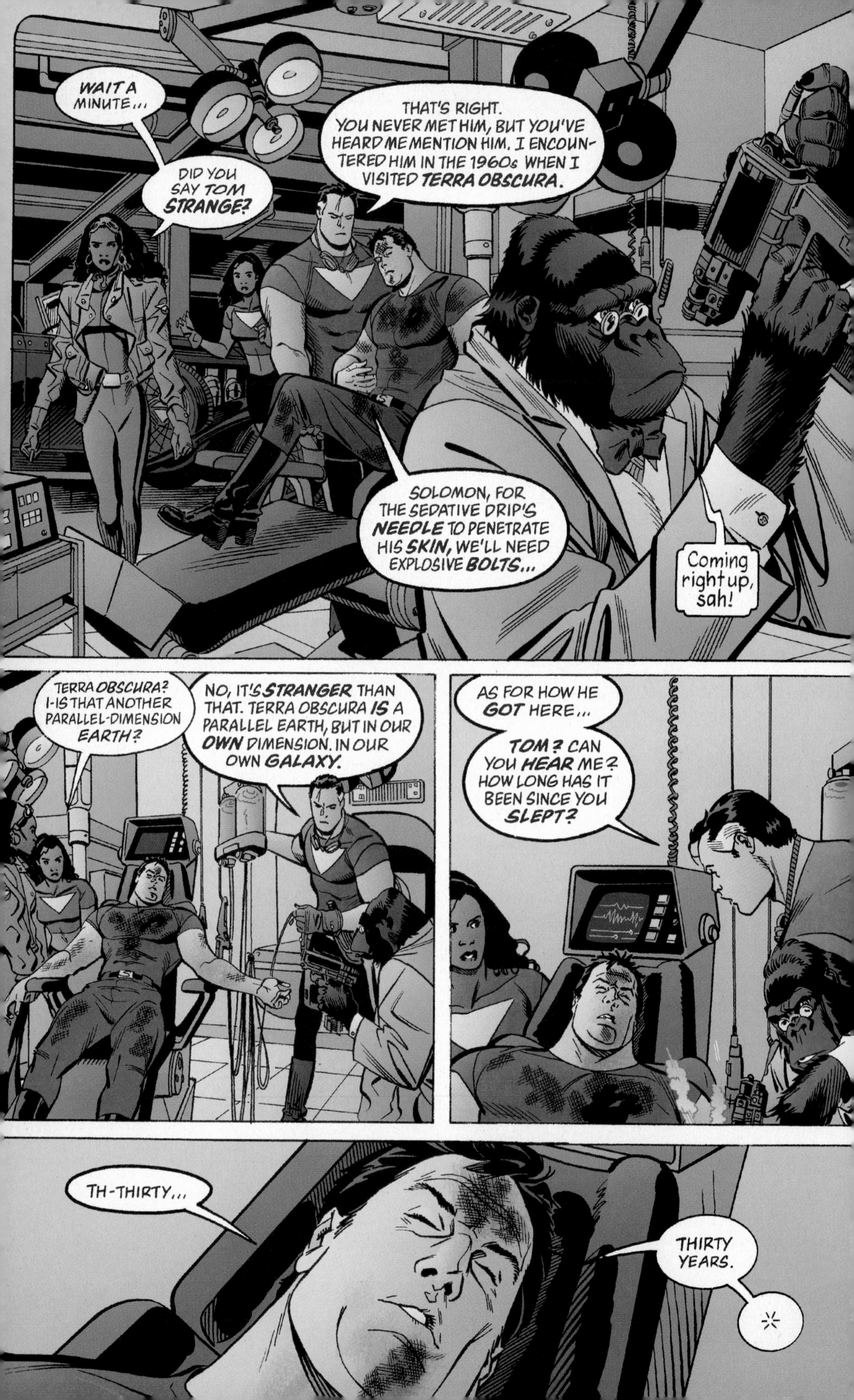
WAIT A MINUTE...
DID YOU SAY TOM STRANGE?
THAT'S RIGHT. YOU NEVER MET HIM, BUT YOU'VE HEARD ME MENTION HIM. I ENCOUNTERED HIM IN THE 1960s WHEN I VISITED TERRA OBSCURA.
SOLOMON, FOR THE SEDATIVE DRIP'S NEEDLE TO PENETRATE HIS SKIN, WE'LL NEED EXPLOSIVE BOLTS...
Coming right up, sah!
TERRA OBSCURA? I-IS THAT ANOTHER PARALLEL-DIMENSION EARTH?
NO, IT'S STRANGER THAN THAT. TERRA OBSCURA IS A PARALLEL EARTH, BUT IN OUR OWN DIMENSION. IN OUR OWN GALAXY.
AS FOR HOW HE GOT HERE...
TOM? CAN YOU HEAR ME? HOW LONG HAS IT BEEN SINCE YOU SLEPT?
TH-THIRTY...
THIRTY YEARS.
*

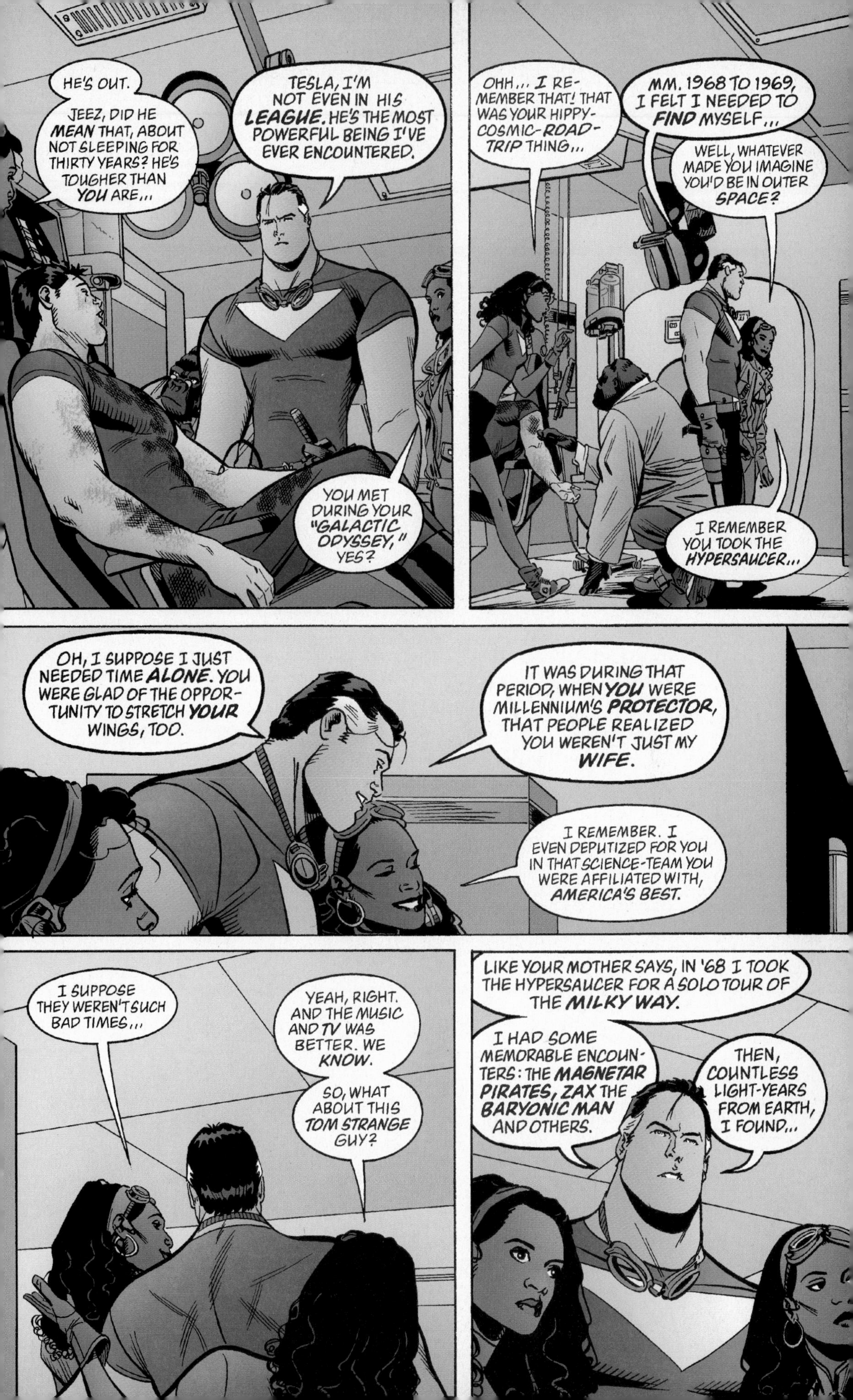
HE'S OUT.
JEEZ, DID HE MEAN THAT, ABOUT NOT SLEEPING FOR THIRTY YEARS? HE'S TOUGHER THAN YOU ARE...
TESLA, I'M NOT EVEN IN HIS LEAGUE. HE'S THE MOST POWERFUL BEING I'VE EVER ENCOUNTERED.
YOU MET DURING YOUR "GALACTIC ODYSSEY," YES?
OHH... I RE-MEMBER THAT! THAT WAS YOUR HIPPY-COSMIC-ROAD-TRIP THING...
MM. 1968 TO 1969, I FELT I NEEDED TO FIND MYSELF...
WELL, WHATEVER MADE YOU IMAGINE YOU'D BE IN OUTER SPACE?
I REMEMBER YOU TOOK THE HYPERSAUCER...
OH, I SUPPOSE I JUST NEEDED TIME ALONE. YOU WERE GLAD OF THE OPPOR-TUNITY TO STRETCH YOUR WINGS, TOO.
IT WAS DURING THAT PERIOD, WHEN YOU WERE MILLENNIUM'S PROTECTOR, THAT PEOPLE REALIZED YOU WEREN'T JUST MY WIFE.
I REMEMBER. I EVEN DEPUTIZED FOR YOU IN THAT SCIENCE-TEAM YOU WERE AFFILIATED WITH, AMERICA'S BEST.
I SUPPOSE THEY WEREN'T SUCH BAD TIMES...
YEAH, RIGHT. AND THE MUSIC AND TV WAS BETTER. WE KNOW.
SO, WHAT ABOUT THIS TOM STRANGE GUY?
LIKE YOUR MOTHER SAYS, IN '68 I TOOK THE HYPERSAUCER FOR A SOLO TOUR OF THE MILKY WAY.
I HAD SOME MEMORABLE ENCOUN-TERS: THE MAGNETAR PIRATES, ZAX THE BARYONIC MAN AND OTHERS.
THEN, COUNTLESS LIGHT-YEARS FROM EARTH, I FOUND...

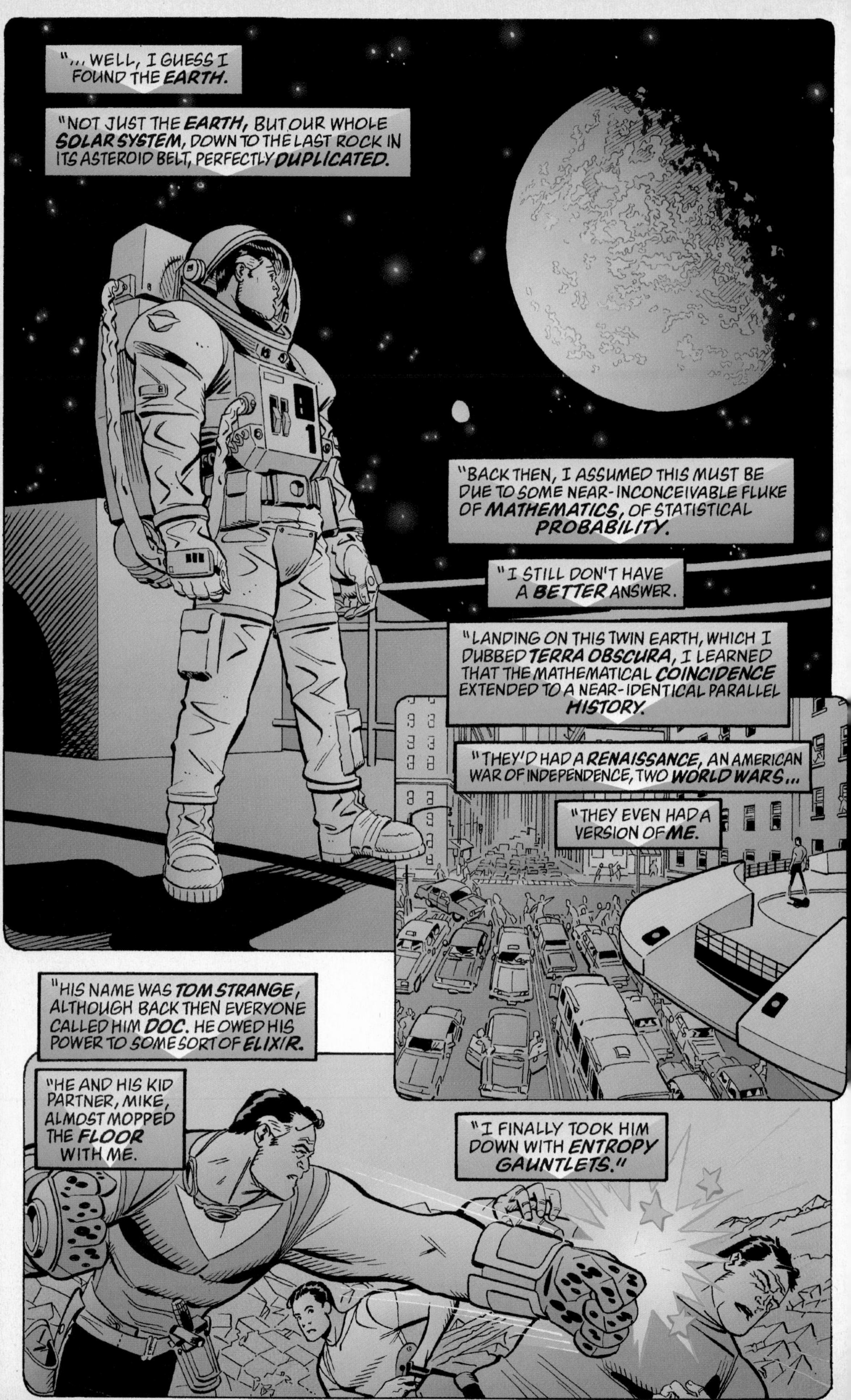
"... WELL, I GUESS I FOUND THE EARTH.
"NOT JUST THE EARTH, BUT OUR WHOLE SOLAR SYSTEM, DOWN TO THE LAST ROCK IN ITS ASTEROID BELT, PERFECTLY DUPLICATED.
"BACK THEN, I ASSUMED THIS MUST BE DUE TO SOME NEAR-INCONCEIVABLE FLUKE OF MATHEMATICS, OF STATISTICAL PROBABILITY.
"I STILL DON'T HAVE A BETTER ANSWER.
"LANDING ON THIS TWIN EARTH, WHICH I DUBBED TERRA OBSCURA, I LEARNED THAT THE MATHEMATICAL COINCIDENCE EXTENDED TO A NEAR-IDENTICAL PARALLEL HISTORY.
"THEY'D HAD A RENAISSANCE, AN AMERICAN WAR OF INDEPENDENCE, TWO WORLD WARS...
"THEY EVEN HAD A VERSION OF ME.
"HIS NAME WAS TOM STRANGE, ALTHOUGH BACK THEN EVERYONE CALLED HIM DOC. HE OWED HIS POWER TO SOME SORT OF ELIXIR.
"HE AND HIS KID PARTNER, MIKE, ALMOST MOPPED THE FLOOR WITH ME.
"I FINALLY TOOK HIM DOWN WITH ENTROPY GAUNTLETS."

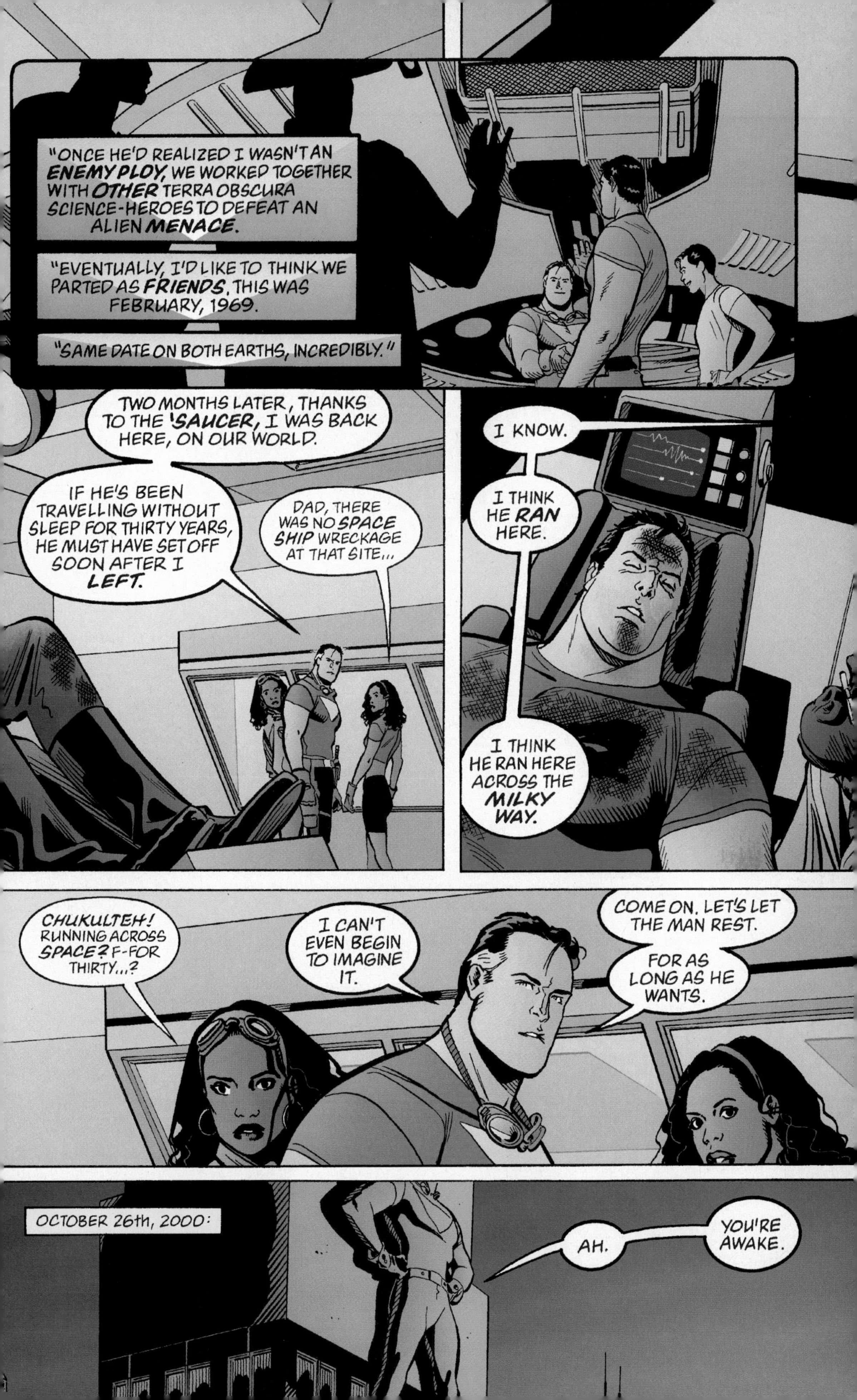
"ONCE HE'D REALIZED I WASN'T AN ENEMY PLOY, WE WORKED TOGETHER WITH OTHER TERRA OBSCURA SCIENCE-HEROES TO DEFEAT AN ALIEN MENACE.
"EVENTUALLY, I'D LIKE TO THINK WE PARTED AS FRIENDS. THIS WAS FEBRUARY, 1969.
"SAME DATE ON BOTH EARTHS, INCREDIBLY."
TWO MONTHS LATER, THANKS TO THE 'SAUCER, I WAS BACK HERE, ON OUR WORLD.
IF HE'S BEEN TRAVELLING WITHOUT SLEEP FOR THIRTY YEARS, HE MUST HAVE SET OFF SOON AFTER I LEFT.
DAD, THERE WAS NO SPACE SHIP WRECKAGE AT THAT SITE...
I KNOW.
I THINK HE RAN HERE.
I THINK HE RAN HERE ACROSS THE MILKY WAY.
CHUKULTEH! RUNNING ACROSS SPACE? F-FOR THIRTY...?
I CAN'T EVEN BEGIN TO IMAGINE IT.
COME ON. LET'S LET THE MAN REST.
FOR AS LONG AS HE WANTS.
OCTOBER 26th, 2000:
AH.
YOU'RE AWAKE.

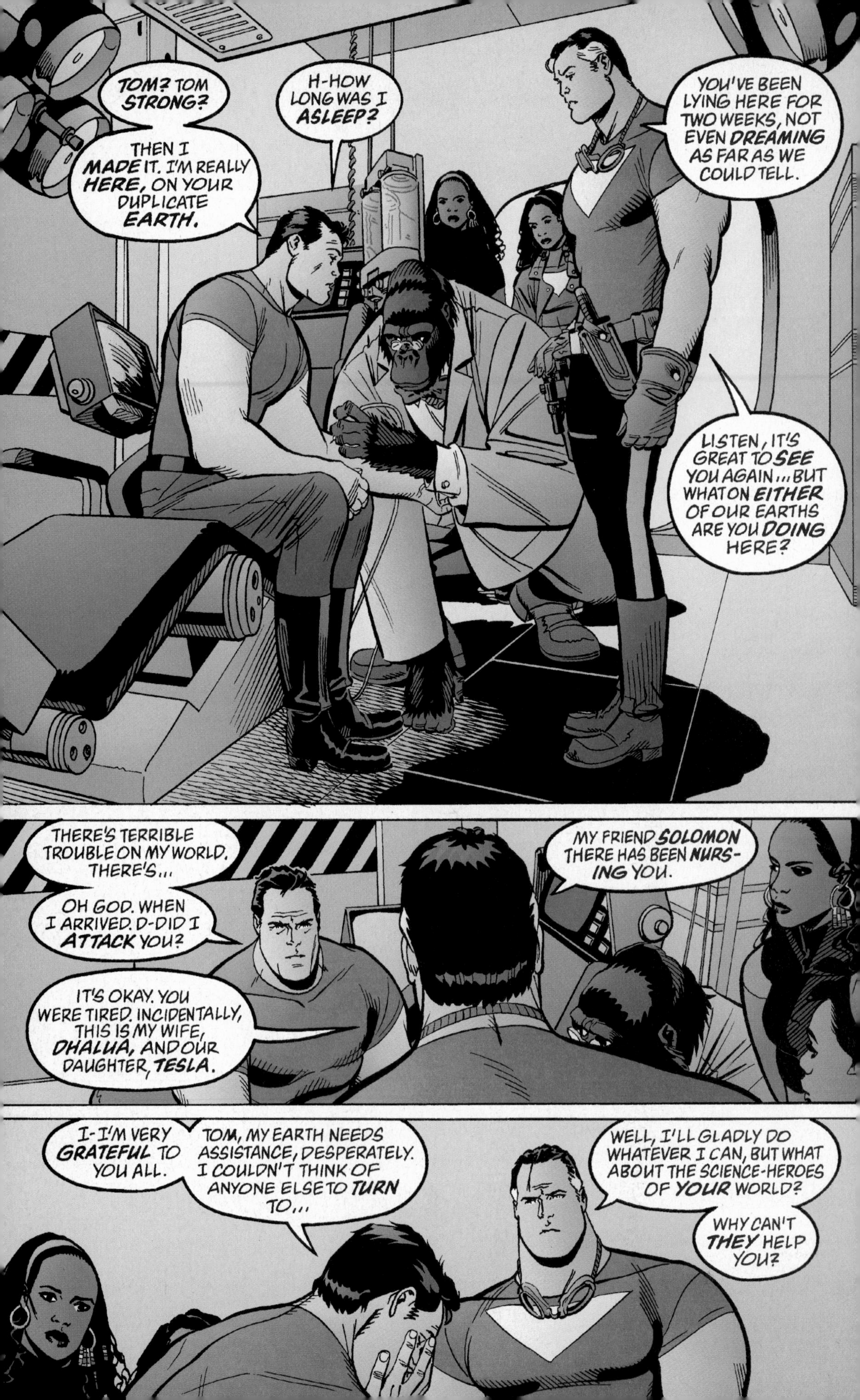
TOM? TOM STRONG?
THEN I MADE IT. I'M REALLY HERE, ON YOUR DUPLICATE EARTH.
H-HOW LONG WAS I ASLEEP?
YOU'VE BEEN LYING HERE FOR TWO WEEKS, NOT EVEN DREAMING AS FAR AS WE COULD TELL.
LISTEN, IT'S GREAT TO SEE YOU AGAIN... BUT WHAT ON EITHER OF OUR EARTHS ARE YOU DOING HERE?
THERE'S TERRIBLE TROUBLE ON MY WORLD. THERE'S...
OH GOD. WHEN I ARRIVED. D-DID I ATTACK YOU?
MY FRIEND SOLOMON THERE HAS BEEN NURSING YOU.
IT'S OKAY. YOU WERE TIRED. INCIDENTALLY, THIS IS MY WIFE, DHALUA, AND OUR DAUGHTER, TESLA.
I-I'M VERY GRATEFUL TO YOU ALL.
TOM, MY EARTH NEEDS ASSISTANCE, DESPERATELY. I COULDN'T THINK OF ANYONE ELSE TO TURN TO...
WELL, I'LL GLADLY DO WHATEVER I CAN, BUT WHAT ABOUT THE SCIENCE-HEROES OF YOUR WORLD?
WHY CAN'T THEY HELP YOU?

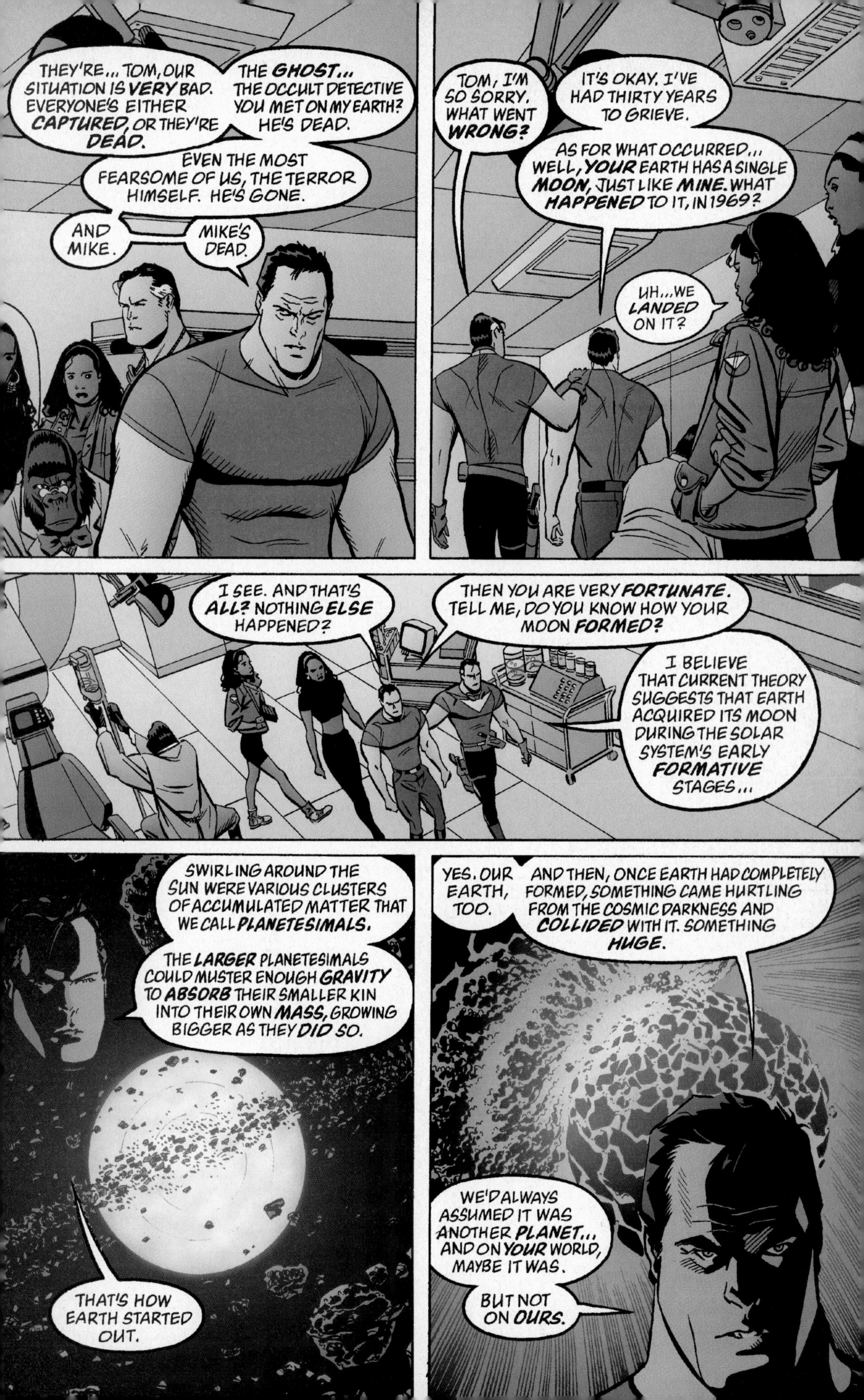
THEY'RE... TOM, OUR SITUATION IS VERY BAD. EVERYONE'S EITHER CAPTURED, OR THEY'RE DEAD.
THE GHOST... THE OCCULT DETECTIVE YOU MET ON MY EARTH? HE'S DEAD.
EVEN THE MOST FEARSOME OF US, THE TERROR HIMSELF. HE'S GONE.
AND MIKE.
MIKE'S DEAD.
TOM, I'M SO SORRY. WHAT WENT WRONG?
IT'S OKAY. I'VE HAD THIRTY YEARS TO GRIEVE.
AS FOR WHAT OCCURRED... WELL, YOUR EARTH HAS A SINGLE MOON, JUST LIKE MINE. WHAT HAPPENED TO IT, IN 1969?
UH... WE LANDED ON IT?
I SEE. AND THAT'S ALL? NOTHING ELSE HAPPENED?
THEN YOU ARE VERY FORTUNATE. TELL ME, DO YOU KNOW HOW YOUR MOON FORMED?
I BELIEVE THAT CURRENT THEORY SUGGESTS THAT EARTH ACQUIRED ITS MOON DURING THE SOLAR SYSTEM'S EARLY FORMATIVE STAGES...
SWIRLING AROUND THE SUN WERE VARIOUS CLUSTERS OF ACCUMULATED MATTER THAT WE CALL PLANETESIMALS.
THE LARGER PLANETESIMALS COULD MUSTER ENOUGH GRAVITY TO ABSORB THEIR SMALLER KIN INTO THEIR OWN MASS, GROWING BIGGER AS THEY DID SO.
THAT'S HOW EARTH STARTED OUT.
YES. OUR EARTH, TOO.
AND THEN, ONCE EARTH HAD COMPLETELY FORMED, SOMETHING CAME HURTLING FROM THE COSMIC DARKNESS AND COLLIDED WITH IT. SOMETHING HUGE.
WE'D ALWAYS ASSUMED IT WAS ANOTHER PLANET... AND ON YOUR WORLD, MAYBE IT WAS.
BUT NOT ON OURS.

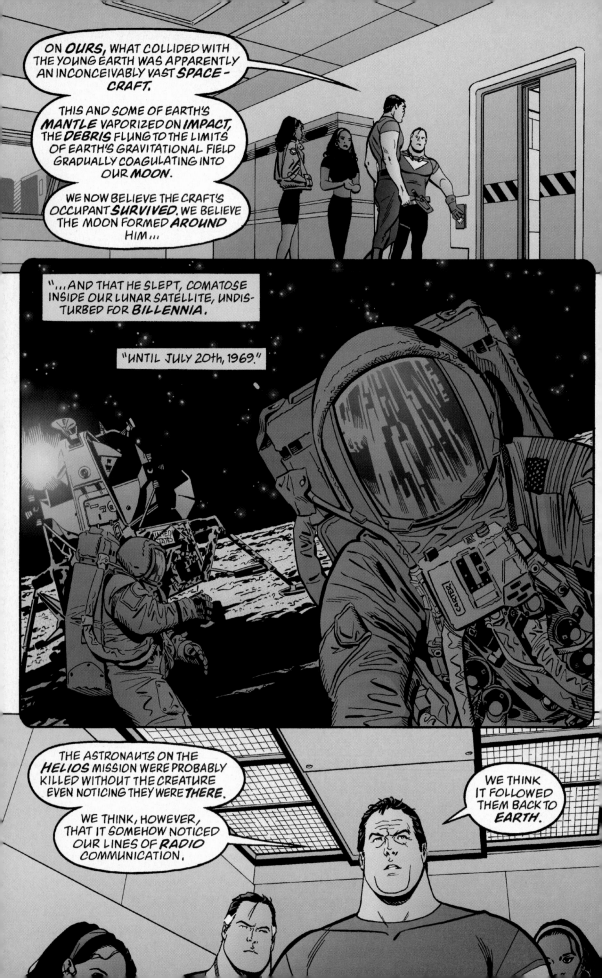

ON **OURS**, WHAT COLLIDED WITH THE YOUNG EARTH WAS APPARENTLY AN INCONCEIVABLY VAST **SPACE-CRAFT**.

THIS AND SOME OF EARTH'S **MANTLE** VAPORIZED ON **IMPACT**, THE **DEBRIS** FLUNG TO THE LIMITS OF EARTH'S GRAVITATIONAL FIELD GRADUALLY COAGULATING INTO OUR **MOON**.

WE NOW BELIEVE THE CRAFT'S OCCUPANT **SURVIVED**. WE BELIEVE THE MOON FORMED **AROUND** HIM...

"...AND THAT HE SLEPT, COMATOSE INSIDE OUR LUNAR SATELLITE, UNDISTURBED FOR **BILLENNIA**."

"UNTIL JULY 20th, 1969."

THE ASTRONAUTS ON THE **HELIOS** MISSION WERE PROBABLY KILLED WITHOUT THE CREATURE EVEN NOTICING THEY WERE **THERE**.

WE THINK, HOWEVER, THAT IT SOMEHOW NOTICED OUR LINES OF **RADIO** COMMUNICATION.

WE THINK IT FOLLOWED THEM BACK TO **EARTH**.

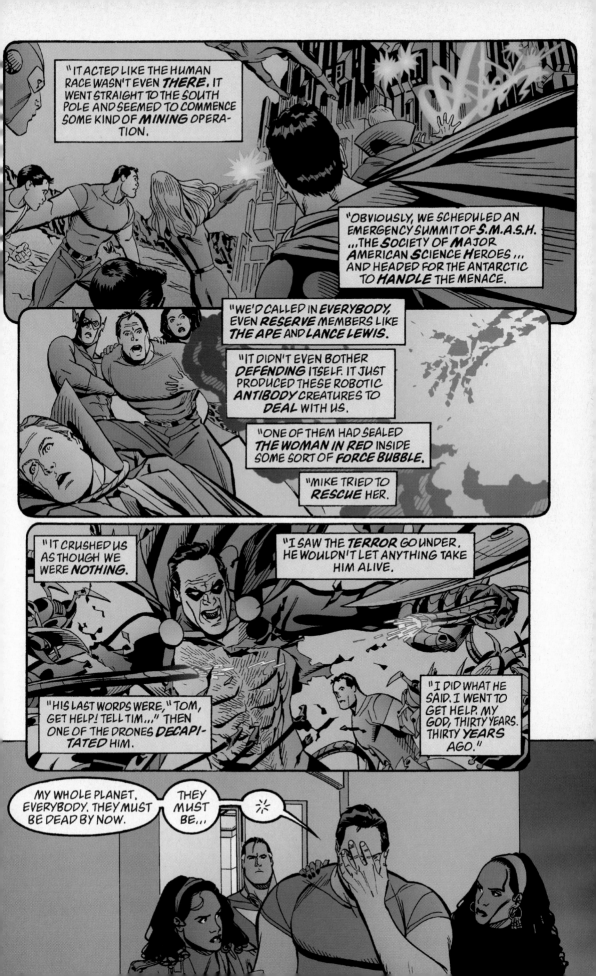

"IT ACTED LIKE THE HUMAN RACE WASN'T EVEN *THERE*. IT WENT STRAIGHT TO THE SOUTH POLE AND SEEMED TO COMMENCE SOME KIND OF *MINING* OPERATION.

"OBVIOUSLY, WE SCHEDULED AN EMERGENCY SUMMIT OF *S.M.A.S.H.* ...THE *SOCIETY OF MAJOR AMERICAN SCIENCE HEROES* ... AND HEADED FOR THE ANTARCTIC TO *HANDLE* THE MENACE.

"WE'D CALLED IN *EVERYBODY*, EVEN *RESERVE* MEMBERS LIKE *THE APE* AND *LANCE LEWIS*.

"IT DIDN'T EVEN BOTHER *DEFENDING* ITSELF. IT JUST PRODUCED THESE ROBOTIC *ANTIBODY* CREATURES TO *DEAL* WITH US.

"ONE OF THEM HAD SEALED *THE WOMAN IN RED* INSIDE SOME SORT OF *FORCE BUBBLE*.

"MIKE TRIED TO *RESCUE* HER.

"IT CRUSHED US AS THOUGH WE WERE *NOTHING*.

"I SAW THE *TERROR* GO UNDER. HE WOULDN'T LET ANYTHING TAKE HIM ALIVE.

"HIS LAST WORDS WERE, "TOM, GET HELP! TELL TIM..." THEN ONE OF THE DRONES *DECAPITATED* HIM.

"I DID WHAT HE SAID. I WENT TO GET HELP. MY GOD, THIRTY YEARS. THIRTY *YEARS* AGO."

MY WHOLE PLANET, EVERYBODY. THEY MUST BE DEAD BY NOW.

THEY MUST BE...

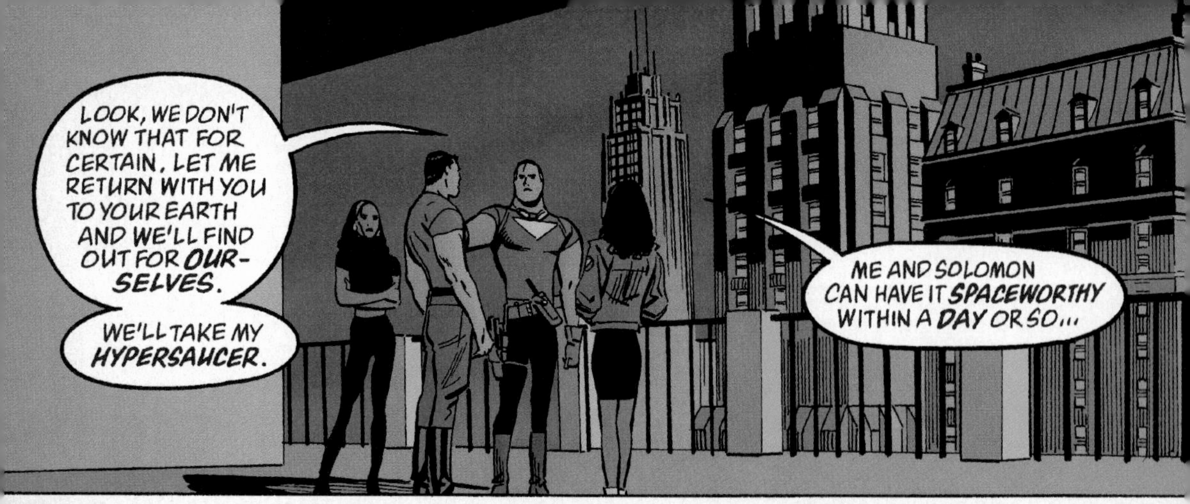
LOOK, WE DON'T KNOW THAT FOR CERTAIN. LET ME RETURN WITH YOU TO YOUR EARTH AND WE'LL FIND OUT FOR OURSELVES.
WE'LL TAKE MY HYPERSAUCER.
ME AND SOLOMON CAN HAVE IT SPACEWORTHY WITHIN A DAY OR SO...

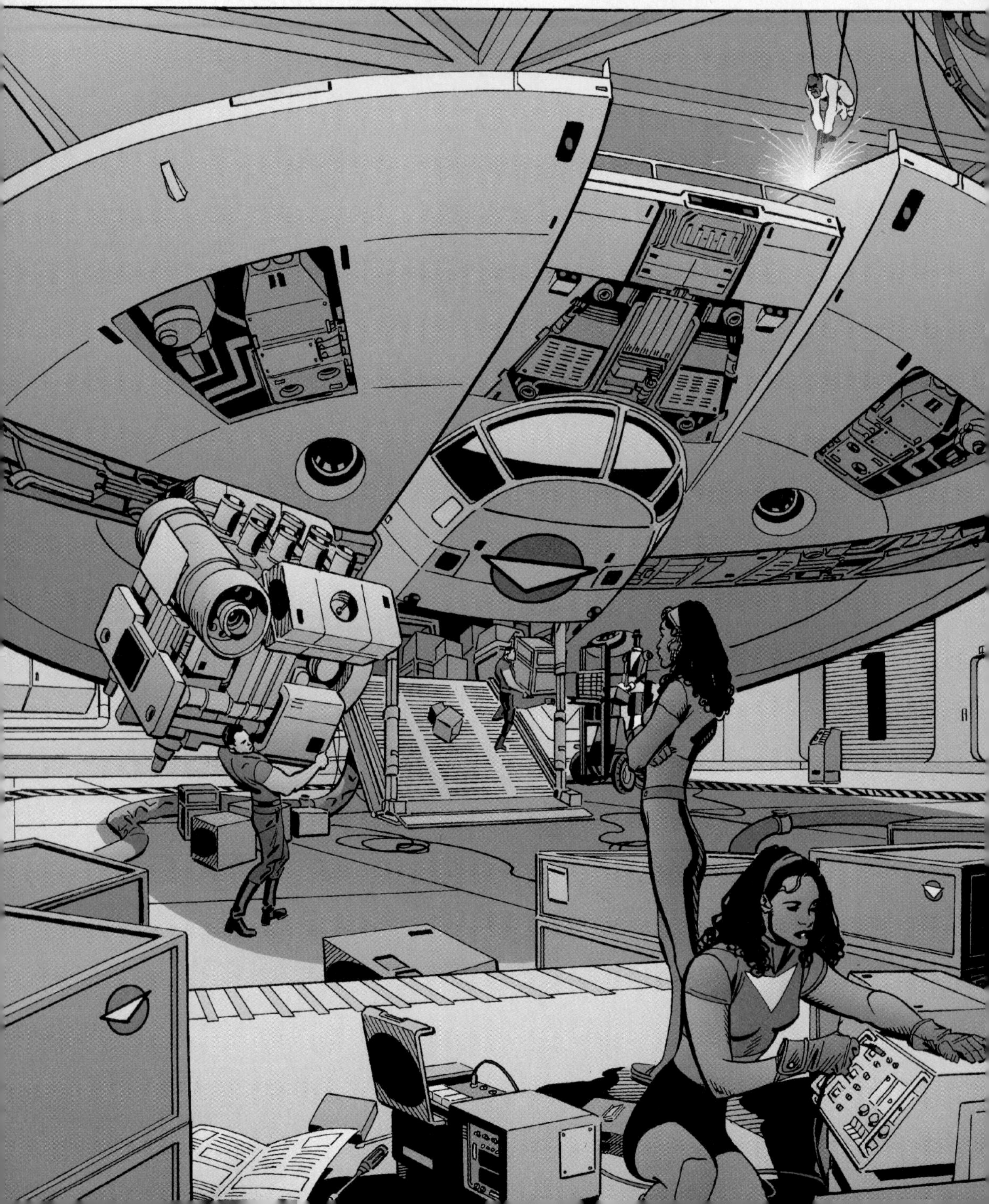

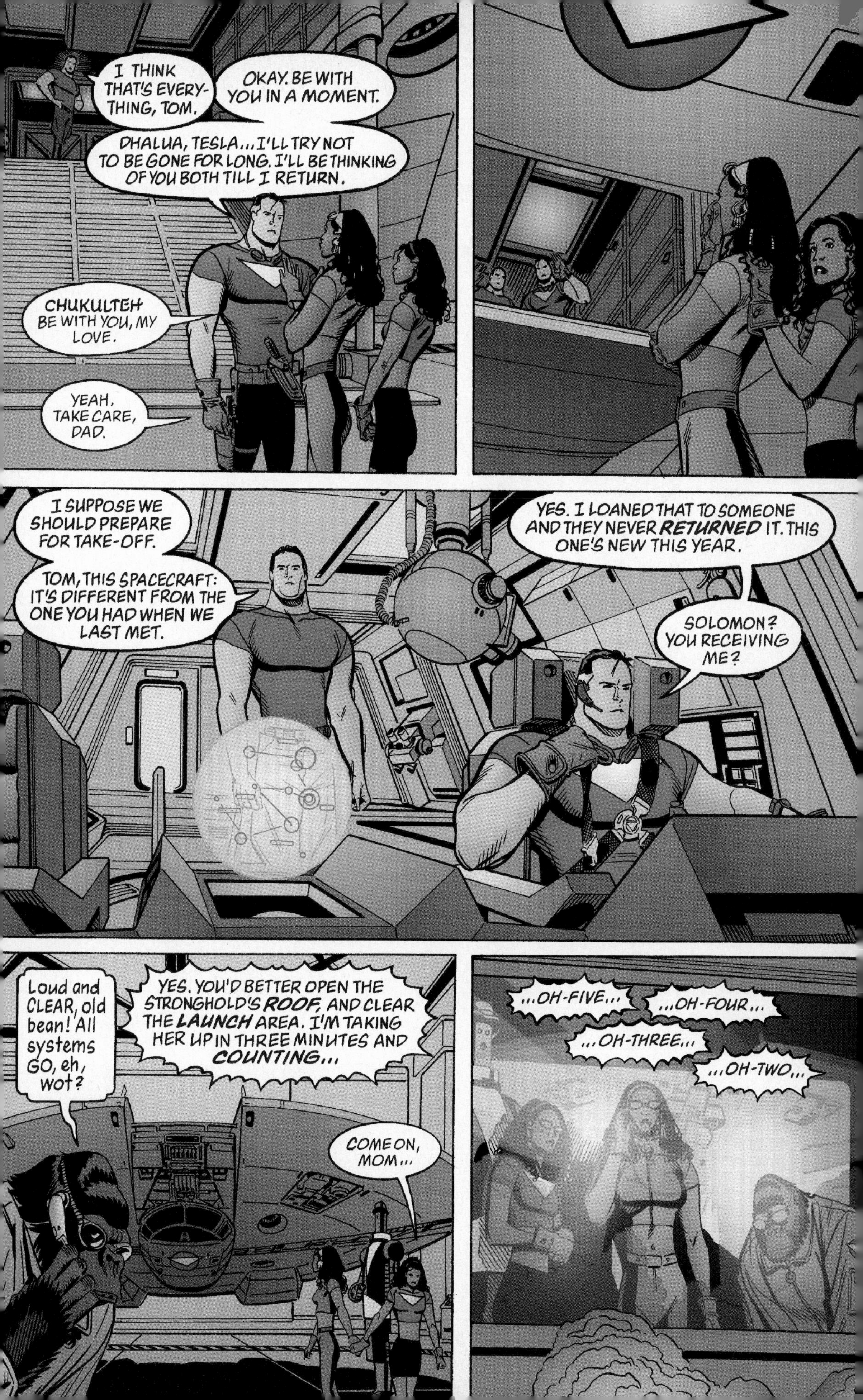
I THINK THAT'S EVERY-THING, TOM.
OKAY. BE WITH YOU IN A MOMENT.
DHALUA, TESLA... I'LL TRY NOT TO BE GONE FOR LONG. I'LL BE THINKING OF YOU BOTH TILL I RETURN.
CHUKULTEH BE WITH YOU, MY LOVE.
YEAH. TAKE CARE, DAD.
I SUPPOSE WE SHOULD PREPARE FOR TAKE-OFF.
TOM, THIS SPACECRAFT: IT'S DIFFERENT FROM THE ONE YOU HAD WHEN WE LAST MET.
YES. I LOANED THAT TO SOMEONE AND THEY NEVER RETURNED IT. THIS ONE'S NEW THIS YEAR.
SOLOMON? YOU RECEIVING ME?
Loud and CLEAR, old bean! All systems GO, eh, wot?
YES. YOU'D BETTER OPEN THE STRONGHOLD'S ROOF, AND CLEAR THE LAUNCH AREA. I'M TAKING HER UP IN THREE MINUTES AND COUNTING...
COME ON, MOM...
...OH-FIVE...
...OH-FOUR...
...OH-THREE...
...OH-TWO...

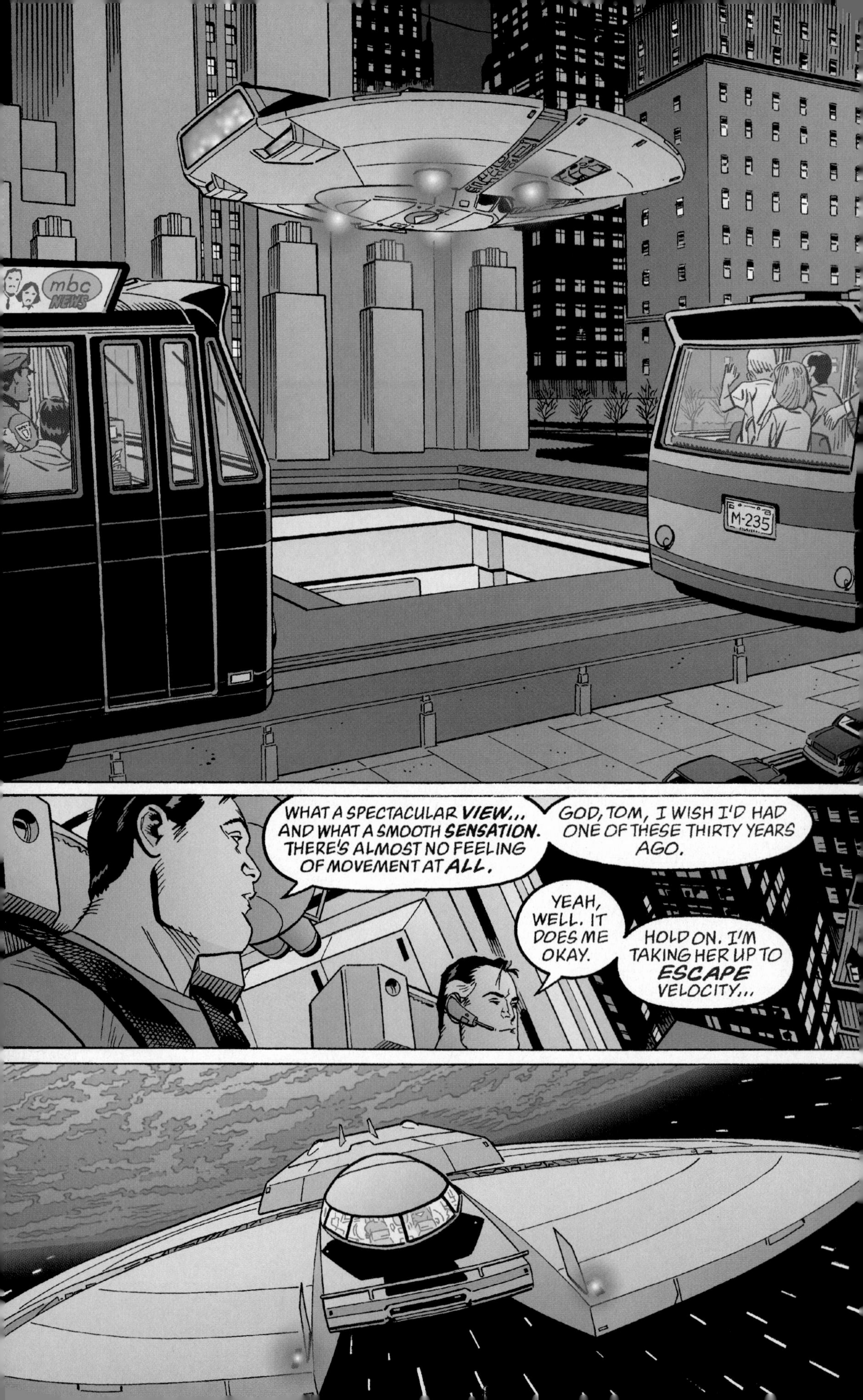
mbc NEWS
M-235
WHAT A SPECTACULAR VIEW... AND WHAT A SMOOTH SENSATION. THERE'S ALMOST NO FEELING OF MOVEMENT AT ALL.
GOD, TOM, I WISH I'D HAD ONE OF THESE THIRTY YEARS AGO.
YEAH, WELL. IT DOES ME OKAY.
HOLD ON. I'M TAKING HER UP TO ESCAPE VELOCITY...

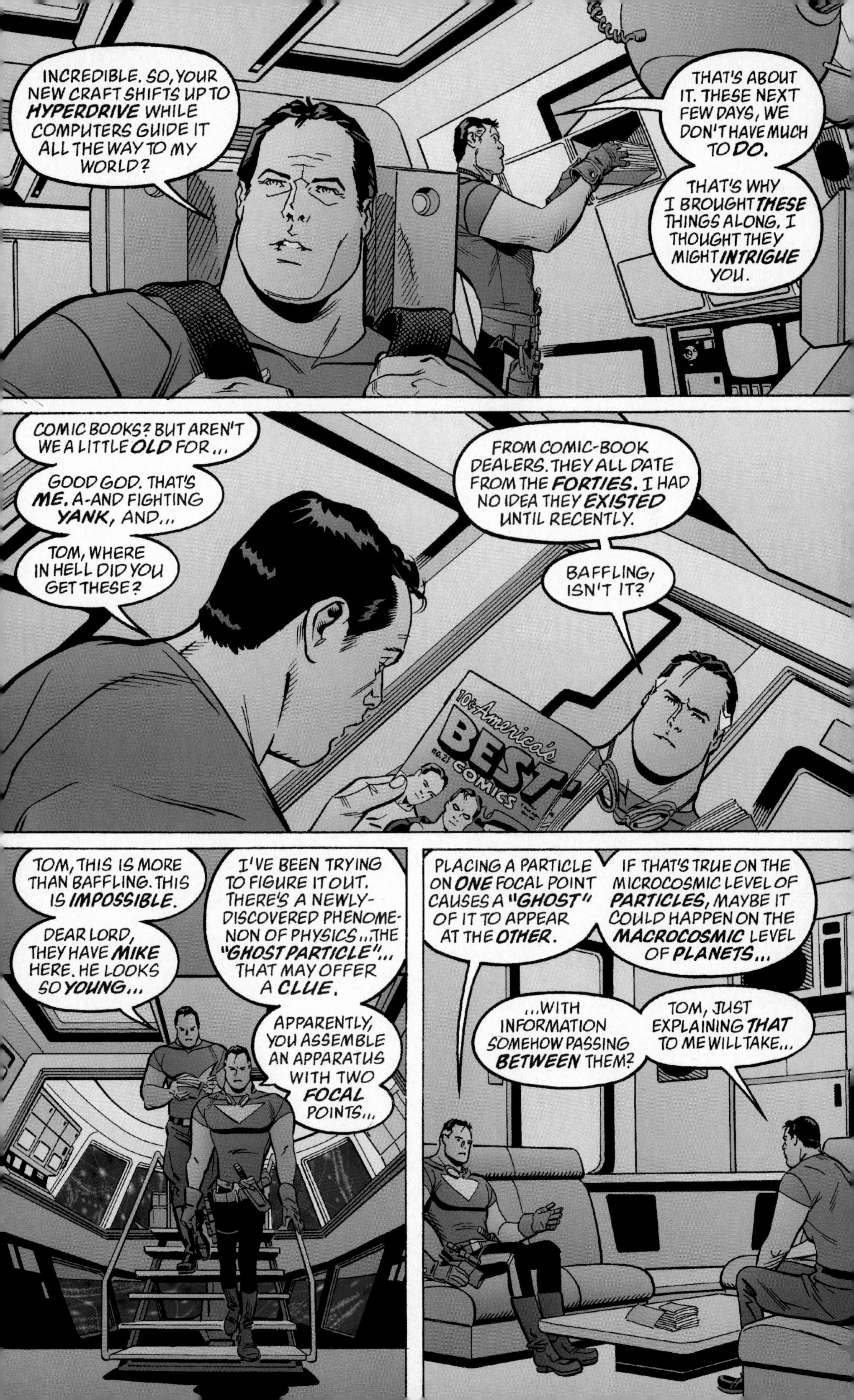

INCREDIBLE. SO, YOUR NEW CRAFT SHIFTS UP TO HYPERDRIVE WHILE COMPUTERS GUIDE IT ALL THE WAY TO MY WORLD?
THAT'S ABOUT IT. THESE NEXT FEW DAYS, WE DON'T HAVE MUCH TO DO.
THAT'S WHY I BROUGHT THESE THINGS ALONG. I THOUGHT THEY MIGHT INTRIGUE YOU.
COMIC BOOKS? BUT AREN'T WE A LITTLE OLD FOR...
GOOD GOD. THAT'S ME. A-AND FIGHTING YANK, AND...
TOM, WHERE IN HELL DID YOU GET THESE?
FROM COMIC-BOOK DEALERS. THEY ALL DATE FROM THE FORTIES. I HAD NO IDEA THEY EXISTED UNTIL RECENTLY.
BAFFLING, ISN'T IT?
10¢ America's BEST COMICS
NO. 21
TOM, THIS IS MORE THAN BAFFLING. THIS IS IMPOSSIBLE.
DEAR LORD, THEY HAVE MIKE HERE. HE LOOKS SO YOUNG...
I'VE BEEN TRYING TO FIGURE IT OUT. THERE'S A NEWLY-DISCOVERED PHENOMENON OF PHYSICS... THE "GHOST PARTICLE"... THAT MAY OFFER A CLUE.
APPARENTLY, YOU ASSEMBLE AN APPARATUS WITH TWO FOCAL POINTS...
PLACING A PARTICLE ON ONE FOCAL POINT CAUSES A "GHOST" OF IT TO APPEAR AT THE OTHER.
IF THAT'S TRUE ON THE MICROCOSMIC LEVEL OF PARTICLES, MAYBE IT COULD HAPPEN ON THE MACROCOSMIC LEVEL OF PLANETS...
...WITH INFORMATION SOMEHOW PASSING BETWEEN THEM?
TOM, JUST EXPLAINING THAT TO ME WILL TAKE...

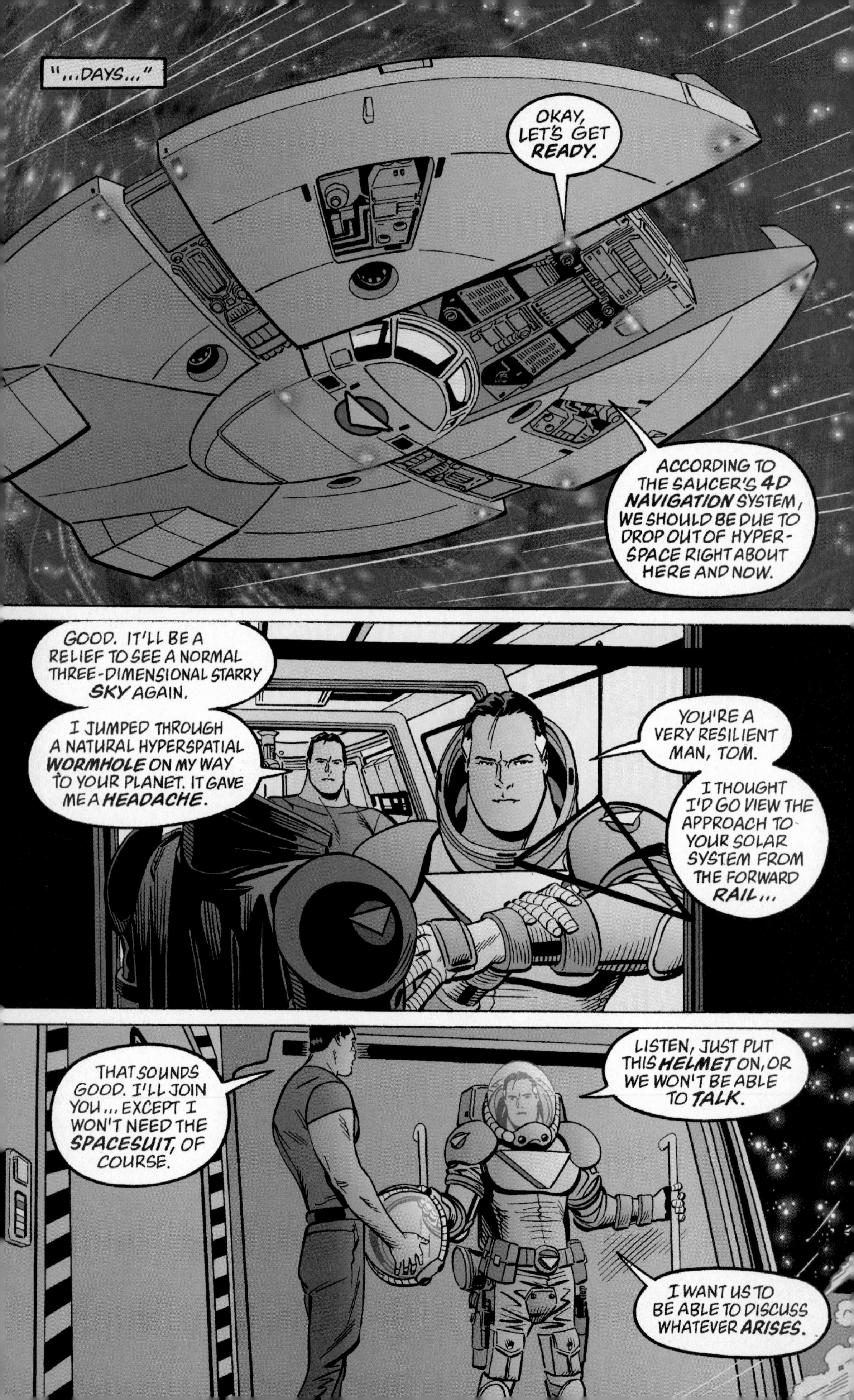
"...DAYS..."
OKAY, LET'S GET READY.
ACCORDING TO THE SAUCER'S 4D NAVIGATION SYSTEM, WE SHOULD BE DUE TO DROP OUT OF HYPER-SPACE RIGHT ABOUT HERE AND NOW.
GOOD. IT'LL BE A RELIEF TO SEE A NORMAL THREE-DIMENSIONAL STARRY SKY AGAIN.
I JUMPED THROUGH A NATURAL HYPERSPATIAL WORMHOLE ON MY WAY TO YOUR PLANET. IT GAVE ME A HEADACHE.
YOU'RE A VERY RESILIENT MAN, TOM.
I THOUGHT I'D GO VIEW THE APPROACH TO YOUR SOLAR SYSTEM FROM THE FORWARD RAIL...
THAT SOUNDS GOOD. I'LL JOIN YOU... EXCEPT I WON'T NEED THE SPACESUIT, OF COURSE.
LISTEN, JUST PUT THIS HELMET ON, OR WE WON'T BE ABLE TO TALK.
I WANT US TO BE ABLE TO DISCUSS WHATEVER ARISES.

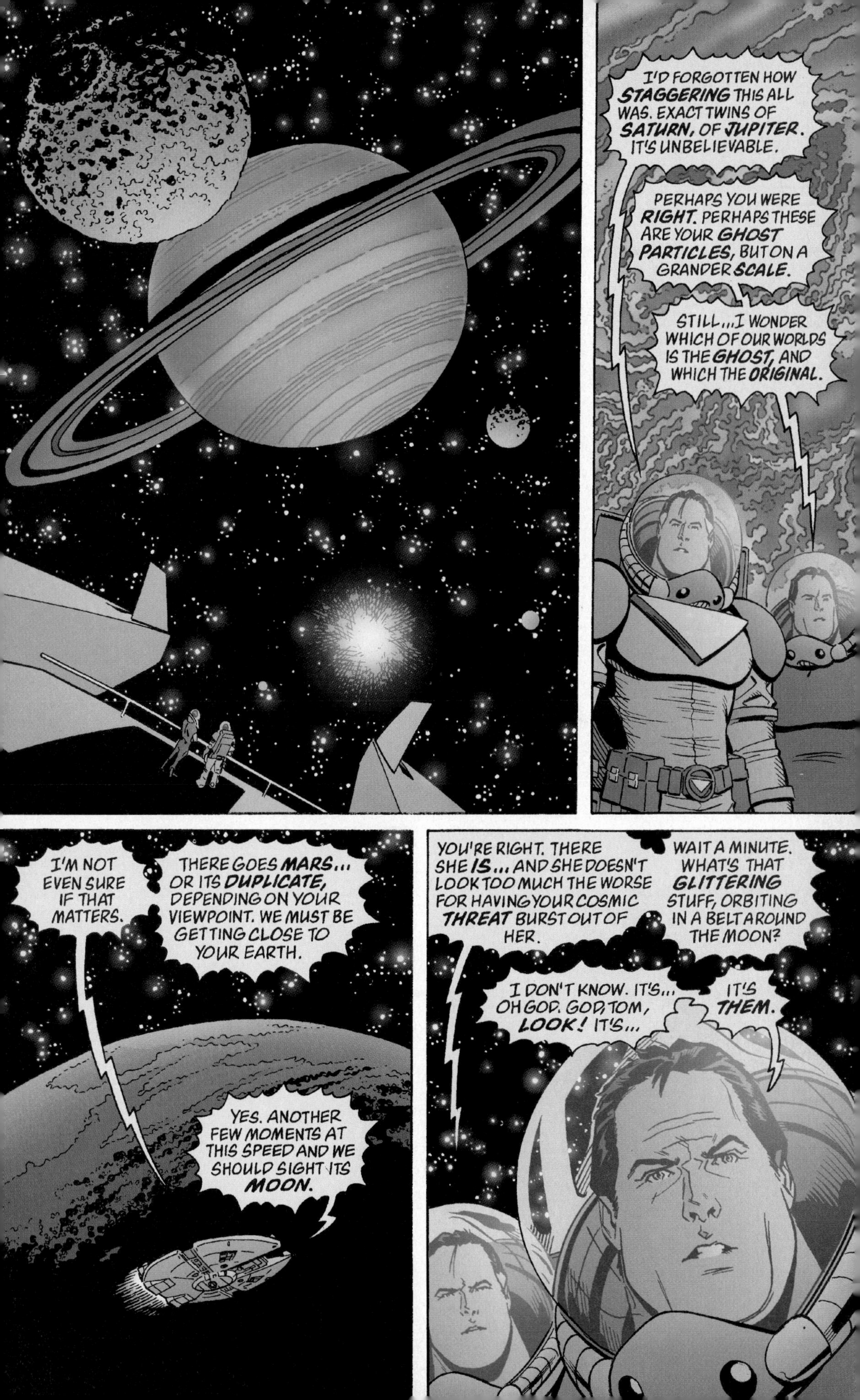
I'D FORGOTTEN HOW STAGGERING THIS ALL WAS. EXACT TWINS OF SATURN, OF JUPITER. IT'S UNBELIEVABLE.
PERHAPS YOU WERE RIGHT. PERHAPS THESE ARE YOUR GHOST PARTICLES, BUT ON A GRANDER SCALE.
STILL... I WONDER WHICH OF OUR WORLDS IS THE GHOST, AND WHICH THE ORIGINAL.
I'M NOT EVEN SURE IF THAT MATTERS.
THERE GOES MARS... OR ITS DUPLICATE, DEPENDING ON YOUR VIEWPOINT. WE MUST BE GETTING CLOSE TO YOUR EARTH.
YES. ANOTHER FEW MOMENTS AT THIS SPEED AND WE SHOULD SIGHT ITS MOON.
YOU'RE RIGHT. THERE SHE IS... AND SHE DOESN'T LOOK TOO MUCH THE WORSE FOR HAVING YOUR COSMIC THREAT BURST OUT OF HER.
WAIT A MINUTE. WHAT'S THAT GLITTERING STUFF, ORBITING IN A BELT AROUND THE MOON?
I DON'T KNOW. IT'S... OH GOD. GOD, TOM, LOOK! IT'S...
IT'S THEM.

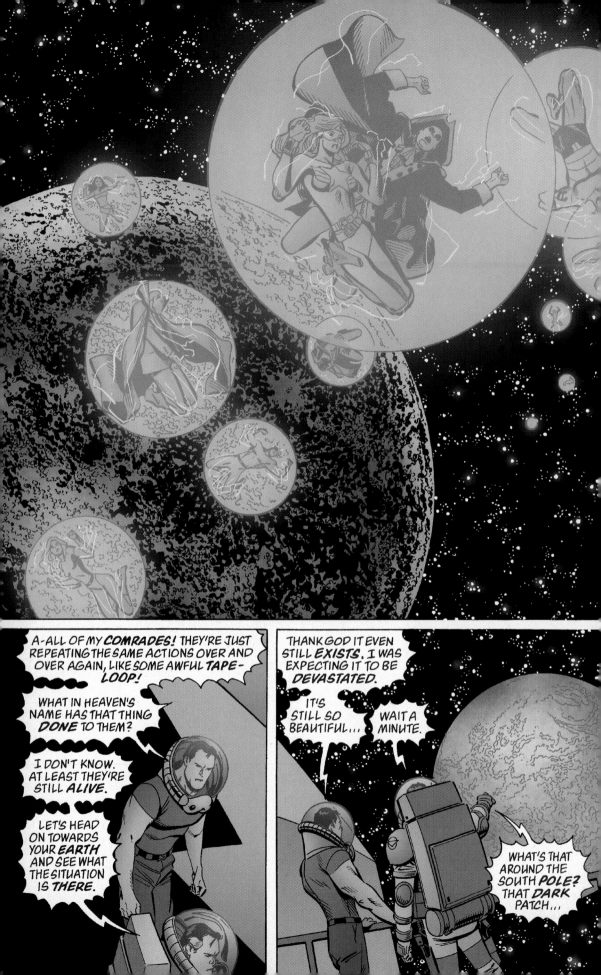

A-ALL OF MY **COMRADES!** THEY'RE JUST REPEATING THE SAME ACTIONS OVER AND OVER AGAIN, LIKE SOME AWFUL **TAPE-LOOP!**

WHAT IN HEAVEN'S NAME HAS THAT THING **DONE** TO THEM?

I DON'T KNOW. AT LEAST THEY'RE STILL **ALIVE.**

LET'S HEAD ON TOWARDS YOUR **EARTH** AND SEE WHAT THE SITUATION IS **THERE.**

THANK GOD IT EVEN STILL **EXISTS.** I WAS EXPECTING IT TO BE **DEVASTATED.**

IT'S STILL SO BEAUTIFUL...

WAIT A MINUTE.

WHAT'S THAT AROUND THE SOUTH **POLE?** THAT **DARK** PATCH...

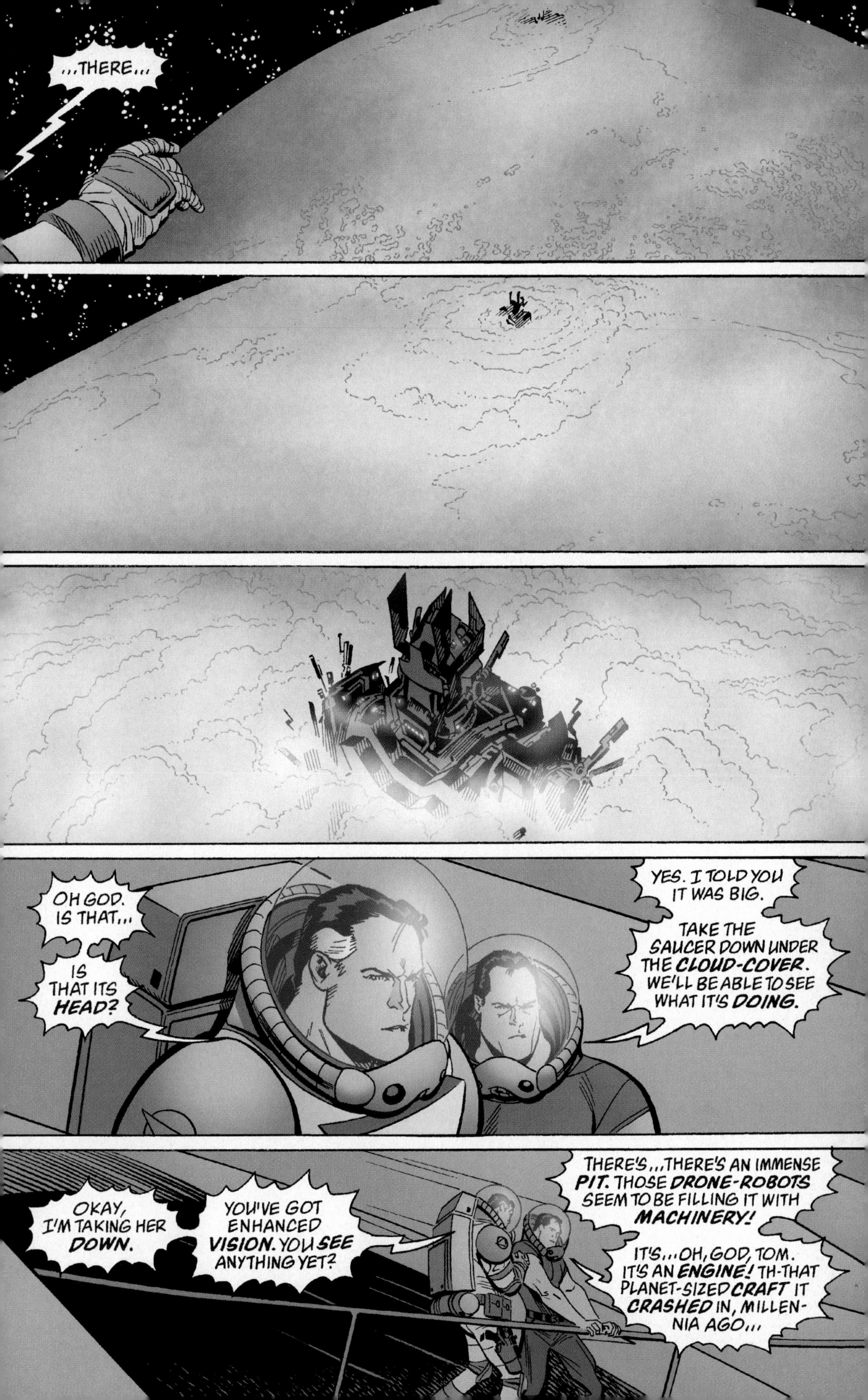
...THERE...
OH GOD. IS THAT...
IS THAT ITS HEAD?
YES. I TOLD YOU IT WAS BIG.
TAKE THE SAUCER DOWN UNDER THE CLOUD-COVER. WE'LL BE ABLE TO SEE WHAT IT'S DOING.
OKAY, I'M TAKING HER DOWN.
YOU'VE GOT ENHANCED VISION. YOU SEE ANYTHING YET?
THERE'S...THERE'S AN IMMENSE PIT. THOSE DRONE-ROBOTS SEEM TO BE FILLING IT WITH MACHINERY!
IT'S...OH, GOD, TOM. IT'S AN ENGINE! TH-THAT PLANET-SIZED CRAFT IT CRASHED IN, MILLENNIA AGO...

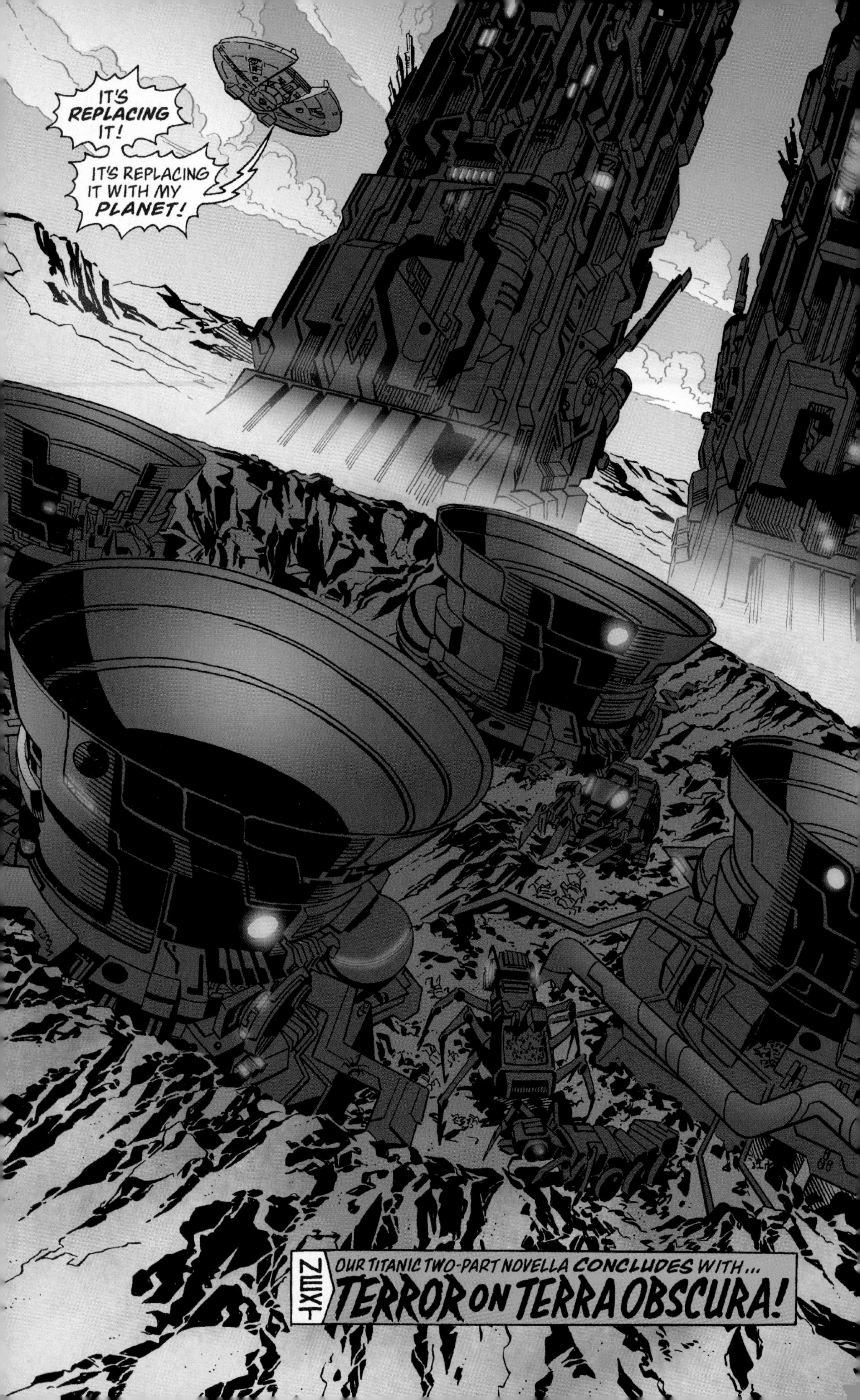
IT'S REPLACING IT!
IT'S REPLACING IT WITH MY PLANET!
NEXT OUR TITANIC TWO-PART NOVELLA CONCLUDES WITH... TERROR ON TERRA OBSCURA!

CHAPTER FIVE

In which both Toms make heroic rescues,
an eerie computer recreates the dead,
and a team of the best faces tall odds.

Cover art:
Chris Sprouse & Al Gordon

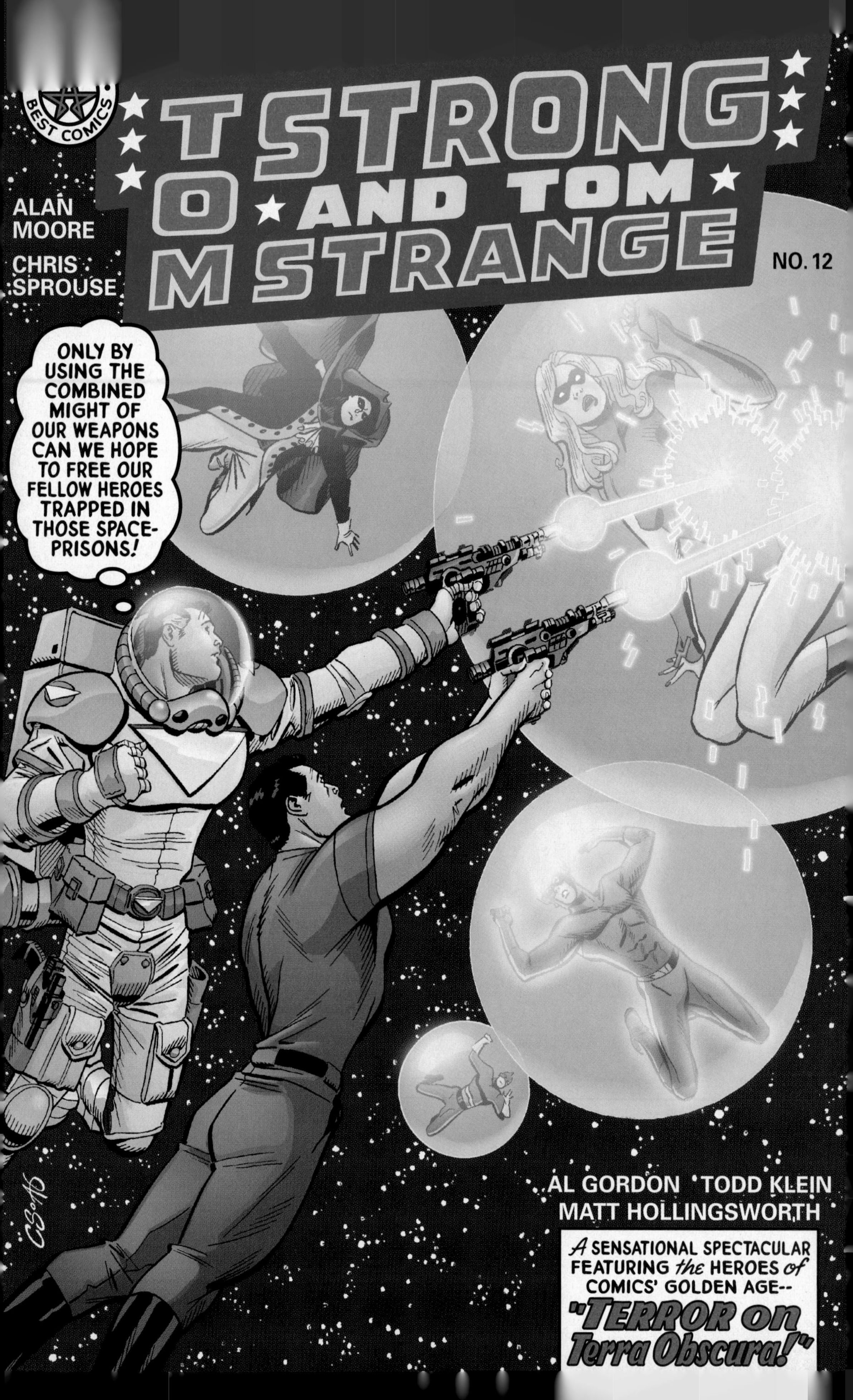
BEST COMICS
TOM STRONG AND TOM STRANGE
ALAN MOORE
CHRIS SPROUSE
NO. 12
ONLY BY USING THE COMBINED MIGHT OF OUR WEAPONS CAN WE HOPE TO FREE OUR FELLOW HEROES TRAPPED IN THOSE SPACE-PRISONS!
AL GORDON TODD KLEIN
MATT HOLLINGSWORTH
A SENSATIONAL SPECTACULAR FEATURING the HEROES of COMICS' GOLDEN AGE--
"TERROR on Terra Obscura!"

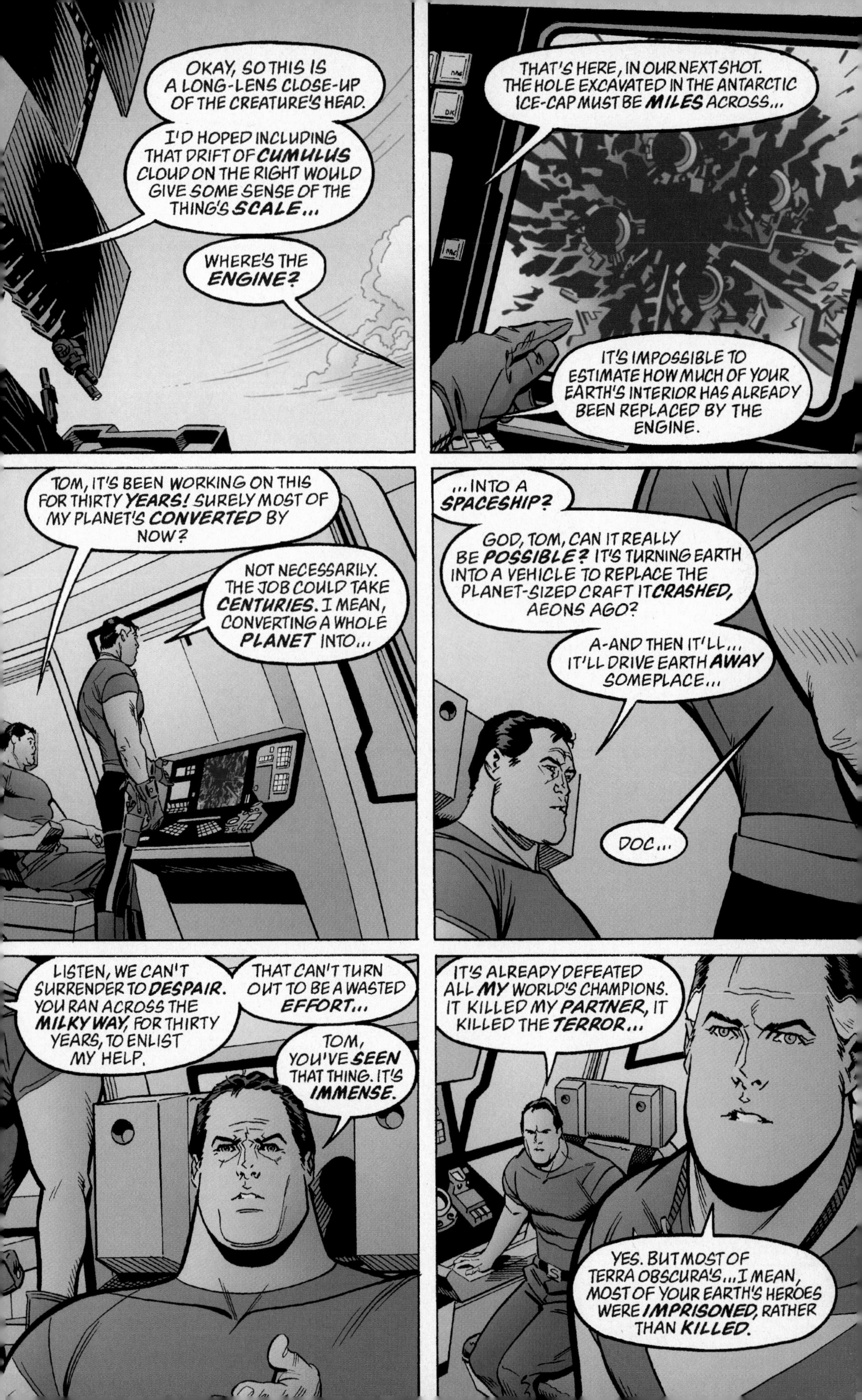

OKAY, SO THIS IS A LONG-LENS CLOSE-UP OF THE CREATURE'S HEAD.
I'D HOPED INCLUDING THAT DRIFT OF CUMULUS CLOUD ON THE RIGHT WOULD GIVE SOME SENSE OF THE THING'S SCALE...
WHERE'S THE ENGINE?
THAT'S HERE, IN OUR NEXT SHOT. THE HOLE EXCAVATED IN THE ANTARCTIC ICE-CAP MUST BE MILES ACROSS...
IT'S IMPOSSIBLE TO ESTIMATE HOW MUCH OF YOUR EARTH'S INTERIOR HAS ALREADY BEEN REPLACED BY THE ENGINE.
TOM, IT'S BEEN WORKING ON THIS FOR THIRTY YEARS! SURELY MOST OF MY PLANET'S CONVERTED BY NOW?
NOT NECESSARILY. THE JOB COULD TAKE CENTURIES. I MEAN, CONVERTING A WHOLE PLANET INTO...
...INTO A SPACESHIP?
GOD, TOM, CAN IT REALLY BE POSSIBLE? IT'S TURNING EARTH INTO A VEHICLE TO REPLACE THE PLANET-SIZED CRAFT IT CRASHED, AEONS AGO?
A-AND THEN IT'LL... IT'LL DRIVE EARTH AWAY SOMEPLACE...
DOC...
LISTEN, WE CAN'T SURRENDER TO DESPAIR. YOU RAN ACROSS THE MILKY WAY, FOR THIRTY YEARS, TO ENLIST MY HELP.
THAT CAN'T TURN OUT TO BE A WASTED EFFORT...
TOM, YOU'VE SEEN THAT THING. IT'S IMMENSE.
IT'S ALREADY DEFEATED ALL MY WORLD'S CHAMPIONS. IT KILLED MY PARTNER, IT KILLED THE TERROR...
YES. BUT MOST OF TERRA OBSCURA'S... I MEAN, MOST OF YOUR EARTH'S HEROES WERE IMPRISONED, RATHER THAN KILLED.

MAYBE WE CAN WORK WITH THAT.

TOM STRONG and TOM STRANGE in our TWO-PART NOVELLA'S incredible CONCLUDING CHAPTER... "TERROR on Terra Obscura!"

ALAN MOORE: script   CHRIS SPROUSE: pencils   AL GORDON: inks   MATT HOLLINGSWORTH: colors   TODD KLEIN: letters   JEFF MARIOTTE: asst editor   SCOTT DUNBIER: editor   MOORE & SPROUSE: creators

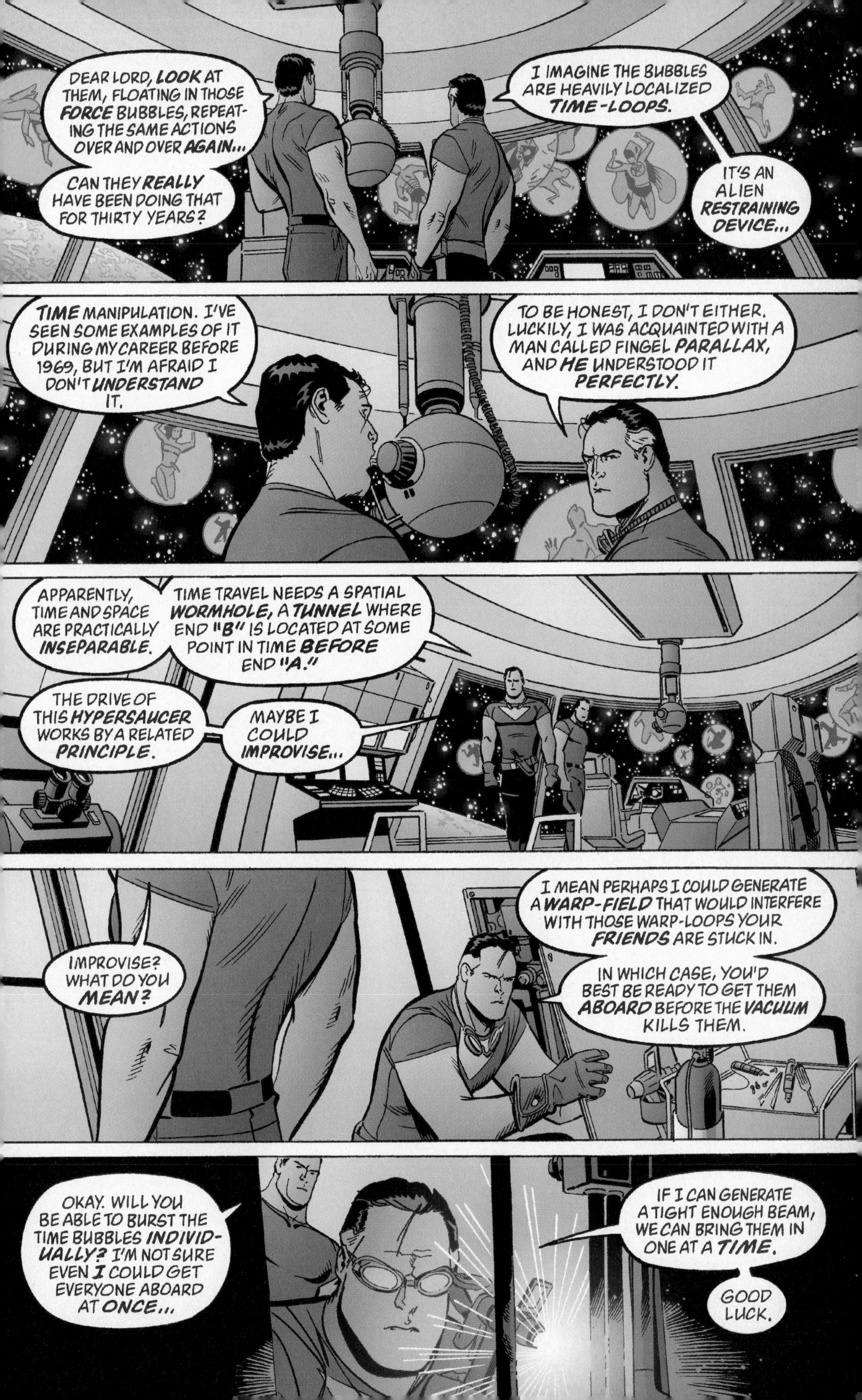
DEAR LORD, LOOK AT THEM, FLOATING IN THOSE FORCE BUBBLES, REPEATING THE SAME ACTIONS OVER AND OVER AGAIN...
CAN THEY REALLY HAVE BEEN DOING THAT FOR THIRTY YEARS?
I IMAGINE THE BUBBLES ARE HEAVILY LOCALIZED TIME-LOOPS.
IT'S AN ALIEN RESTRAINING DEVICE...
TIME MANIPULATION. I'VE SEEN SOME EXAMPLES OF IT DURING MY CAREER BEFORE 1969, BUT I'M AFRAID I DON'T UNDERSTAND IT.
TO BE HONEST, I DON'T EITHER. LUCKILY, I WAS ACQUAINTED WITH A MAN CALLED FINGEL PARALLAX, AND HE UNDERSTOOD IT PERFECTLY.
APPARENTLY, TIME AND SPACE ARE PRACTICALLY INSEPARABLE.
TIME TRAVEL NEEDS A SPATIAL WORMHOLE, A TUNNEL WHERE END "B" IS LOCATED AT SOME POINT IN TIME BEFORE END "A."
THE DRIVE OF THIS HYPERSAUCER WORKS BY A RELATED PRINCIPLE.
MAYBE I COULD IMPROVISE...
IMPROVISE? WHAT DO YOU MEAN?
I MEAN PERHAPS I COULD GENERATE A WARP-FIELD THAT WOULD INTERFERE WITH THOSE WARP-LOOPS YOUR FRIENDS ARE STUCK IN.
IN WHICH CASE, YOU'D BEST BE READY TO GET THEM ABOARD BEFORE THE VACUUM KILLS THEM.
OKAY. WILL YOU BE ABLE TO BURST THE TIME BUBBLES INDIVIDUALLY? I'M NOT SURE EVEN I COULD GET EVERYONE ABOARD AT ONCE...
IF I CAN GENERATE A TIGHT ENOUGH BEAM, WE CAN BRING THEM IN ONE AT A TIME.
GOOD LUCK.

LOG UPDATE: I'M CURRENTLY ON BOARD, MANIPULATING THE *WARP FIELD* TO DISRUPT THE *TIME KNOTS* THAT TERRA OBSCURA'S *HEROES* ARE APPARENTLY CAUGHT IN.

TOM STRANGE IS OUTSIDE RETRIEVING THE LIBERATED CHAMPIONS. HOPEFULLY, OUR COMBINED POWERS AND WEAPONS WILL BE SUFFICIENT TO *FREE* THEM.

OKAY, I'M PREPARING THE AIRLOCK...

ALL RIGHT. ONE DOWN, DOZENS TO GO.

TOM, THIS IS *DICK MARTIN*, BETTER KNOWN AS *PYROMAN*. HE'S GOING TO NEED SOME HELP *ADJUSTING*. YOU COULD START BY TELLING HIM TODAY'S *DATE*.

LEAVE HIM WITH ME. YOU CATCH YOUR BREATH, THEN TAKE CARE OF THE *OTHERS*.

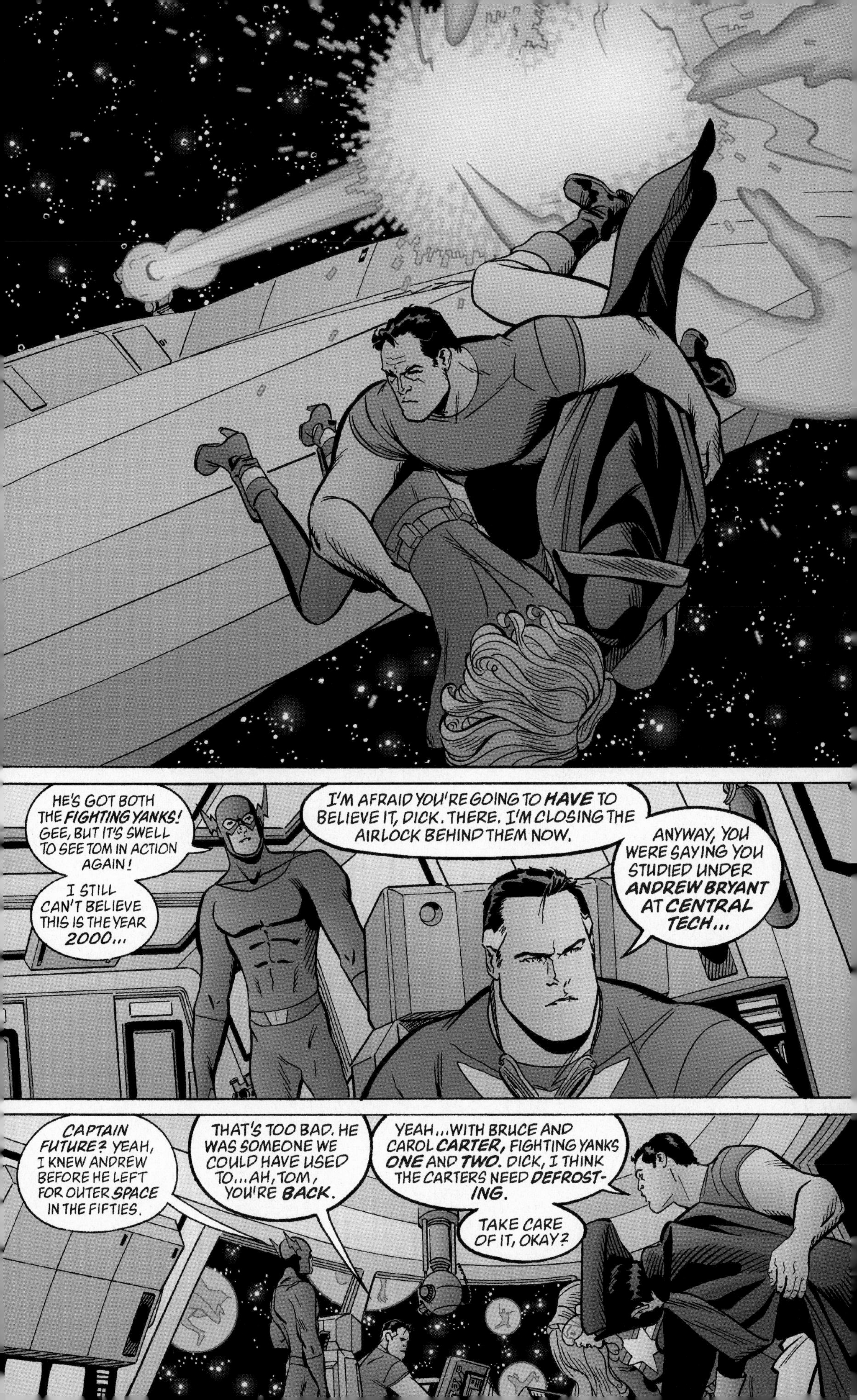
HE'S GOT BOTH THE FIGHTING YANKS! GEE, BUT IT'S SWELL TO SEE TOM IN ACTION AGAIN!
I STILL CAN'T BELIEVE THIS IS THE YEAR 2000...
I'M AFRAID YOU'RE GOING TO HAVE TO BELIEVE IT, DICK. THERE. I'M CLOSING THE AIRLOCK BEHIND THEM NOW.
ANYWAY, YOU WERE SAYING YOU STUDIED UNDER ANDREW BRYANT AT CENTRAL TECH...
CAPTAIN FUTURE? YEAH, I KNEW ANDREW BEFORE HE LEFT FOR OUTER SPACE IN THE FIFTIES.
THAT'S TOO BAD. HE WAS SOMEONE WE COULD HAVE USED TO... AH, TOM, YOU'RE BACK.
YEAH... WITH BRUCE AND CAROL CARTER, FIGHTING YANKS ONE AND TWO. DICK, I THINK THE CARTERS NEED DEFROST-ING.
TAKE CARE OF IT, OKAY?

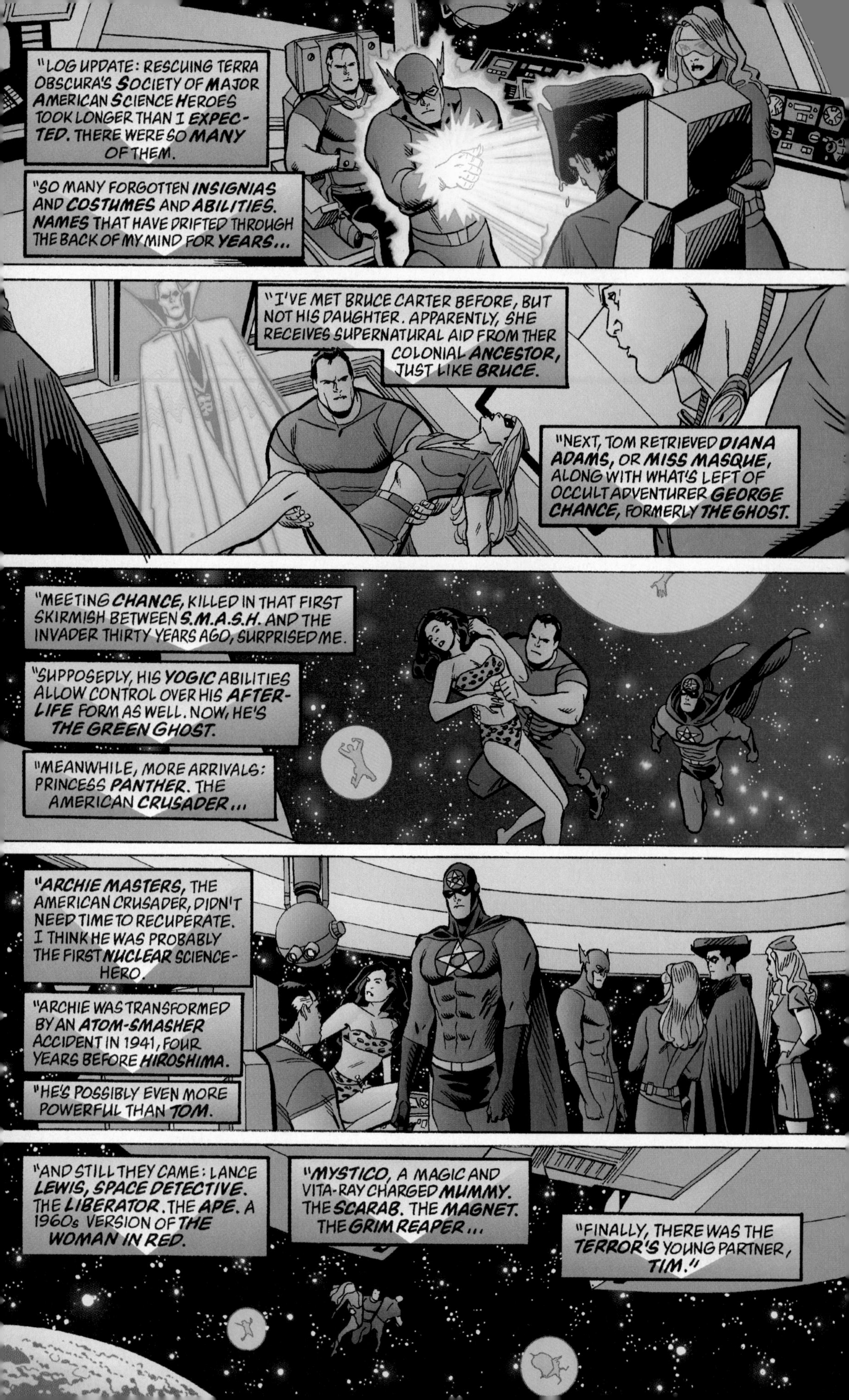
"LOG UPDATE: RESCUING TERRA OBSCURA'S SOCIETY OF MAJOR AMERICAN SCIENCE HEROES TOOK LONGER THAN I EXPECTED. THERE WERE SO MANY OF THEM.
"SO MANY FORGOTTEN INSIGNIAS AND COSTUMES AND ABILITIES. NAMES THAT HAVE DRIFTED THROUGH THE BACK OF MY MIND FOR YEARS...
"I'VE MET BRUCE CARTER BEFORE, BUT NOT HIS DAUGHTER. APPARENTLY, SHE RECEIVES SUPERNATURAL AID FROM THER COLONIAL ANCESTOR, JUST LIKE BRUCE.
"NEXT, TOM RETRIEVED DIANA ADAMS, OR MISS MASQUE, ALONG WITH WHAT'S LEFT OF OCCULT ADVENTURER GEORGE CHANCE, FORMERLY THE GHOST.
"MEETING CHANCE, KILLED IN THAT FIRST SKIRMISH BETWEEN S.M.A.S.H. AND THE INVADER THIRTY YEARS AGO, SURPRISED ME.
"SUPPOSEDLY, HIS YOGIC ABILITIES ALLOW CONTROL OVER HIS AFTER-LIFE FORM AS WELL. NOW, HE'S THE GREEN GHOST.
"MEANWHILE, MORE ARRIVALS: PRINCESS PANTHER. THE AMERICAN CRUSADER...
"ARCHIE MASTERS, THE AMERICAN CRUSADER, DIDN'T NEED TIME TO RECUPERATE. I THINK HE WAS PROBABLY THE FIRST NUCLEAR SCIENCE-HERO.
"ARCHIE WAS TRANSFORMED BY AN ATOM-SMASHER ACCIDENT IN 1941, FOUR YEARS BEFORE HIROSHIMA.
"HE'S POSSIBLY EVEN MORE POWERFUL THAN TOM.
"AND STILL THEY CAME: LANCE LEWIS, SPACE DETECTIVE. THE LIBERATOR. THE APE. A 1960s VERSION OF THE WOMAN IN RED.
"MYSTICO, A MAGIC AND VITA-RAY CHARGED MUMMY. THE SCARAB. THE MAGNET. THE GRIM REAPER...
"FINALLY, THERE WAS THE TERROR'S YOUNG PARTNER, TIM."

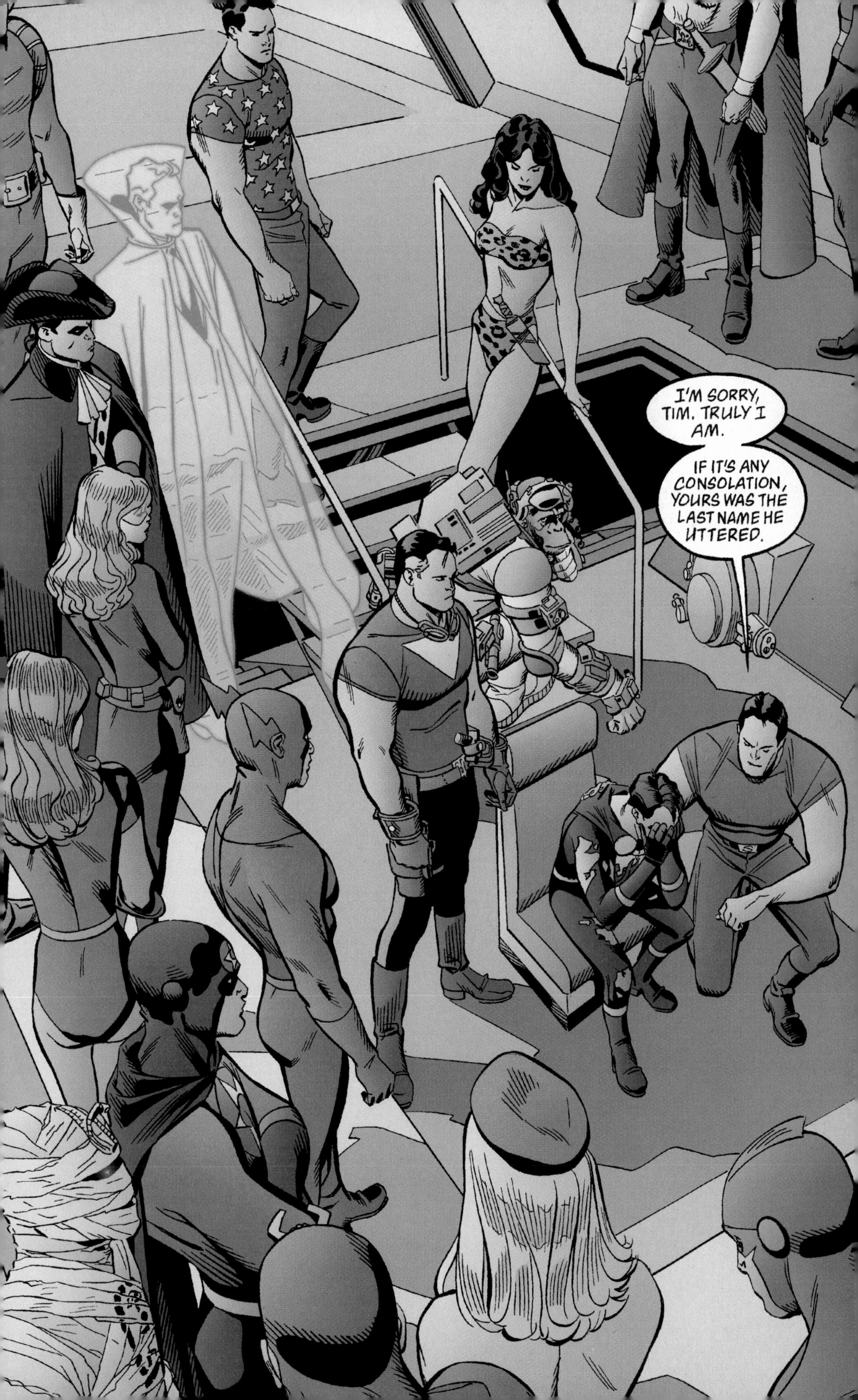
I'M SORRY, TIM. TRULY I AM.
IF IT'S ANY CONSOLATION, YOURS WAS THE LAST NAME HE UTTERED.

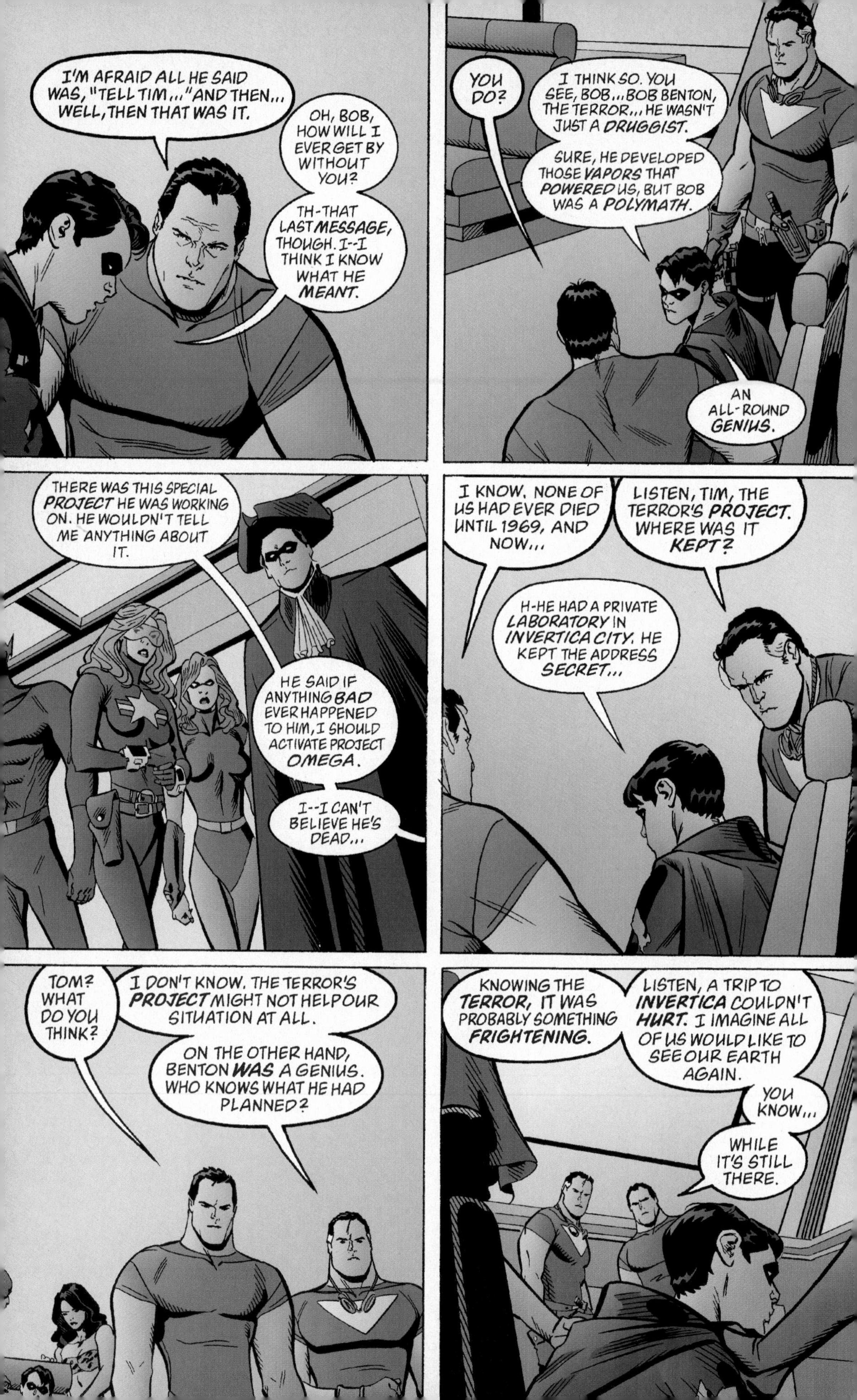
I'M AFRAID ALL HE SAID WAS, "TELL TIM..." AND THEN... WELL, THEN THAT WAS IT.
OH, BOB, HOW WILL I EVER GET BY WITHOUT YOU?
TH-THAT LAST MESSAGE, THOUGH. I--I THINK I KNOW WHAT HE MEANT.
YOU DO?
I THINK SO. YOU SEE, BOB... BOB BENTON, THE TERROR... HE WASN'T JUST A DRUGGIST.
SURE, HE DEVELOPED THOSE VAPORS THAT POWERED US, BUT BOB WAS A POLYMATH.
AN ALL-ROUND GENIUS.
THERE WAS THIS SPECIAL PROJECT HE WAS WORKING ON. HE WOULDN'T TELL ME ANYTHING ABOUT IT.
HE SAID IF ANYTHING BAD EVER HAPPENED TO HIM, I SHOULD ACTIVATE PROJECT OMEGA.
I--I CAN'T BELIEVE HE'S DEAD...
I KNOW. NONE OF US HAD EVER DIED UNTIL 1969, AND NOW...
LISTEN, TIM, THE TERROR'S PROJECT. WHERE WAS IT KEPT?
H-HE HAD A PRIVATE LABORATORY IN INVERTICA CITY. HE KEPT THE ADDRESS SECRET...
TOM? WHAT DO YOU THINK?
I DON'T KNOW. THE TERROR'S PROJECT MIGHT NOT HELP OUR SITUATION AT ALL.
ON THE OTHER HAND, BENTON WAS A GENIUS. WHO KNOWS WHAT HE HAD PLANNED?
KNOWING THE TERROR, IT WAS PROBABLY SOMETHING FRIGHTENING.
LISTEN, A TRIP TO INVERTICA COULDN'T HURT. I IMAGINE ALL OF US WOULD LIKE TO SEE OUR EARTH AGAIN.
YOU KNOW...
WHILE IT'S STILL THERE.

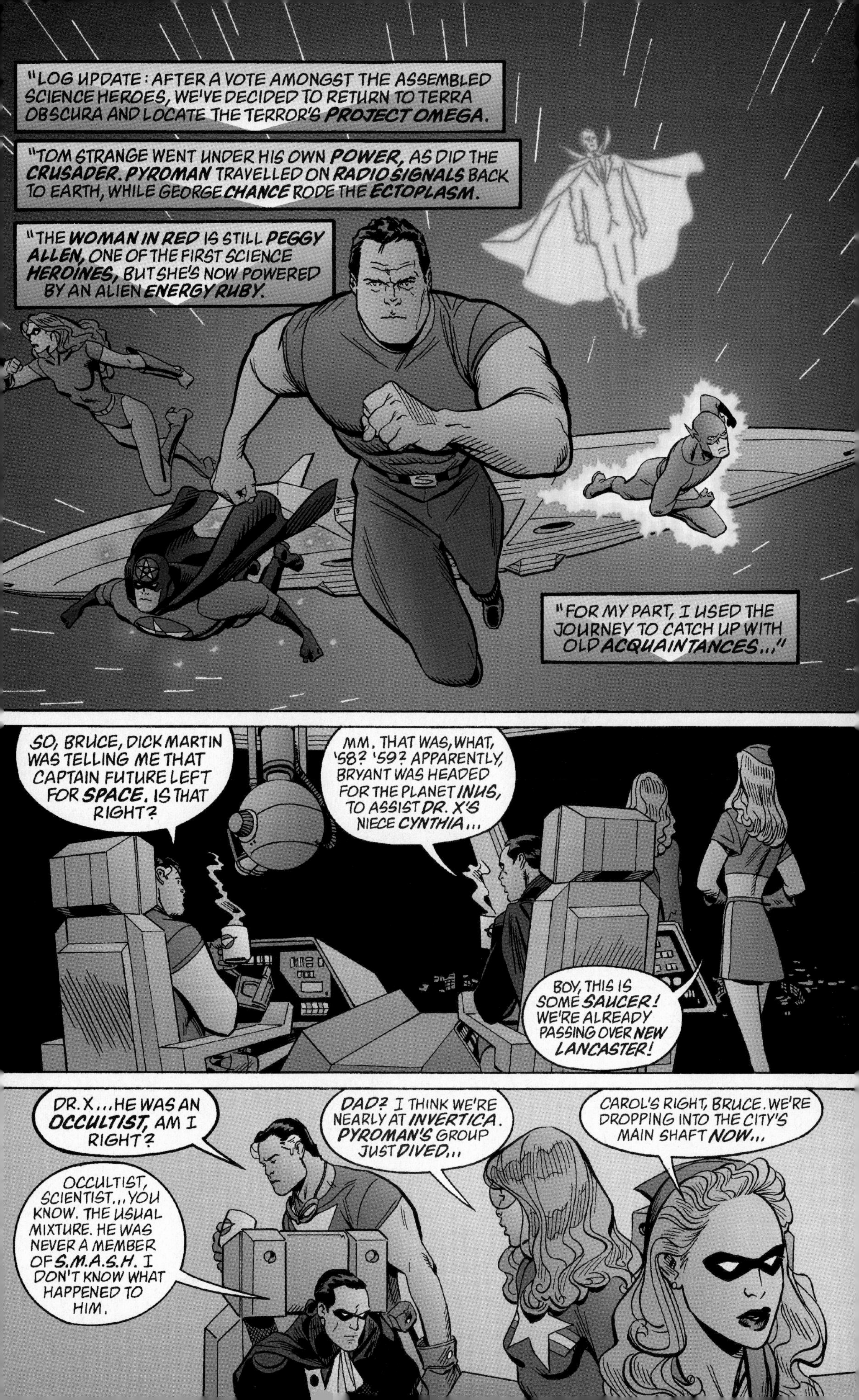
"LOG UPDATE: AFTER A VOTE AMONGST THE ASSEMBLED SCIENCE HEROES, WE'VE DECIDED TO RETURN TO TERRA OBSCURA AND LOCATE THE TERROR'S PROJECT OMEGA.
"TOM STRANGE WENT UNDER HIS OWN POWER, AS DID THE CRUSADER. PYROMAN TRAVELLED ON RADIO SIGNALS BACK TO EARTH, WHILE GEORGE CHANCE RODE THE ECTOPLASM.
"THE WOMAN IN RED IS STILL PEGGY ALLEN, ONE OF THE FIRST SCIENCE HEROINES, BUT SHE'S NOW POWERED BY AN ALIEN ENERGY RUBY.
"FOR MY PART, I USED THE JOURNEY TO CATCH UP WITH OLD ACQUAINTANCES..."
SO, BRUCE, DICK MARTIN WAS TELLING ME THAT CAPTAIN FUTURE LEFT FOR SPACE. IS THAT RIGHT?
MM. THAT WAS, WHAT, '58? '59? APPARENTLY, BRYANT WAS HEADED FOR THE PLANET INUS, TO ASSIST DR. X'S NIECE CYNTHIA...
BOY, THIS IS SOME SAUCER! WE'RE ALREADY PASSING OVER NEW LANCASTER!
DR. X... HE WAS AN OCCULTIST, AM I RIGHT?
OCCULTIST, SCIENTIST... YOU KNOW. THE USUAL MIXTURE. HE WAS NEVER A MEMBER OF S.M.A.S.H. I DON'T KNOW WHAT HAPPENED TO HIM.
DAD? I THINK WE'RE NEARLY AT INVERTICA. PYROMAN'S GROUP JUST DIVED...
CAROL'S RIGHT, BRUCE. WE'RE DROPPING INTO THE CITY'S MAIN SHAFT NOW...

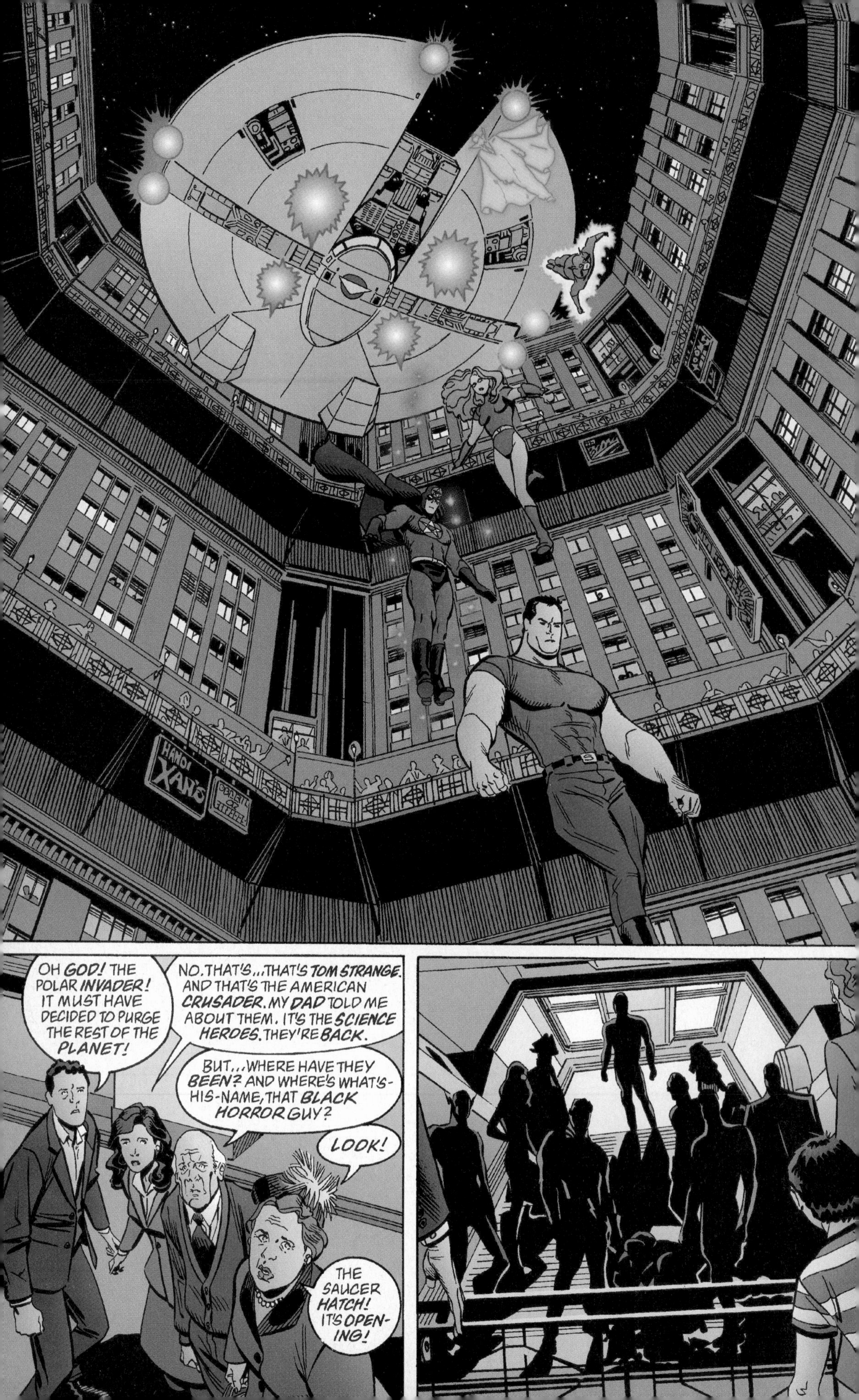
OH GOD! THE POLAR INVADER! IT MUST HAVE DECIDED TO PURGE THE REST OF THE PLANET!
NO. THAT'S... THAT'S TOM STRANGE. AND THAT'S THE AMERICAN CRUSADER. MY DAD TOLD ME ABOUT THEM. IT'S THE SCIENCE HEROES. THEY'RE BACK.
BUT... WHERE HAVE THEY BEEN? AND WHERE'S WHAT'S-HIS-NAME, THAT BLACK HORROR GUY?
LOOK!
THE SAUCER HATCH! IT'S OPENING!

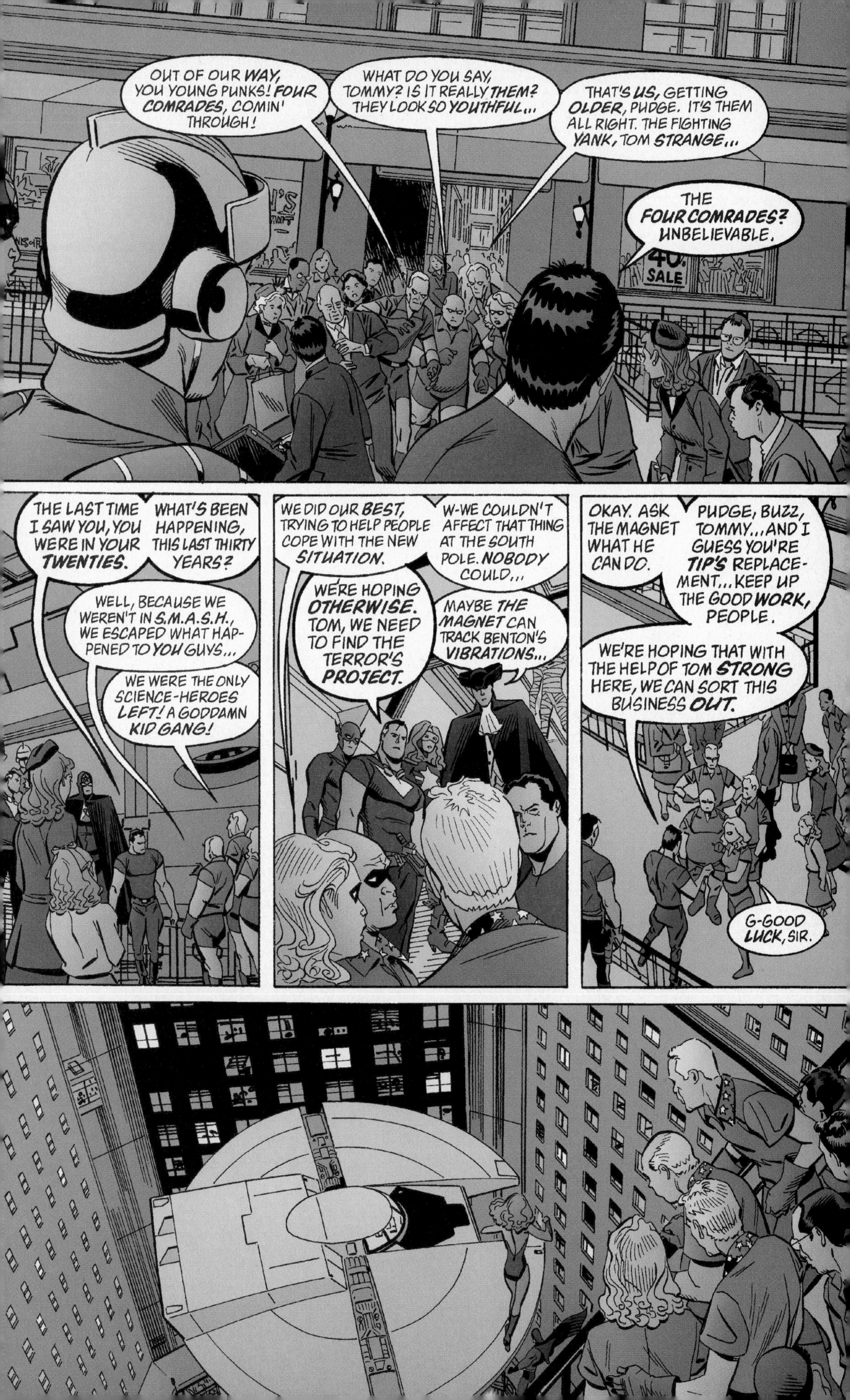
OUT OF OUR WAY, YOU YOUNG PUNKS! FOUR COMRADES, COMIN' THROUGH!
WHAT DO YOU SAY, TOMMY? IS IT REALLY THEM? THEY LOOK SO YOUTHFUL...
THAT'S US, GETTING OLDER, PUDGE. IT'S THEM ALL RIGHT. THE FIGHTING YANK, TOM STRANGE...
THE FOUR COMRADES? UNBELIEVABLE.
40% SALE
THE LAST TIME I SAW YOU, YOU WERE IN YOUR TWENTIES.
WHAT'S BEEN HAPPENING, THIS LAST THIRTY YEARS?
WELL, BECAUSE WE WEREN'T IN S.M.A.S.H., WE ESCAPED WHAT HAPPENED TO YOU GUYS...
WE WERE THE ONLY SCIENCE-HEROES LEFT! A GODDAMN KID GANG!
WE DID OUR BEST, TRYING TO HELP PEOPLE COPE WITH THE NEW SITUATION.
W-WE COULDN'T AFFECT THAT THING AT THE SOUTH POLE. NOBODY COULD...
WE'RE HOPING OTHERWISE. TOM, WE NEED TO FIND THE TERROR'S PROJECT.
MAYBE THE MAGNET CAN TRACK BENTON'S VIBRATIONS...
OKAY. ASK THE MAGNET WHAT HE CAN DO.
PUDGE, BUZZ, TOMMY... AND I GUESS YOU'RE TIP'S REPLACEMENT... KEEP UP THE GOOD WORK, PEOPLE.
WE'RE HOPING THAT WITH THE HELP OF TOM STRONG HERE, WE CAN SORT THIS BUSINESS OUT.
G-GOOD LUCK, SIR.

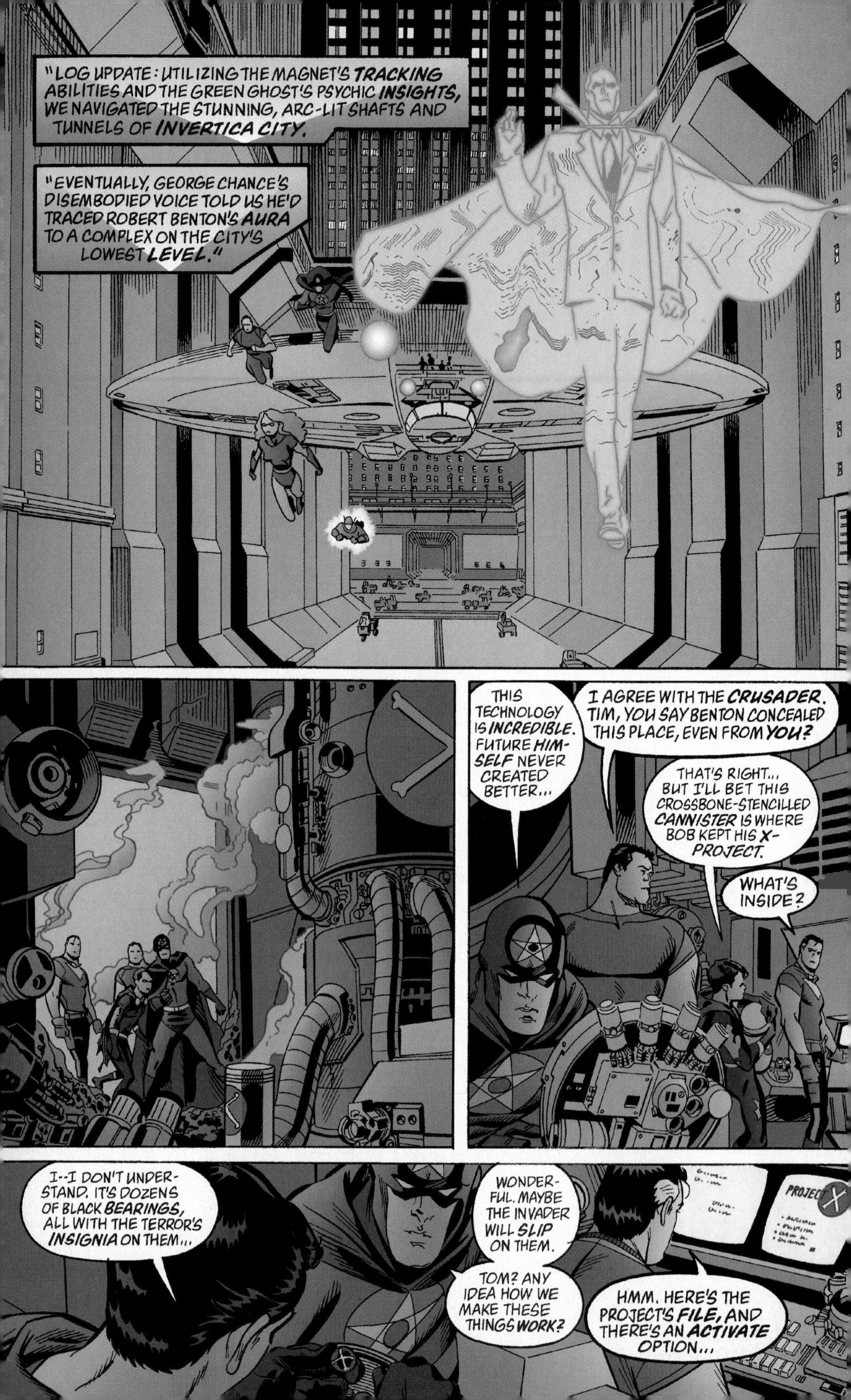
"LOG UPDATE: UTILIZING THE MAGNET'S TRACKING ABILITIES AND THE GREEN GHOST'S PSYCHIC INSIGHTS, WE NAVIGATED THE STUNNING, ARC-LIT SHAFTS AND TUNNELS OF INVERTICA CITY.
"EVENTUALLY, GEORGE CHANCE'S DISEMBODIED VOICE TOLD US HE'D TRACED ROBERT BENTON'S AURA TO A COMPLEX ON THE CITY'S LOWEST LEVEL."
THIS TECHNOLOGY IS INCREDIBLE. FUTURE HIM-SELF NEVER CREATED BETTER...
I AGREE WITH THE CRUSADER. TIM, YOU SAY BENTON CONCEALED THIS PLACE, EVEN FROM YOU?
THAT'S RIGHT... BUT I'LL BET THIS CROSSBONE-STENCILLED CANNISTER IS WHERE BOB KEPT HIS X-PROJECT.
WHAT'S INSIDE?
I--I DON'T UNDER-STAND. IT'S DOZENS OF BLACK BEARINGS, ALL WITH THE TERROR'S INSIGNIA ON THEM...
WONDER-FUL. MAYBE THE INVADER WILL SLIP ON THEM.
TOM? ANY IDEA HOW WE MAKE THESE THINGS WORK?
HMM. HERE'S THE PROJECT'S FILE, AND THERE'S AN ACTIVATE OPTION...
PROJECT X

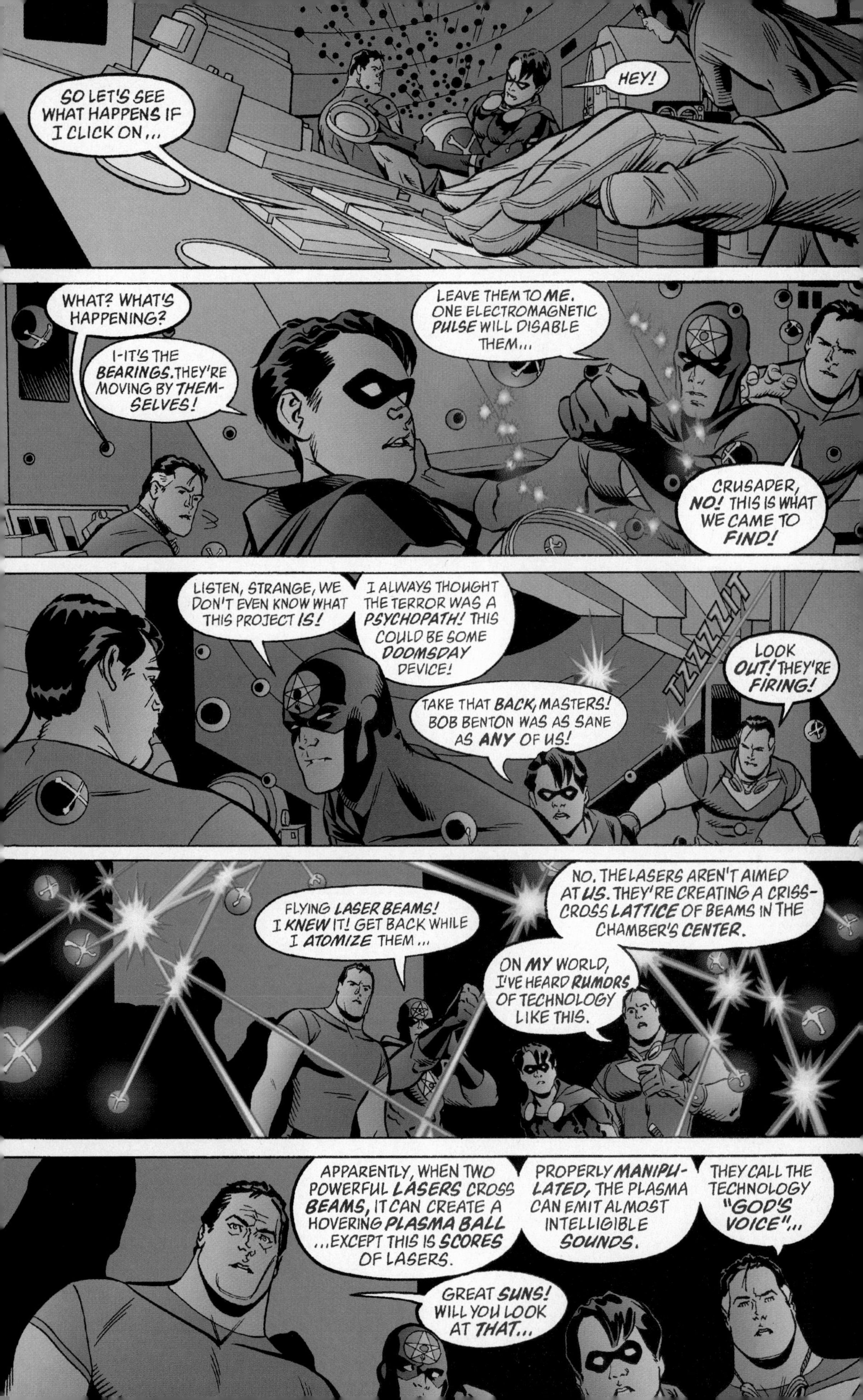
SO LET'S SEE WHAT HAPPENS IF I CLICK ON...
HEY!
WHAT? WHAT'S HAPPENING?
I-IT'S THE BEARINGS. THEY'RE MOVING BY THEMSELVES!
LEAVE THEM TO ME. ONE ELECTROMAGNETIC PULSE WILL DISABLE THEM...
CRUSADER, NO! THIS IS WHAT WE CAME TO FIND!
LISTEN, STRANGE, WE DON'T EVEN KNOW WHAT THIS PROJECT IS!
I ALWAYS THOUGHT THE TERROR WAS A PSYCHOPATH! THIS COULD BE SOME DOOMSDAY DEVICE!
TAKE THAT BACK, MASTERS! BOB BENTON WAS AS SANE AS ANY OF US!
TZZZZZIT
LOOK OUT! THEY'RE FIRING!
FLYING LASER BEAMS! I KNEW IT! GET BACK WHILE I ATOMIZE THEM...
NO. THE LASERS AREN'T AIMED AT US. THEY'RE CREATING A CRISS-CROSS LATTICE OF BEAMS IN THE CHAMBER'S CENTER.
ON MY WORLD, I'VE HEARD RUMORS OF TECHNOLOGY LIKE THIS.
APPARENTLY, WHEN TWO POWERFUL LASERS CROSS BEAMS, IT CAN CREATE A HOVERING PLASMA BALL ...EXCEPT THIS IS SCORES OF LASERS.
PROPERLY MANIPULATED, THE PLASMA CAN EMIT ALMOST INTELLIGIBLE SOUNDS.
THEY CALL THE TECHNOLOGY "GOD'S VOICE"...
GREAT SUNS! WILL YOU LOOK AT THAT...

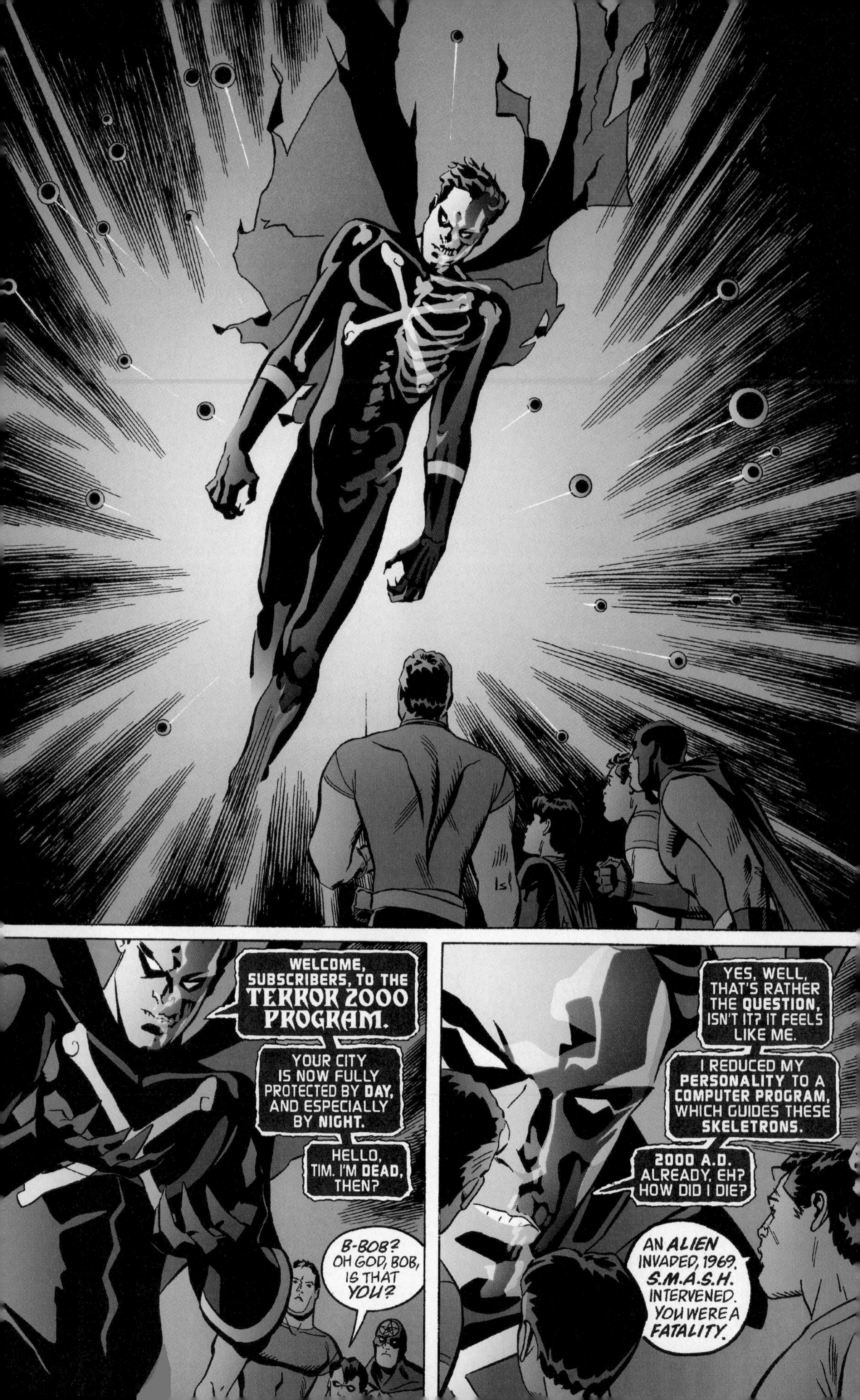

WELCOME, SUBSCRIBERS, TO THE TERROR 2000 PROGRAM.
YOUR CITY IS NOW FULLY PROTECTED BY DAY, AND ESPECIALLY BY NIGHT.
HELLO, TIM. I'M DEAD, THEN?
B-BOB? OH GOD, BOB, IS THAT YOU?
YES, WELL, THAT'S RATHER THE QUESTION, ISN'T IT? IT FEELS LIKE ME.
I REDUCED MY PERSONALITY TO A COMPUTER PROGRAM, WHICH GUIDES THESE SKELETRONS.
2000 A.D. ALREADY, EH? HOW DID I DIE?
AN ALIEN INVADED, 1969. S.M.A.S.H. INTERVENED. YOU WERE A FATALITY.

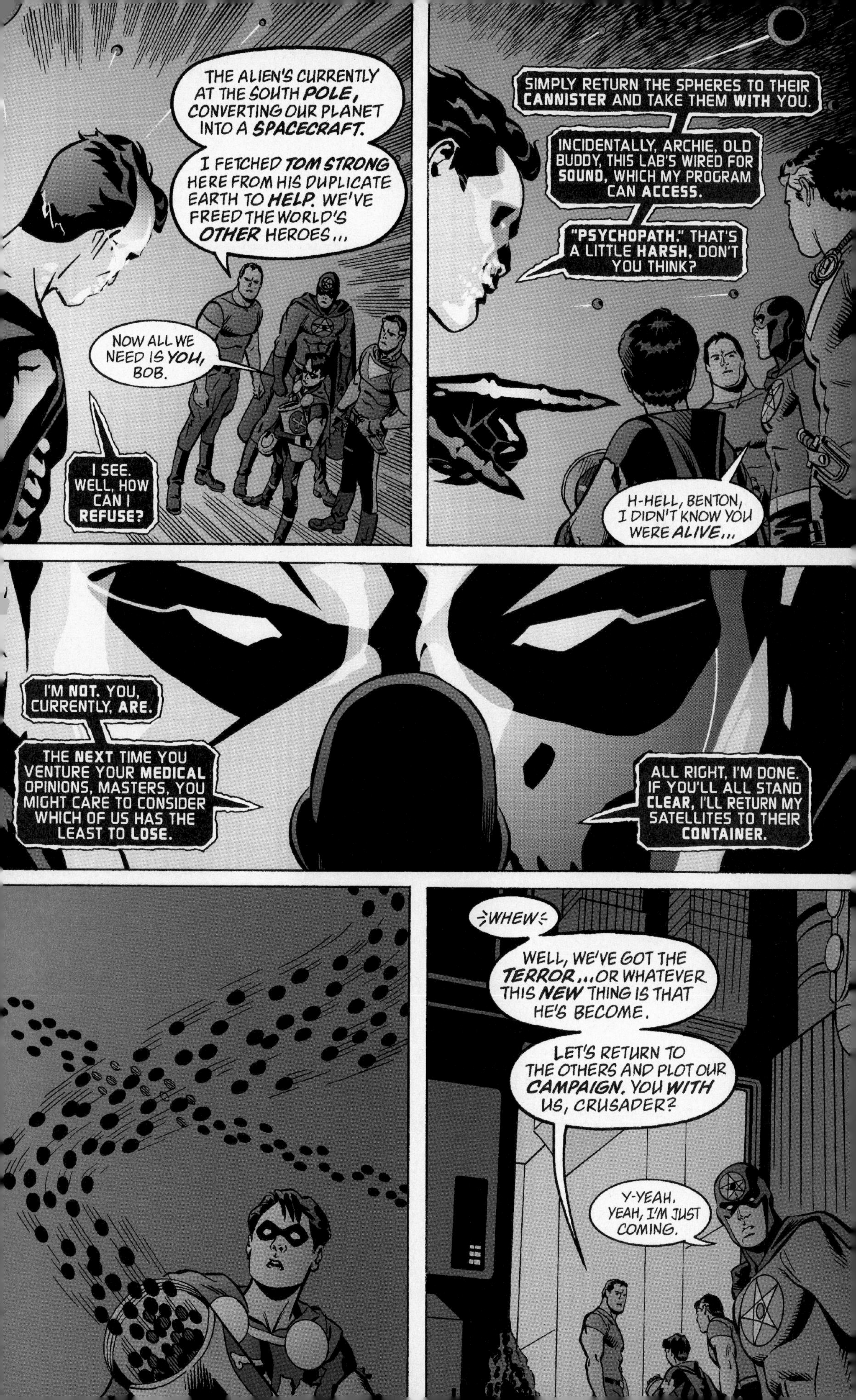
THE ALIEN'S CURRENTLY AT THE SOUTH POLE, CONVERTING OUR PLANET INTO A SPACECRAFT.
I FETCHED TOM STRONG HERE FROM HIS DUPLICATE EARTH TO HELP. WE'VE FREED THE WORLD'S OTHER HEROES...
NOW ALL WE NEED IS YOU, BOB.
I SEE. WELL, HOW CAN I REFUSE?
SIMPLY RETURN THE SPHERES TO THEIR CANNISTER AND TAKE THEM WITH YOU.
INCIDENTALLY, ARCHIE, OLD BUDDY, THIS LAB'S WIRED FOR SOUND, WHICH MY PROGRAM CAN ACCESS.
"PSYCHOPATH." THAT'S A LITTLE HARSH, DON'T YOU THINK?
H-HELL, BENTON, I DIDN'T KNOW YOU WERE ALIVE...
I'M NOT. YOU, CURRENTLY, ARE.
THE NEXT TIME YOU VENTURE YOUR MEDICAL OPINIONS, MASTERS, YOU MIGHT CARE TO CONSIDER WHICH OF US HAS THE LEAST TO LOSE.
ALL RIGHT, I'M DONE. IF YOU'LL ALL STAND CLEAR, I'LL RETURN MY SATELLITES TO THEIR CONTAINER.
WHEW
WELL, WE'VE GOT THE TERROR...OR WHATEVER THIS NEW THING IS THAT HE'S BECOME.
LET'S RETURN TO THE OTHERS AND PLOT OUR CAMPAIGN. YOU WITH US, CRUSADER?
Y-YEAH. YEAH, I'M JUST COMING.

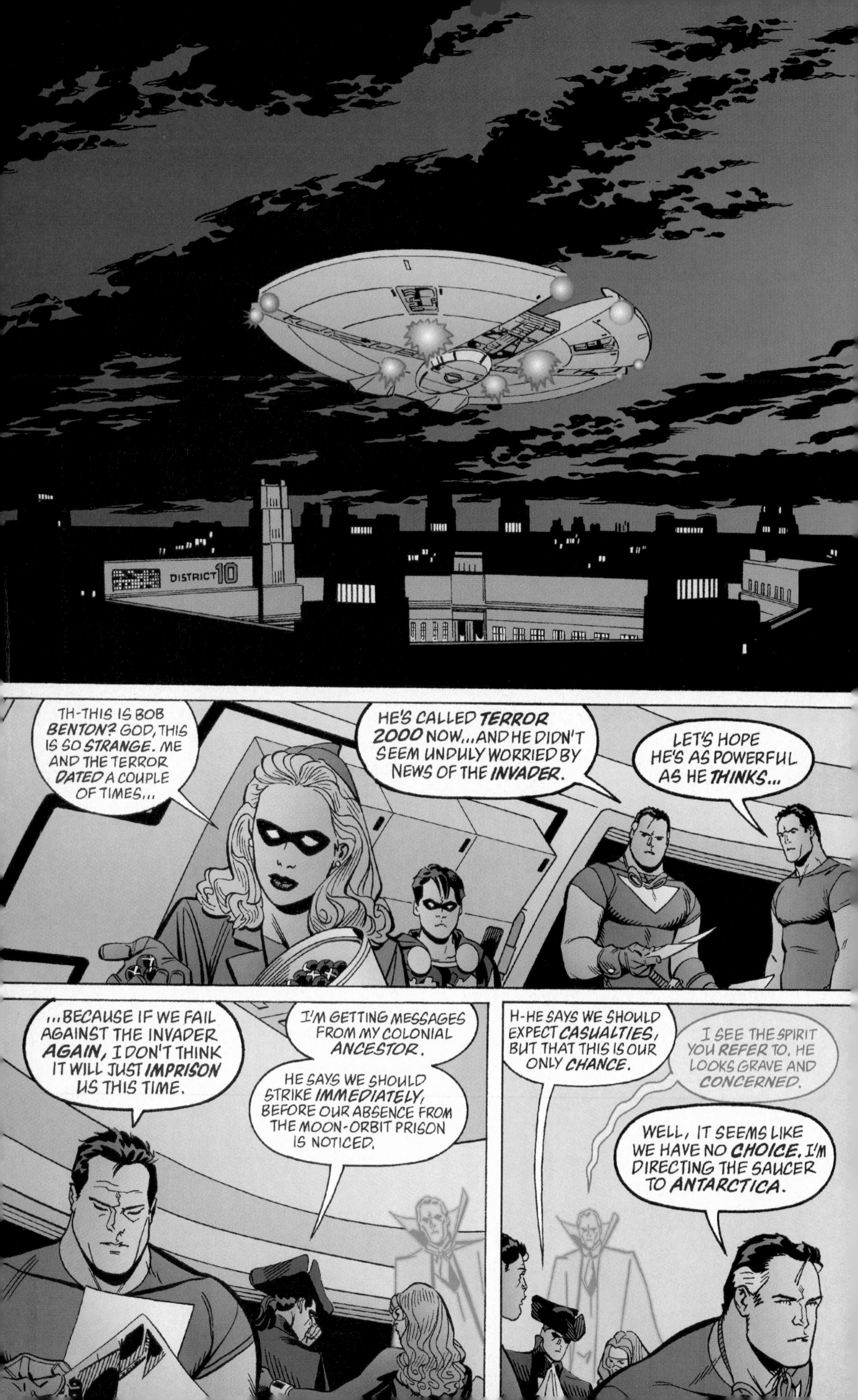
DISTRICT 10
TH-THIS IS BOB BENTON? GOD, THIS IS SO STRANGE. ME AND THE TERROR DATED A COUPLE OF TIMES...
HE'S CALLED TERROR 2000 NOW...AND HE DIDN'T SEEM UNDULY WORRIED BY NEWS OF THE INVADER.
LET'S HOPE HE'S AS POWERFUL AS HE THINKS...
...BECAUSE IF WE FAIL AGAINST THE INVADER AGAIN, I DON'T THINK IT WILL JUST IMPRISON US THIS TIME.
I'M GETTING MESSAGES FROM MY COLONIAL ANCESTOR.
HE SAYS WE SHOULD STRIKE IMMEDIATELY, BEFORE OUR ABSENCE FROM THE MOON-ORBIT PRISON IS NOTICED.
H-HE SAYS WE SHOULD EXPECT CASUALTIES, BUT THAT THIS IS OUR ONLY CHANCE.
I SEE THE SPIRIT YOU REFER TO. HE LOOKS GRAVE AND CONCERNED.
WELL, IT SEEMS LIKE WE HAVE NO CHOICE. I'M DIRECTING THE SAUCER TO ANTARCTICA.

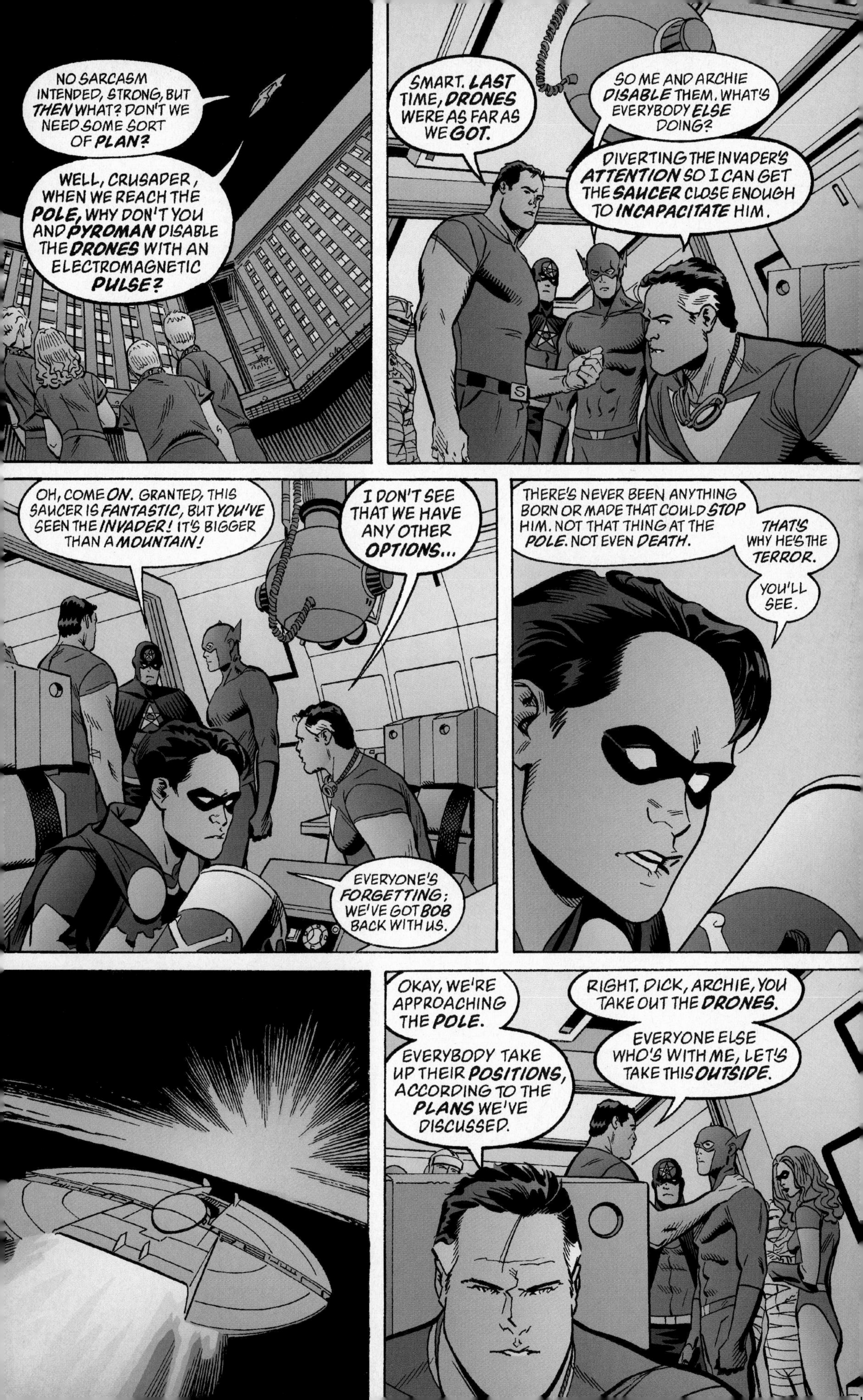
NO SARCASM INTENDED, STRONG, BUT THEN WHAT? DON'T WE NEED SOME SORT OF PLAN?
WELL, CRUSADER, WHEN WE REACH THE POLE, WHY DON'T YOU AND PYROMAN DISABLE THE DRONES WITH AN ELECTROMAGNETIC PULSE?
SMART. LAST TIME, DRONES WERE AS FAR AS WE GOT.
SO ME AND ARCHIE DISABLE THEM. WHAT'S EVERYBODY ELSE DOING?
DIVERTING THE INVADER'S ATTENTION SO I CAN GET THE SAUCER CLOSE ENOUGH TO INCAPACITATE HIM.
OH, COME ON. GRANTED, THIS SAUCER IS FANTASTIC, BUT YOU'VE SEEN THE INVADER! IT'S BIGGER THAN A MOUNTAIN!
I DON'T SEE THAT WE HAVE ANY OTHER OPTIONS...
EVERYONE'S FORGETTING; WE'VE GOT BOB BACK WITH US.
THERE'S NEVER BEEN ANYTHING BORN OR MADE THAT COULD STOP HIM. NOT THAT THING AT THE POLE. NOT EVEN DEATH.
THAT'S WHY HE'S THE TERROR.
YOU'LL SEE.
OKAY, WE'RE APPROACHING THE POLE.
EVERYBODY TAKE UP THEIR POSITIONS, ACCORDING TO THE PLANS WE'VE DISCUSSED.
RIGHT. DICK, ARCHIE, YOU TAKE OUT THE DRONES.
EVERYONE ELSE WHO'S WITH ME, LET'S TAKE THIS OUTSIDE.

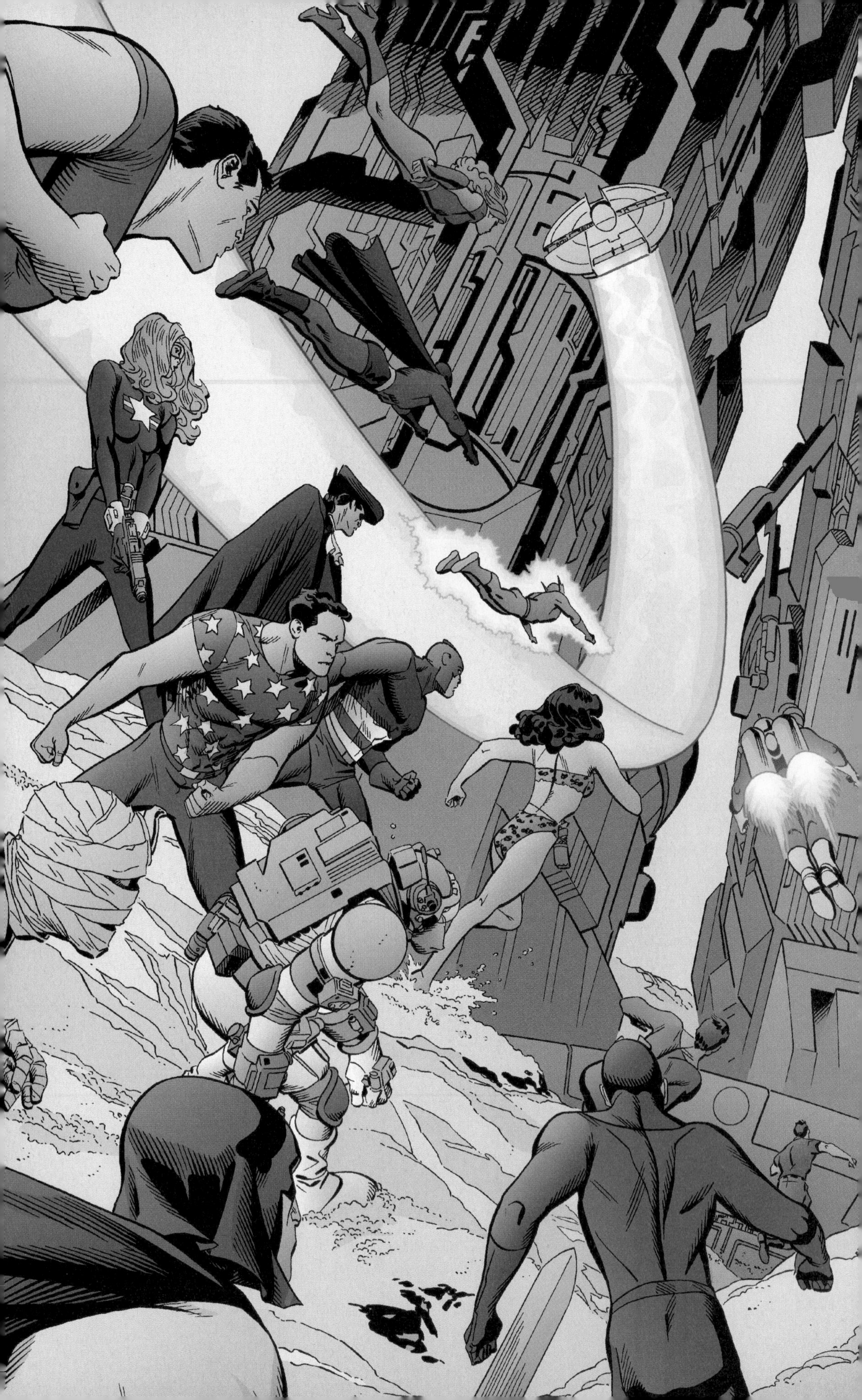

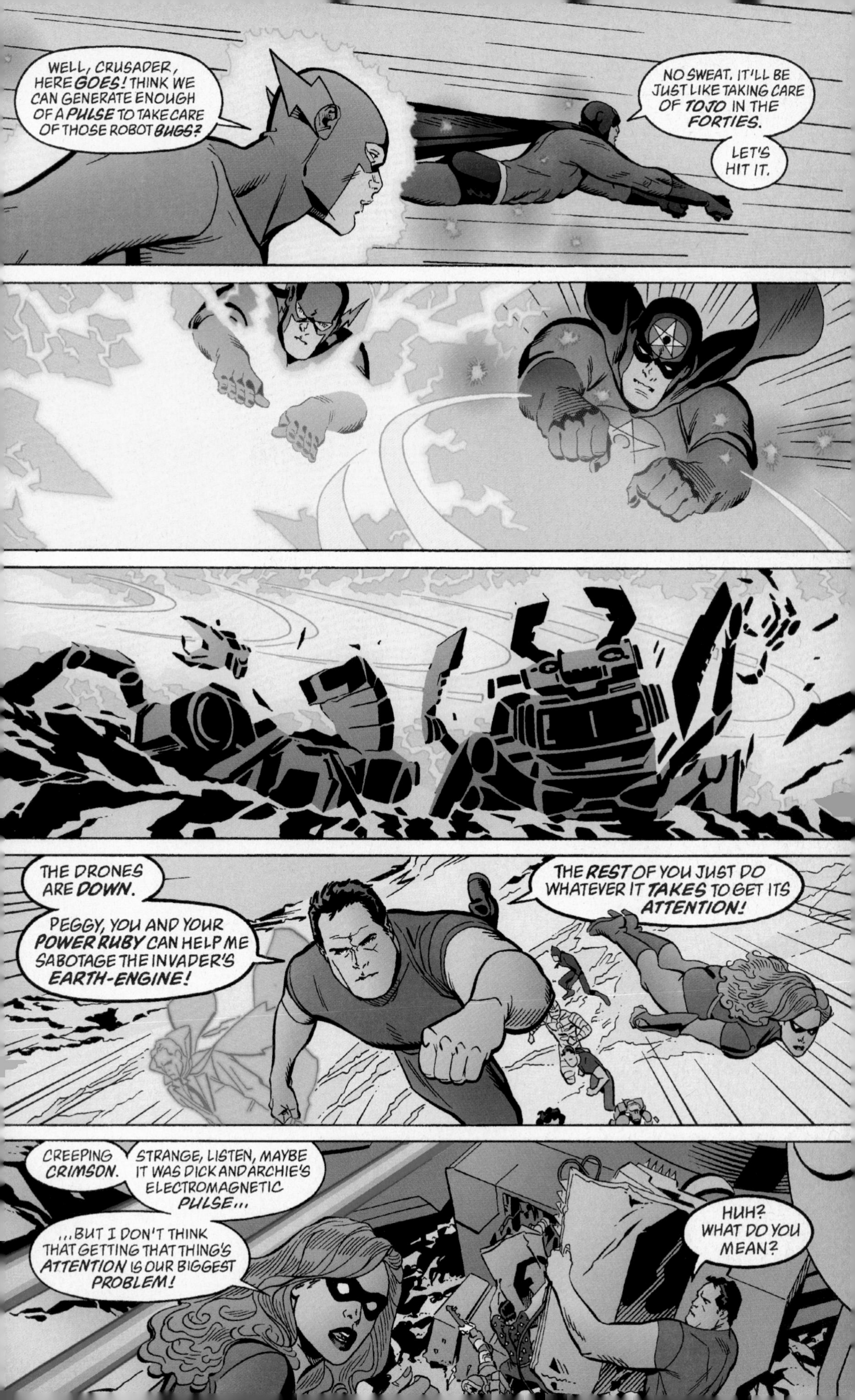
WELL, CRUSADER, HERE GOES! THINK WE CAN GENERATE ENOUGH OF A PULSE TO TAKE CARE OF THOSE ROBOT BUGS?
NO SWEAT. IT'LL BE JUST LIKE TAKING CARE OF TOJO IN THE FORTIES.
LET'S HIT IT.
THE DRONES ARE DOWN.
PEGGY, YOU AND YOUR POWER RUBY CAN HELP ME SABOTAGE THE INVADER'S EARTH-ENGINE!
THE REST OF YOU JUST DO WHATEVER IT TAKES TO GET ITS ATTENTION!
CREEPING CRIMSON.
STRANGE, LISTEN, MAYBE IT WAS DICK AND ARCHIE'S ELECTROMAGNETIC PULSE...
...BUT I DON'T THINK THAT GETTING THAT THING'S ATTENTION IS OUR BIGGEST PROBLEM!
HUH? WHAT DO YOU MEAN?

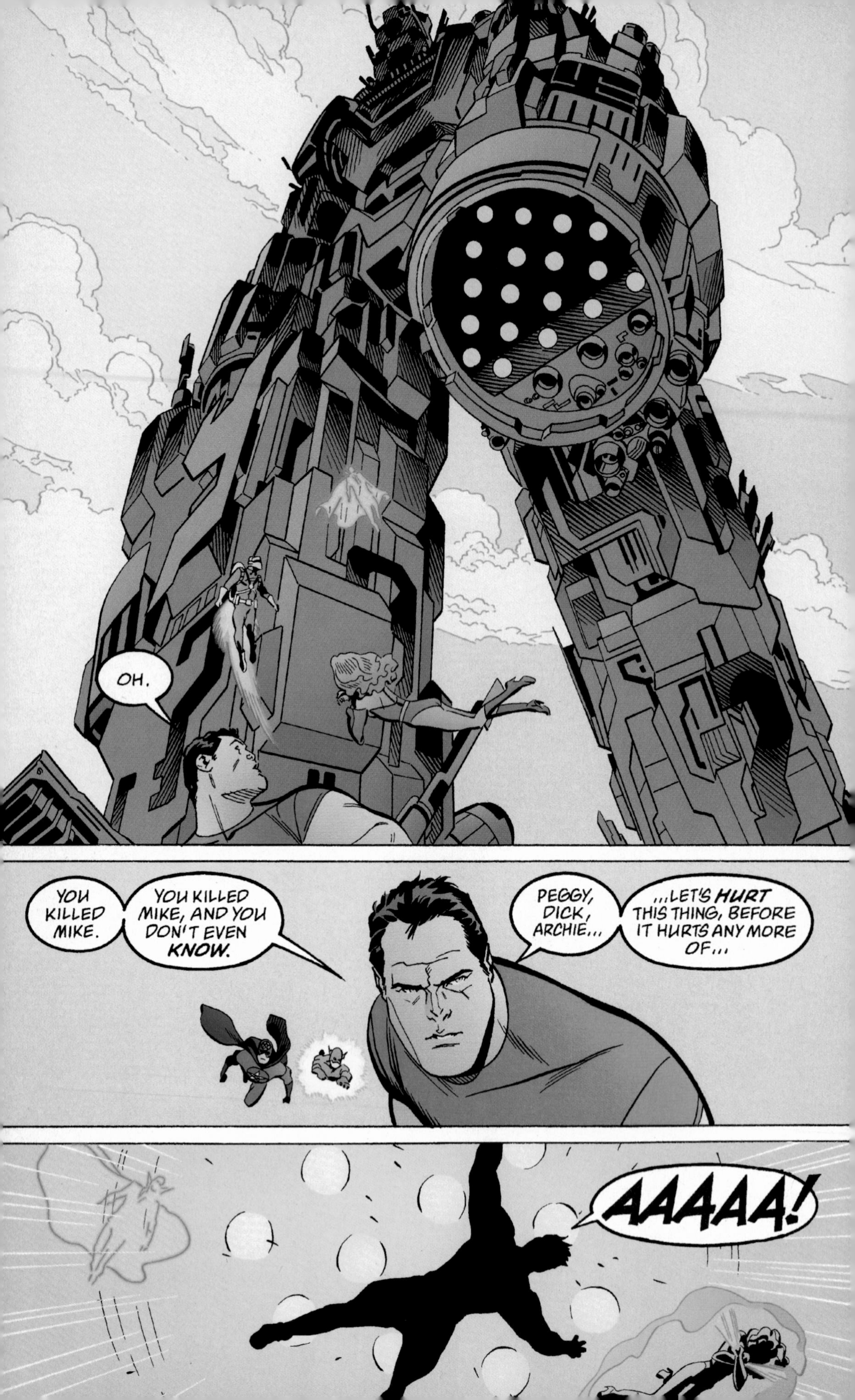
OH.
YOU KILLED MIKE.
YOU KILLED MIKE, AND YOU DON'T EVEN **KNOW**.
PEGGY, DICK, ARCHIE...
...LET'S **HURT** THIS THING, BEFORE IT HURTS ANY MORE OF...
AAAAA!

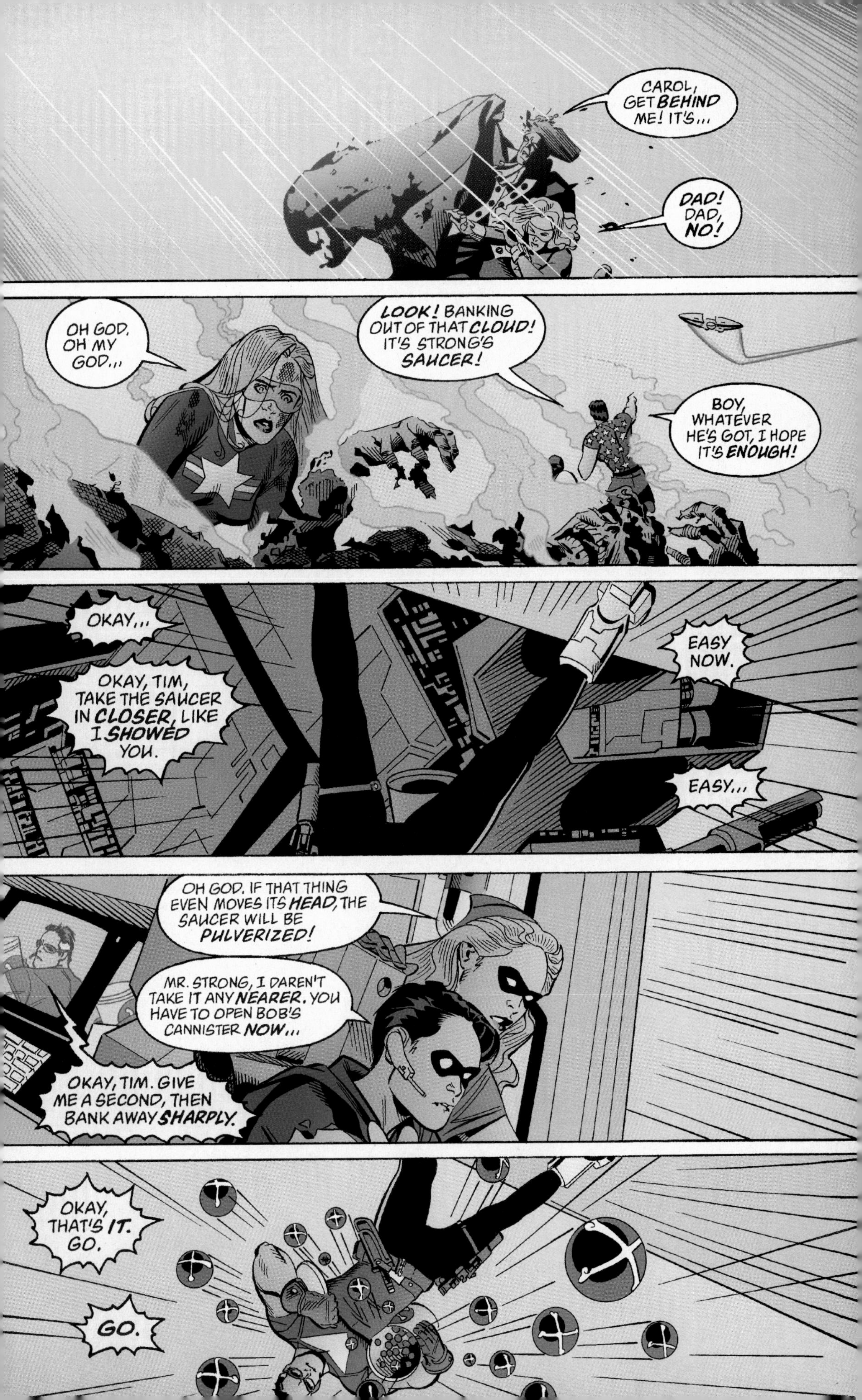
CAROL, GET BEHIND ME! IT'S...
DAD! DAD, NO!
OH GOD, OH MY GOD...
LOOK! BANKING OUT OF THAT CLOUD! IT'S STRONG'S SAUCER!
BOY, WHATEVER HE'S GOT, I HOPE IT'S ENOUGH!
OKAY...
OKAY, TIM, TAKE THE SAUCER IN CLOSER, LIKE I SHOWED YOU.
EASY NOW.
EASY...
OH GOD. IF THAT THING EVEN MOVES ITS HEAD, THE SAUCER WILL BE PULVERIZED!
MR. STRONG, I DAREN'T TAKE IT ANY NEARER. YOU HAVE TO OPEN BOB'S CANNISTER NOW...
OKAY, TIM. GIVE ME A SECOND, THEN BANK AWAY SHARPLY.
OKAY, THAT'S IT. GO.
GO.

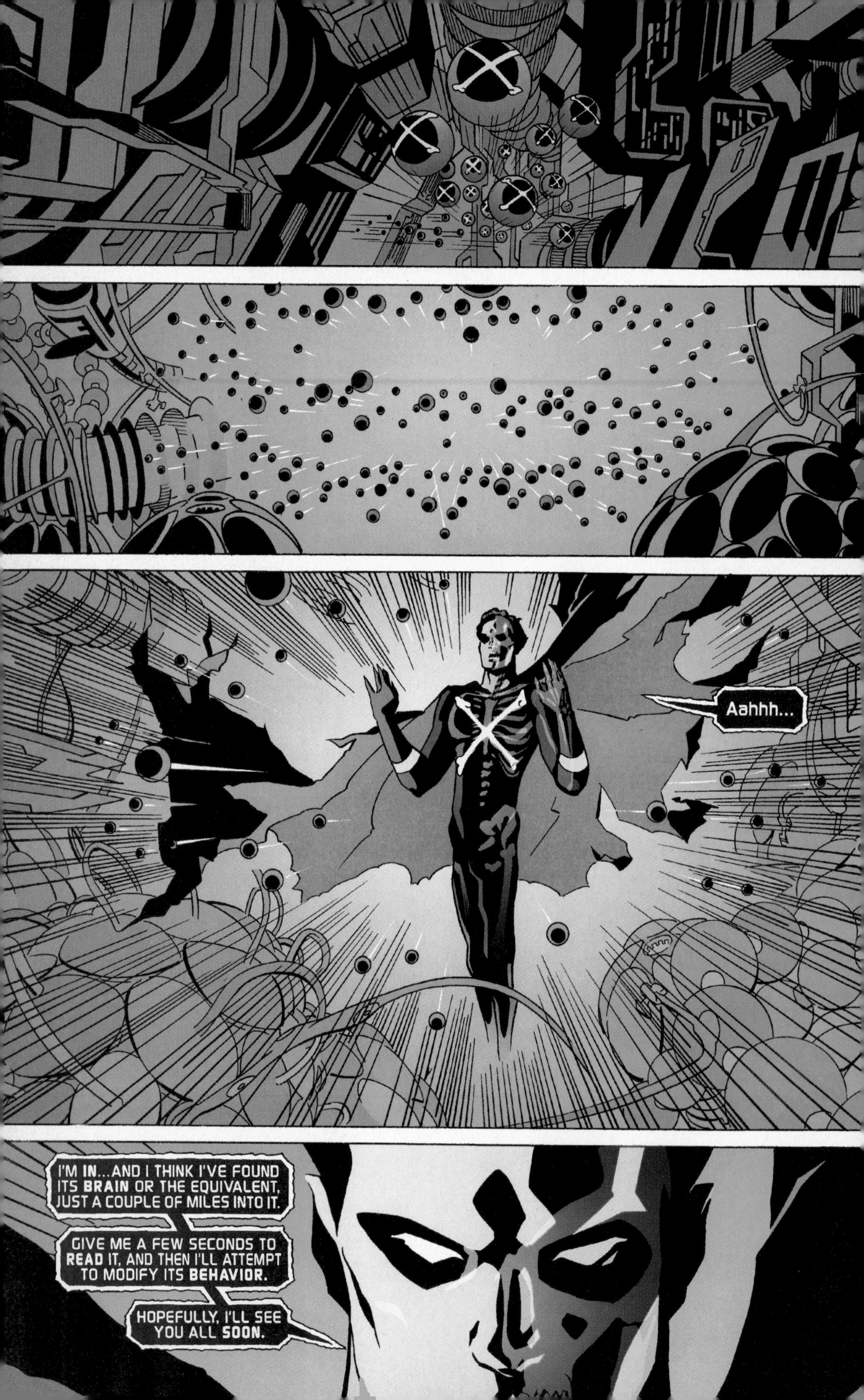
Aahhh...
I'M IN...AND I THINK I'VE FOUND ITS BRAIN OR THE EQUIVALENT, JUST A COUPLE OF MILES INTO IT.
GIVE ME A FEW SECONDS TO READ IT, AND THEN I'LL ATTEMPT TO MODIFY ITS BEHAVIOR.
HOPEFULLY, I'LL SEE YOU ALL SOON.

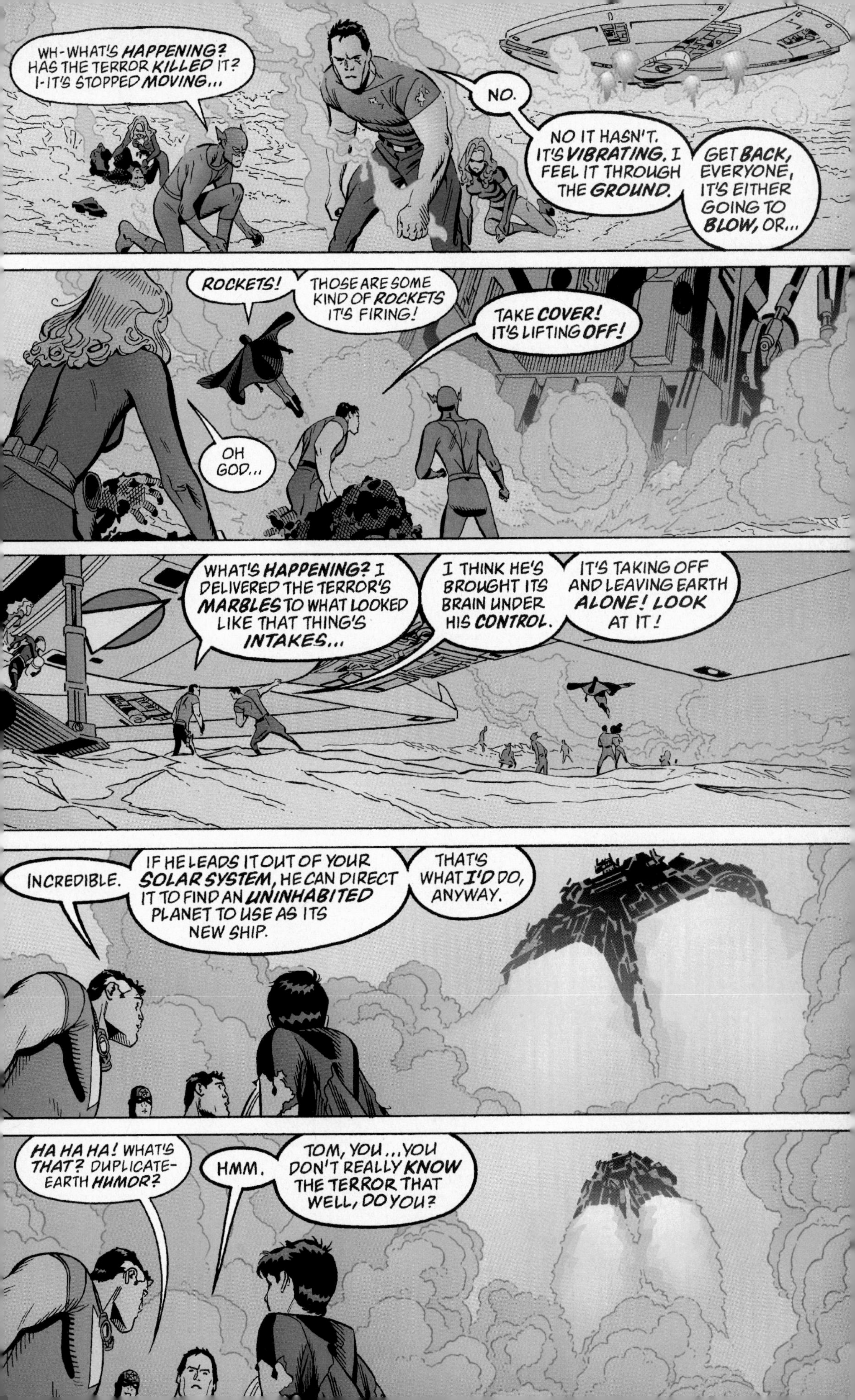

WH-WHAT'S HAPPENING? HAS THE TERROR KILLED IT? I-IT'S STOPPED MOVING...
NO.
NO IT HASN'T. IT'S VIBRATING. I FEEL IT THROUGH THE GROUND.
GET BACK, EVERYONE, IT'S EITHER GOING TO BLOW, OR...
ROCKETS!
THOSE ARE SOME KIND OF ROCKETS IT'S FIRING!
TAKE COVER! IT'S LIFTING OFF!
OH GOD...
WHAT'S HAPPENING? I DELIVERED THE TERROR'S MARBLES TO WHAT LOOKED LIKE THAT THING'S INTAKES...
I THINK HE'S BROUGHT ITS BRAIN UNDER HIS CONTROL.
IT'S TAKING OFF AND LEAVING EARTH ALONE! LOOK AT IT!
INCREDIBLE.
IF HE LEADS IT OUT OF YOUR SOLAR SYSTEM, HE CAN DIRECT IT TO FIND AN UNINHABITED PLANET TO USE AS ITS NEW SHIP.
THAT'S WHAT I'D DO, ANYWAY.
HA HA HA! WHAT'S THAT? DUPLICATE-EARTH HUMOR?
HMM.
TOM, YOU...YOU DON'T REALLY KNOW THE TERROR THAT WELL, DO YOU?

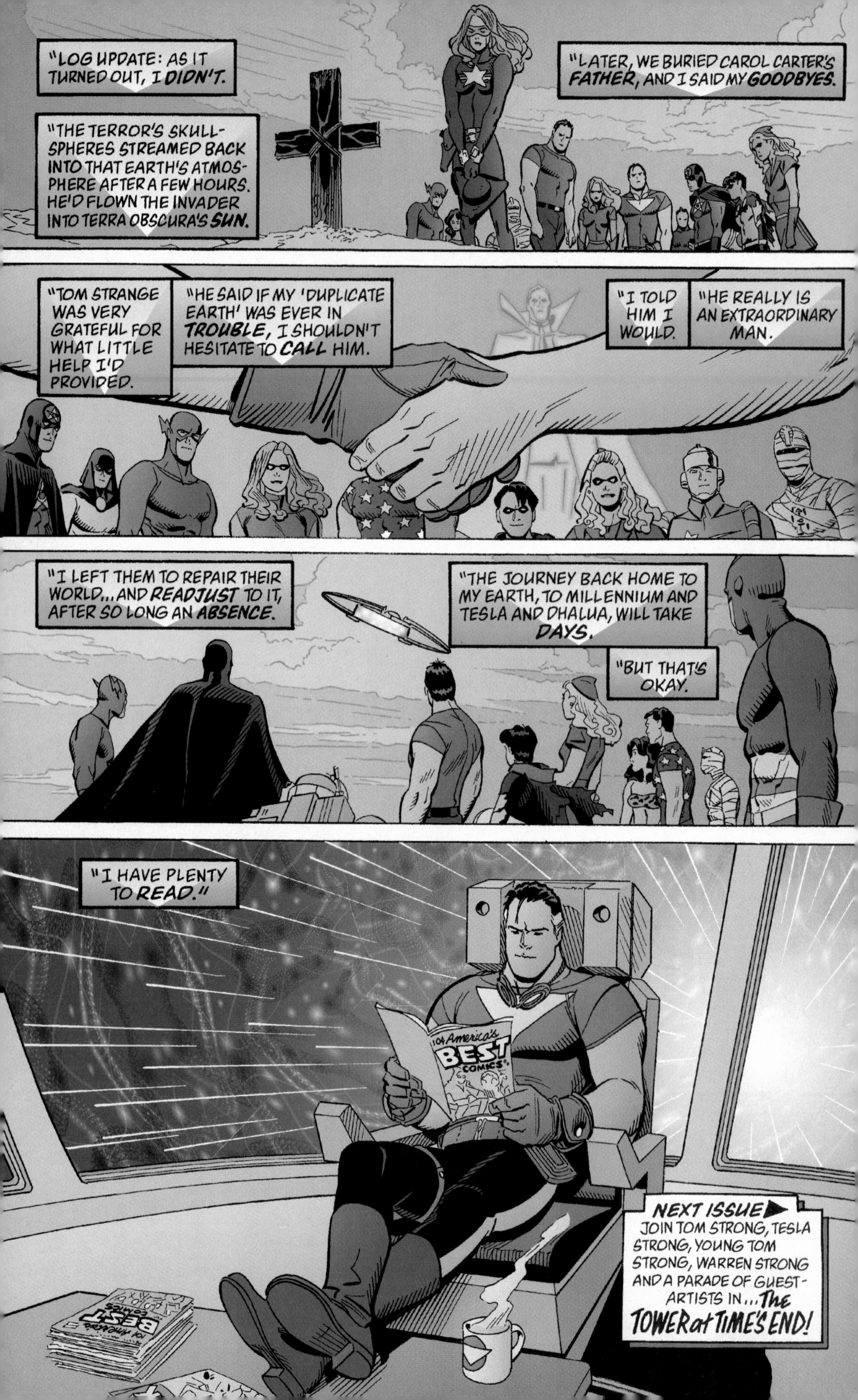
"LOG UPDATE: AS IT TURNED OUT, I DIDN'T.
"THE TERROR'S SKULL-SPHERES STREAMED BACK INTO THAT EARTH'S ATMOSPHERE AFTER A FEW HOURS. HE'D FLOWN THE INVADER INTO TERRA OBSCURA'S SUN.
"LATER, WE BURIED CAROL CARTER'S FATHER, AND I SAID MY GOODBYES.
"TOM STRANGE WAS VERY GRATEFUL FOR WHAT LITTLE HELP I'D PROVIDED.
"HE SAID IF MY 'DUPLICATE EARTH' WAS EVER IN TROUBLE, I SHOULDN'T HESITATE TO CALL HIM.
"I TOLD HIM I WOULD.
"HE REALLY IS AN EXTRAORDINARY MAN.
"I LEFT THEM TO REPAIR THEIR WORLD... AND READJUST TO IT, AFTER SO LONG AN ABSENCE.
"THE JOURNEY BACK HOME TO MY EARTH, TO MILLENNIUM AND TESLA AND DHALUA, WILL TAKE DAYS.
"BUT THAT'S OKAY.
"I HAVE PLENTY TO READ."
104 America's BEST COMICS
NEXT ISSUE ▶ JOIN TOM STRONG, TESLA STRONG, YOUNG TOM STRONG, WARREN STRONG AND A PARADE OF GUEST-ARTISTS IN... The TOWER at TIME'S END!

CHAPTER SIX

In which Tom and Tesla reach an embattled tower,
Young Tom and Warren Strong join the fray,
and the whole family runs out of time!

Cover art:
Chris Sprouse & Al Gordon

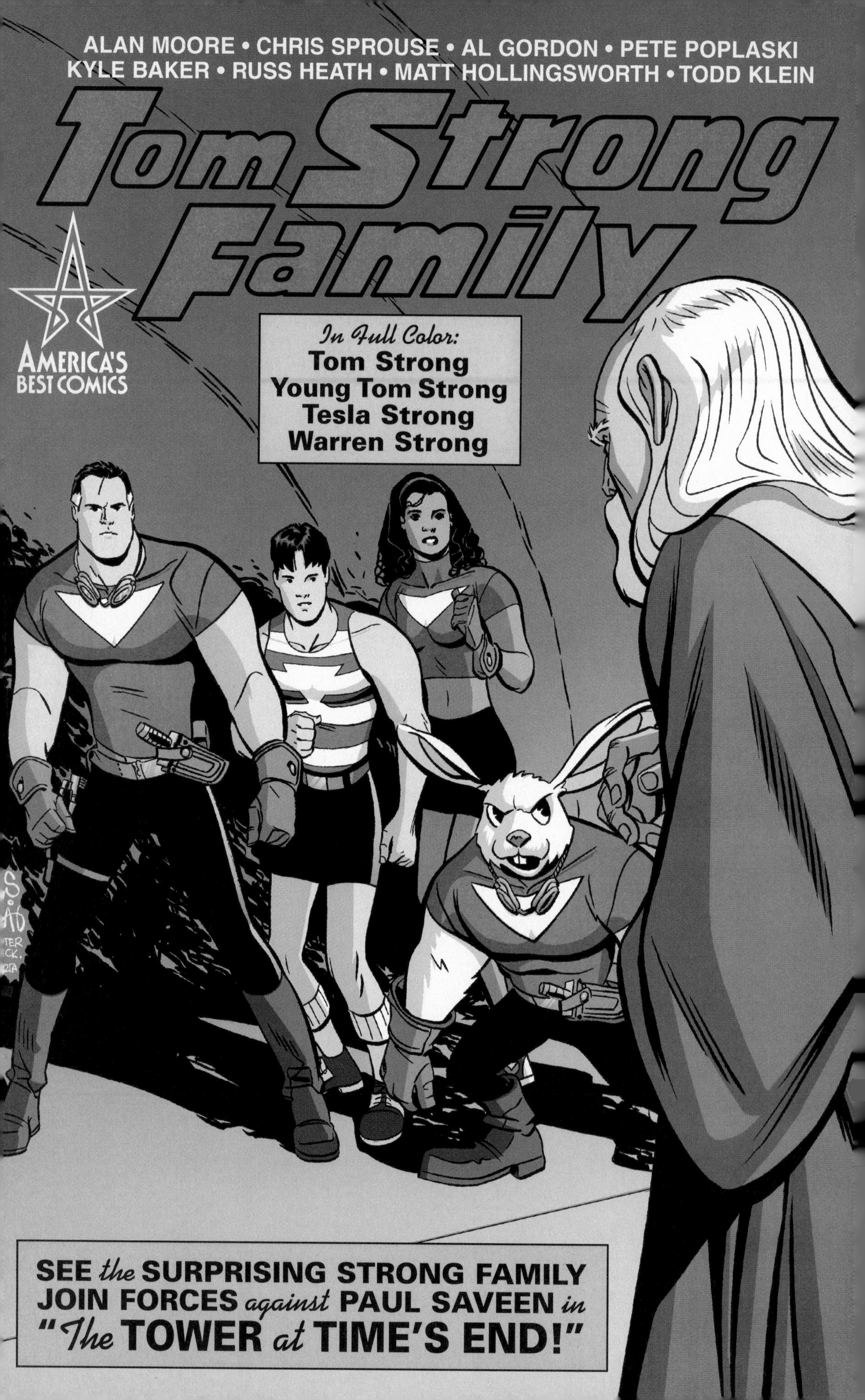

ALAN MOORE • CHRIS SPROUSE • AL GORDON • PETE POPLASKI
KYLE BAKER • RUSS HEATH • MATT HOLLINGSWORTH • TODD KLEIN
Tom Strong Family
AMERICA'S BEST COMICS
In Full Color:
Tom Strong
Young Tom Strong
Tesla Strong
Warren Strong
SEE the SURPRISING STRONG FAMILY
JOIN FORCES against PAUL SAVEEN in
"The TOWER at TIME'S END!"

WHOLESOME ENTERTAINMENT APPROVED READING

ALAN MOORE: writer · AL GORDON: inker, Sprouse Pages · TODD KLEIN: letters
MATT HOLLINGSWORTH: colors

The Family Strong

artists:
CHRIS SPROUSE
KYLE BAKER
RUSS HEATH
PETE POPLASKI

JEFF MARIOTTE: assistant editor
SCOTT DUNBIER: editor

MOORE & SPROUSE: creators

AND THE TOWER AT TIME'S END!

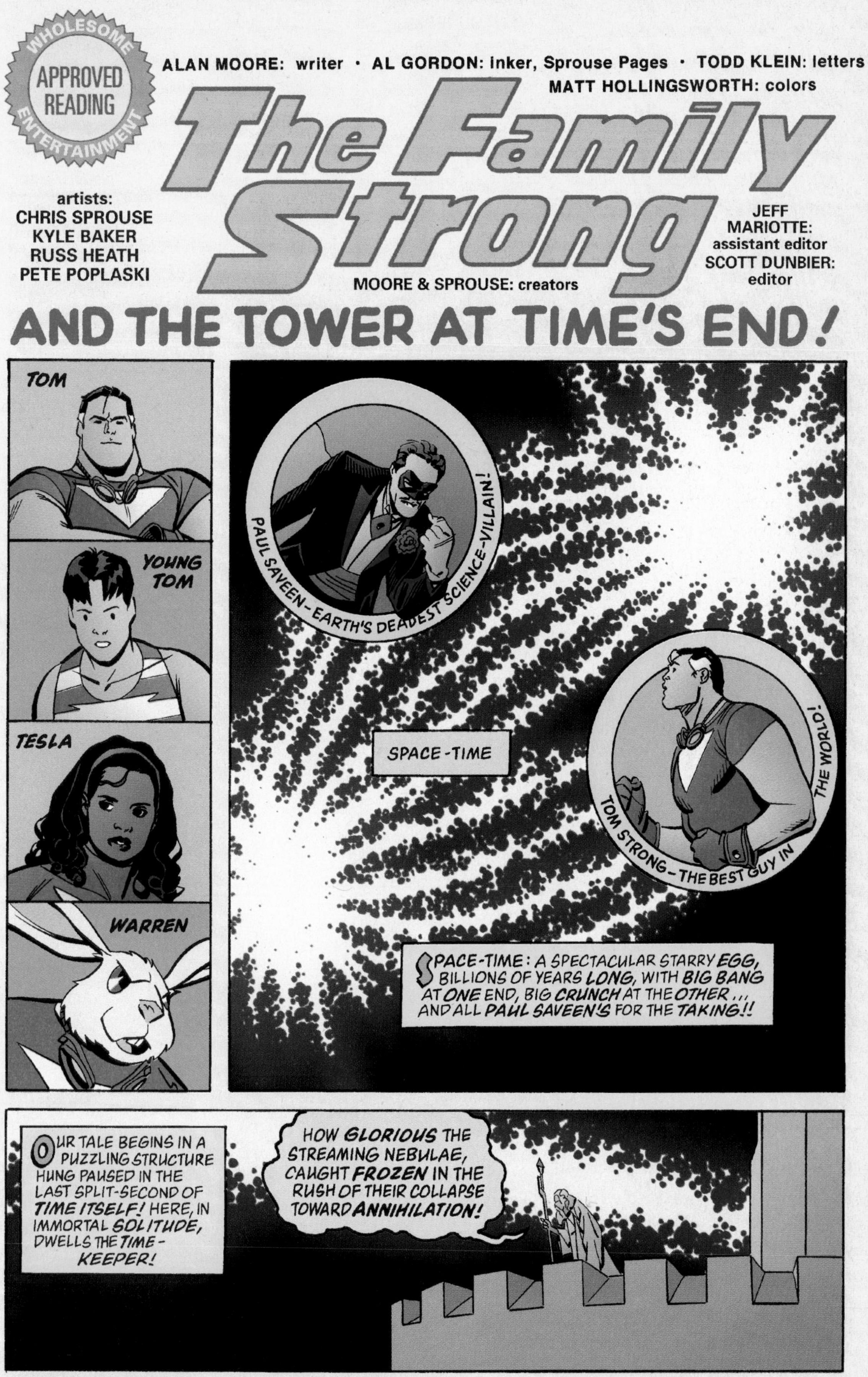
TOM
YOUNG TOM
TESLA
WARREN
PAUL SAVEEN - EARTH'S DEADEST SCIENCE-VILLAIN!
SPACE-TIME
TOM STRONG - THE BEST GUY IN THE WORLD!
SPACE-TIME: A SPECTACULAR STARRY EGG, BILLIONS OF YEARS LONG, WITH BIG BANG AT ONE END, BIG CRUNCH AT THE OTHER... AND ALL PAUL SAVEEN'S FOR THE TAKING!!
OUR TALE BEGINS IN A PUZZLING STRUCTURE HUNG PAUSED IN THE LAST SPLIT-SECOND OF TIME ITSELF! HERE, IN IMMORTAL SOLITUDE, DWELLS THE TIME-KEEPER!
HOW GLORIOUS THE STREAMING NEBULAE, CAUGHT FROZEN IN THE RUSH OF THEIR COLLAPSE TOWARD ANNIHILATION!

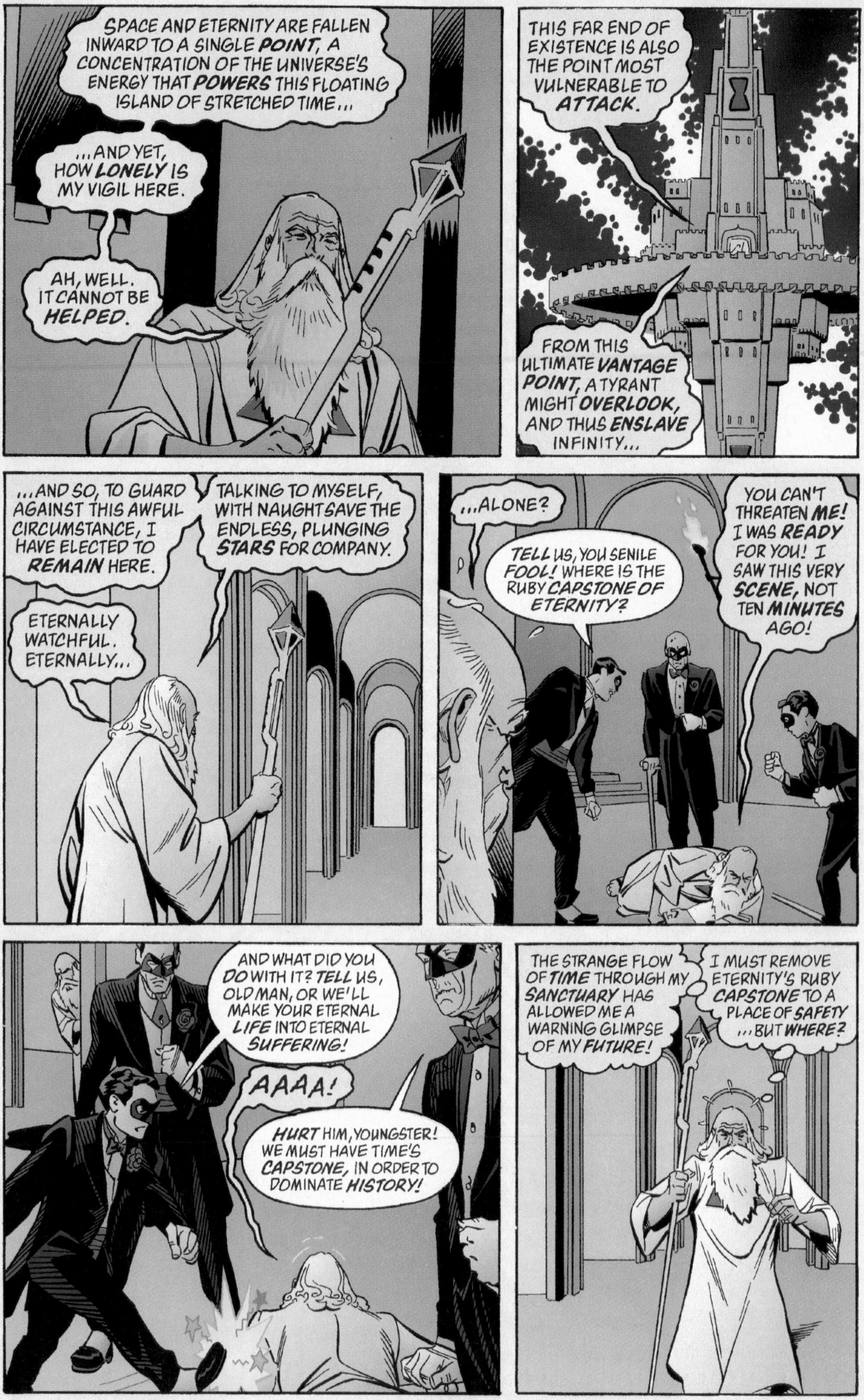

SPACE AND ETERNITY ARE FALLEN INWARD TO A SINGLE POINT, A CONCENTRATION OF THE UNIVERSE'S ENERGY THAT POWERS THIS FLOATING ISLAND OF STRETCHED TIME...
...AND YET, HOW LONELY IS MY VIGIL HERE.
AH, WELL. IT CANNOT BE HELPED.
THIS FAR END OF EXISTENCE IS ALSO THE POINT MOST VULNERABLE TO ATTACK.
FROM THIS ULTIMATE VANTAGE POINT, A TYRANT MIGHT OVERLOOK, AND THUS ENSLAVE INFINITY...
...AND SO, TO GUARD AGAINST THIS AWFUL CIRCUMSTANCE, I HAVE ELECTED TO REMAIN HERE.
TALKING TO MYSELF, WITH NAUGHT SAVE THE ENDLESS, PLUNGING STARS FOR COMPANY.
ETERNALLY WATCHFUL. ETERNALLY...
...ALONE?
TELL US, YOU SENILE FOOL! WHERE IS THE RUBY CAPSTONE OF ETERNITY?
YOU CAN'T THREATEN ME! I WAS READY FOR YOU! I SAW THIS VERY SCENE, NOT TEN MINUTES AGO!
AND WHAT DID YOU DO WITH IT? TELL US, OLD MAN, OR WE'LL MAKE YOUR ETERNAL LIFE INTO ETERNAL SUFFERING!
AAAA!
HURT HIM, YOUNGSTER! WE MUST HAVE TIME'S CAPSTONE, IN ORDER TO DOMINATE HISTORY!
THE STRANGE FLOW OF TIME THROUGH MY SANCTUARY HAS ALLOWED ME A WARNING GLIMPSE OF MY FUTURE!
I MUST REMOVE ETERNITY'S RUBY CAPSTONE TO A PLACE OF SAFETY ...BUT WHERE?

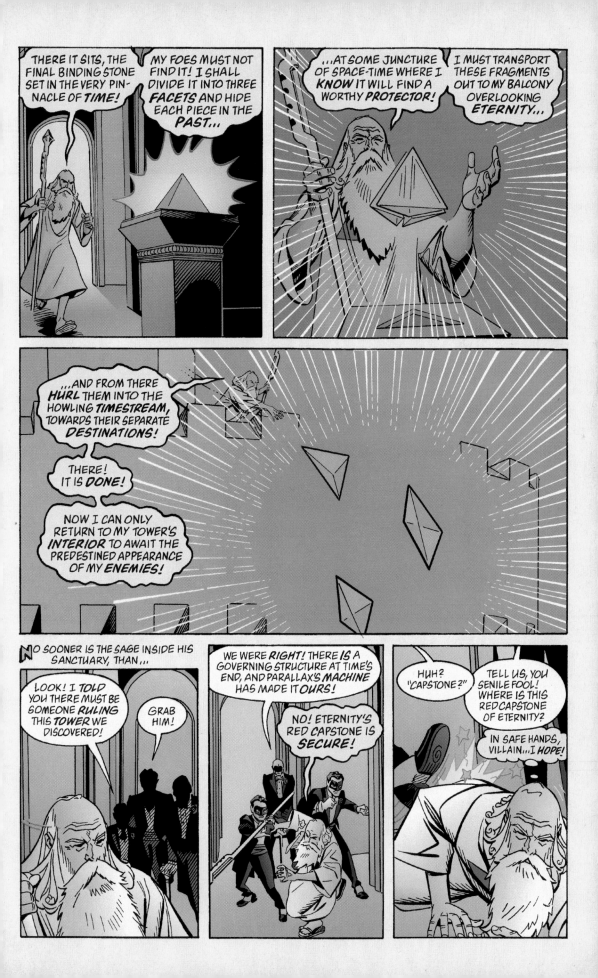

THERE IT SITS, THE FINAL BINDING STONE SET IN THE VERY PINNACLE OF *TIME!*

MY FOES MUST NOT FIND IT! I SHALL DIVIDE IT INTO THREE *FACETS* AND HIDE EACH PIECE IN THE *PAST...*

...AT SOME JUNCTURE OF SPACE-TIME WHERE I *KNOW* IT WILL FIND A WORTHY *PROTECTOR!*

I MUST TRANSPORT THESE FRAGMENTS OUT TO MY BALCONY OVERLOOKING *ETERNITY...*

...AND FROM THERE *HURL* THEM INTO THE HOWLING *TIMESTREAM,* TOWARDS THEIR SEPARATE *DESTINATIONS!*

THERE! IT IS *DONE!*

NOW I CAN ONLY RETURN TO MY TOWER'S *INTERIOR* TO AWAIT THE PREDESTINED APPEARANCE OF MY *ENEMIES!*

NO SOONER IS THE SAGE INSIDE HIS SANCTUARY, THAN...

LOOK! I *TOLD* YOU THERE MUST BE SOMEONE *RULING* THIS *TOWER* WE DISCOVERED!

GRAB HIM!

WE WERE *RIGHT!* THERE *IS* A GOVERNING STRUCTURE AT TIME'S END, AND PARALLAX'S *MACHINE* HAS MADE IT *OURS!*

NO! ETERNITY'S RED CAPSTONE IS *SECURE!*

HUH? "CAPSTONE?"

TELL US, YOU SENILE FOOL! WHERE IS THIS RED CAPSTONE OF ETERNITY?

IN SAFE HANDS, VILLAIN...I *HOPE!*

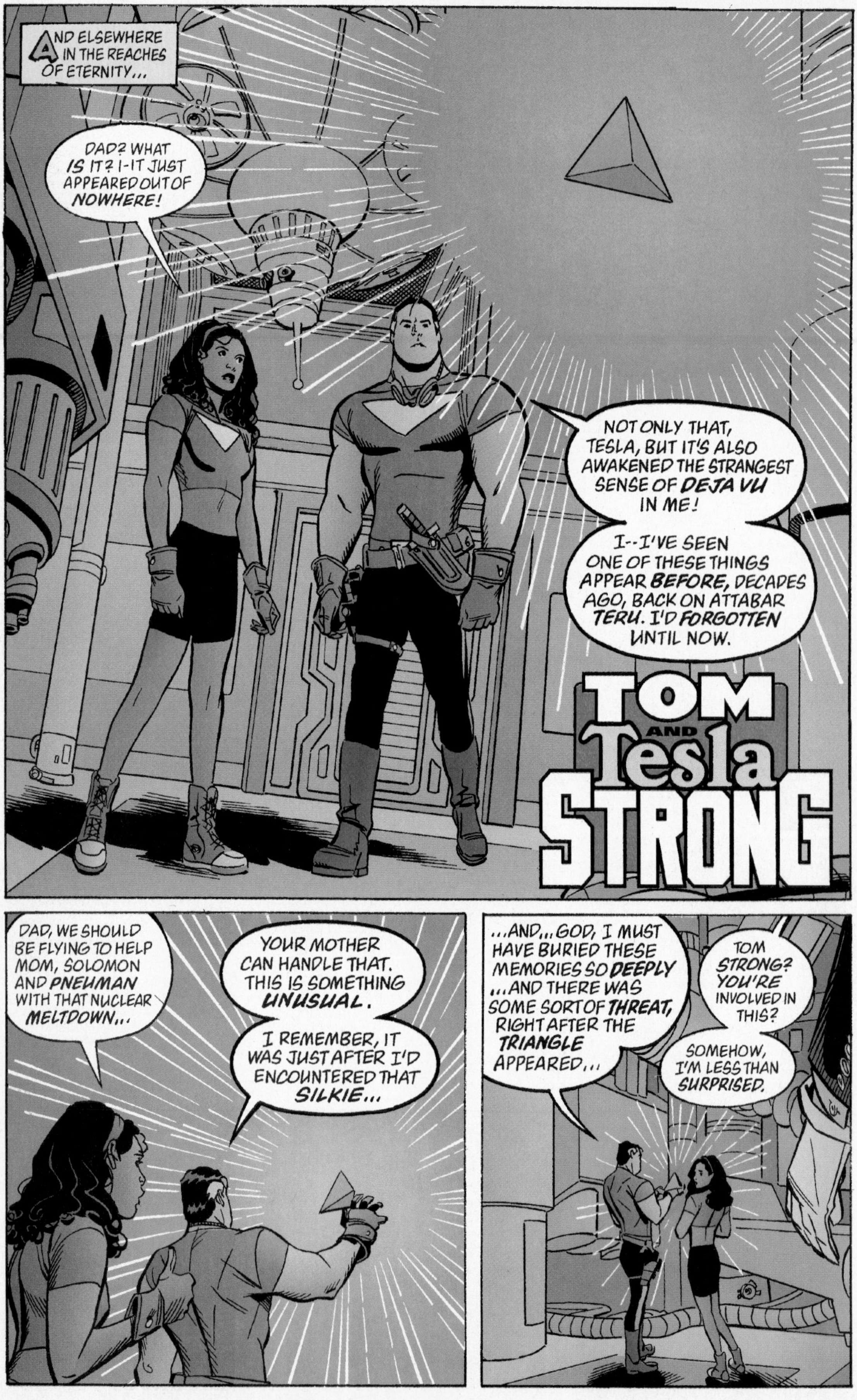
AND ELSEWHERE IN THE REACHES OF ETERNITY...
DAD? WHAT IS IT? I-IT JUST APPEARED OUT OF NOWHERE!
NOT ONLY THAT, TESLA, BUT IT'S ALSO AWAKENED THE STRANGEST SENSE OF DEJA VU IN ME!
I--I'VE SEEN ONE OF THESE THINGS APPEAR BEFORE, DECADES AGO, BACK ON ATTABAR TERU. I'D FORGOTTEN UNTIL NOW.
TOM AND Tesla STRONG
DAD, WE SHOULD BE FLYING TO HELP MOM, SOLOMON AND PNEUMAN WITH THAT NUCLEAR MELTDOWN...
YOUR MOTHER CAN HANDLE THAT. THIS IS SOMETHING UNUSUAL.
I REMEMBER, IT WAS JUST AFTER I'D ENCOUNTERED THAT SILKIE...
...AND... GOD, I MUST HAVE BURIED THESE MEMORIES SO DEEPLY ...AND THERE WAS SOME SORT OF THREAT, RIGHT AFTER THE TRIANGLE APPEARED...
TOM STRONG? YOU'RE INVOLVED IN THIS?
SOMEHOW, I'M LESS THAN SURPRISED.

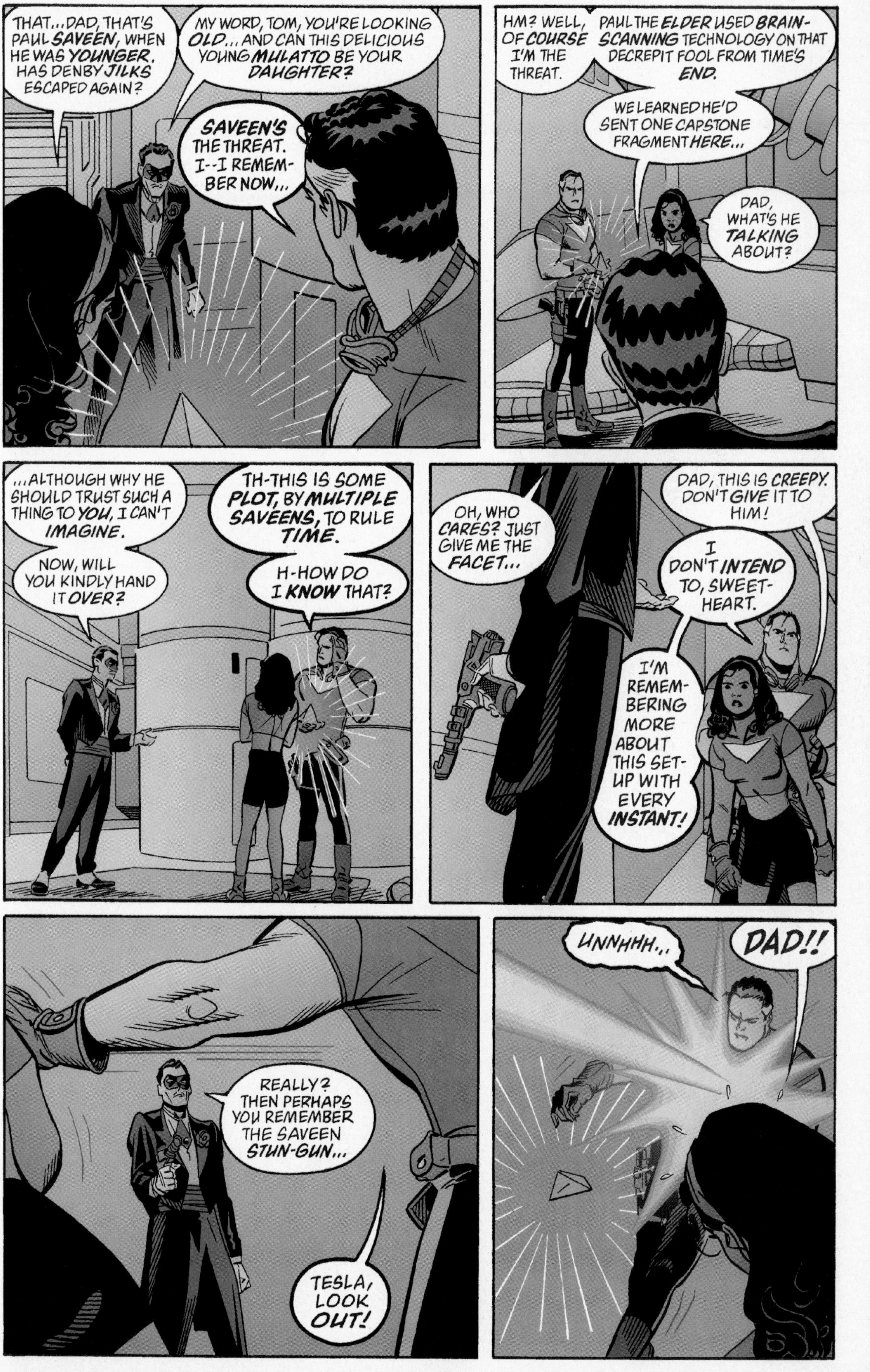
THAT...DAD, THAT'S PAUL SAVEEN, WHEN HE WAS YOUNGER. HAS DENBY JILKS ESCAPED AGAIN?
MY WORD, TOM, YOU'RE LOOKING OLD... AND CAN THIS DELICIOUS YOUNG MULATTO BE YOUR DAUGHTER?
SAVEEN'S THE THREAT. I--I REMEMBER NOW...
HM? WELL, OF COURSE I'M THE THREAT.
PAUL THE ELDER USED BRAIN-SCANNING TECHNOLOGY ON THAT DECREPIT FOOL FROM TIME'S END.
WE LEARNED HE'D SENT ONE CAPSTONE FRAGMENT HERE...
DAD, WHAT'S HE TALKING ABOUT?
...ALTHOUGH WHY HE SHOULD TRUST SUCH A THING TO YOU, I CAN'T IMAGINE.
NOW, WILL YOU KINDLY HAND IT OVER?
TH-THIS IS SOME PLOT, BY MULTIPLE SAVEENS, TO RULE TIME.
H-HOW DO I KNOW THAT?
OH, WHO CARES? JUST GIVE ME THE FACET...
DAD, THIS IS CREEPY. DON'T GIVE IT TO HIM!
I DON'T INTEND TO, SWEETHEART.
I'M REMEMBERING MORE ABOUT THIS SET-UP WITH EVERY INSTANT!
REALLY? THEN PERHAPS YOU REMEMBER THE SAVEEN STUN-GUN...
TESLA, LOOK OUT!
UNNHHH...
DAD!!

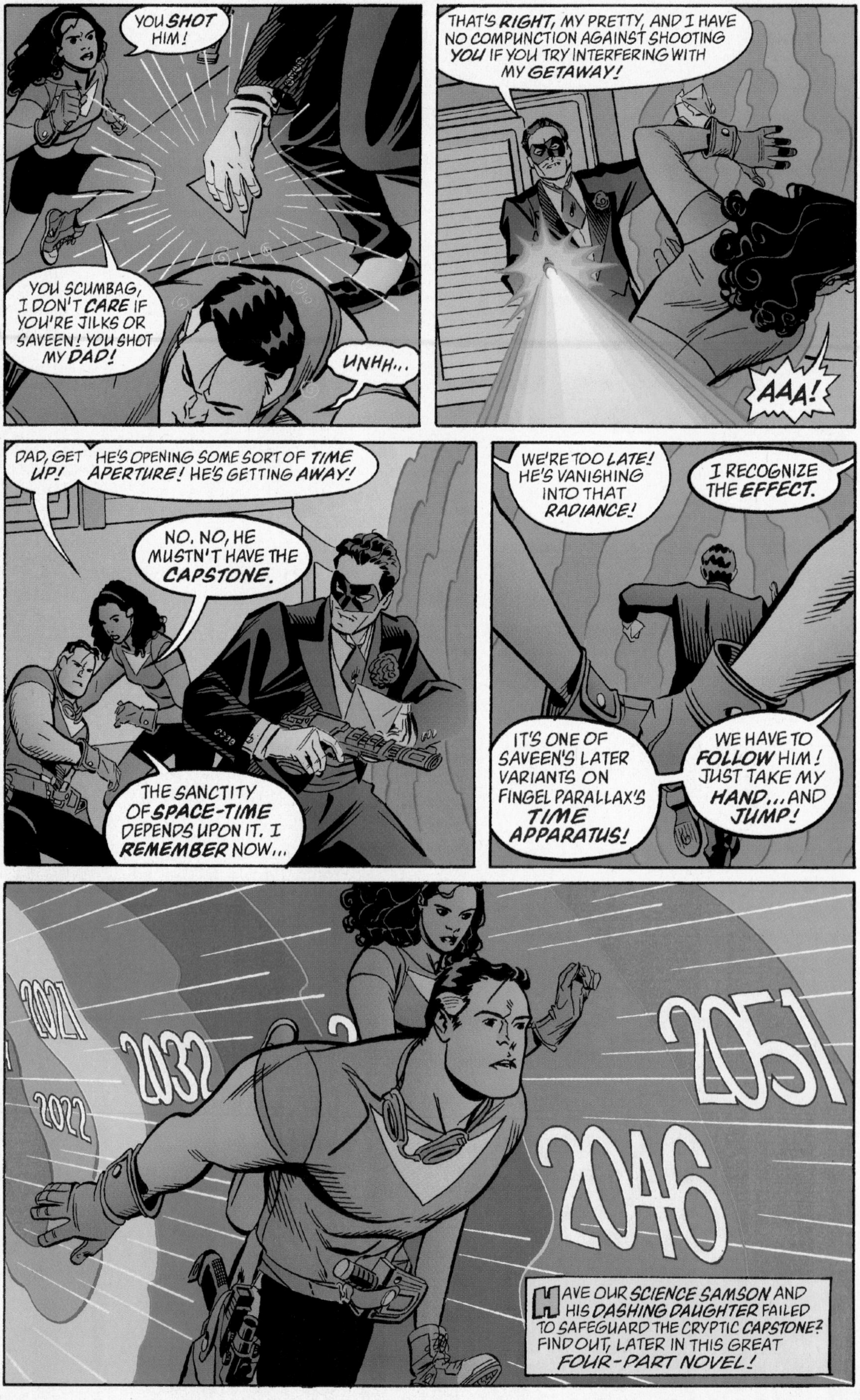
YOU SHOT HIM!
YOU SCUMBAG, I DON'T CARE IF YOU'RE JILKS OR SAVEEN! YOU SHOT MY DAD!
UNHH...
THAT'S RIGHT, MY PRETTY, AND I HAVE NO COMPUNCTION AGAINST SHOOTING YOU IF YOU TRY INTERFERING WITH MY GETAWAY!
AAA!
DAD, GET UP!
HE'S OPENING SOME SORT OF TIME APERTURE! HE'S GETTING AWAY!
NO. NO, HE MUSTN'T HAVE THE CAPSTONE.
THE SANCTITY OF SPACE-TIME DEPENDS UPON IT. I REMEMBER NOW...
WE'RE TOO LATE! HE'S VANISHING INTO THAT RADIANCE!
I RECOGNIZE THE EFFECT.
IT'S ONE OF SAVEEN'S LATER VARIANTS ON FINGEL PARALLAX'S TIME APPARATUS!
WE HAVE TO FOLLOW HIM! JUST TAKE MY HAND...AND JUMP!
2021
2032
2022
2051
2046
HAVE OUR SCIENCE SAMSON AND HIS DASHING DAUGHTER FAILED TO SAFEGUARD THE CRYPTIC CAPSTONE? FIND OUT, LATER IN THIS GREAT FOUR-PART NOVEL!

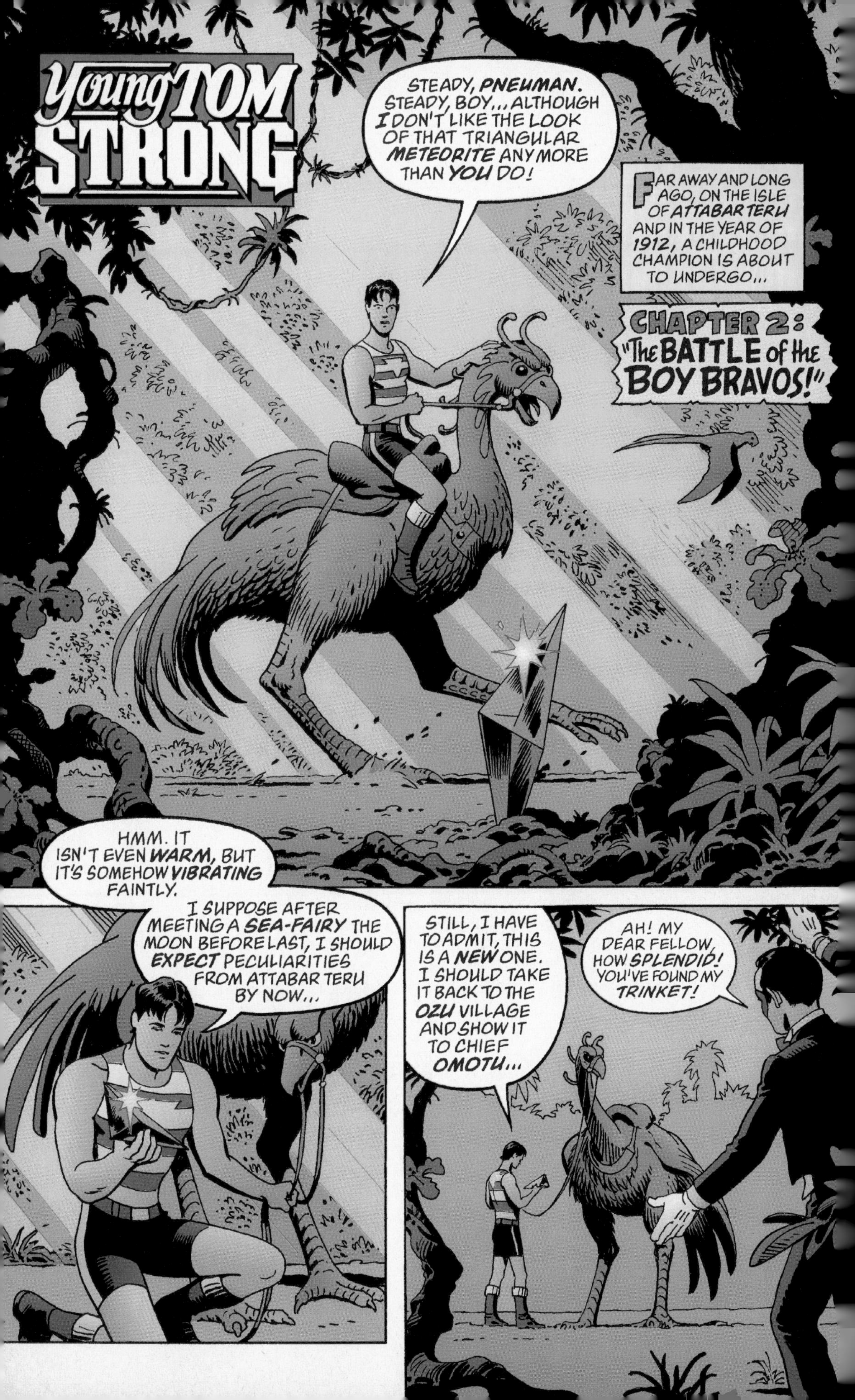
Young TOM STRONG
STEADY, PNEUMAN. STEADY, BOY... ALTHOUGH I DON'T LIKE THE LOOK OF THAT TRIANGULAR METEORITE ANY MORE THAN YOU DO!
FAR AWAY AND LONG AGO, ON THE ISLE OF ATTABAR TERU AND IN THE YEAR OF 1912, A CHILDHOOD CHAMPION IS ABOUT TO UNDERGO...
CHAPTER 2: "The BATTLE of the BOY BRAVOS!"
HMM. IT ISN'T EVEN WARM, BUT IT'S SOMEHOW VIBRATING FAINTLY.
I SUPPOSE AFTER MEETING A SEA-FAIRY THE MOON BEFORE LAST, I SHOULD EXPECT PECULIARITIES FROM ATTABAR TERU BY NOW...
STILL, I HAVE TO ADMIT, THIS IS A NEW ONE. I SHOULD TAKE IT BACK TO THE OZU VILLAGE AND SHOW IT TO CHIEF OMOTU...
AH! MY DEAR FELLOW, HOW SPLENDID! YOU'VE FOUND MY TRINKET!

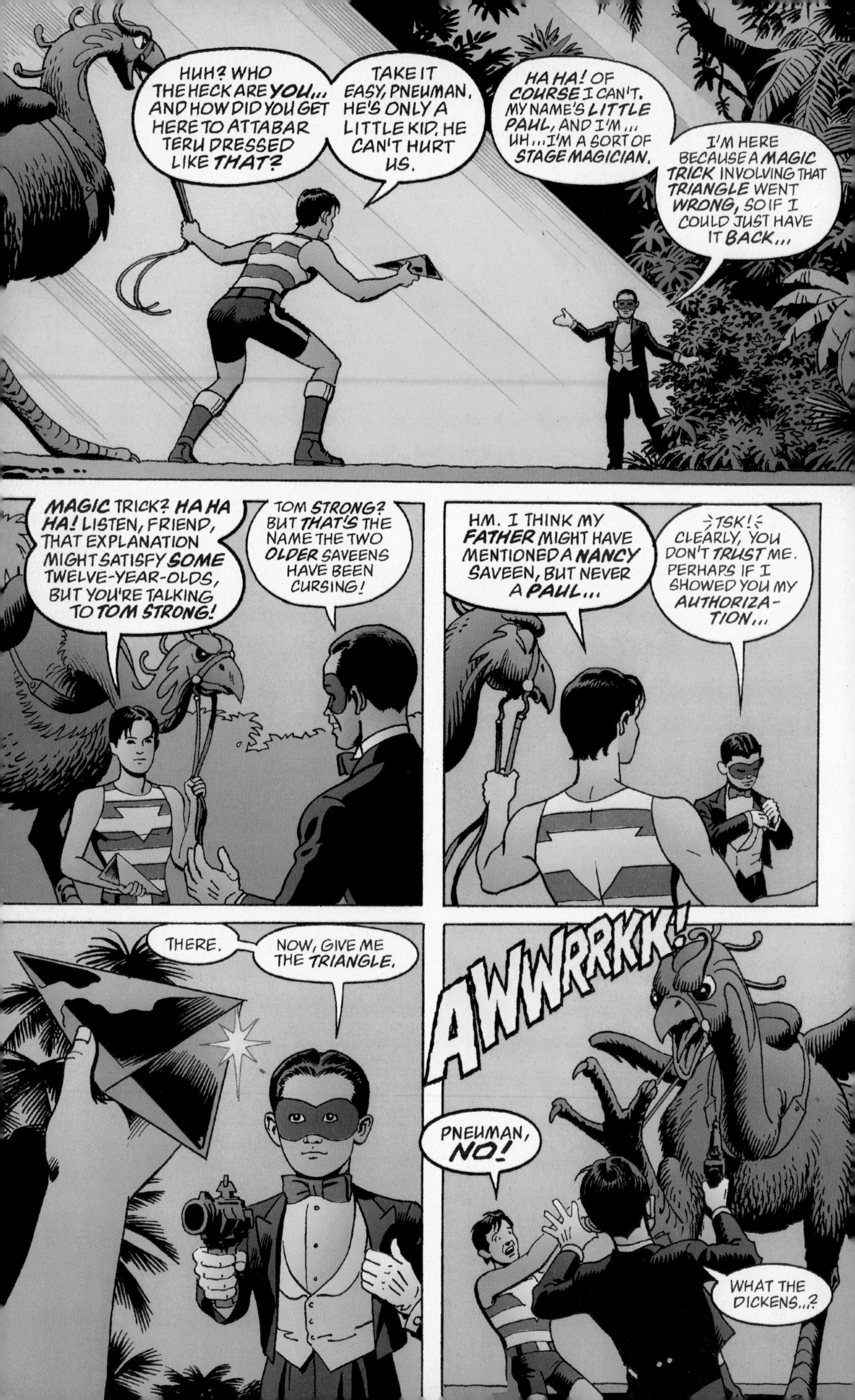
HUH? WHO THE HECK ARE YOU... AND HOW DID YOU GET HERE TO ATTABAR TERU DRESSED LIKE THAT?
TAKE IT EASY, PNEUMAN. HE'S ONLY A LITTLE KID. HE CAN'T HURT US.
HA HA! OF COURSE I CAN'T. MY NAME'S LITTLE PAUL, AND I'M... UH... I'M A SORT OF STAGE MAGICIAN.
I'M HERE BECAUSE A MAGIC TRICK INVOLVING THAT TRIANGLE WENT WRONG, SO IF I COULD JUST HAVE IT BACK...
MAGIC TRICK? HA HA HA! LISTEN, FRIEND, THAT EXPLANATION MIGHT SATISFY SOME TWELVE-YEAR-OLDS, BUT YOU'RE TALKING TO TOM STRONG!
TOM STRONG? BUT THAT'S THE NAME THE TWO OLDER SAVEENS HAVE BEEN CURSING!
HM. I THINK MY FATHER MIGHT HAVE MENTIONED A NANCY SAVEEN, BUT NEVER A PAUL...
TSK! CLEARLY, YOU DON'T TRUST ME. PERHAPS IF I SHOWED YOU MY AUTHORIZATION...
THERE.
NOW, GIVE ME THE TRIANGLE.
AWWRRKK!
PNEUMAN, NO!
WHAT THE DICKENS...?

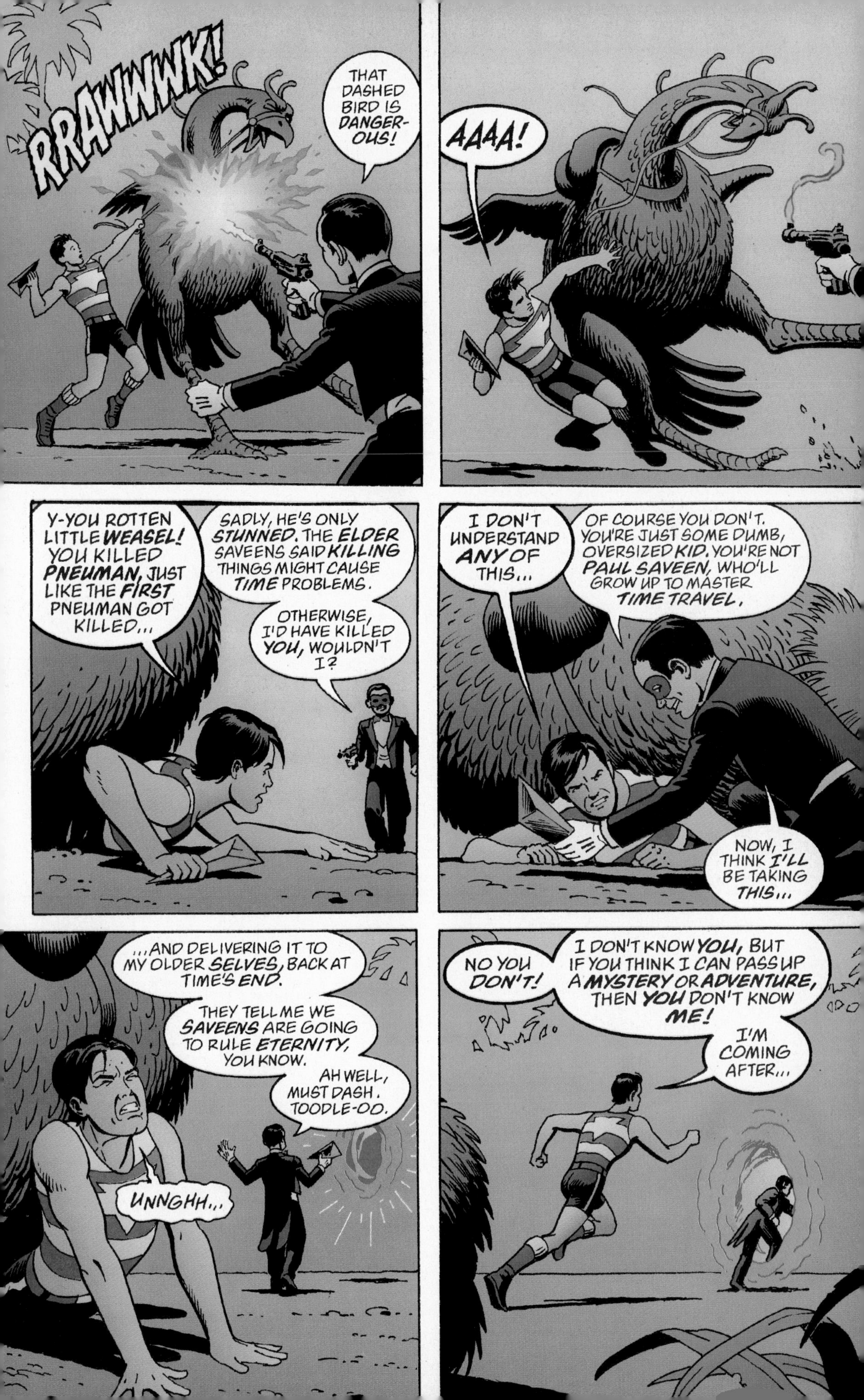
RRAWWWK!
THAT DASHED BIRD IS DANGER-OUS!
AAAA!
Y-YOU ROTTEN LITTLE WEASEL! YOU KILLED PNEUMAN, JUST LIKE THE FIRST PNEUMAN GOT KILLED...
SADLY, HE'S ONLY STUNNED. THE ELDER SAVEENS SAID KILLING THINGS MIGHT CAUSE TIME PROBLEMS.
OTHERWISE, I'D HAVE KILLED YOU, WOULDN'T I?
I DON'T UNDERSTAND ANY OF THIS...
OF COURSE YOU DON'T. YOU'RE JUST SOME DUMB, OVERSIZED KID. YOU'RE NOT PAUL SAVEEN, WHO'LL GROW UP TO MASTER TIME TRAVEL.
NOW, I THINK I'LL BE TAKING THIS...
...AND DELIVERING IT TO MY OLDER SELVES, BACK AT TIME'S END.
THEY TELL ME WE SAVEENS ARE GOING TO RULE ETERNITY, YOU KNOW.
AH WELL, MUST DASH. TOODLE-OO.
UNNGHH...
NO YOU DON'T!
I DON'T KNOW YOU, BUT IF YOU THINK I CAN PASS UP A MYSTERY OR ADVENTURE, THEN YOU DON'T KNOW ME!
I'M COMING AFTER...

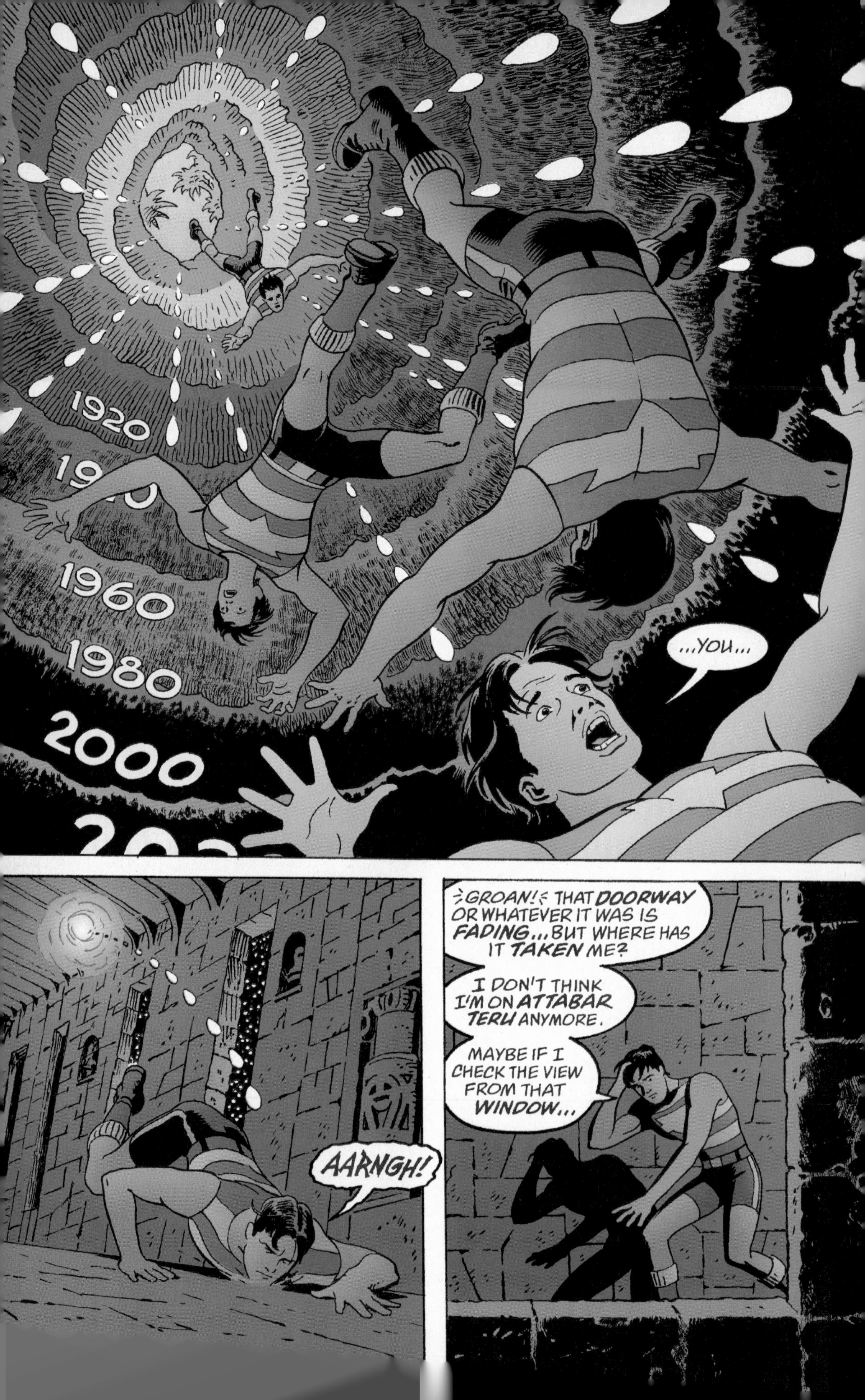
1920
1960
1980
2000
...YOU...
AARNGH!
GROAN! THAT DOORWAY OR WHATEVER IT WAS IS FADING... BUT WHERE HAS IT TAKEN ME?
I DON'T THINK I'M ON ATTABAR TERU ANYMORE.
MAYBE IF I CHECK THE VIEW FROM THAT WINDOW...

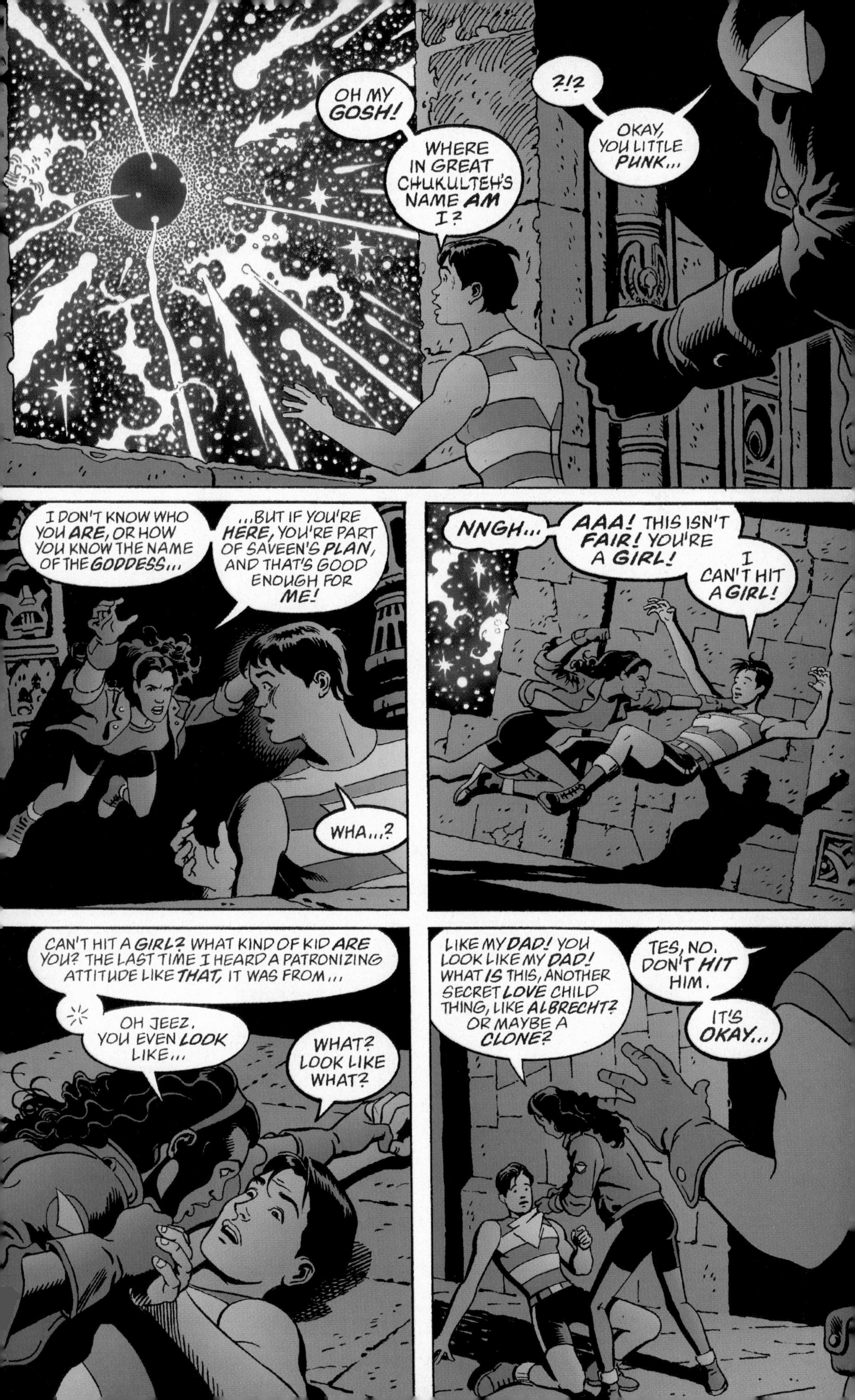
OH MY GOSH!
WHERE IN GREAT CHUKULTEH'S NAME AM I?
?!?
OKAY, YOU LITTLE PUNK...
I DON'T KNOW WHO YOU ARE, OR HOW YOU KNOW THE NAME OF THE GODDESS...
...BUT IF YOU'RE HERE, YOU'RE PART OF SAVEEN'S PLAN, AND THAT'S GOOD ENOUGH FOR ME!
WHA...?
NNGH...
AAA! THIS ISN'T FAIR! YOU'RE A GIRL!
I CAN'T HIT A GIRL!
CAN'T HIT A GIRL? WHAT KIND OF KID ARE YOU? THE LAST TIME I HEARD A PATRONIZING ATTITUDE LIKE THAT, IT WAS FROM...
OH JEEZ. YOU EVEN LOOK LIKE...
WHAT? LOOK LIKE WHAT?
LIKE MY DAD! YOU LOOK LIKE MY DAD! WHAT IS THIS, ANOTHER SECRET LOVE CHILD THING, LIKE ALBRECHT? OR MAYBE A CLONE?
TES, NO. DON'T HIT HIM.
IT'S OKAY...

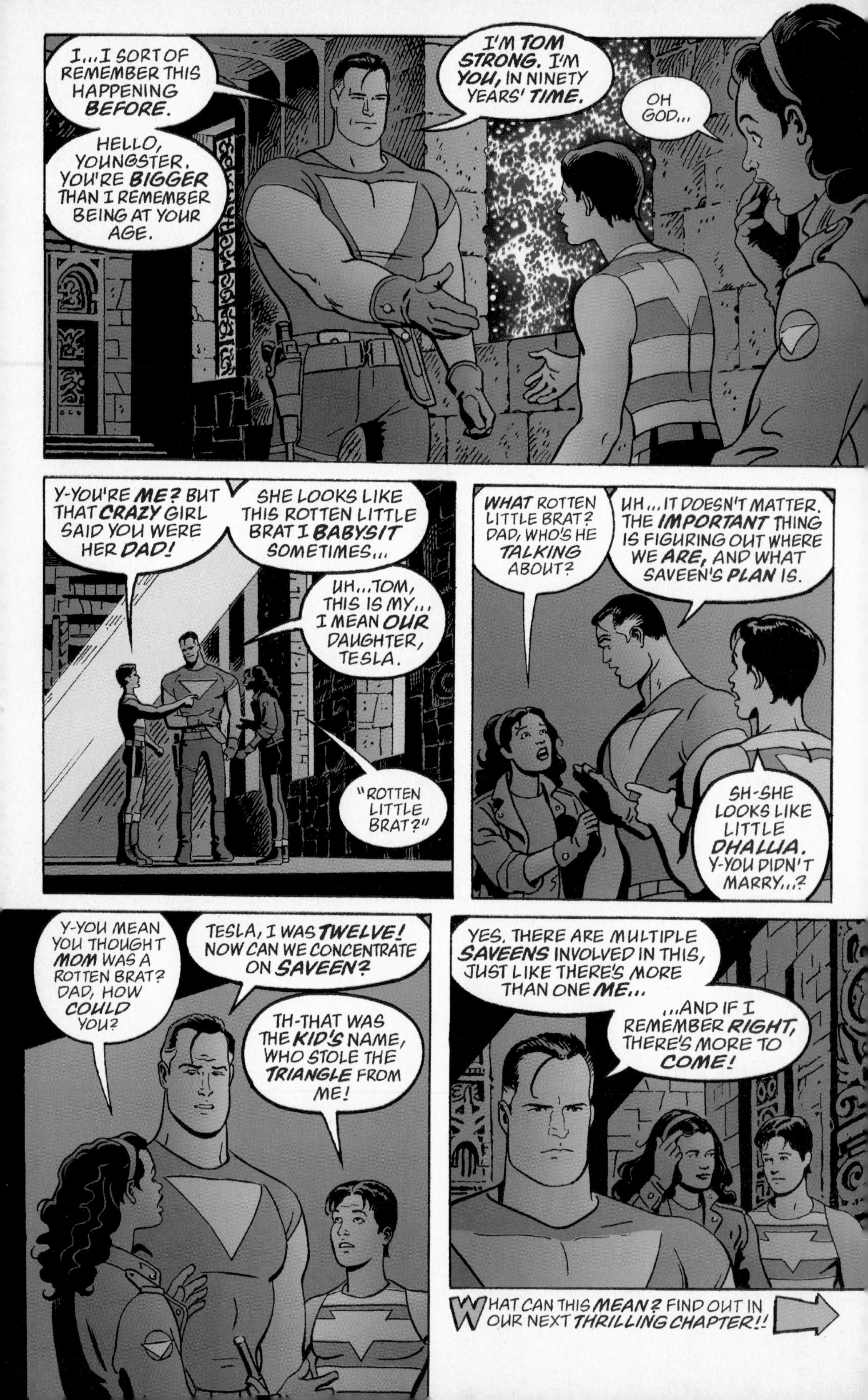
I... I SORT OF REMEMBER THIS HAPPENING BEFORE.
HELLO, YOUNGSTER. YOU'RE BIGGER THAN I REMEMBER BEING AT YOUR AGE.
I'M TOM STRONG. I'M YOU, IN NINETY YEARS' TIME.
OH GOD...
Y-YOU'RE ME? BUT THAT CRAZY GIRL SAID YOU WERE HER DAD!
SHE LOOKS LIKE THIS ROTTEN LITTLE BRAT I BABYSIT SOMETIMES...
UH... TOM, THIS IS MY... I MEAN OUR DAUGHTER, TESLA.
"ROTTEN LITTLE BRAT?"
WHAT ROTTEN LITTLE BRAT? DAD, WHO'S HE TALKING ABOUT?
UH... IT DOESN'T MATTER. THE IMPORTANT THING IS FIGURING OUT WHERE WE ARE, AND WHAT SAVEEN'S PLAN IS.
SH-SHE LOOKS LIKE LITTLE DHALLIA. Y-YOU DIDN'T MARRY...?
Y-YOU MEAN YOU THOUGHT MOM WAS A ROTTEN BRAT? DAD, HOW COULD YOU?
TESLA, I WAS TWELVE! NOW CAN WE CONCENTRATE ON SAVEEN?
TH-THAT WAS THE KID'S NAME, WHO STOLE THE TRIANGLE FROM ME!
YES. THERE ARE MULTIPLE SAVEENS INVOLVED IN THIS, JUST LIKE THERE'S MORE THAN ONE ME...
...AND IF I REMEMBER RIGHT, THERE'S MORE TO COME!
WHAT CAN THIS MEAN? FIND OUT IN OUR NEXT THRILLING CHAPTER!!

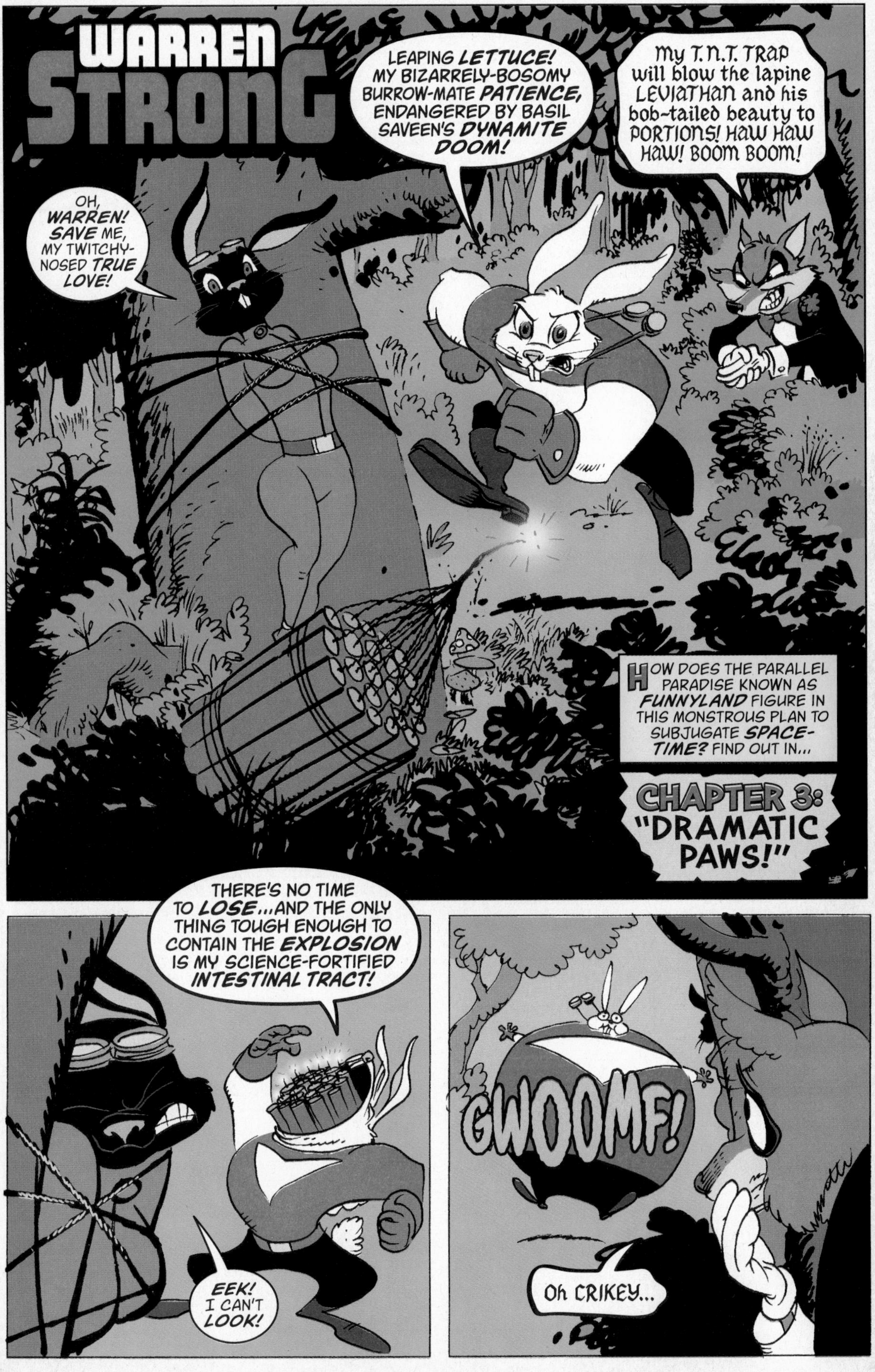

WARREN STRONG
LEAPING LETTUCE! MY BIZARRELY-BOSOMY BURROW-MATE PATIENCE, ENDANGERED BY BASIL SAVEEN'S DYNAMITE DOOM!
My T.N.T. TRAP will blow the lapine LEVIATHAN and his bob-tailed beauty to PORTIONS! HAW HAW HAW! BOOM BOOM!
OH, WARREN! SAVE ME, MY TWITCHY-NOSED TRUE LOVE!
HOW DOES THE PARALLEL PARADISE KNOWN AS FUNNYLAND FIGURE IN THIS MONSTROUS PLAN TO SUBJUGATE SPACE-TIME? FIND OUT IN...
CHAPTER 3: "DRAMATIC PAWS!"
THERE'S NO TIME TO LOSE...AND THE ONLY THING TOUGH ENOUGH TO CONTAIN THE EXPLOSION IS MY SCIENCE-FORTIFIED INTESTINAL TRACT!
EEK! I CAN'T LOOK!
GWOOMF!
Oh CRIKEY...

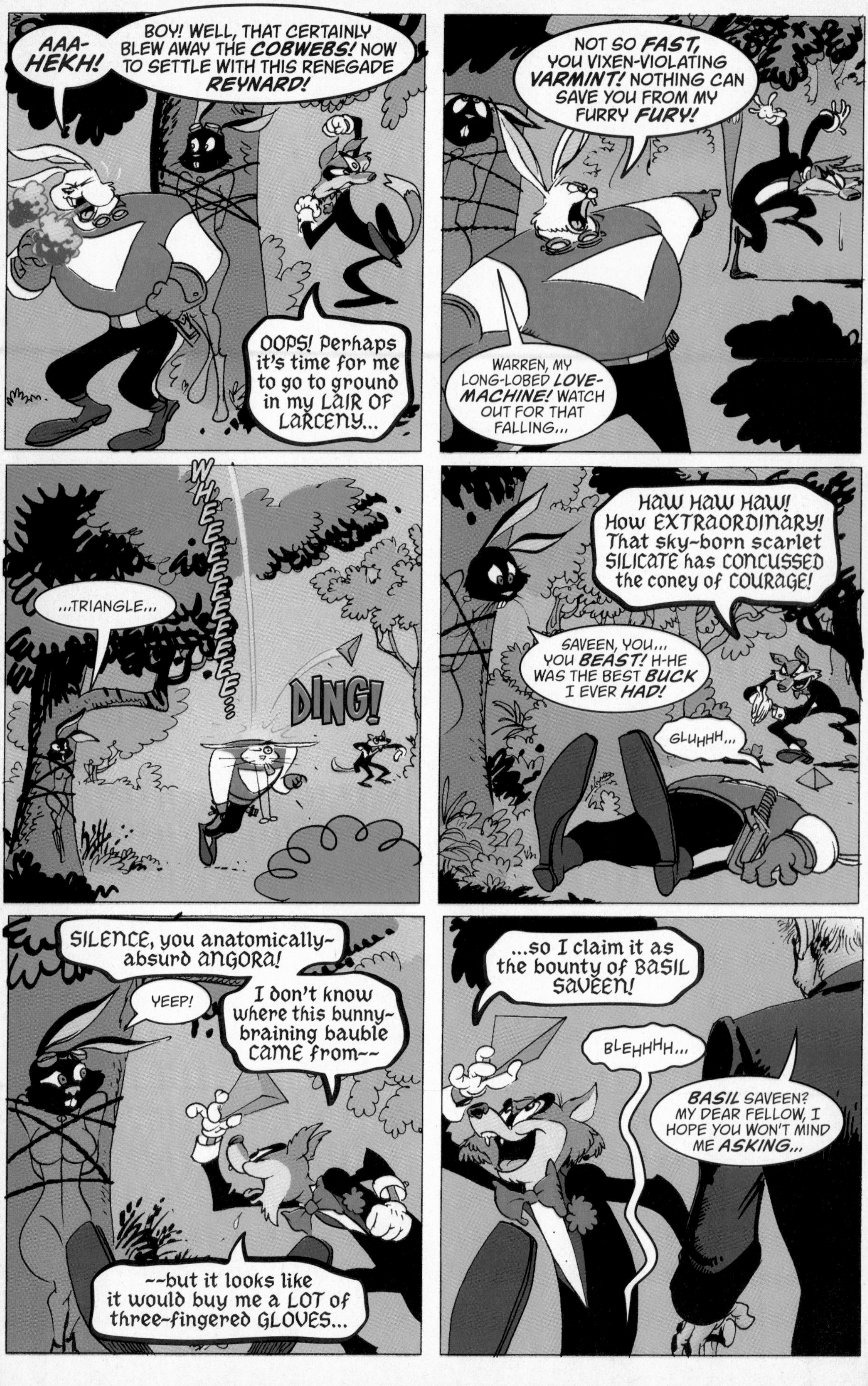
AAA-HEKH!
BOY! WELL, THAT CERTAINLY BLEW AWAY THE COBWEBS! NOW TO SETTLE WITH THIS RENEGADE REYNARD!
OOPS! Perhaps it's time for me to go to ground in my LAIR OF LARCENY...
NOT SO FAST, YOU VIXEN-VIOLATING VARMINT! NOTHING CAN SAVE YOU FROM MY FURRY FURY!
WARREN, MY LONG-LOBED LOVE-MACHINE! WATCH OUT FOR THAT FALLING...
...TRIANGLE...
WHEEEEEEEEEEEEEooo
DING!
HAW HAW HAW! How EXTRAORDINARY! That sky-born scarlet SILICATE has CONCUSSED the coney of COURAGE!
SAVEEN, YOU... YOU BEAST! H-HE WAS THE BEST BUCK I EVER HAD!
GLUHHH...
SILENCE, you anatomically-absurd ANGORA!
YEEP!
I don't know where this bunny-braining bauble CAME from--
--but it looks like it would buy me a LOT of three-fingered GLOVES...
...so I claim it as the bounty of BASIL SAVEEN!
BLEHHHH...
BASIL SAVEEN? MY DEAR FELLOW, I HOPE YOU WON'T MIND ME ASKING...

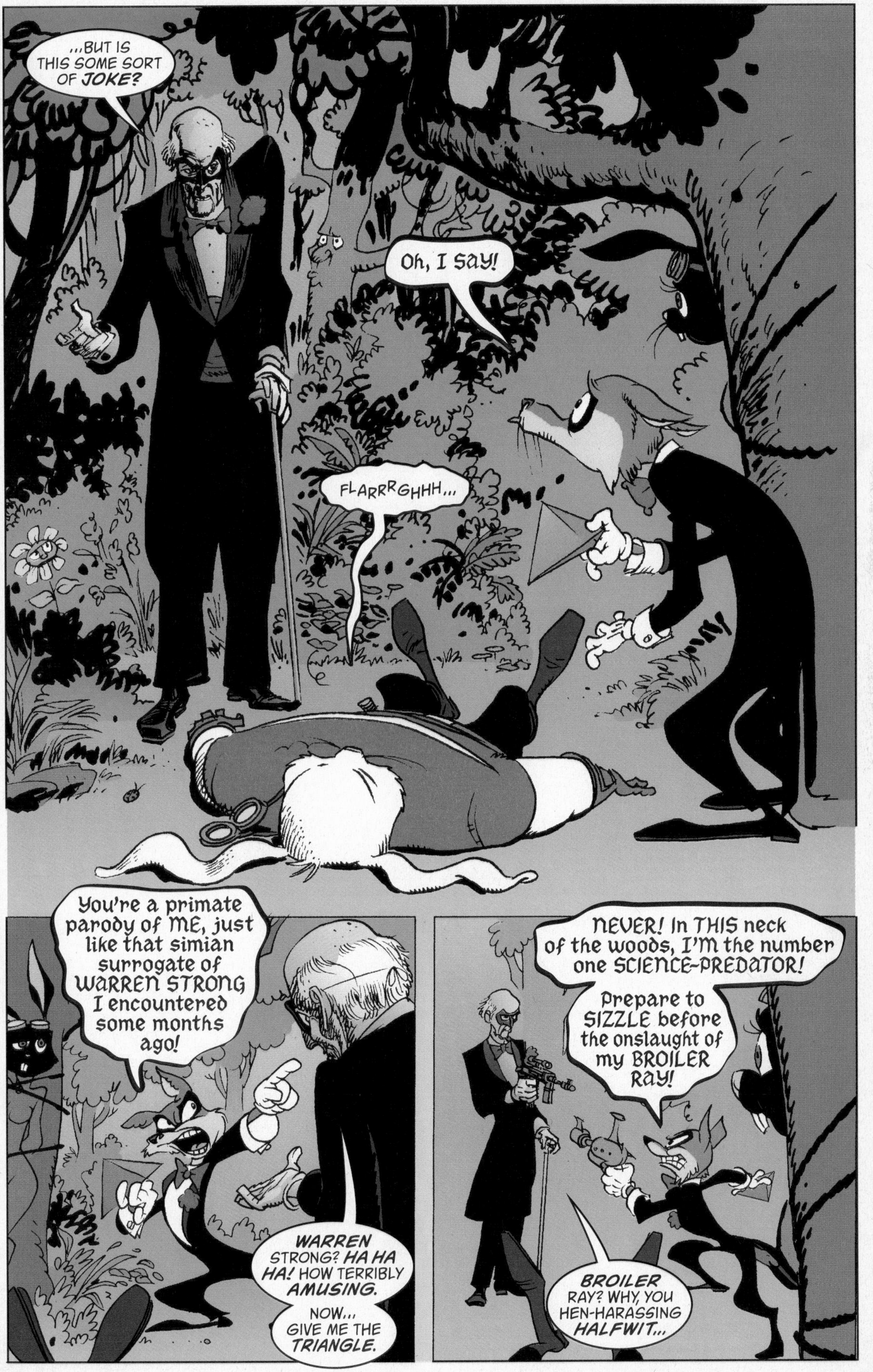
...BUT IS THIS SOME SORT OF JOKE?
Oh, I say!
FLARRRGHHH...
You're a primate parody of ME, just like that simian surrogate of WARREN STRONG I encountered some months ago!
WARREN STRONG? HA HA HA! HOW TERRIBLY AMUSING.
NOW... GIVE ME THE TRIANGLE.
NEVER! In THIS neck of the woods, I'M the number one SCIENCE-PREDATOR!
Prepare to SIZZLE before the onslaught of my BROILER RAY!
BROILER RAY? WHY, YOU HEN-HARASSING HALFWIT...

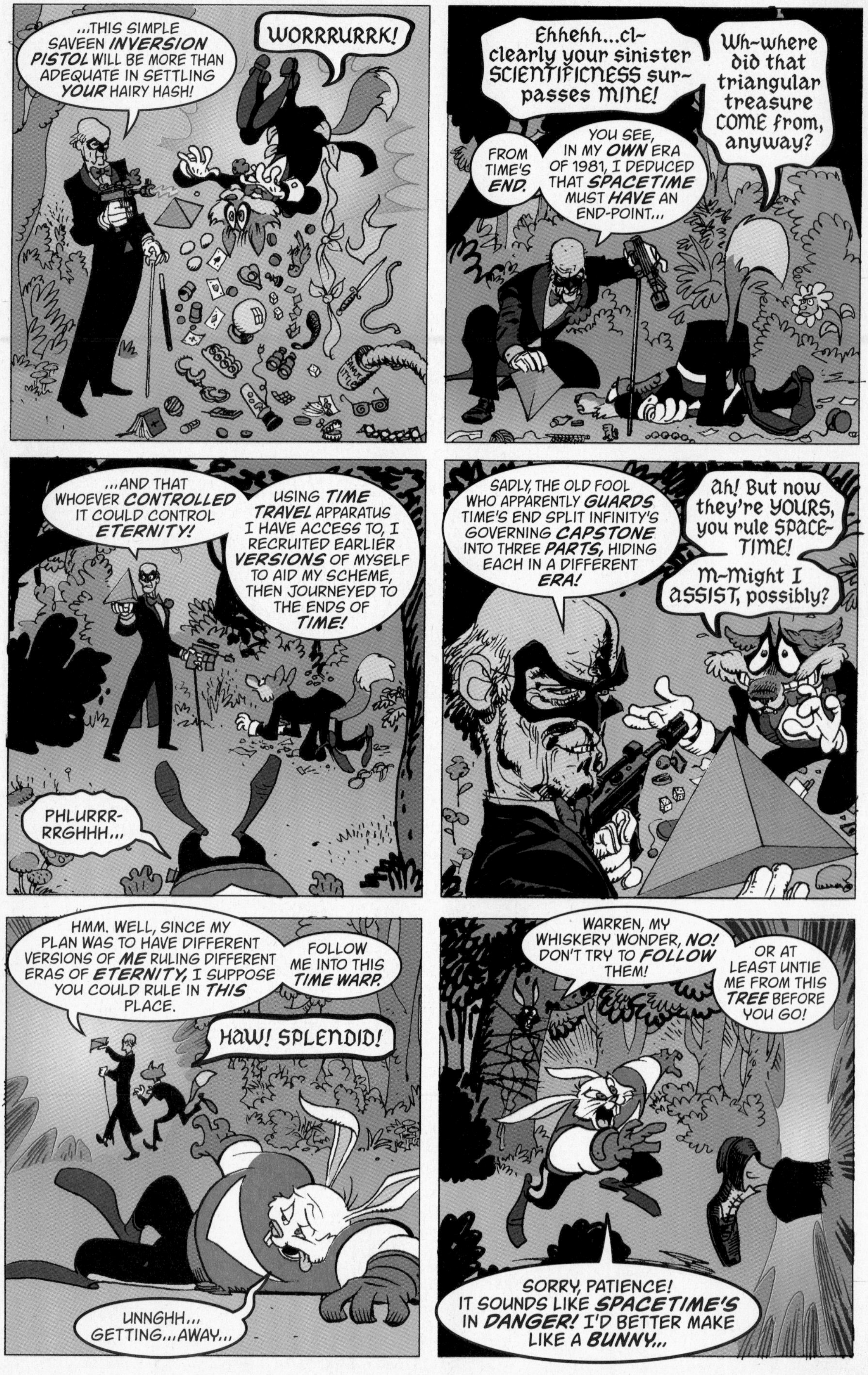
...THIS SIMPLE SAVEEN INVERSION PISTOL WILL BE MORE THAN ADEQUATE IN SETTLING YOUR HAIRY HASH!
WORRRURRK!
Ehhehh...cl-clearly your sinister SCIENTIFICNESS sur-passes MINE!
Wh-where did that triangular treasure COME from, anyway?
FROM TIME'S END.
YOU SEE, IN MY OWN ERA OF 1981, I DEDUCED THAT SPACETIME MUST HAVE AN END-POINT...
...AND THAT WHOEVER CONTROLLED IT COULD CONTROL ETERNITY!
USING TIME TRAVEL APPARATUS I HAVE ACCESS TO, I RECRUITED EARLIER VERSIONS OF MYSELF TO AID MY SCHEME, THEN JOURNEYED TO THE ENDS OF TIME!
PHLURRR-RRGHHH...
SADLY, THE OLD FOOL WHO APPARENTLY GUARDS TIME'S END SPLIT INFINITY'S GOVERNING CAPSTONE INTO THREE PARTS, HIDING EACH IN A DIFFERENT ERA!
ah! But now they're YOURS, you rule SPACE-TIME!
M-Might I ASSIST, possibly?
HMM. WELL, SINCE MY PLAN WAS TO HAVE DIFFERENT VERSIONS OF ME RULING DIFFERENT ERAS OF ETERNITY, I SUPPOSE YOU COULD RULE IN THIS PLACE.
FOLLOW ME INTO THIS TIME WARP.
HaW! SPLENDID!
UNNGHH... GETTING...AWAY...
WARREN, MY WHISKERY WONDER, NO! DON'T TRY TO FOLLOW THEM!
OR AT LEAST UNTIE ME FROM THIS TREE BEFORE YOU GO!
SORRY, PATIENCE! IT SOUNDS LIKE SPACETIME'S IN DANGER! I'D BETTER MAKE LIKE A BUNNY...

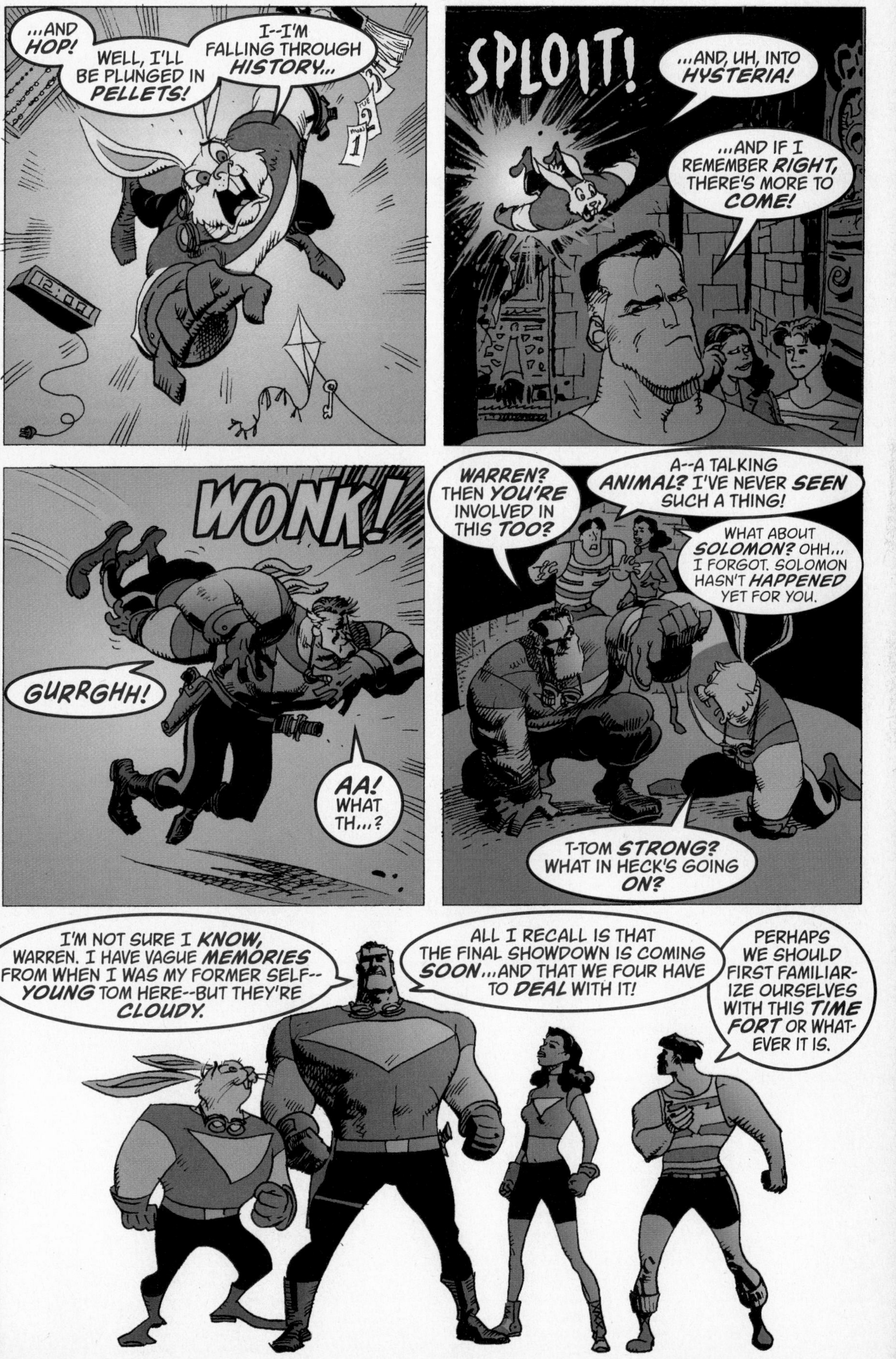
...AND HOP!
WELL, I'LL BE PLUNGED IN PELLETS!
I--I'M FALLING THROUGH HISTORY...
SPLOIT!
...AND, UH, INTO HYSTERIA!
...AND IF I REMEMBER RIGHT, THERE'S MORE TO COME!
WONK!
GURRGHH!
AA! WHAT TH...?
WARREN? THEN YOU'RE INVOLVED IN THIS TOO?
A--A TALKING ANIMAL? I'VE NEVER SEEN SUCH A THING!
WHAT ABOUT SOLOMON? OHH... I FORGOT. SOLOMON HASN'T HAPPENED YET FOR YOU.
T-TOM STRONG? WHAT IN HECK'S GOING ON?
I'M NOT SURE I KNOW, WARREN. I HAVE VAGUE MEMORIES FROM WHEN I WAS MY FORMER SELF-- YOUNG TOM HERE--BUT THEY'RE CLOUDY.
ALL I RECALL IS THAT THE FINAL SHOWDOWN IS COMING SOON...AND THAT WE FOUR HAVE TO DEAL WITH IT!
PERHAPS WE SHOULD FIRST FAMILIAR-IZE OURSELVES WITH THIS TIME FORT OR WHAT-EVER IT IS.

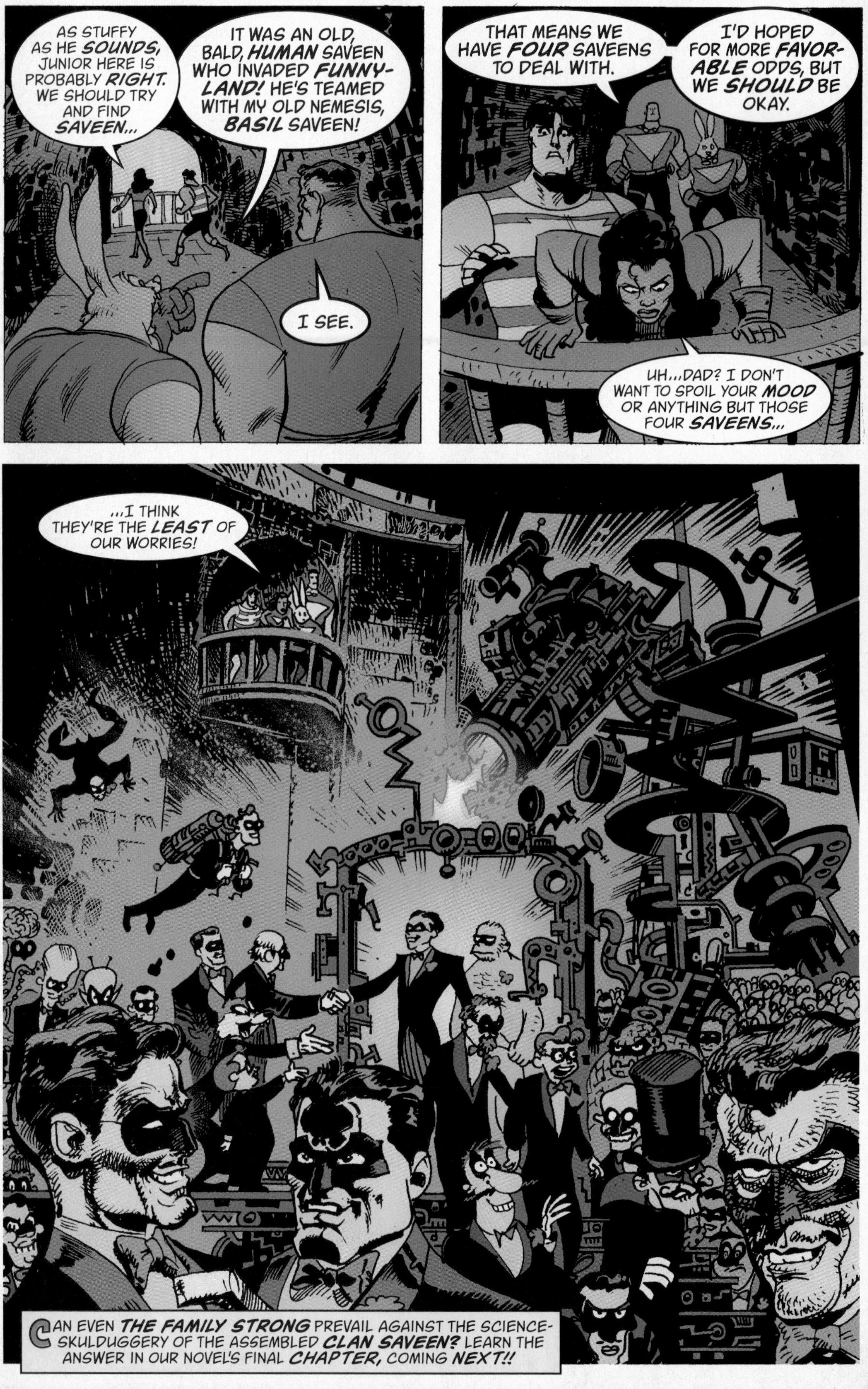
AS STUFFY AS HE SOUNDS, JUNIOR HERE IS PROBABLY RIGHT. WE SHOULD TRY AND FIND SAVEEN...
IT WAS AN OLD, BALD, HUMAN SAVEEN WHO INVADED FUNNY-LAND! HE'S TEAMED WITH MY OLD NEMESIS, BASIL SAVEEN!
I SEE.
THAT MEANS WE HAVE FOUR SAVEENS TO DEAL WITH.
I'D HOPED FOR MORE FAVOR-ABLE ODDS, BUT WE SHOULD BE OKAY.
UH...DAD? I DON'T WANT TO SPOIL YOUR MOOD OR ANYTHING BUT THOSE FOUR SAVEENS...
...I THINK THEY'RE THE LEAST OF OUR WORRIES!
CAN EVEN THE FAMILY STRONG PREVAIL AGAINST THE SCIENCE-SKULDUGGERY OF THE ASSEMBLED CLAN SAVEEN? LEARN THE ANSWER IN OUR NOVEL'S FINAL CHAPTER, COMING NEXT!!

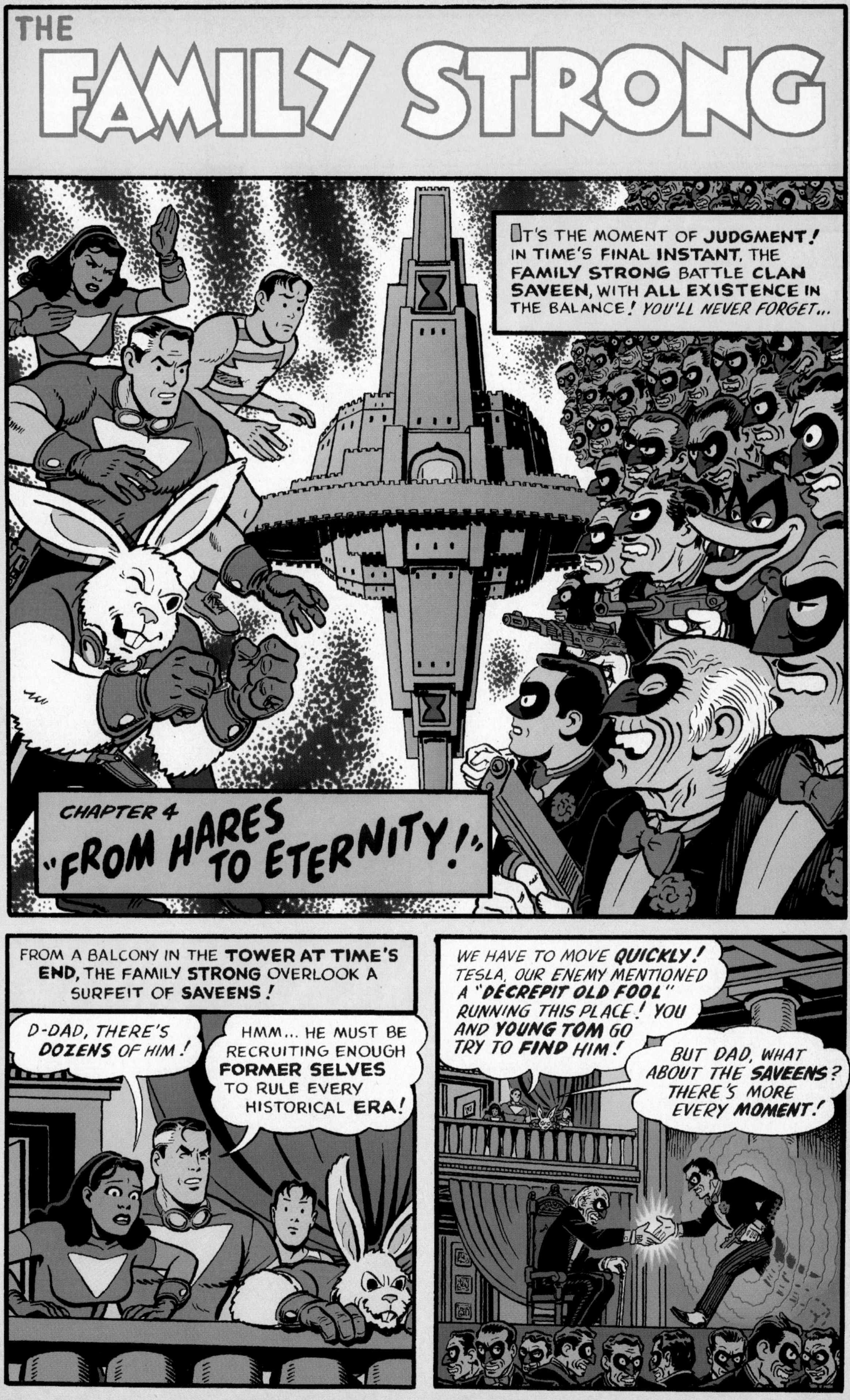
THE FAMILY STRONG
IT'S THE MOMENT OF JUDGMENT! IN TIME'S FINAL INSTANT, THE FAMILY STRONG BATTLE CLAN SAVEEN, WITH ALL EXISTENCE IN THE BALANCE! YOU'LL NEVER FORGET...
CHAPTER 4
"FROM HARES TO ETERNITY!"
FROM A BALCONY IN THE TOWER AT TIME'S END, THE FAMILY STRONG OVERLOOK A SURFEIT OF SAVEENS!
D-DAD, THERE'S DOZENS OF HIM!
HMM... HE MUST BE RECRUITING ENOUGH FORMER SELVES TO RULE EVERY HISTORICAL ERA!
WE HAVE TO MOVE QUICKLY! TESLA, OUR ENEMY MENTIONED A "DECREPIT OLD FOOL" RUNNING THIS PLACE! YOU AND YOUNG TOM GO TRY TO FIND HIM!
BUT DAD, WHAT ABOUT THE SAVEENS? THERE'S MORE EVERY MOMENT!

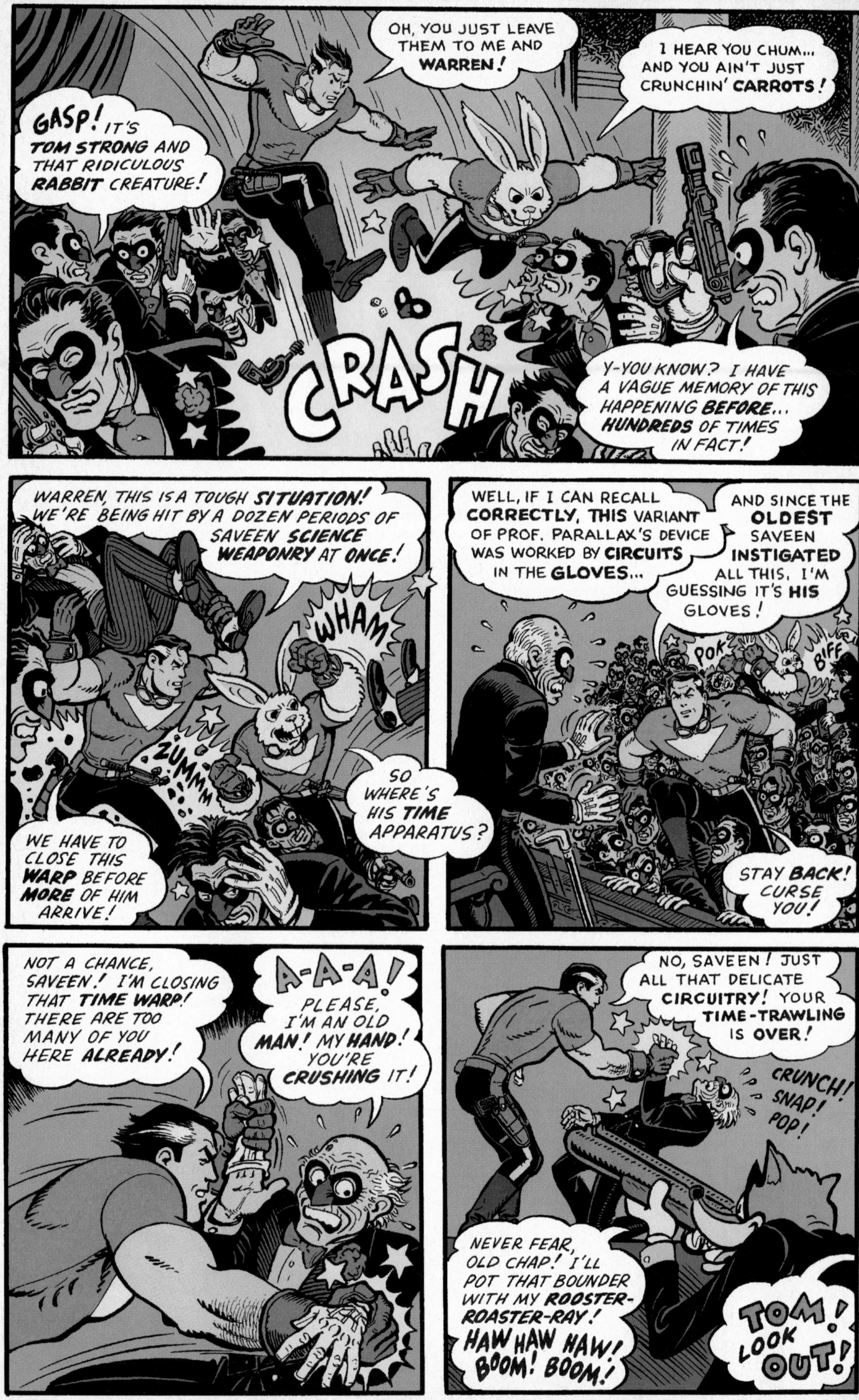
GASP! IT'S TOM STRONG AND THAT RIDICULOUS RABBIT CREATURE!
OH, YOU JUST LEAVE THEM TO ME AND WARREN!
I HEAR YOU CHUM... AND YOU AIN'T JUST CRUNCHIN' CARROTS!
CRASH
Y-YOU KNOW? I HAVE A VAGUE MEMORY OF THIS HAPPENING BEFORE... HUNDREDS OF TIMES IN FACT!
WARREN, THIS IS A TOUGH SITUATION! WE'RE BEING HIT BY A DOZEN PERIODS OF SAVEEN SCIENCE WEAPONRY AT ONCE!
WHAM
ZUMMM
SO WHERE'S HIS TIME APPARATUS?
WE HAVE TO CLOSE THIS WARP BEFORE MORE OF HIM ARRIVE!
WELL, IF I CAN RECALL CORRECTLY, THIS VARIANT OF PROF. PARALLAX'S DEVICE WAS WORKED BY CIRCUITS IN THE GLOVES...
AND SINCE THE OLDEST SAVEEN INSTIGATED ALL THIS, I'M GUESSING IT'S HIS GLOVES!
POK
BIFF
STAY BACK! CURSE YOU!
NOT A CHANCE, SAVEEN! I'M CLOSING THAT TIME WARP! THERE ARE TOO MANY OF YOU HERE ALREADY!
A-A-A! PLEASE, I'M AN OLD MAN! MY HAND! YOU'RE CRUSHING IT!
NO, SAVEEN! JUST ALL THAT DELICATE CIRCUITRY! YOUR TIME-TRAWLING IS OVER!
CRUNCH! SNAP! POP!
NEVER FEAR, OLD CHAP! I'LL POT THAT BOUNDER WITH MY ROOSTER-ROASTER-RAY! HAW HAW HAW! BOOM! BOOM!
TOM! LOOK OUT!

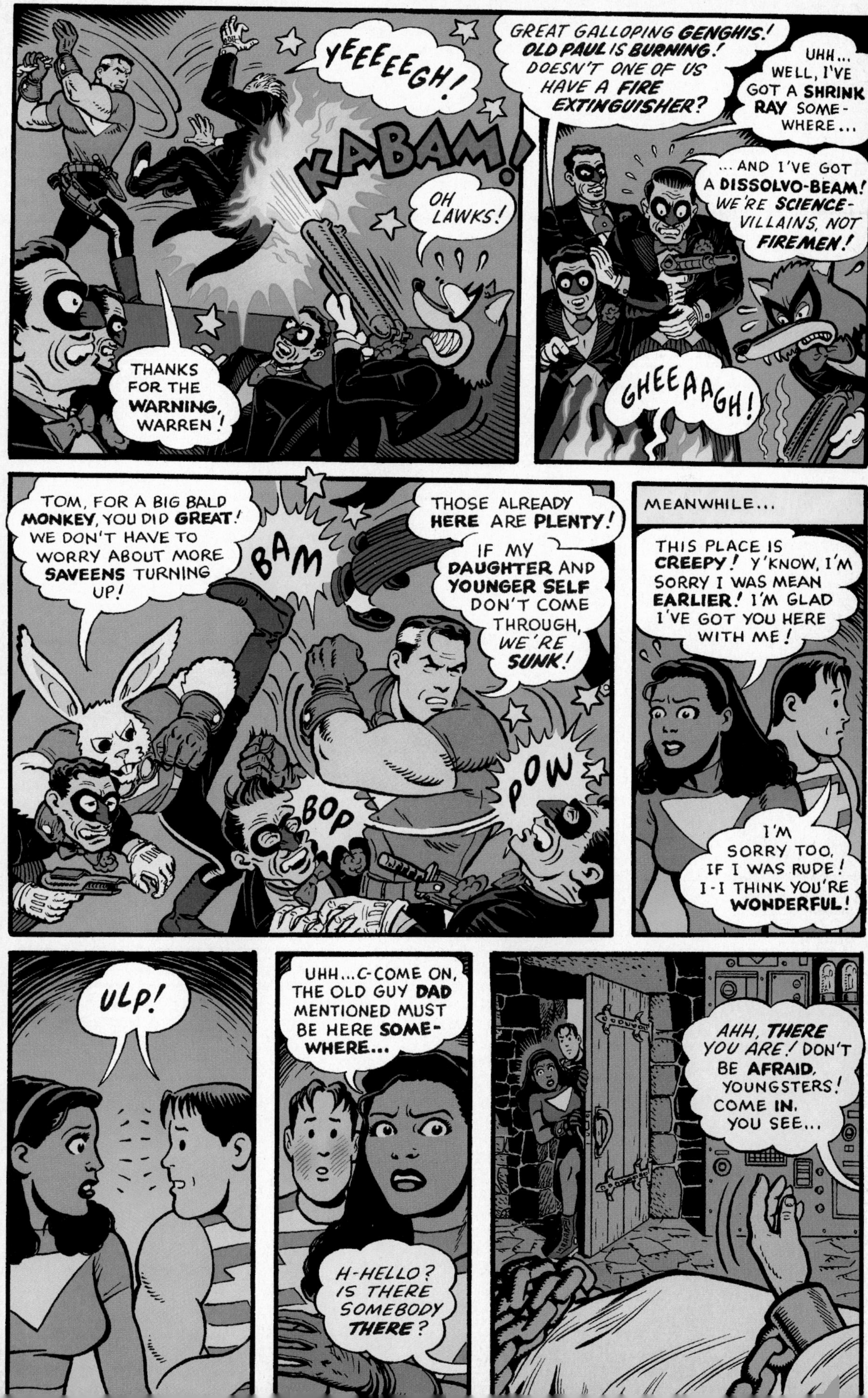
YEEEEEGH!
KABAM!
OH LAWKS!
THANKS FOR THE WARNING, WARREN!
GREAT GALLOPING GENGHIS! OLD PAUL IS BURNING! DOESN'T ONE OF US HAVE A FIRE EXTINGUISHER?
UHH... WELL, I'VE GOT A SHRINK RAY SOME-WHERE...
...AND I'VE GOT A DISSOLVO-BEAM! WE'RE SCIENCE-VILLAINS, NOT FIREMEN!
GHEEAAGH!
TOM, FOR A BIG BALD MONKEY, YOU DID GREAT! WE DON'T HAVE TO WORRY ABOUT MORE SAVEENS TURNING UP!
BAM
THOSE ALREADY HERE ARE PLENTY!
IF MY DAUGHTER AND YOUNGER SELF DON'T COME THROUGH, WE'RE SUNK!
BOP
POW
MEANWHILE...
THIS PLACE IS CREEPY! Y'KNOW, I'M SORRY I WAS MEAN EARLIER! I'M GLAD I'VE GOT YOU HERE WITH ME!
I'M SORRY TOO, IF I WAS RUDE! I-I THINK YOU'RE WONDERFUL!
ULP!
UHH...C-COME ON, THE OLD GUY DAD MENTIONED MUST BE HERE SOME-WHERE...
H-HELLO? IS THERE SOMEBODY THERE?
AHH, THERE YOU ARE! DON'T BE AFRAID, YOUNGSTERS! COME IN. YOU SEE...

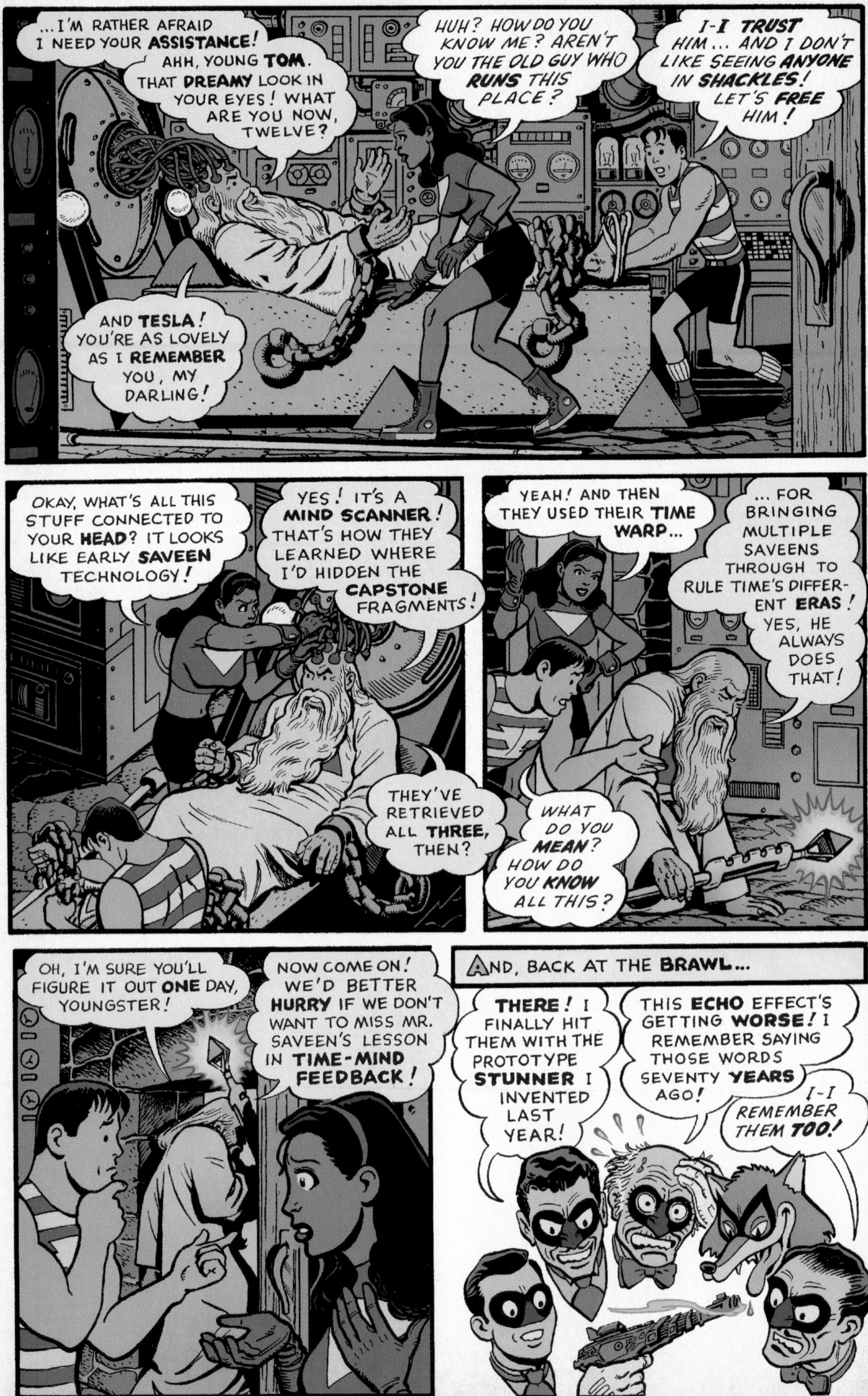
...I'M RATHER AFRAID I NEED YOUR ASSISTANCE!
AHH, YOUNG TOM. THAT DREAMY LOOK IN YOUR EYES! WHAT ARE YOU NOW, TWELVE?
HUH? HOW DO YOU KNOW ME? AREN'T YOU THE OLD GUY WHO RUNS THIS PLACE?
I-I TRUST HIM... AND I DON'T LIKE SEEING ANYONE IN SHACKLES! LET'S FREE HIM!
AND TESLA! YOU'RE AS LOVELY AS I REMEMBER YOU, MY DARLING!
OKAY, WHAT'S ALL THIS STUFF CONNECTED TO YOUR HEAD? IT LOOKS LIKE EARLY SAVEEN TECHNOLOGY!
YES! IT'S A MIND SCANNER! THAT'S HOW THEY LEARNED WHERE I'D HIDDEN THE CAPSTONE FRAGMENTS!
THEY'VE RETRIEVED ALL THREE, THEN?
YEAH! AND THEN THEY USED THEIR TIME WARP...
...FOR BRINGING MULTIPLE SAVEENS THROUGH TO RULE TIME'S DIFFERENT ERAS! YES, HE ALWAYS DOES THAT!
WHAT DO YOU MEAN? HOW DO YOU KNOW ALL THIS?
OH, I'M SURE YOU'LL FIGURE IT OUT ONE DAY, YOUNGSTER!
NOW COME ON! WE'D BETTER HURRY IF WE DON'T WANT TO MISS MR. SAVEEN'S LESSON IN TIME-MIND FEEDBACK!
AND, BACK AT THE BRAWL...
THERE! I FINALLY HIT THEM WITH THE PROTOTYPE STUNNER I INVENTED LAST YEAR!
THIS ECHO EFFECT'S GETTING WORSE! I REMEMBER SAYING THOSE WORDS SEVENTY YEARS AGO!
I-I REMEMBER THEM TOO!

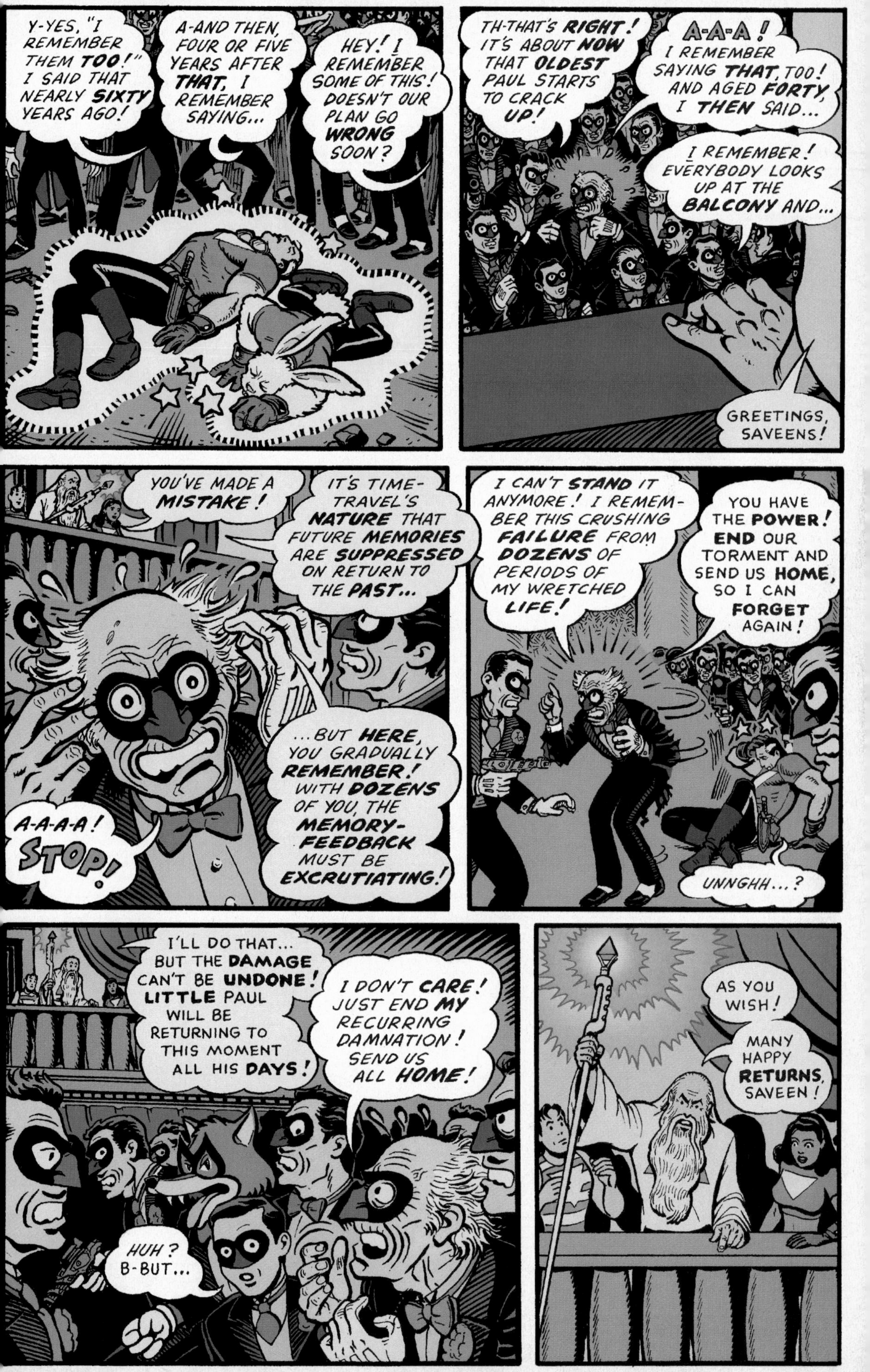

Y-YES, "I REMEMBER THEM TOO!" I SAID THAT NEARLY SIXTY YEARS AGO!
A-AND THEN, FOUR OR FIVE YEARS AFTER THAT, I REMEMBER SAYING...
HEY! I REMEMBER SOME OF THIS! DOESN'T OUR PLAN GO WRONG SOON?
TH-THAT'S RIGHT! IT'S ABOUT NOW THAT OLDEST PAUL STARTS TO CRACK UP!
A-A-A! I REMEMBER SAYING THAT, TOO! AND AGED FORTY, I THEN SAID...
I REMEMBER! EVERYBODY LOOKS UP AT THE BALCONY AND...
GREETINGS, SAVEENS!
YOU'VE MADE A MISTAKE!
IT'S TIME-TRAVEL'S NATURE THAT FUTURE MEMORIES ARE SUPPRESSED ON RETURN TO THE PAST...
...BUT HERE, YOU GRADUALLY REMEMBER! WITH DOZENS OF YOU, THE MEMORY-FEEDBACK MUST BE EXCRUTIATING!
A-A-A-A! STOP!
I CAN'T STAND IT ANYMORE! I REMEMBER THIS CRUSHING FAILURE FROM DOZENS OF PERIODS OF MY WRETCHED LIFE!
YOU HAVE THE POWER! END OUR TORMENT AND SEND US HOME, SO I CAN FORGET AGAIN!
UNNGHH...?
I'LL DO THAT... BUT THE DAMAGE CAN'T BE UNDONE! LITTLE PAUL WILL BE RETURNING TO THIS MOMENT ALL HIS DAYS!
I DON'T CARE! JUST END MY RECURRING DAMNATION! SEND US ALL HOME!
HUH? B-BUT...
AS YOU WISH!
MANY HAPPY RETURNS, SAVEEN!

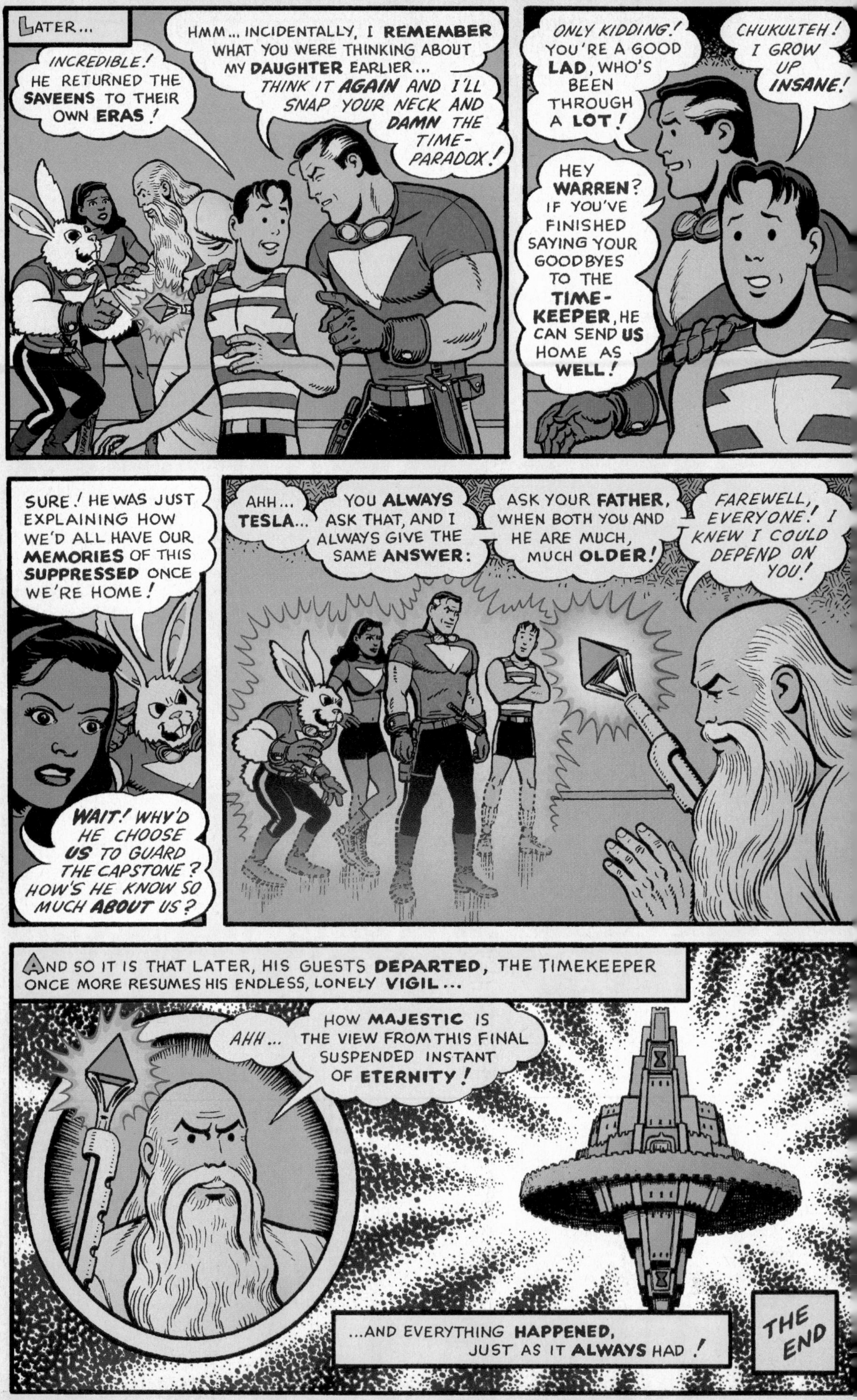

LATER...
INCREDIBLE! HE RETURNED THE SAVEENS TO THEIR OWN ERAS!
HMM... INCIDENTALLY, I REMEMBER WHAT YOU WERE THINKING ABOUT MY DAUGHTER EARLIER... THINK IT AGAIN AND I'LL SNAP YOUR NECK AND DAMN THE TIME-PARADOX!
ONLY KIDDING! YOU'RE A GOOD LAD, WHO'S BEEN THROUGH A LOT!
CHUKULTEH! I GROW UP INSANE!
HEY WARREN? IF YOU'VE FINISHED SAYING YOUR GOODBYES TO THE TIME-KEEPER, HE CAN SEND US HOME AS WELL!
SURE! HE WAS JUST EXPLAINING HOW WE'D ALL HAVE OUR MEMORIES OF THIS SUPPRESSED ONCE WE'RE HOME!
WAIT! WHY'D HE CHOOSE US TO GUARD THE CAPSTONE? HOW'S HE KNOW SO MUCH ABOUT US?
AHH... TESLA...
YOU ALWAYS ASK THAT, AND I ALWAYS GIVE THE SAME ANSWER:
ASK YOUR FATHER, WHEN BOTH YOU AND HE ARE MUCH, MUCH OLDER!
FAREWELL, EVERYONE! I KNEW I COULD DEPEND ON YOU!
AND SO IT IS THAT LATER, HIS GUESTS DEPARTED, THE TIMEKEEPER ONCE MORE RESUMES HIS ENDLESS, LONELY VIGIL...
AHH...
HOW MAJESTIC IS THE VIEW FROM THIS FINAL SUSPENDED INSTANT OF ETERNITY!
...AND EVERYTHING HAPPENED, JUST AS IT ALWAYS HAD!
THE END

CHAPTER SEVEN

**In which the Strong Family takes a vacation,
Tom and Dhalua recapture their youth,
and Tom leaps ahead with Johnny Future.**

**Cover art:
Tom McWeeney**

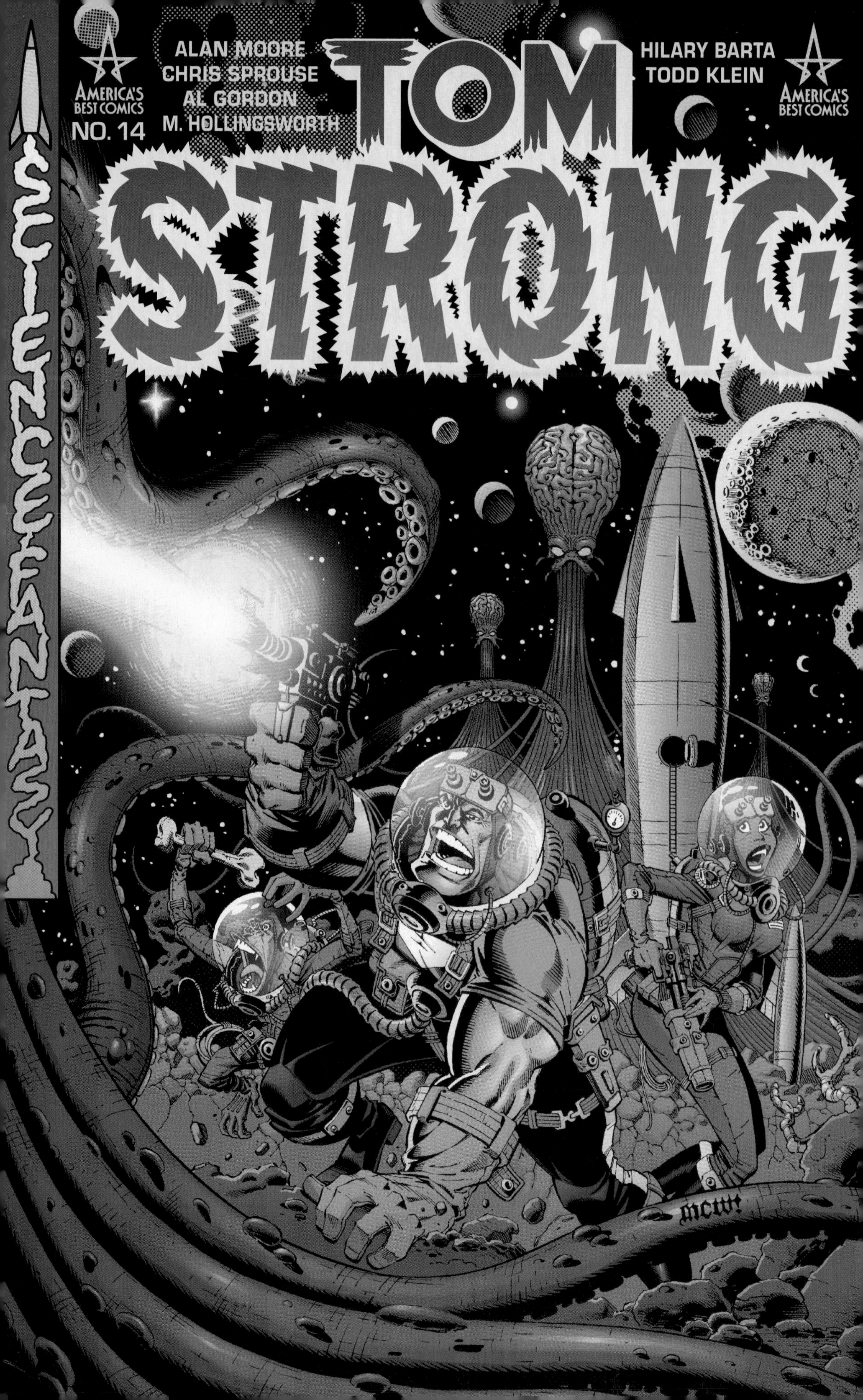
AMERICA'S BEST COMICS
NO. 14
ALAN MOORE
CHRIS SPROUSE
AL GORDON
M. HOLLINGSWORTH
TOM STRONG
HILARY BARTA
TODD KLEIN
AMERICA'S BEST COMICS
SCIENCEFANTASY

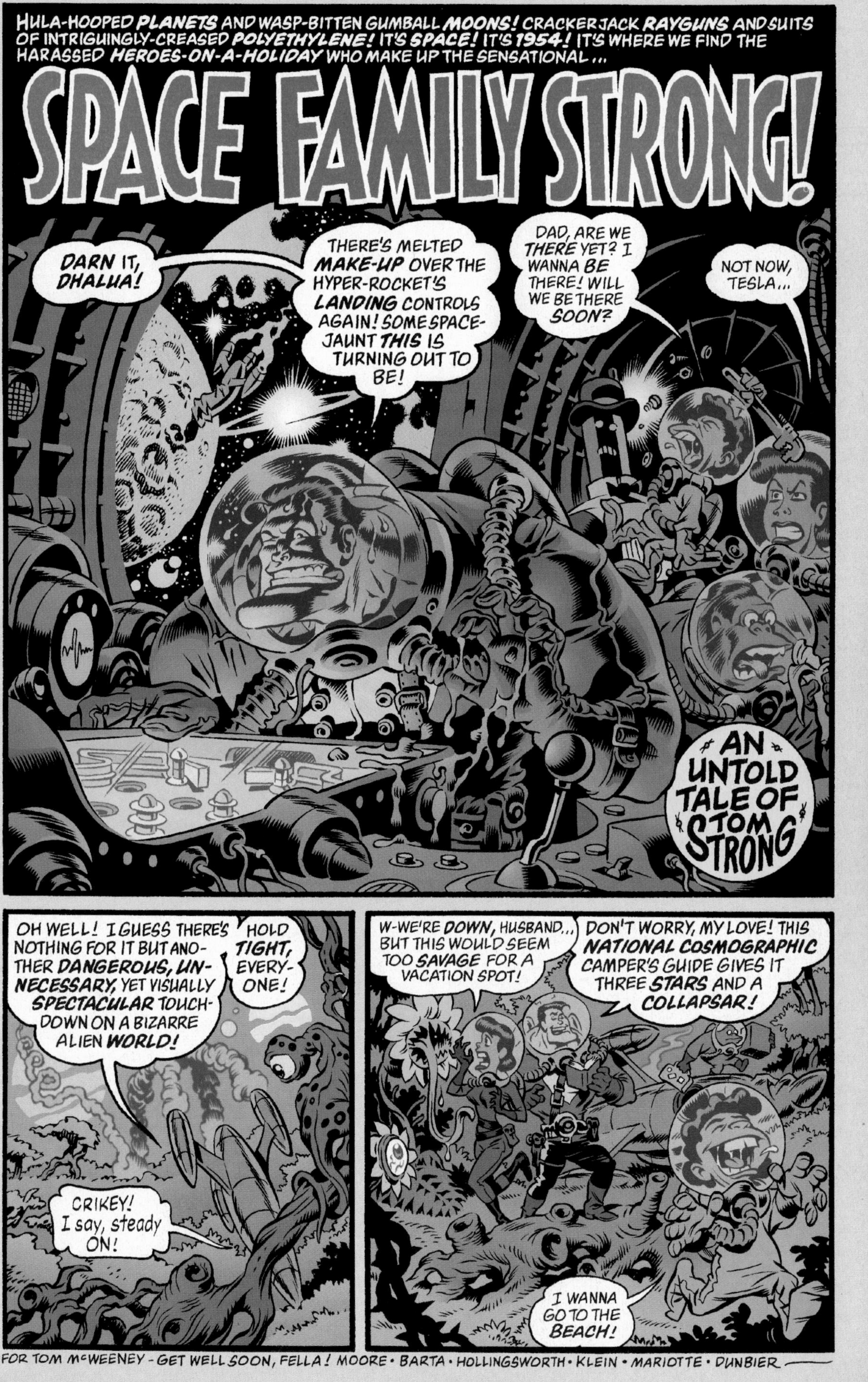
HULA-HOOPED PLANETS AND WASP-BITTEN GUMBALL MOONS! CRACKERJACK RAYGUNS AND SUITS OF INTRIGUINGLY-CREASED POLYETHYLENE! IT'S SPACE! IT'S 1954! IT'S WHERE WE FIND THE HARASSED HEROES-ON-A-HOLIDAY WHO MAKE UP THE SENSATIONAL...
SPACE FAMILY STRONG!
DARN IT, DHALUA!
THERE'S MELTED MAKE-UP OVER THE HYPER-ROCKET'S LANDING CONTROLS AGAIN! SOME SPACE-JAUNT THIS IS TURNING OUT TO BE!
DAD, ARE WE THERE YET? I WANNA BE THERE! WILL WE BE THERE SOON?
NOT NOW, TESLA...
AN UNTOLD TALE OF TOM STRONG
OH WELL! I GUESS THERE'S NOTHING FOR IT BUT ANOTHER DANGEROUS, UNNECESSARY, YET VISUALLY SPECTACULAR TOUCHDOWN ON A BIZARRE ALIEN WORLD!
HOLD TIGHT, EVERYONE!
CRIKEY! I say, steady ON!
W-WE'RE DOWN, HUSBAND... BUT THIS WOULD SEEM TOO SAVAGE FOR A VACATION SPOT!
DON'T WORRY, MY LOVE! THIS NATIONAL COSMOGRAPHIC CAMPER'S GUIDE GIVES IT THREE STARS AND A COLLAPSAR!
I WANNA GO TO THE BEACH!

FOR TOM McWEENEY - GET WELL SOON, FELLA! MOORE • BARTA • HOLLINGSWORTH • KLEIN • MARIOTTE • DUNBIER

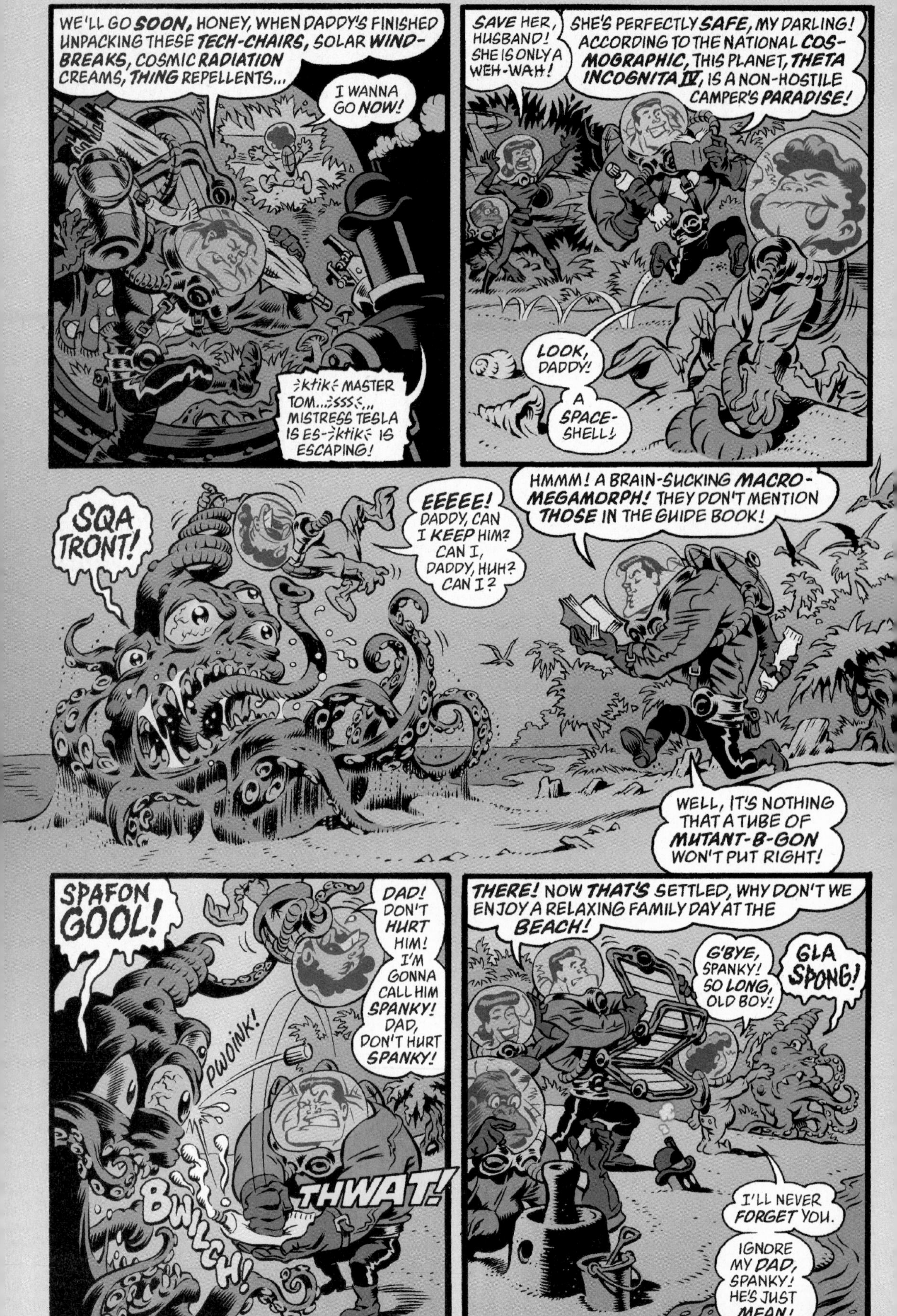

WE'LL GO SOON, HONEY, WHEN DADDY'S FINISHED UNPACKING THESE TECH-CHAIRS, SOLAR WIND-BREAKS, COSMIC RADIATION CREAMS, THING REPELLENTS...
I WANNA GO NOW!
ktik MASTER TOM...sss... MISTRESS TESLA IS ES-ktik IS ESCAPING!
SAVE HER, HUSBAND! SHE IS ONLY A WEH-WAH!
SHE'S PERFECTLY SAFE, MY DARLING! ACCORDING TO THE NATIONAL COS-MOGRAPHIC, THIS PLANET, THETA INCOGNITA IV, IS A NON-HOSTILE CAMPER'S PARADISE!
LOOK, DADDY!
A SPACE-SHELL!
SQA TRONT!
EEEEE! DADDY, CAN I KEEP HIM? CAN I, DADDY, HUH? CAN I?
HMMM! A BRAIN-SUCKING MACRO-MEGAMORPH! THEY DON'T MENTION THOSE IN THE GUIDE BOOK!
WELL, IT'S NOTHING THAT A TUBE OF MUTANT-B-GON WON'T PUT RIGHT!
SPAFON GOOL!
DAD! DON'T HURT HIM! I'M GONNA CALL HIM SPANKY! DAD, DON'T HURT SPANKY!
PWOINK!
THWAT!
BWILCH!
THERE! NOW THAT'S SETTLED, WHY DON'T WE ENJOY A RELAXING FAMILY DAY AT THE BEACH!
G'BYE, SPANKY! SO LONG, OLD BOY!
GLA SPONG!
I'LL NEVER FORGET YOU.
IGNORE MY DAD, SPANKY! HE'S JUST MEAN!

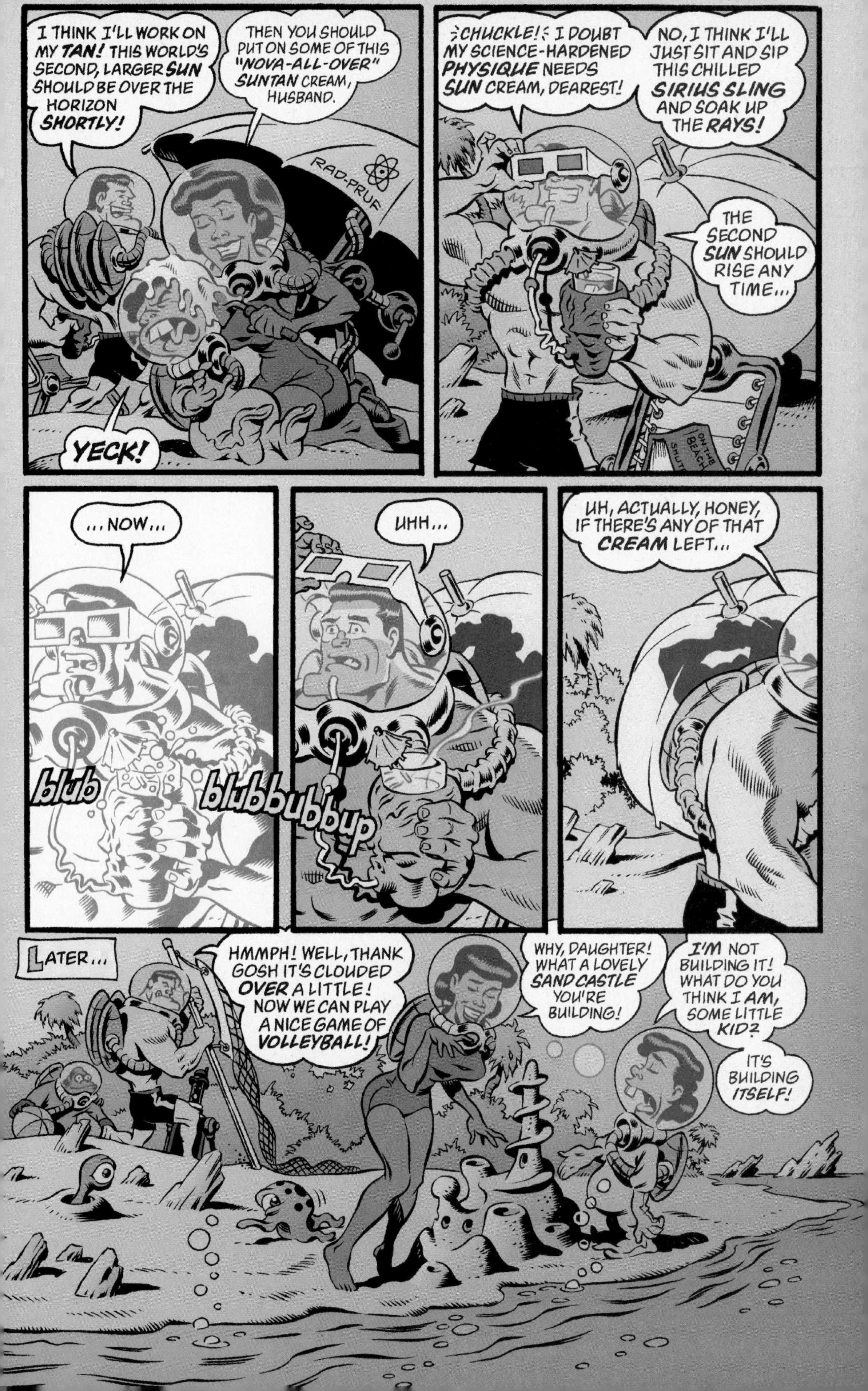
I THINK I'LL WORK ON MY TAN! THIS WORLD'S SECOND, LARGER SUN SHOULD BE OVER THE HORIZON SHORTLY!
THEN YOU SHOULD PUT ON SOME OF THIS "NOVA-ALL-OVER" SUNTAN CREAM, HUSBAND.
RAD-PRUF
YECK!
CHUCKLE! I DOUBT MY SCIENCE-HARDENED PHYSIQUE NEEDS SUN CREAM, DEAREST!
NO, I THINK I'LL JUST SIT AND SIP THIS CHILLED SIRIUS SLING AND SOAK UP THE RAYS!
THE SECOND SUN SHOULD RISE ANY TIME...
...NOW...
blub
blubbubbup
UHH...
UH, ACTUALLY, HONEY, IF THERE'S ANY OF THAT CREAM LEFT...
LATER...
HMMPH! WELL, THANK GOSH IT'S CLOUDED OVER A LITTLE! NOW WE CAN PLAY A NICE GAME OF VOLLEYBALL!
WHY, DAUGHTER! WHAT A LOVELY SAND CASTLE YOU'RE BUILDING!
I'M NOT BUILDING IT! WHAT DO YOU THINK I AM, SOME LITTLE KID?
IT'S BUILDING ITSELF!

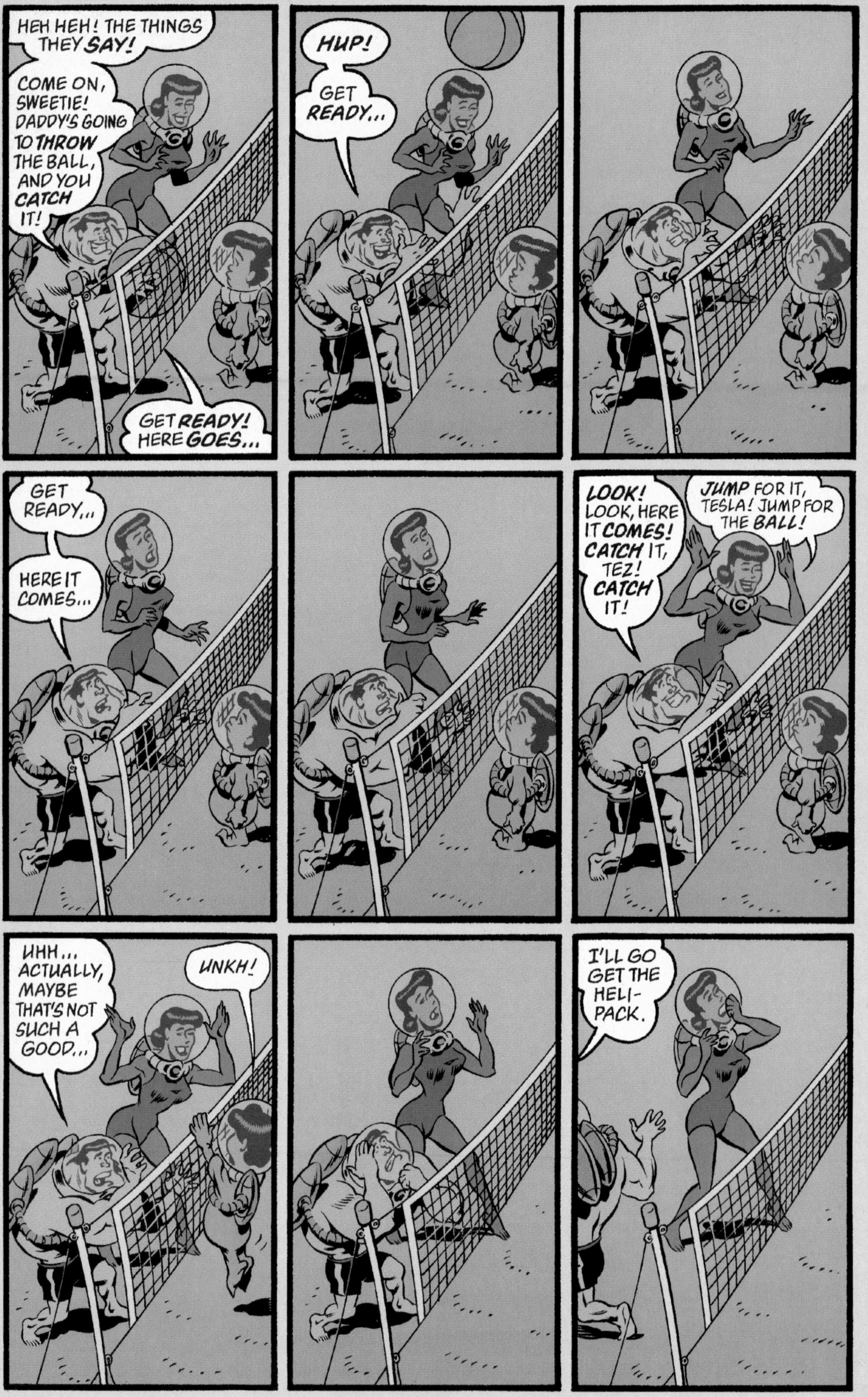
HEH HEH! THE THINGS THEY SAY!
COME ON, SWEETIE! DADDY'S GOING TO THROW THE BALL, AND YOU CATCH IT!
GET READY! HERE GOES...
HUP!
GET READY...
GET READY...
HERE IT COMES...
LOOK! LOOK, HERE IT COMES! CATCH IT, TEZ! CATCH IT!
JUMP FOR IT, TESLA! JUMP FOR THE BALL!
UHH... ACTUALLY, MAYBE THAT'S NOT SUCH A GOOD...
UNKH!
I'LL GO GET THE HELI-PACK.

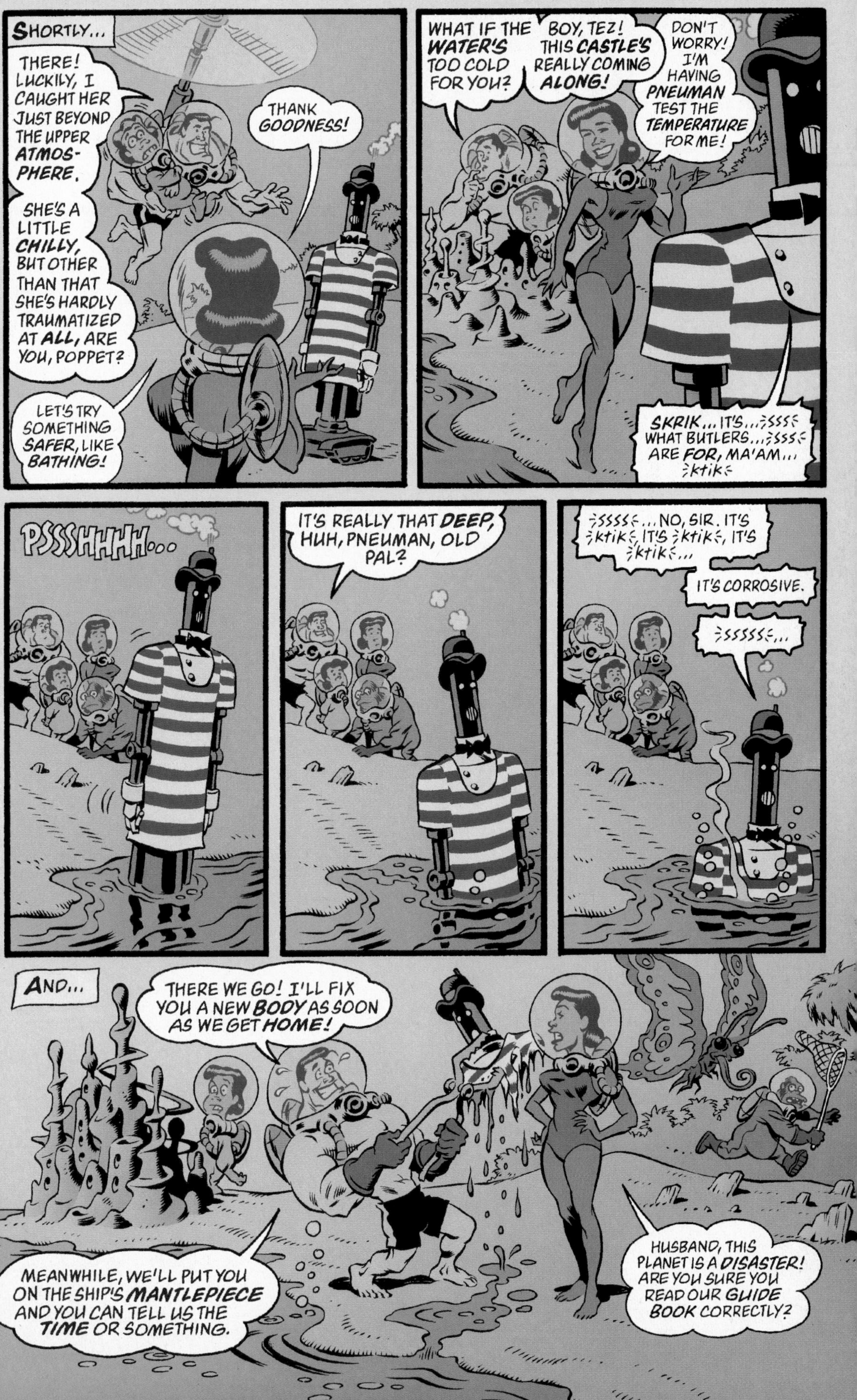
SHORTLY...
THERE! LUCKILY, I CAUGHT HER JUST BEYOND THE UPPER ATMOSPHERE.
SHE'S A LITTLE CHILLY, BUT OTHER THAN THAT SHE'S HARDLY TRAUMATIZED AT ALL, ARE YOU, POPPET?
THANK GOODNESS!
LET'S TRY SOMETHING SAFER, LIKE BATHING!
WHAT IF THE WATER'S TOO COLD FOR YOU?
BOY, TEZ! THIS CASTLE'S REALLY COMING ALONG!
DON'T WORRY! I'M HAVING PNEUMAN TEST THE TEMPERATURE FOR ME!
SKRIK... IT'S... SSSS WHAT BUTLERS... SSSS ARE FOR, MA'AM... ktik
PSSSHHHH...
IT'S REALLY THAT DEEP, HUH, PNEUMAN, OLD PAL?
SSSSS... NO, SIR. IT'S ktik, IT'S ktik, IT'S ktik...
IT'S CORROSIVE.
SSSSSS...
AND...
THERE WE GO! I'LL FIX YOU A NEW BODY AS SOON AS WE GET HOME!
MEANWHILE, WE'LL PUT YOU ON THE SHIP'S MANTLEPIECE AND YOU CAN TELL US THE TIME OR SOMETHING.
HUSBAND, THIS PLANET IS A DISASTER! ARE YOU SURE YOU READ OUR GUIDE BOOK CORRECTLY?

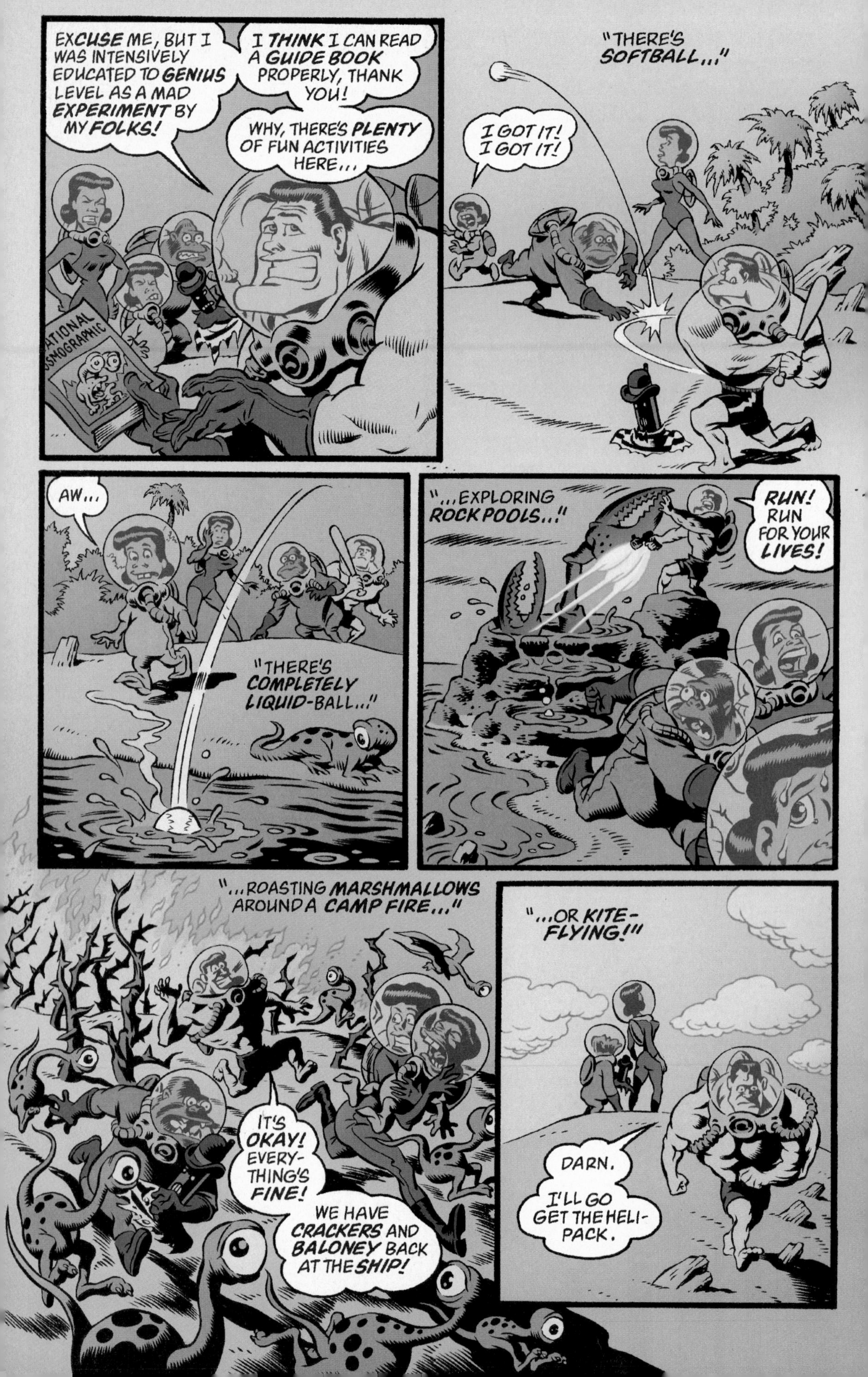
EXCUSE ME, BUT I WAS INTENSIVELY EDUCATED TO GENIUS LEVEL AS A MAD EXPERIMENT BY MY FOLKS!
I THINK I CAN READ A GUIDE BOOK PROPERLY, THANK YOU!
WHY, THERE'S PLENTY OF FUN ACTIVITIES HERE...
"THERE'S SOFTBALL..."
I GOT IT! I GOT IT!
AW...
"THERE'S COMPLETELY LIQUID-BALL..."
"...EXPLORING ROCK POOLS..."
RUN! RUN FOR YOUR LIVES!
"...ROASTING MARSHMALLOWS AROUND A CAMP FIRE..."
IT'S OKAY! EVERYTHING'S FINE!
WE HAVE CRACKERS AND BALONEY BACK AT THE SHIP!
"...OR KITE-FLYING!"
DARN.
I'LL GO GET THE HELI-PACK.

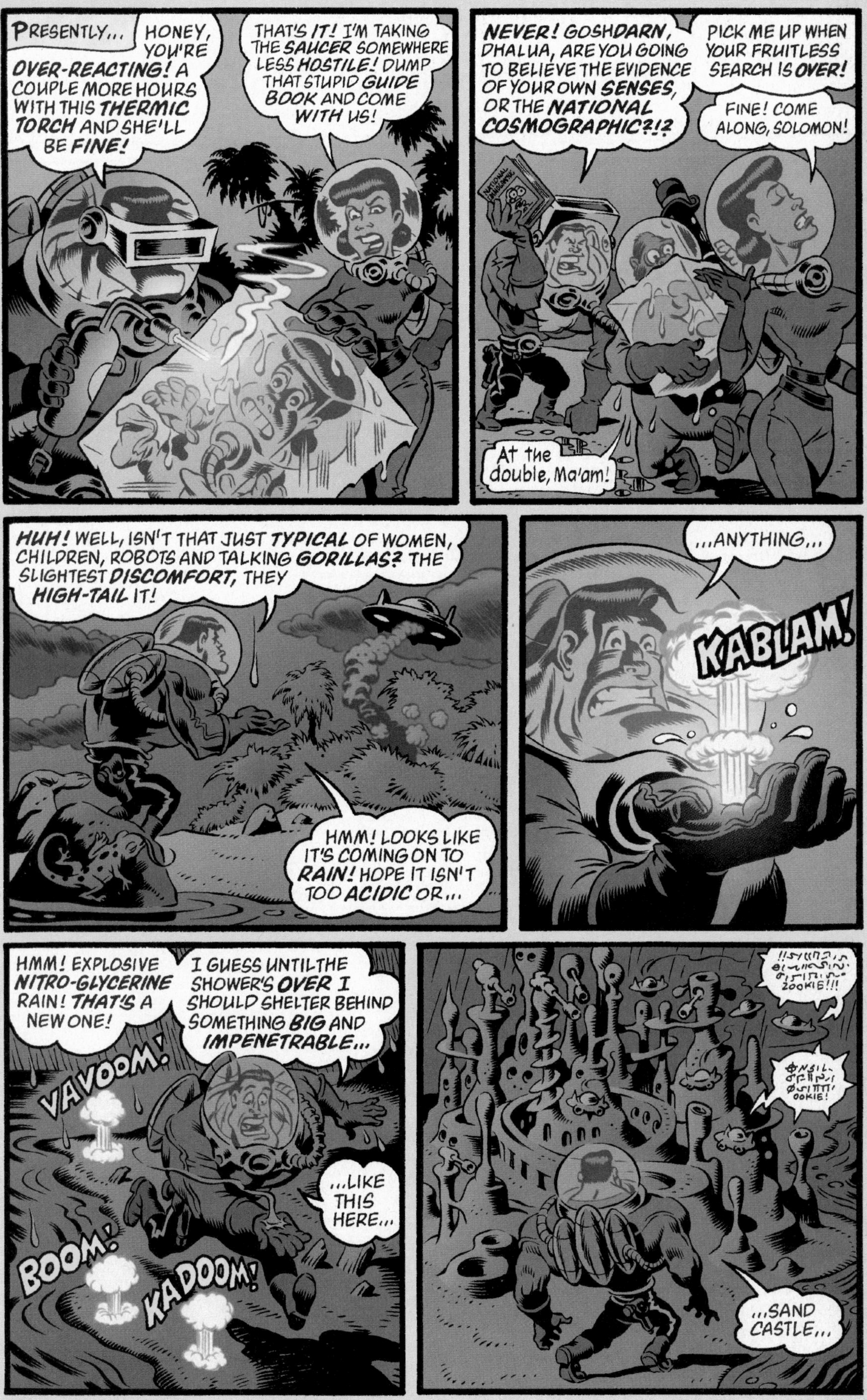
PRESENTLY...
HONEY, YOU'RE OVER-REACTING! A COUPLE MORE HOURS WITH THIS THERMIC TORCH AND SHE'LL BE FINE!
THAT'S IT! I'M TAKING THE SAUCER SOMEWHERE LESS HOSTILE! DUMP THAT STUPID GUIDE BOOK AND COME WITH US!
NEVER! GOSHDARN, DHALUA, ARE YOU GOING TO BELIEVE THE EVIDENCE OF YOUR OWN SENSES, OR THE NATIONAL COSMOGRAPHIC?!?
PICK ME UP WHEN YOUR FRUITLESS SEARCH IS OVER!
FINE! COME ALONG, SOLOMON!
At the double, Ma'am!
HUH! WELL, ISN'T THAT JUST TYPICAL OF WOMEN, CHILDREN, ROBOTS AND TALKING GORILLAS? THE SLIGHTEST DISCOMFORT, THEY HIGH-TAIL IT!
HMM! LOOKS LIKE IT'S COMING ON TO RAIN! HOPE IT ISN'T TOO ACIDIC OR...
...ANYTHING...
KABLAM!
HMM! EXPLOSIVE NITRO-GLYCERINE RAIN! THAT'S A NEW ONE!
I GUESS UNTIL THE SHOWER'S OVER I SHOULD SHELTER BEHIND SOMETHING BIG AND IMPENETRABLE...
VAVOOM!
...LIKE THIS HERE...
BOOM!
KADOOM!
ZOOKIE!!!
OOKIE!
...SAND CASTLE...

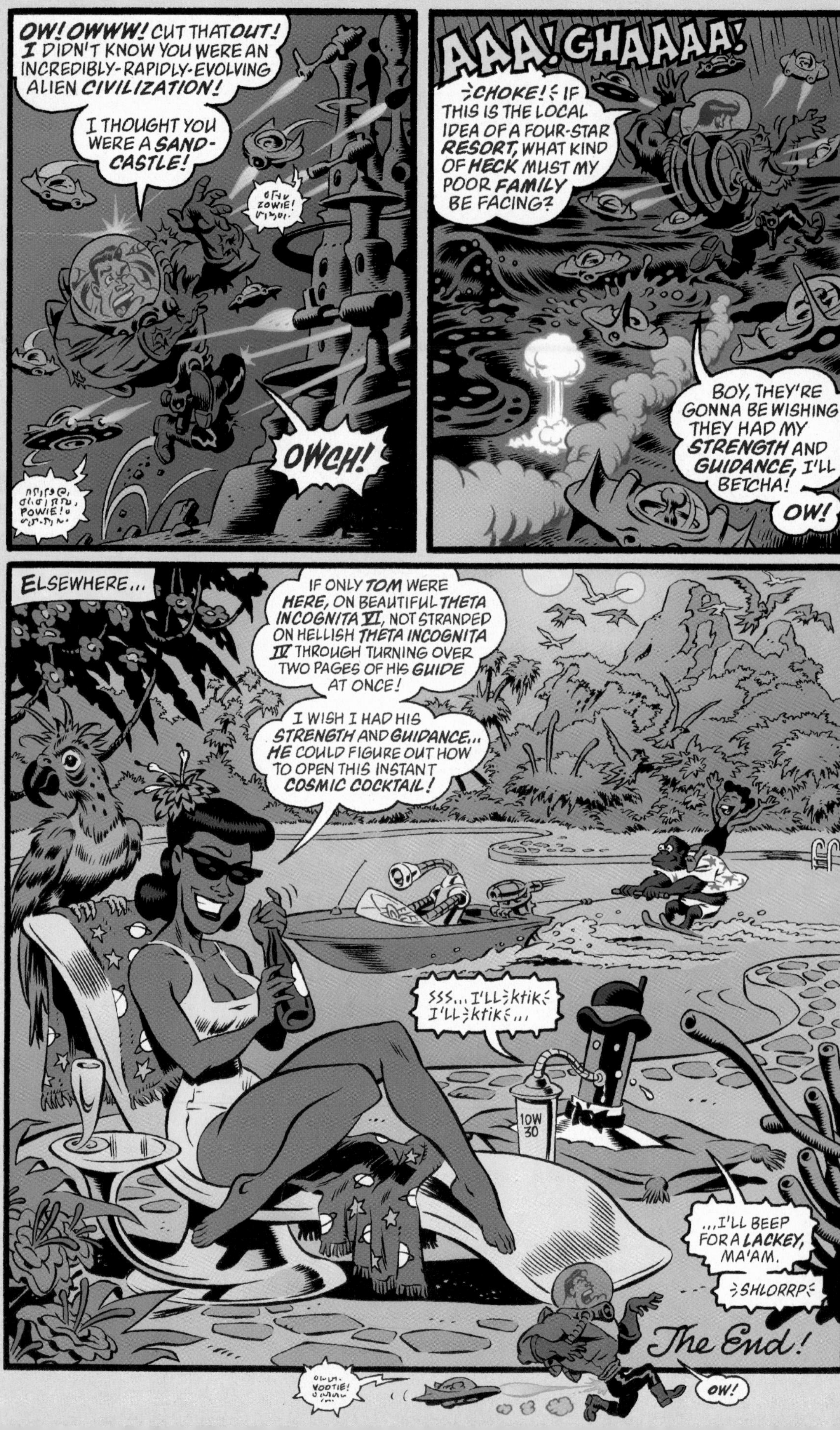

OW! OWWW! CUT THAT OUT! I DIDN'T KNOW YOU WERE AN INCREDIBLY-RAPIDLY-EVOLVING ALIEN CIVILIZATION!
I THOUGHT YOU WERE A SAND-CASTLE!
ZOWIE!
OWCH!
POWIE!
AAA! GHAAAA!
CHOKE! IF THIS IS THE LOCAL IDEA OF A FOUR-STAR RESORT, WHAT KIND OF HECK MUST MY POOR FAMILY BE FACING?
BOY, THEY'RE GONNA BE WISHING THEY HAD MY STRENGTH AND GUIDANCE, I'LL BETCHA!
OW!
ELSEWHERE...
IF ONLY TOM WERE HERE, ON BEAUTIFUL THETA INCOGNITA VI, NOT STRANDED ON HELLISH THETA INCOGNITA IV THROUGH TURNING OVER TWO PAGES OF HIS GUIDE AT ONCE!
I WISH I HAD HIS STRENGTH AND GUIDANCE... HE COULD FIGURE OUT HOW TO OPEN THIS INSTANT COSMIC COCKTAIL!
SSS... I'LL ktik I'LL ktik...
10W 30
...I'LL BEEP FOR A LACKEY, MA'AM.
SHLORRP
The End!
VOOTIE!
OW!

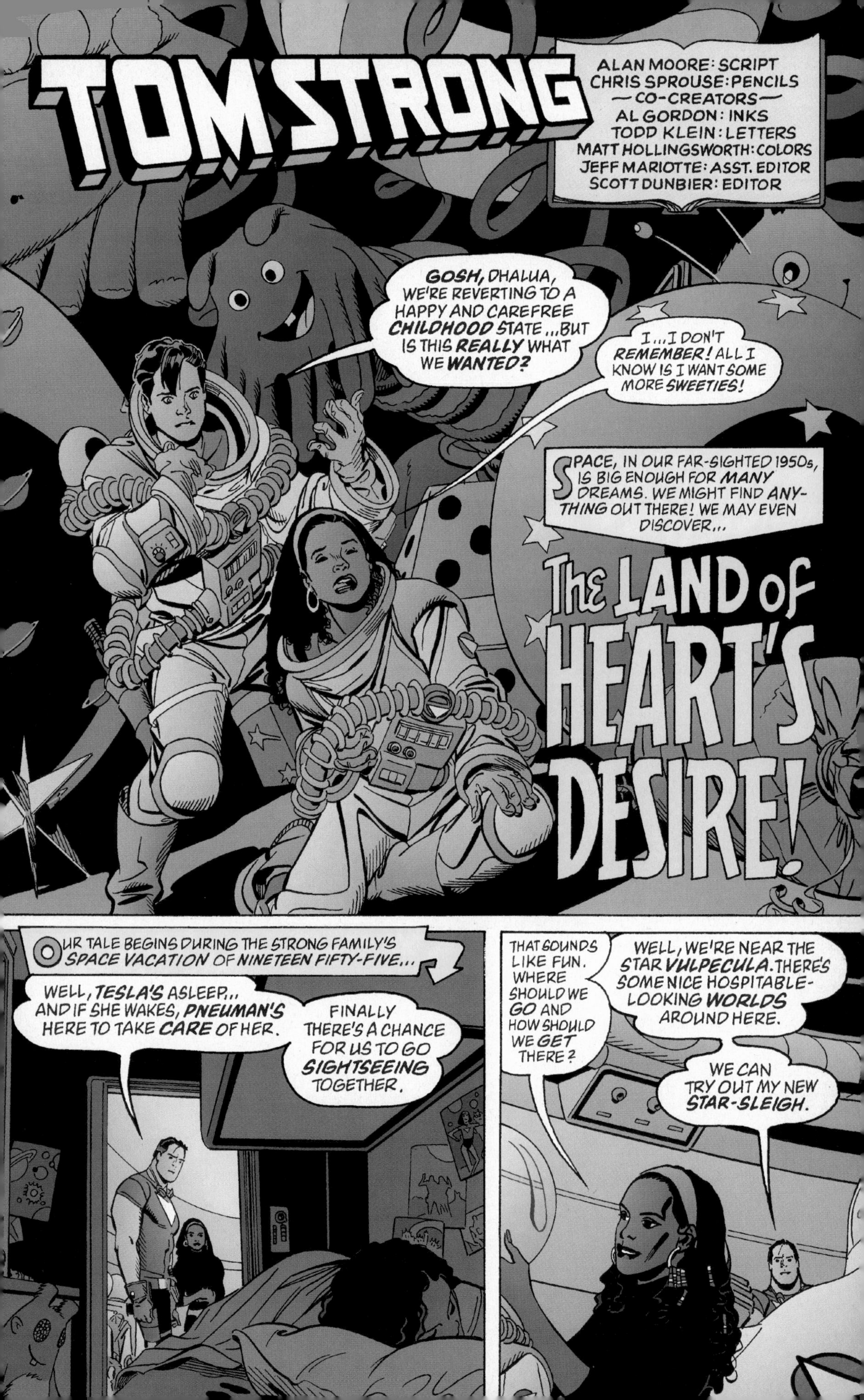
TOM STRONG
ALAN MOORE: SCRIPT
CHRIS SPROUSE: PENCILS
—CO-CREATORS—
AL GORDON: INKS
TODD KLEIN: LETTERS
MATT HOLLINGSWORTH: COLORS
JEFF MARIOTTE: ASST. EDITOR
SCOTT DUNBIER: EDITOR
GOSH, DHALUA, WE'RE REVERTING TO A HAPPY AND CAREFREE CHILDHOOD STATE ...BUT IS THIS REALLY WHAT WE WANTED?
I...I DON'T REMEMBER! ALL I KNOW IS I WANT SOME MORE SWEETIES!
SPACE, IN OUR FAR-SIGHTED 1950s, IS BIG ENOUGH FOR MANY DREAMS. WE MIGHT FIND ANYTHING OUT THERE! WE MAY EVEN DISCOVER...
The LAND of HEART'S DESIRE!
OUR TALE BEGINS DURING THE STRONG FAMILY'S SPACE VACATION OF NINETEEN FIFTY-FIVE...
WELL, TESLA'S ASLEEP... AND IF SHE WAKES, PNEUMAN'S HERE TO TAKE CARE OF HER.
FINALLY THERE'S A CHANCE FOR US TO GO SIGHTSEEING TOGETHER.
THAT SOUNDS LIKE FUN. WHERE SHOULD WE GO AND HOW SHOULD WE GET THERE?
WELL, WE'RE NEAR THE STAR VULPECULA. THERE'S SOME NICE HOSPITABLE-LOOKING WORLDS AROUND HERE.
WE CAN TRY OUT MY NEW STAR-SLEIGH.

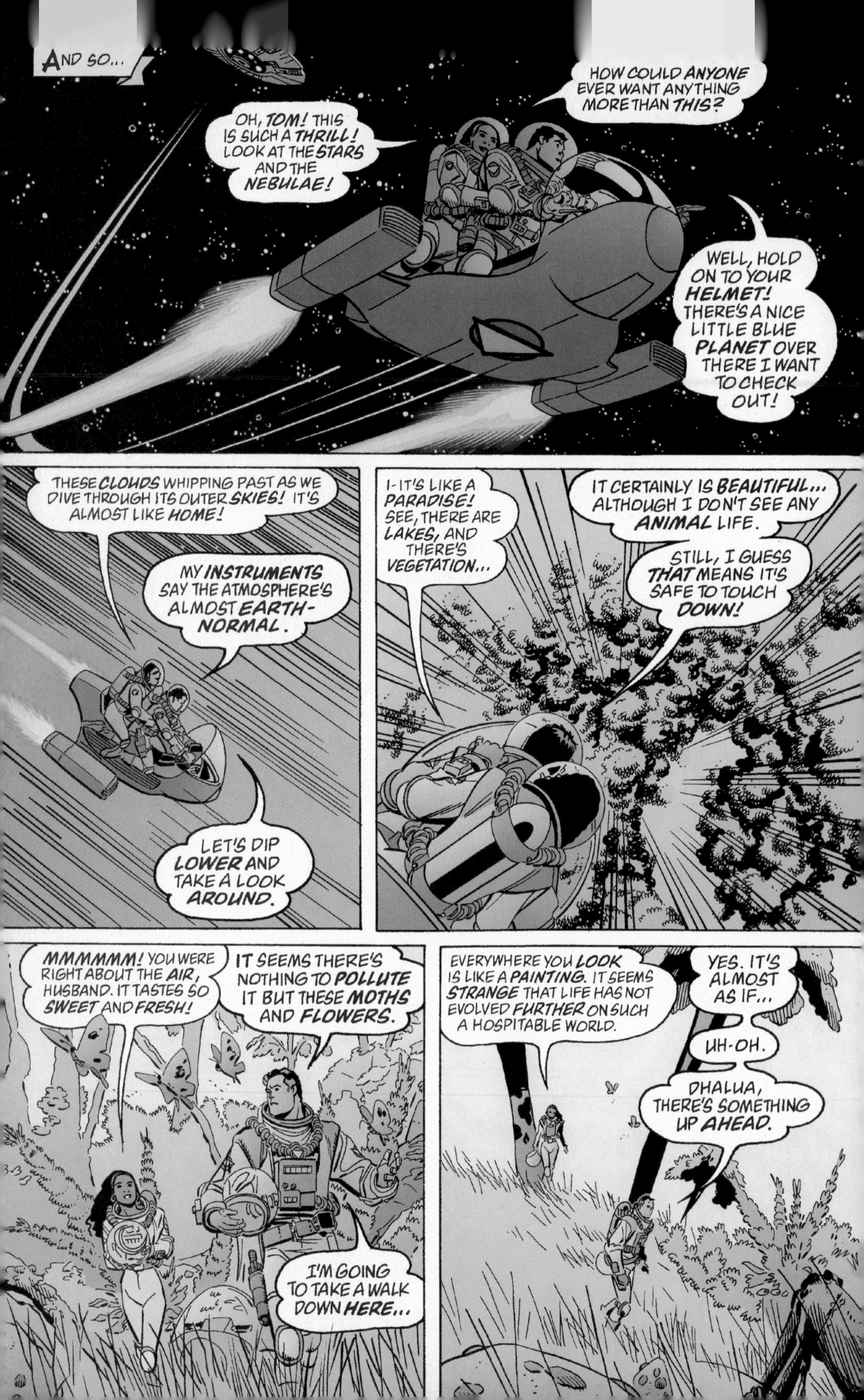
AND SO...
OH, TOM! THIS IS SUCH A THRILL! LOOK AT THE STARS AND THE NEBULAE!
HOW COULD ANYONE EVER WANT ANYTHING MORE THAN THIS?
WELL, HOLD ON TO YOUR HELMET! THERE'S A NICE LITTLE BLUE PLANET OVER THERE I WANT TO CHECK OUT!
THESE CLOUDS WHIPPING PAST AS WE DIVE THROUGH ITS OUTER SKIES! IT'S ALMOST LIKE HOME!
MY INSTRUMENTS SAY THE ATMOSPHERE'S ALMOST EARTH-NORMAL.
LET'S DIP LOWER AND TAKE A LOOK AROUND.
I-IT'S LIKE A PARADISE! SEE, THERE ARE LAKES, AND THERE'S VEGETATION...
IT CERTAINLY IS BEAUTIFUL... ALTHOUGH I DON'T SEE ANY ANIMAL LIFE.
STILL, I GUESS THAT MEANS IT'S SAFE TO TOUCH DOWN!
MMMMMM! YOU WERE RIGHT ABOUT THE AIR, HUSBAND. IT TASTES SO SWEET AND FRESH!
IT SEEMS THERE'S NOTHING TO POLLUTE IT BUT THESE MOTHS AND FLOWERS.
I'M GOING TO TAKE A WALK DOWN HERE...
EVERYWHERE YOU LOOK IS LIKE A PAINTING. IT SEEMS STRANGE THAT LIFE HAS NOT EVOLVED FURTHER ON SUCH A HOSPITABLE WORLD.
YES. IT'S ALMOST AS IF...
UH-OH.
DHALUA, THERE'S SOMETHING UP AHEAD.

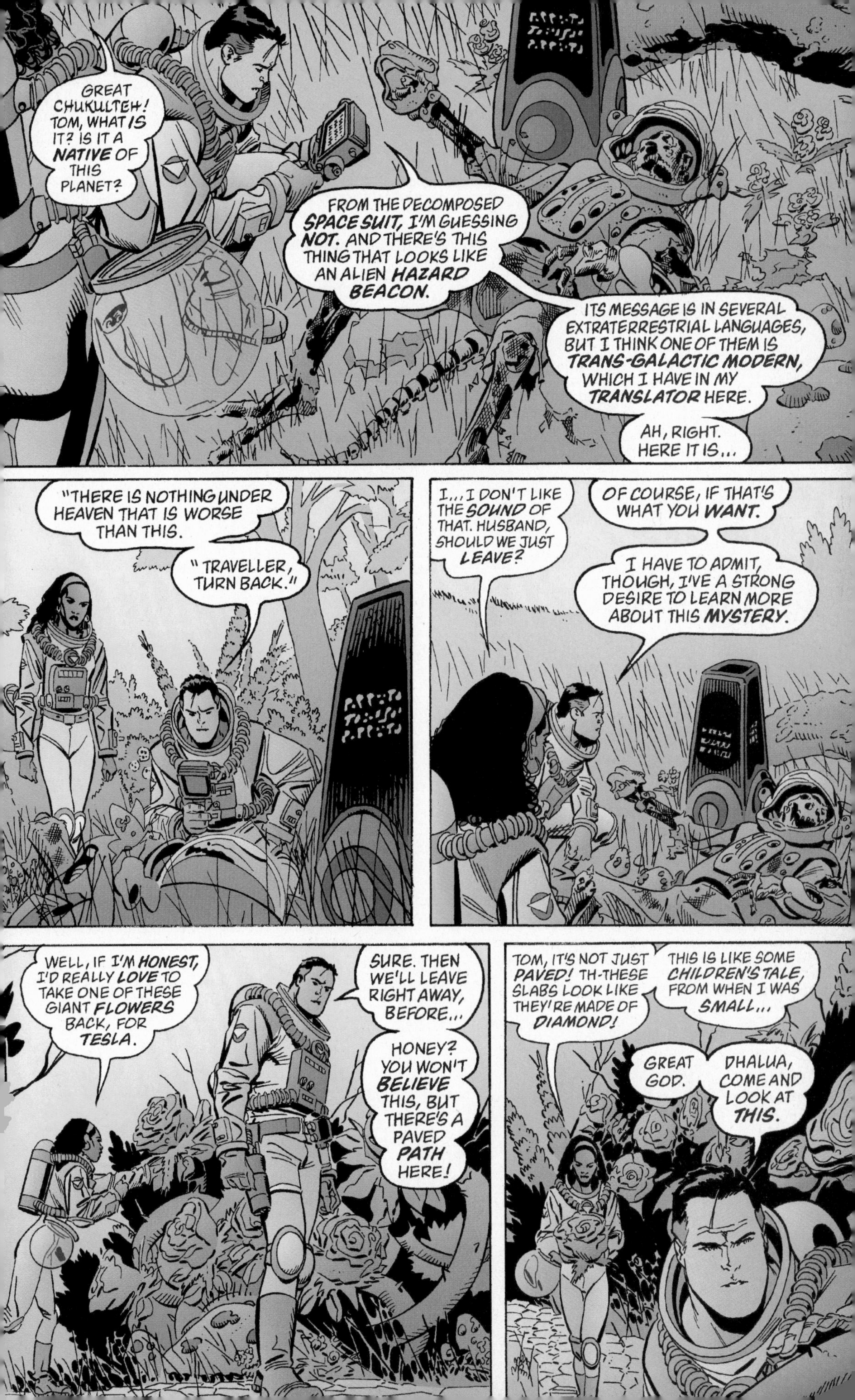
GREAT CHUKULTEH! TOM, WHAT IS IT? IS IT A NATIVE OF THIS PLANET?
FROM THE DECOMPOSED SPACE SUIT, I'M GUESSING NOT. AND THERE'S THIS THING THAT LOOKS LIKE AN ALIEN HAZARD BEACON.
ITS MESSAGE IS IN SEVERAL EXTRATERRESTRIAL LANGUAGES, BUT I THINK ONE OF THEM IS TRANS-GALACTIC MODERN, WHICH I HAVE IN MY TRANSLATOR HERE.
AH, RIGHT. HERE IT IS...
"THERE IS NOTHING UNDER HEAVEN THAT IS WORSE THAN THIS.
"TRAVELLER, TURN BACK."
I... I DON'T LIKE THE SOUND OF THAT. HUSBAND, SHOULD WE JUST LEAVE?
OF COURSE, IF THAT'S WHAT YOU WANT.
I HAVE TO ADMIT, THOUGH, I'VE A STRONG DESIRE TO LEARN MORE ABOUT THIS MYSTERY.
WELL, IF I'M HONEST, I'D REALLY LOVE TO TAKE ONE OF THESE GIANT FLOWERS BACK, FOR TESLA.
SURE. THEN WE'LL LEAVE RIGHT AWAY, BEFORE...
HONEY? YOU WON'T BELIEVE THIS, BUT THERE'S A PAVED PATH HERE!
TOM, IT'S NOT JUST PAVED! TH-THESE SLABS LOOK LIKE THEY'RE MADE OF DIAMOND!
THIS IS LIKE SOME CHILDREN'S TALE, FROM WHEN I WAS SMALL...
GREAT GOD.
DHALUA, COME AND LOOK AT THIS.

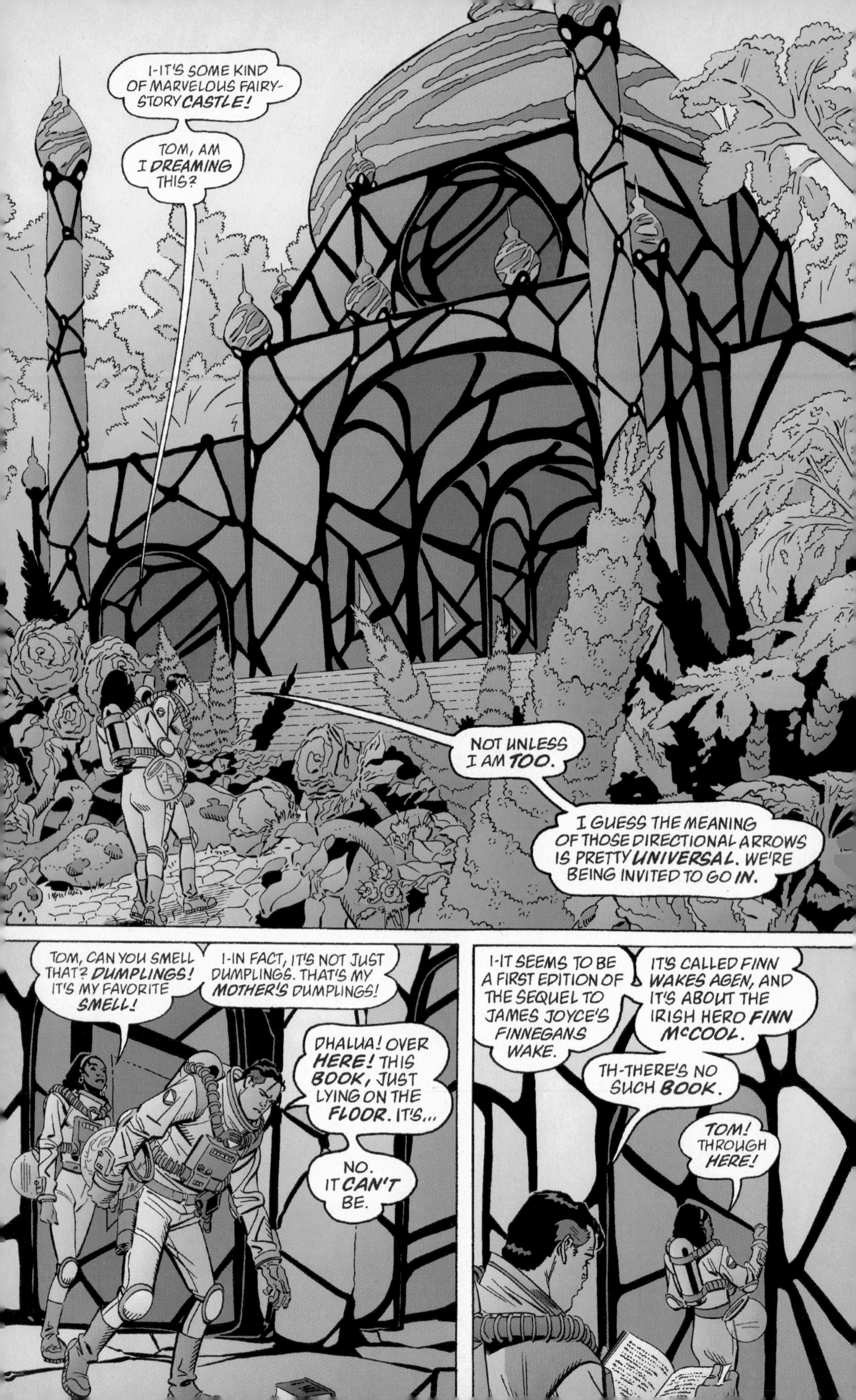
I-IT'S SOME KIND OF MARVELOUS FAIRY-STORY CASTLE!
TOM, AM I DREAMING THIS?
NOT UNLESS I AM TOO.
I GUESS THE MEANING OF THOSE DIRECTIONAL ARROWS IS PRETTY UNIVERSAL. WE'RE BEING INVITED TO GO IN.
TOM, CAN YOU SMELL THAT? DUMPLINGS! IT'S MY FAVORITE SMELL!
I-IN FACT, IT'S NOT JUST DUMPLINGS. THAT'S MY MOTHER'S DUMPLINGS!
DHALUA! OVER HERE! THIS BOOK, JUST LYING ON THE FLOOR. IT'S...
NO. IT CAN'T BE.
I-IT SEEMS TO BE A FIRST EDITION OF THE SEQUEL TO JAMES JOYCE'S FINNEGANS WAKE.
IT'S CALLED FINN WAKES AGEN, AND IT'S ABOUT THE IRISH HERO FINN McCOOL.
TH-THERE'S NO SUCH BOOK.
TOM! THROUGH HERE!

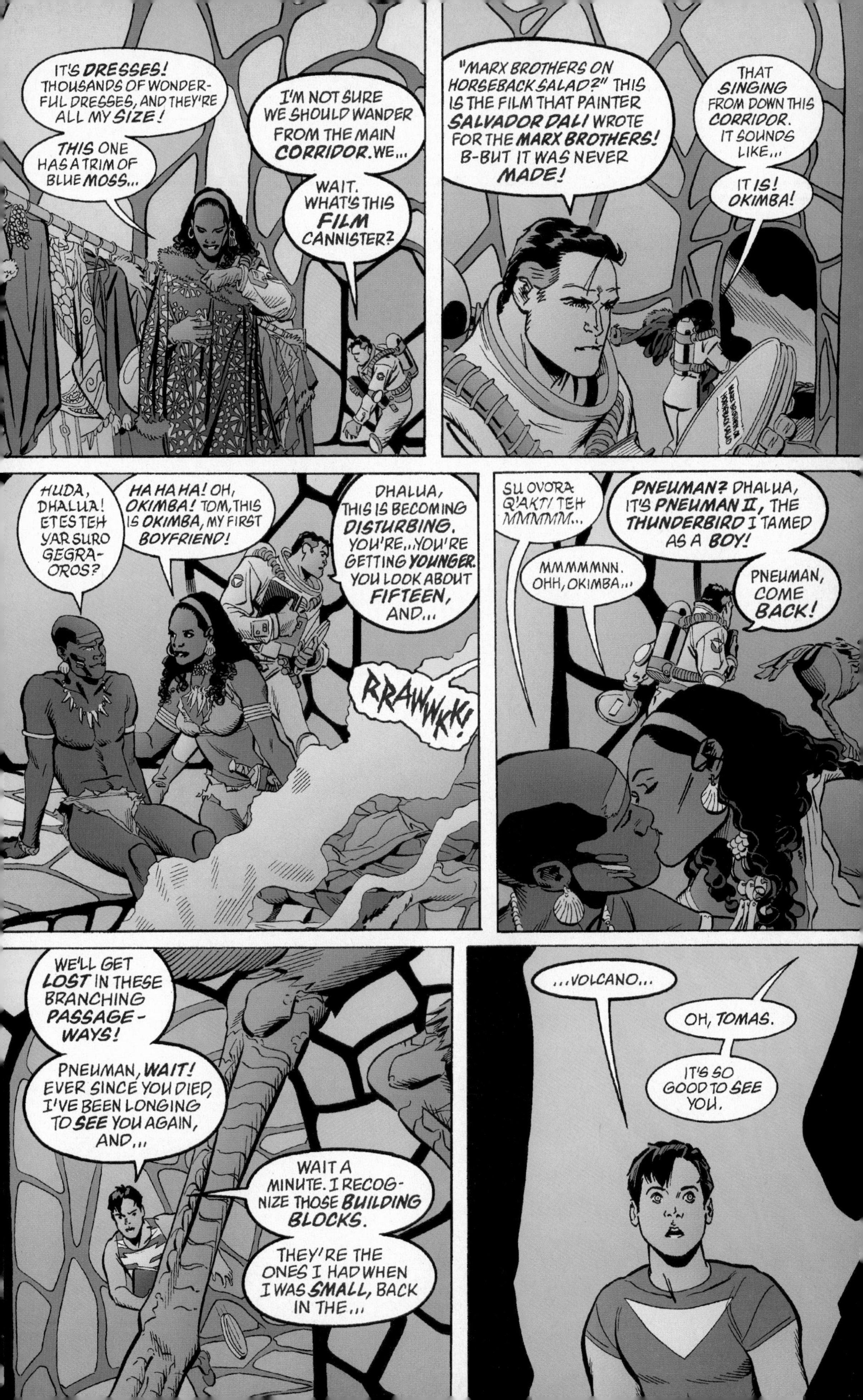
IT'S DRESSES! THOUSANDS OF WONDERFUL DRESSES, AND THEY'RE ALL MY SIZE!
THIS ONE HAS A TRIM OF BLUE MOSS...
I'M NOT SURE WE SHOULD WANDER FROM THE MAIN CORRIDOR. WE...
WAIT. WHAT'S THIS FILM CANNISTER?
"MARX BROTHERS ON HORSEBACK SALAD?" THIS IS THE FILM THAT PAINTER SALVADOR DALI WROTE FOR THE MARX BROTHERS! B-BUT IT WAS NEVER MADE!
THAT SINGING FROM DOWN THIS CORRIDOR. IT SOUNDS LIKE...
IT IS! OKIMBA!
HUDA, DHALUA! ETES TEH YAR SURO GEGRA-OROS?
HA HA HA! OH, OKIMBA! TOM, THIS IS OKIMBA, MY FIRST BOYFRIEND!
DHALUA, THIS IS BECOMING DISTURBING. YOU'RE... YOU'RE GETTING YOUNGER. YOU LOOK ABOUT FIFTEEN, AND...
RRAWWKK!
SU OVORA Q'AKT/ TEH MMMMM...
PNEUMAN? DHALUA, IT'S PNEUMAN II, THE THUNDERBIRD I TAMED AS A BOY!
MMMMMNN. OHH, OKIMBA...
PNEUMAN, COME BACK!
WE'LL GET LOST IN THESE BRANCHING PASSAGE-WAYS!
PNEUMAN, WAIT! EVER SINCE YOU DIED, I'VE BEEN LONGING TO SEE YOU AGAIN, AND...
WAIT A MINUTE. I RECOGNIZE THOSE BUILDING BLOCKS.
THEY'RE THE ONES I HAD WHEN I WAS SMALL, BACK IN THE...
...VOLCANO...
OH, TOMAS.
IT'S SO GOOD TO SEE YOU.

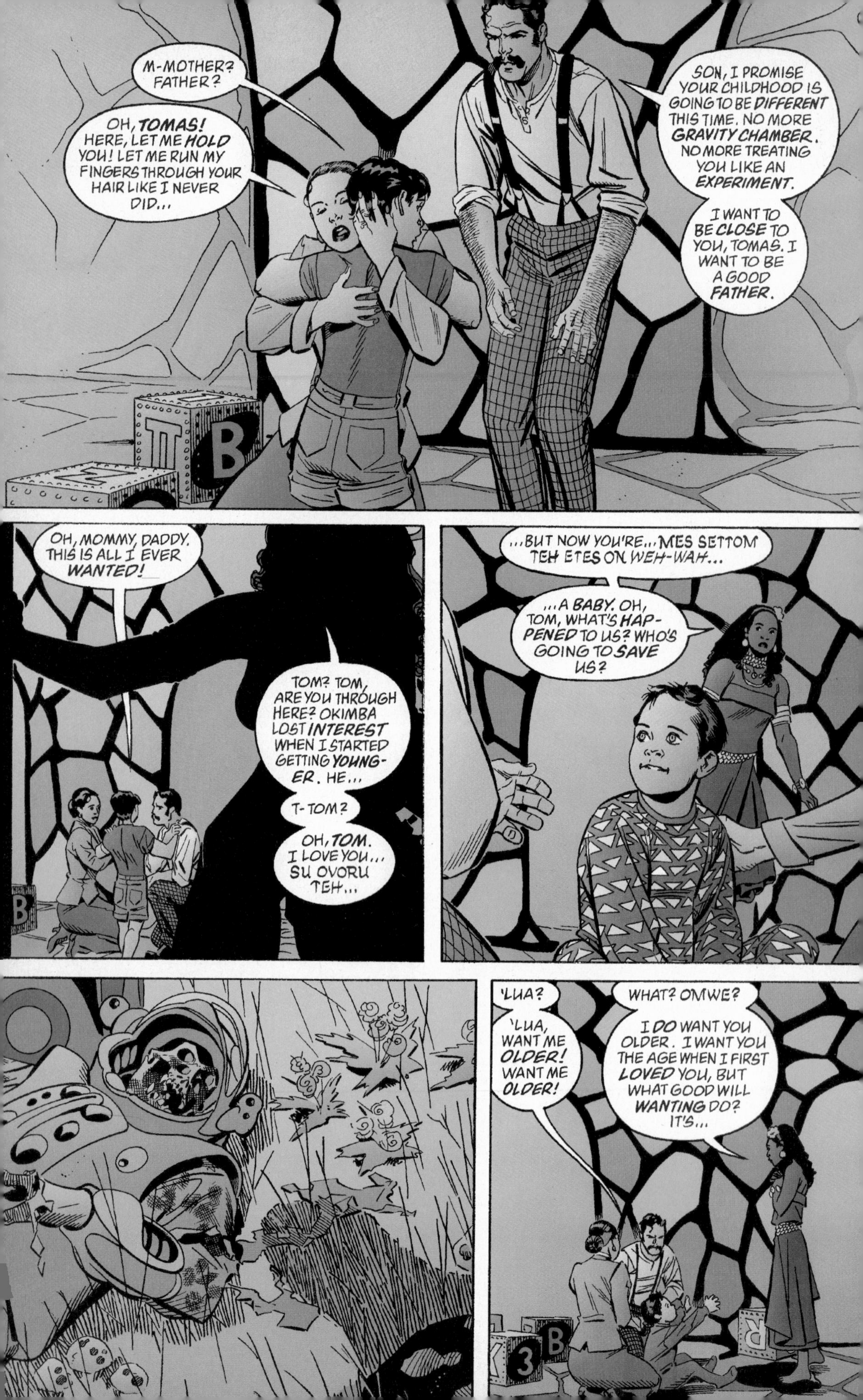
M-MOTHER? FATHER?
OH, TOMAS! HERE, LET ME HOLD YOU! LET ME RUN MY FINGERS THROUGH YOUR HAIR LIKE I NEVER DID...
SON, I PROMISE YOUR CHILDHOOD IS GOING TO BE DIFFERENT THIS TIME. NO MORE GRAVITY CHAMBER. NO MORE TREATING YOU LIKE AN EXPERIMENT.
I WANT TO BE CLOSE TO YOU, TOMAS. I WANT TO BE A GOOD FATHER.
OH, MOMMY, DADDY. THIS IS ALL I EVER WANTED!
TOM? TOM, ARE YOU THROUGH HERE? OKIMBA LOST INTEREST WHEN I STARTED GETTING YOUNGER. HE...
T-TOM?
OH, TOM. I LOVE YOU... SU OVORU TEH...
...BUT NOW YOU'RE... MES SETTOM TEH ETES ON WEH-WAH...
...A BABY. OH, TOM, WHAT'S HAPPENED TO US? WHO'S GOING TO SAVE US?
'LUA?
WHAT? OMWE?
'LUA, WANT ME OLDER! WANT ME OLDER!
I DO WANT YOU OLDER. I WANT YOU THE AGE WHEN I FIRST LOVED YOU, BUT WHAT GOOD WILL WANTING DO? IT'S...

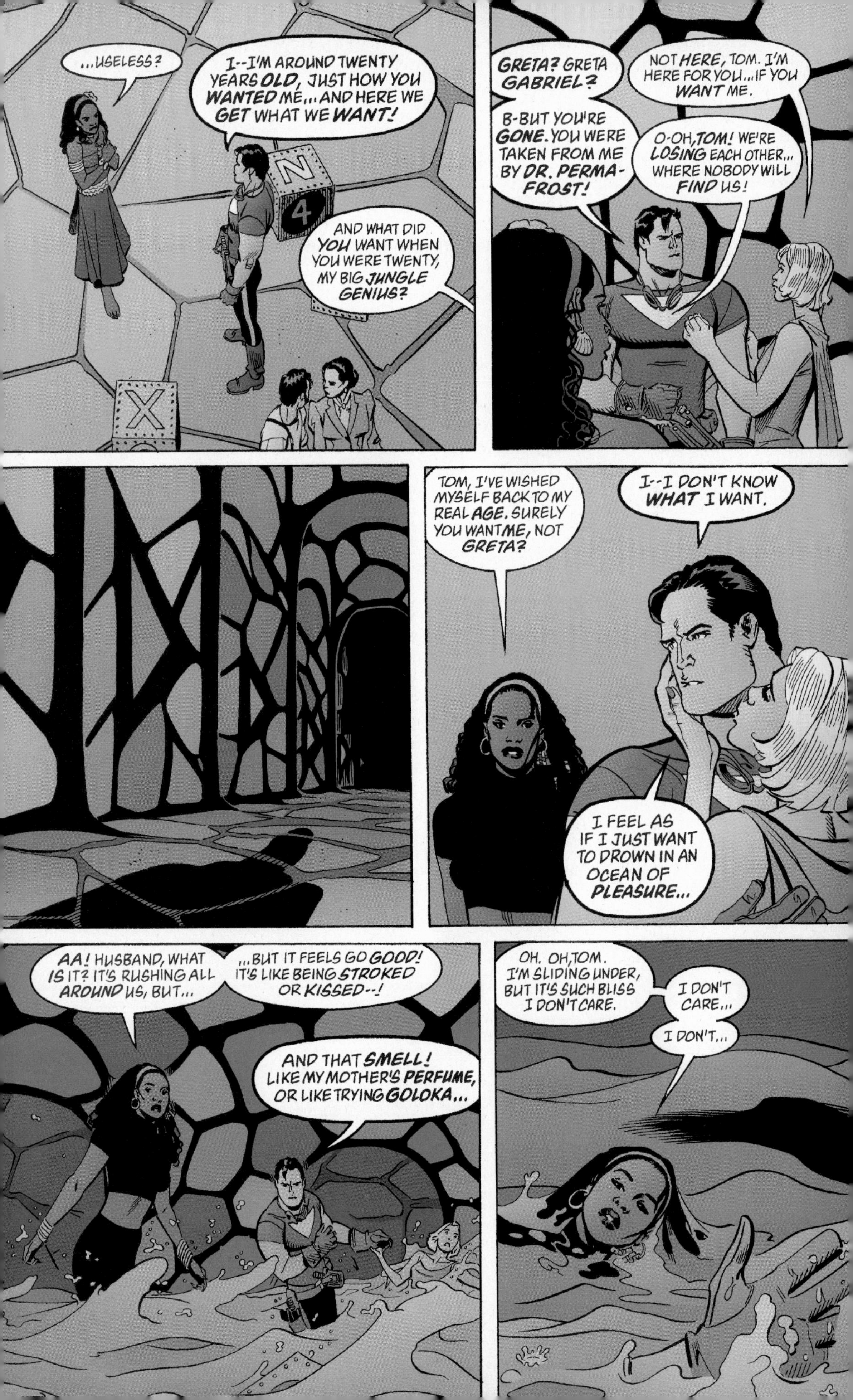

...USELESS?
I--I'M AROUND TWENTY YEARS OLD, JUST HOW YOU WANTED ME... AND HERE WE GET WHAT WE WANT!
AND WHAT DID YOU WANT WHEN YOU WERE TWENTY, MY BIG JUNGLE GENIUS?
GRETA? GRETA GABRIEL?
B-BUT YOU'RE GONE. YOU WERE TAKEN FROM ME BY DR. PERMA-FROST!
NOT HERE, TOM. I'M HERE FOR YOU... IF YOU WANT ME.
O-OH, TOM! WE'RE LOSING EACH OTHER... WHERE NOBODY WILL FIND US!
TOM, I'VE WISHED MYSELF BACK TO MY REAL AGE. SURELY YOU WANT ME, NOT GRETA?
I--I DON'T KNOW WHAT I WANT.
I FEEL AS IF I JUST WANT TO DROWN IN AN OCEAN OF PLEASURE...
AA! HUSBAND, WHAT IS IT? IT'S RUSHING ALL AROUND US, BUT...
...BUT IT FEELS SO GOOD! IT'S LIKE BEING STROKED OR KISSED--!
AND THAT SMELL! LIKE MY MOTHER'S PERFUME, OR LIKE TRYING GOLOKA...
OH. OH, TOM. I'M SLIDING UNDER, BUT IT'S SUCH BLISS I DON'T CARE.
I DON'T CARE...
I DON'T...

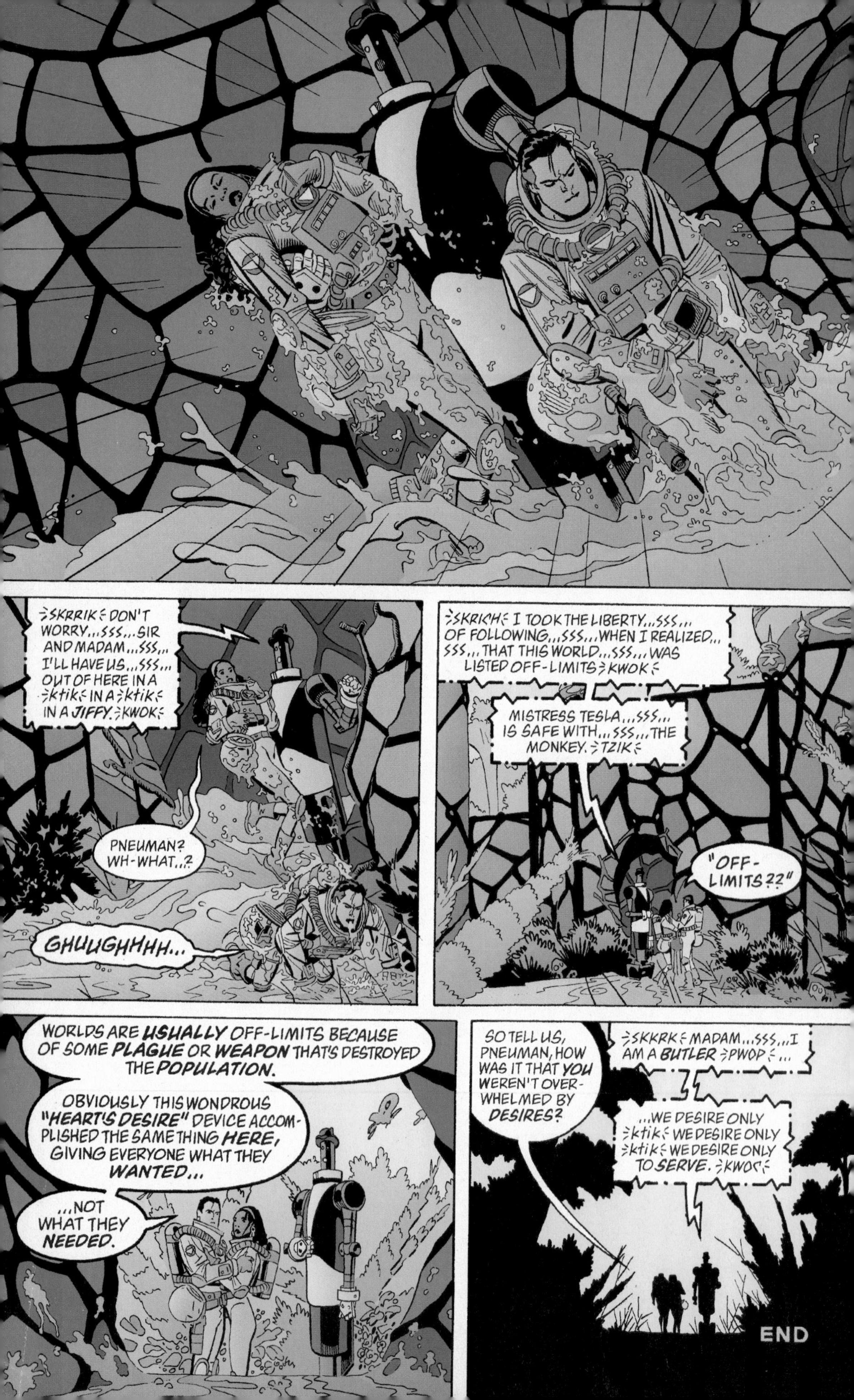

⇾SKRRIK⇽ DON'T WORRY...SSS...SIR AND MADAM...SSS... I'LL HAVE US...SSS... OUT OF HERE IN A ⇾ktik⇽ IN A ⇾ktik⇽ IN A JIFFY. ⇾KWOK⇽
PNEUMAN? WH-WHAT...?
GHUUGHHHH...
⇾SKRICH⇽ I TOOK THE LIBERTY...SSS... OF FOLLOWING...SSS... WHEN I REALIZED... SSS... THAT THIS WORLD...SSS... WAS LISTED OFF-LIMITS ⇾KWOK⇽
MISTRESS TESLA...SSS... IS SAFE WITH...SSS... THE MONKEY. ⇾TZIK⇽
"OFF-LIMITS??"
WORLDS ARE USUALLY OFF-LIMITS BECAUSE OF SOME PLAGUE OR WEAPON THAT'S DESTROYED THE POPULATION.
OBVIOUSLY THIS WONDROUS "HEART'S DESIRE" DEVICE ACCOMPLISHED THE SAME THING HERE, GIVING EVERYONE WHAT THEY WANTED...
...NOT WHAT THEY NEEDED.
SO TELL US, PNEUMAN, HOW WAS IT THAT YOU WEREN'T OVERWHELMED BY DESIRES?
⇾SKKRK⇽ MADAM...SSS...I AM A BUTLER ⇾PWOP⇽ ...
...WE DESIRE ONLY ⇾ktik⇽ WE DESIRE ONLY ⇾ktik⇽ WE DESIRE ONLY TO SERVE. ⇾KWOC⇽
END

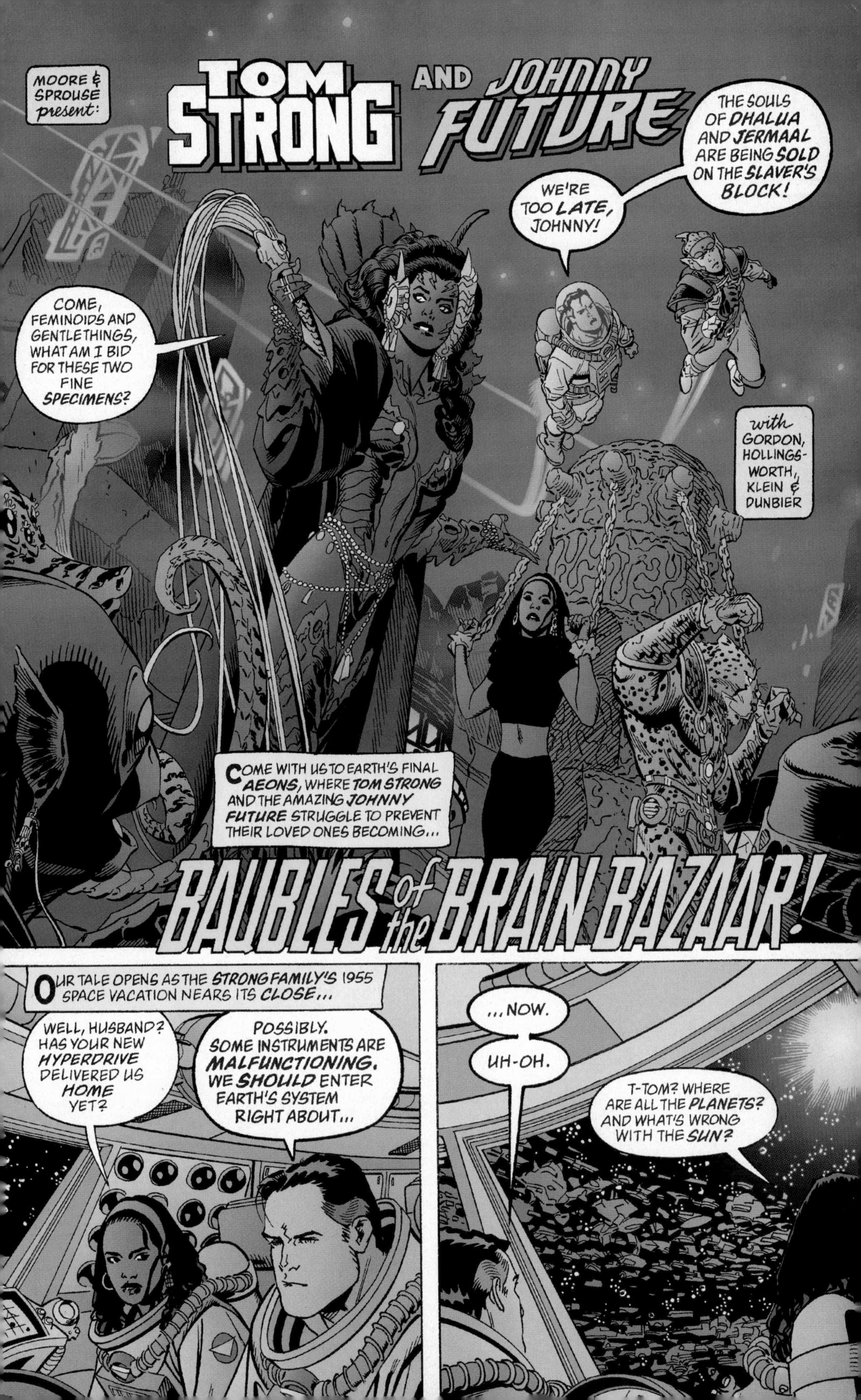
MOORE & SPROUSE present:
TOM STRONG AND JOHNNY FUTURE
THE SOULS OF DHALUA AND JERMAAL ARE BEING SOLD ON THE SLAVER'S BLOCK!
WE'RE TOO LATE, JOHNNY!
COME, FEMINOIDS AND GENTLETHINGS, WHAT AM I BID FOR THESE TWO FINE SPECIMENS?
with GORDON, HOLLINGSWORTH, KLEIN & DUNBIER
COME WITH US TO EARTH'S FINAL AEONS, WHERE TOM STRONG AND THE AMAZING JOHNNY FUTURE STRUGGLE TO PREVENT THEIR LOVED ONES BECOMING...
BAUBLES of the BRAIN BAZAAR!
OUR TALE OPENS AS THE STRONG FAMILY'S 1955 SPACE VACATION NEARS ITS CLOSE...
WELL, HUSBAND? HAS YOUR NEW HYPERDRIVE DELIVERED US HOME YET?
POSSIBLY. SOME INSTRUMENTS ARE MALFUNCTIONING. WE SHOULD ENTER EARTH'S SYSTEM RIGHT ABOUT...
...NOW.
UH-OH.
T-TOM? WHERE ARE ALL THE PLANETS? AND WHAT'S WRONG WITH THE SUN?

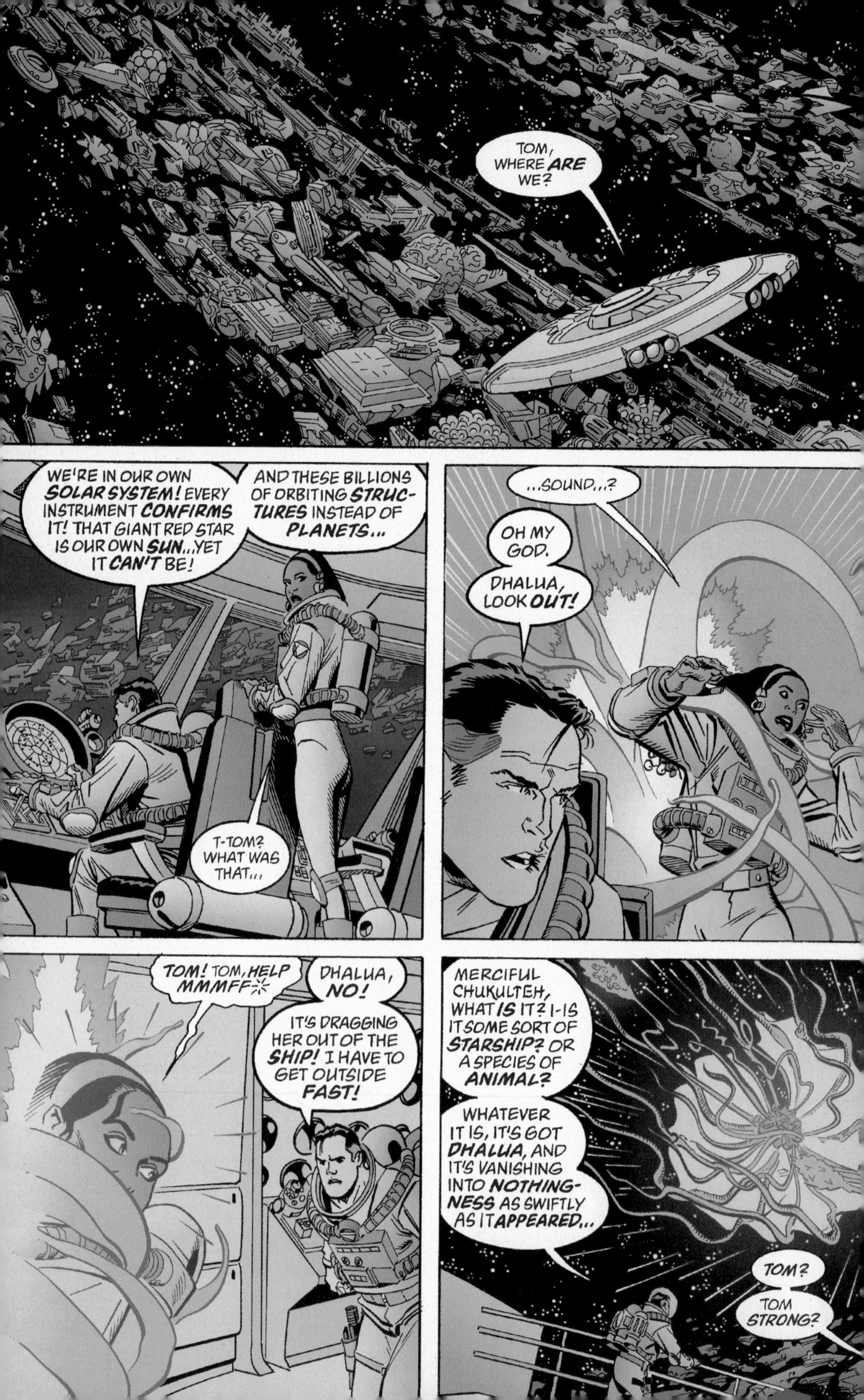
TOM, WHERE ARE WE?
WE'RE IN OUR OWN SOLAR SYSTEM! EVERY INSTRUMENT CONFIRMS IT! THAT GIANT RED STAR IS OUR OWN SUN...YET IT CAN'T BE!
AND THESE BILLIONS OF ORBITING STRUCTURES INSTEAD OF PLANETS...
T-TOM? WHAT WAS THAT...
...SOUND...?
OH MY GOD.
DHALUA, LOOK OUT!
TOM! TOM, HELP MMMFF
DHALUA, NO!
IT'S DRAGGING HER OUT OF THE SHIP! I HAVE TO GET OUTSIDE FAST!
MERCIFUL CHUKULTEH, WHAT IS IT? I-IS IT SOME SORT OF STARSHIP? OR A SPECIES OF ANIMAL?
WHATEVER IT IS, IT'S GOT DHALUA, AND IT'S VANISHING INTO NOTHINGNESS AS SWIFTLY AS IT APPEARED...
TOM?
TOM STRONG?

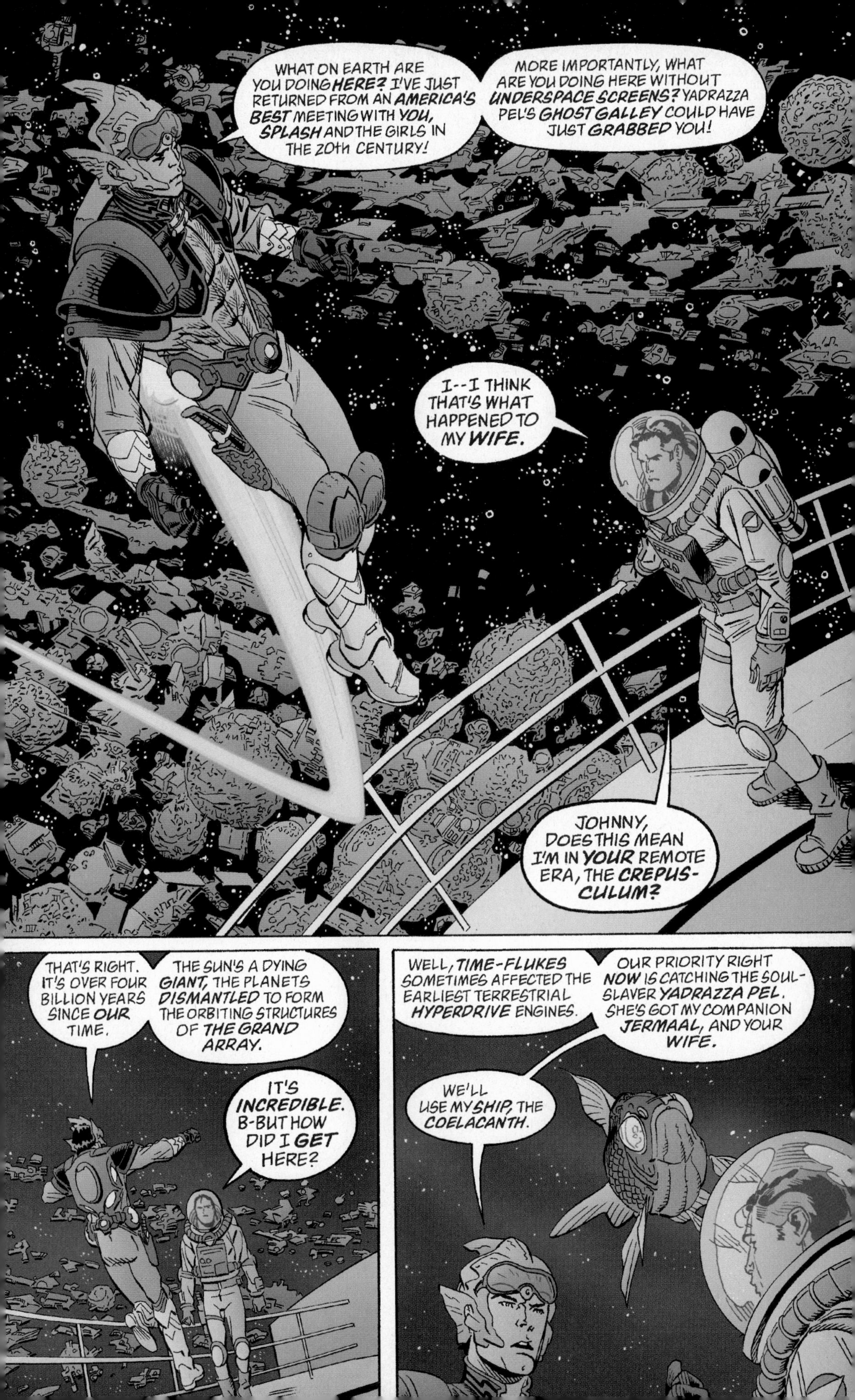
WHAT ON EARTH ARE YOU DOING HERE? I'VE JUST RETURNED FROM AN AMERICA'S BEST MEETING WITH YOU, SPLASH AND THE GIRLS IN THE 20th CENTURY!
MORE IMPORTANTLY, WHAT ARE YOU DOING HERE WITHOUT UNDERSPACE SCREENS? YADRAZZA PEL'S GHOST GALLEY COULD HAVE JUST GRABBED YOU!
I--I THINK THAT'S WHAT HAPPENED TO MY WIFE.
JOHNNY, DOES THIS MEAN I'M IN YOUR REMOTE ERA, THE CREPUS-CULUM?
THAT'S RIGHT. IT'S OVER FOUR BILLION YEARS SINCE OUR TIME.
THE SUN'S A DYING GIANT, THE PLANETS DISMANTLED TO FORM THE ORBITING STRUCTURES OF THE GRAND ARRAY.
IT'S INCREDIBLE. B-BUT HOW DID I GET HERE?
WELL, TIME-FLUKES SOMETIMES AFFECTED THE EARLIEST TERRESTRIAL HYPERDRIVE ENGINES.
OUR PRIORITY RIGHT NOW IS CATCHING THE SOUL-SLAVER YADRAZZA PEL. SHE'S GOT MY COMPANION JERMAAL, AND YOUR WIFE.
WE'LL USE MY SHIP, THE COELACANTH.

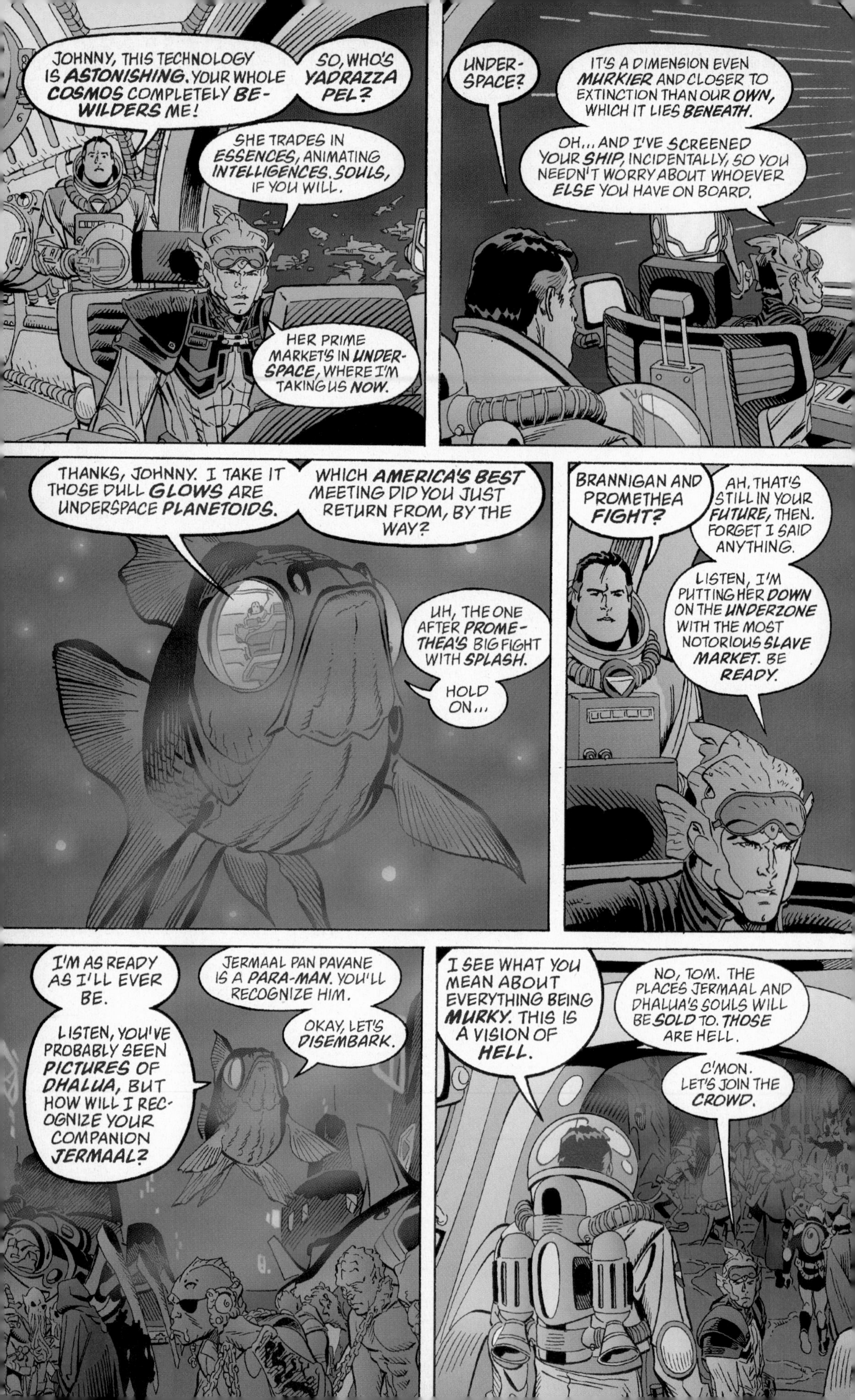
JOHNNY, THIS TECHNOLOGY IS ASTONISHING. YOUR WHOLE COSMOS COMPLETELY BE-WILDERS ME!
SO, WHO'S YADRAZZA PEL?
SHE TRADES IN ESSENCES, ANIMATING INTELLIGENCES. SOULS, IF YOU WILL.
HER PRIME MARKET'S IN UNDER-SPACE, WHERE I'M TAKING US NOW.
UNDER-SPACE?
IT'S A DIMENSION EVEN MURKIER AND CLOSER TO EXTINCTION THAN OUR OWN, WHICH IT LIES BENEATH.
OH... AND I'VE SCREENED YOUR SHIP, INCIDENTALLY, SO YOU NEEDN'T WORRY ABOUT WHOEVER ELSE YOU HAVE ON BOARD.
THANKS, JOHNNY. I TAKE IT THOSE DULL GLOWS ARE UNDERSPACE PLANETOIDS.
WHICH AMERICA'S BEST MEETING DID YOU JUST RETURN FROM, BY THE WAY?
UH, THE ONE AFTER PROME-THEA'S BIG FIGHT WITH SPLASH.
HOLD ON...
BRANNIGAN AND PROMETHEA FIGHT?
AH. THAT'S STILL IN YOUR FUTURE, THEN. FORGET I SAID ANYTHING.
LISTEN, I'M PUTTING HER DOWN ON THE UNDERZONE WITH THE MOST NOTORIOUS SLAVE MARKET. BE READY.
I'M AS READY AS I'LL EVER BE.
LISTEN, YOU'VE PROBABLY SEEN PICTURES OF DHALUA, BUT HOW WILL I REC-OGNIZE YOUR COMPANION JERMAAL?
JERMAAL PAN PAVANE IS A PARA-MAN. YOU'LL RECOGNIZE HIM.
OKAY, LET'S DISEMBARK.
I SEE WHAT YOU MEAN ABOUT EVERYTHING BEING MURKY. THIS IS A VISION OF HELL.
NO, TOM. THE PLACES JERMAAL AND DHALUA'S SOULS WILL BE SOLD TO. THOSE ARE HELL.
C'MON. LET'S JOIN THE CROWD.

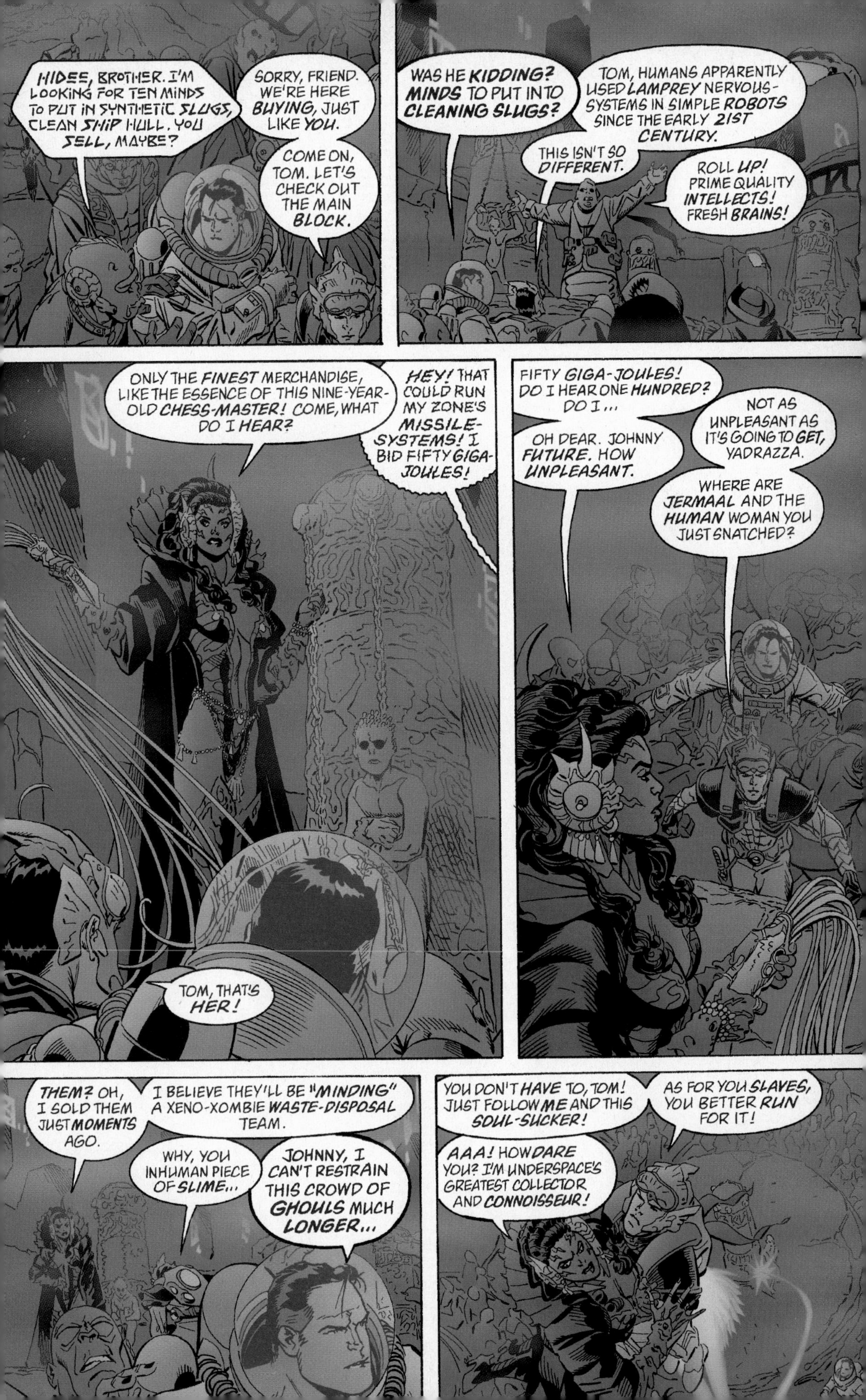
HIDEE, BROTHER. I'M LOOKING FOR TEN MINDS TO PUT IN SYNTHETIC SLUGS, CLEAN SHIP HULL. YOU SELL, MAYBE?
SORRY, FRIEND. WE'RE HERE BUYING, JUST LIKE YOU.
COME ON, TOM. LET'S CHECK OUT THE MAIN BLOCK.
WAS HE KIDDING? MINDS TO PUT INTO CLEANING SLUGS?
TOM, HUMANS APPARENTLY USED LAMPREY NERVOUS-SYSTEMS IN SIMPLE ROBOTS SINCE THE EARLY 21ST CENTURY.
THIS ISN'T SO DIFFERENT.
ROLL UP! PRIME QUALITY INTELLECTS! FRESH BRAINS!
ONLY THE FINEST MERCHANDISE, LIKE THE ESSENCE OF THIS NINE-YEAR-OLD CHESS-MASTER! COME, WHAT DO I HEAR?
HEY! THAT COULD RUN MY ZONE'S MISSILE-SYSTEMS! I BID FIFTY GIGA-JOULES!
TOM, THAT'S HER!
FIFTY GIGA-JOULES! DO I HEAR ONE HUNDRED? DO I...
OH DEAR. JOHNNY FUTURE. HOW UNPLEASANT.
NOT AS UNPLEASANT AS IT'S GOING TO GET, YADRAZZA.
WHERE ARE JERMAAL AND THE HUMAN WOMAN YOU JUST SNATCHED?
THEM? OH, I SOLD THEM JUST MOMENTS AGO.
I BELIEVE THEY'LL BE "MINDING" A XENO-XOMBIE WASTE-DISPOSAL TEAM.
WHY, YOU INHUMAN PIECE OF SLIME...
JOHNNY, I CAN'T RESTRAIN THIS CROWD OF GHOULS MUCH LONGER...
YOU DON'T HAVE TO, TOM! JUST FOLLOW ME AND THIS SOUL-SUCKER!
AS FOR YOU SLAVES, YOU BETTER RUN FOR IT!
AAA! HOW DARE YOU? I'M UNDERSPACE'S GREATEST COLLECTOR AND CONNOISSEUR!

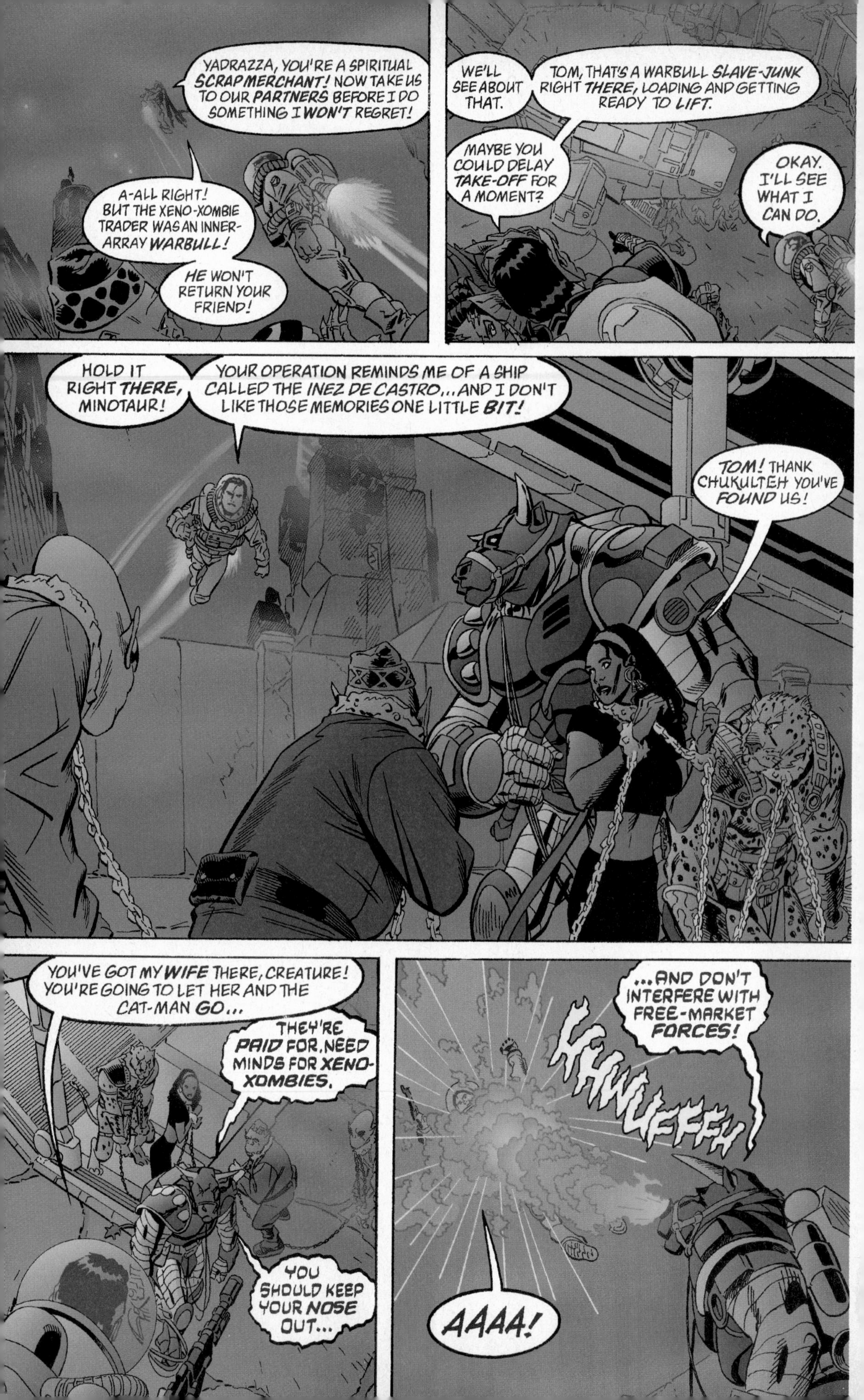
YADRAZZA, YOU'RE A SPIRITUAL SCRAP MERCHANT! NOW TAKE US TO OUR PARTNERS BEFORE I DO SOMETHING I WON'T REGRET!
A-ALL RIGHT! BUT THE XENO-XOMBIE TRADER WAS AN INNER-ARRAY WARBULL!
HE WON'T RETURN YOUR FRIEND!
WE'LL SEE ABOUT THAT.
TOM, THAT'S A WARBULL SLAVE-JUNK RIGHT THERE, LOADING AND GETTING READY TO LIFT.
MAYBE YOU COULD DELAY TAKE-OFF FOR A MOMENT?
OKAY. I'LL SEE WHAT I CAN DO.
HOLD IT RIGHT THERE, MINOTAUR!
YOUR OPERATION REMINDS ME OF A SHIP CALLED THE INEZ DE CASTRO,... AND I DON'T LIKE THOSE MEMORIES ONE LITTLE BIT!
TOM! THANK CHUKULTEH YOU'VE FOUND US!
YOU'VE GOT MY WIFE THERE, CREATURE! YOU'RE GOING TO LET HER AND THE CAT-MAN GO...
THEY'RE PAID FOR. NEED MINDS FOR XENO-XOMBIES.
YOU SHOULD KEEP YOUR NOSE OUT...
...AND DON'T INTERFERE WITH FREE-MARKET FORCES!
HHHNUFFFH
AAAA!

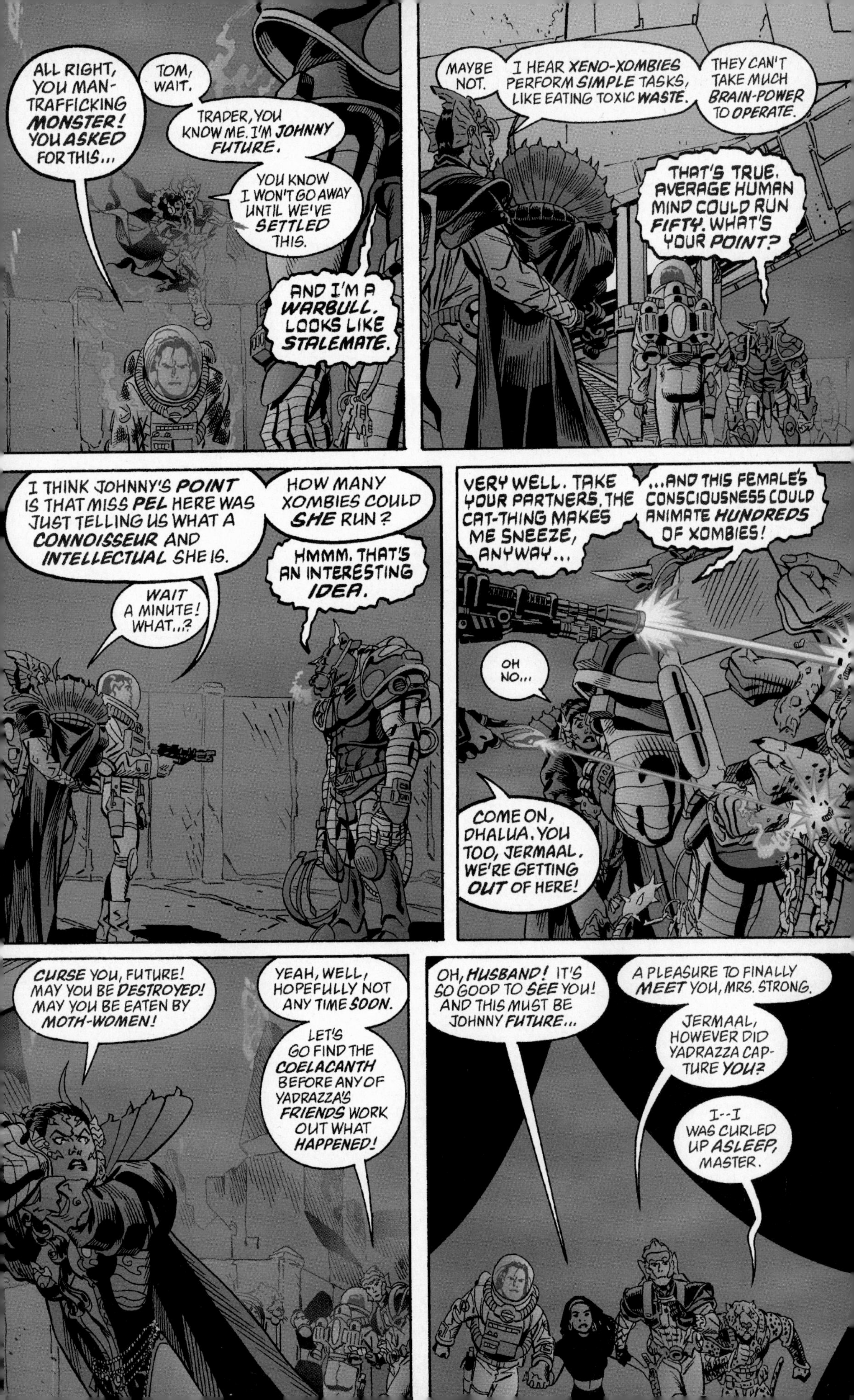
ALL RIGHT, YOU MAN-TRAFFICKING MONSTER! YOU ASKED FOR THIS...
TOM, WAIT.
TRADER, YOU KNOW ME. I'M JOHNNY FUTURE.
YOU KNOW I WON'T GO AWAY UNTIL WE'VE SETTLED THIS.
AND I'M A WARBULL. LOOKS LIKE STALEMATE.
MAYBE NOT.
I HEAR XENO-XOMBIES PERFORM SIMPLE TASKS, LIKE EATING TOXIC WASTE.
THEY CAN'T TAKE MUCH BRAIN-POWER TO OPERATE.
THAT'S TRUE. AVERAGE HUMAN MIND COULD RUN FIFTY. WHAT'S YOUR POINT?
I THINK JOHNNY'S POINT IS THAT MISS PEL HERE WAS JUST TELLING US WHAT A CONNOISSEUR AND INTELLECTUAL SHE IS.
HOW MANY XOMBIES COULD SHE RUN?
HMMM. THAT'S AN INTERESTING IDEA.
WAIT A MINUTE! WHAT...?
VERY WELL. TAKE YOUR PARTNERS. THE CAT-THING MAKES ME SNEEZE, ANYWAY...
...AND THIS FEMALE'S CONSCIOUSNESS COULD ANIMATE HUNDREDS OF XOMBIES!
OH NO...
COME ON, DHALUA. YOU TOO, JERMAAL. WE'RE GETTING OUT OF HERE!
CURSE YOU, FUTURE! MAY YOU BE DESTROYED! MAY YOU BE EATEN BY MOTH-WOMEN!
YEAH, WELL, HOPEFULLY NOT ANY TIME SOON.
LET'S GO FIND THE COELACANTH BEFORE ANY OF YADRAZZA'S FRIENDS WORK OUT WHAT HAPPENED!
OH, HUSBAND! IT'S SO GOOD TO SEE YOU! AND THIS MUST BE JOHNNY FUTURE...
A PLEASURE TO FINALLY MEET YOU, MRS. STRONG.
JERMAAL, HOWEVER DID YADRAZZA CAPTURE YOU?
I--I WAS CURLED UP ASLEEP, MASTER.

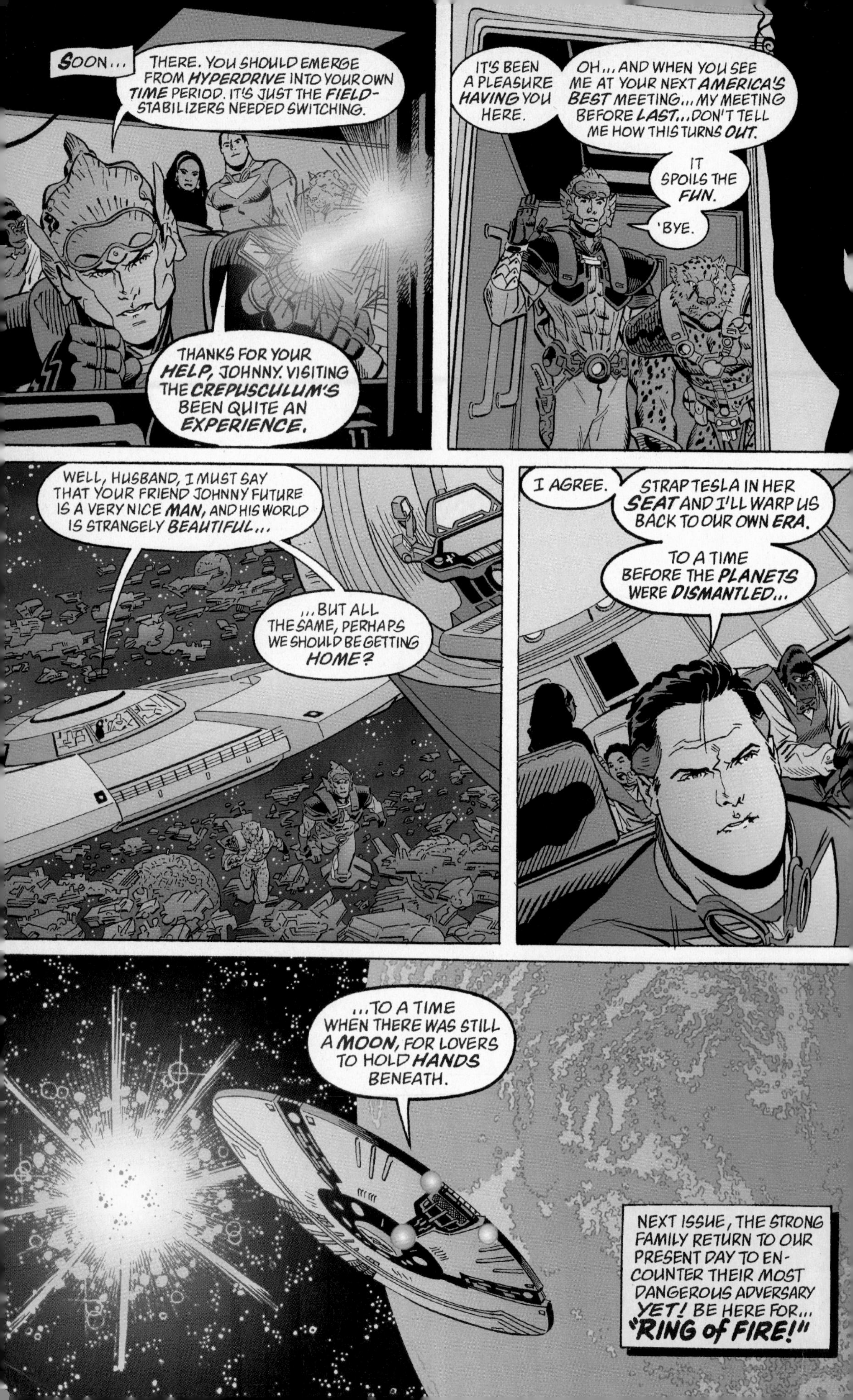
SOON...
THERE. YOU SHOULD EMERGE FROM HYPERDRIVE INTO YOUR OWN TIME PERIOD. IT'S JUST THE FIELD-STABILIZERS NEEDED SWITCHING.
THANKS FOR YOUR HELP, JOHNNY. VISITING THE CREPUSCULUM'S BEEN QUITE AN EXPERIENCE.
IT'S BEEN A PLEASURE HAVING YOU HERE.
OH... AND WHEN YOU SEE ME AT YOUR NEXT AMERICA'S BEST MEETING... MY MEETING BEFORE LAST... DON'T TELL ME HOW THIS TURNS OUT.
IT SPOILS THE FUN.
'BYE.
WELL, HUSBAND, I MUST SAY THAT YOUR FRIEND JOHNNY FUTURE IS A VERY NICE MAN, AND HIS WORLD IS STRANGELY BEAUTIFUL...
...BUT ALL THE SAME, PERHAPS WE SHOULD BE GETTING HOME?
I AGREE.
STRAP TESLA IN HER SEAT AND I'LL WARP US BACK TO OUR OWN ERA.
TO A TIME BEFORE THE PLANETS WERE DISMANTLED...
...TO A TIME WHEN THERE WAS STILL A MOON, FOR LOVERS TO HOLD HANDS BENEATH.
NEXT ISSUE, THE STRONG FAMILY RETURN TO OUR PRESENT DAY TO ENCOUNTER THEIR MOST DANGEROUS ADVERSARY YET! BE HERE FOR... "RING of FIRE!"

TOM STRONG GALLERY

Designs by ALAN WEISS for his take on the character in Chapter One

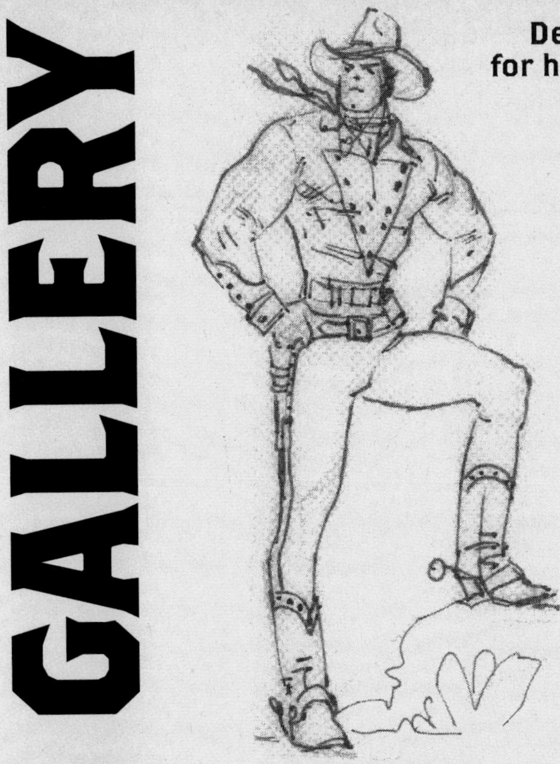

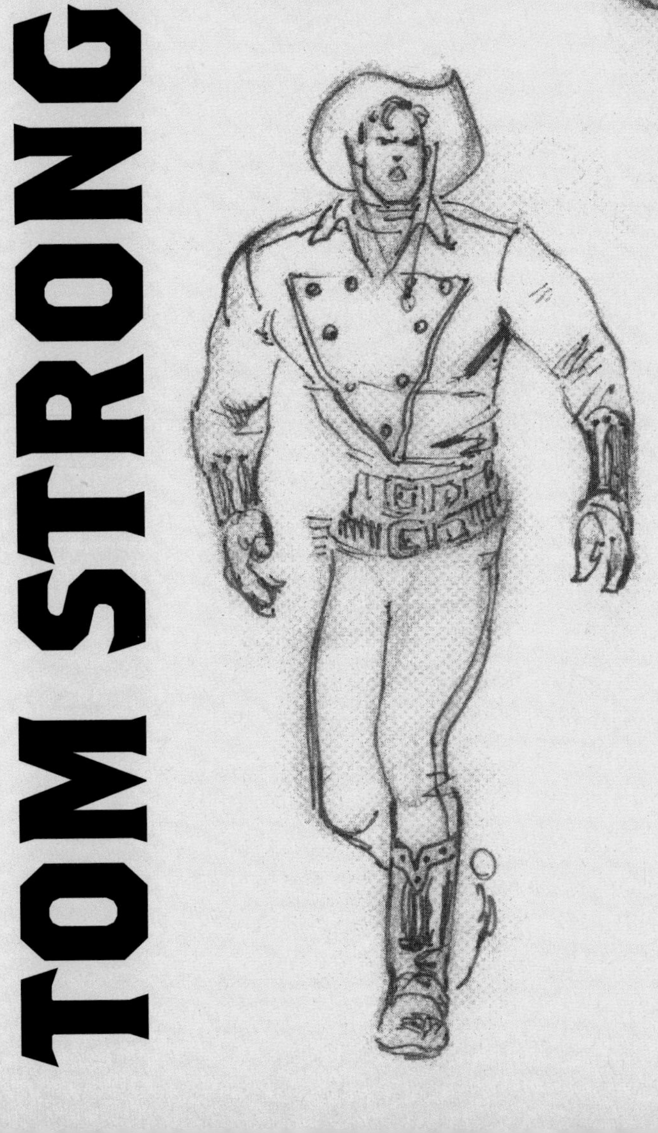

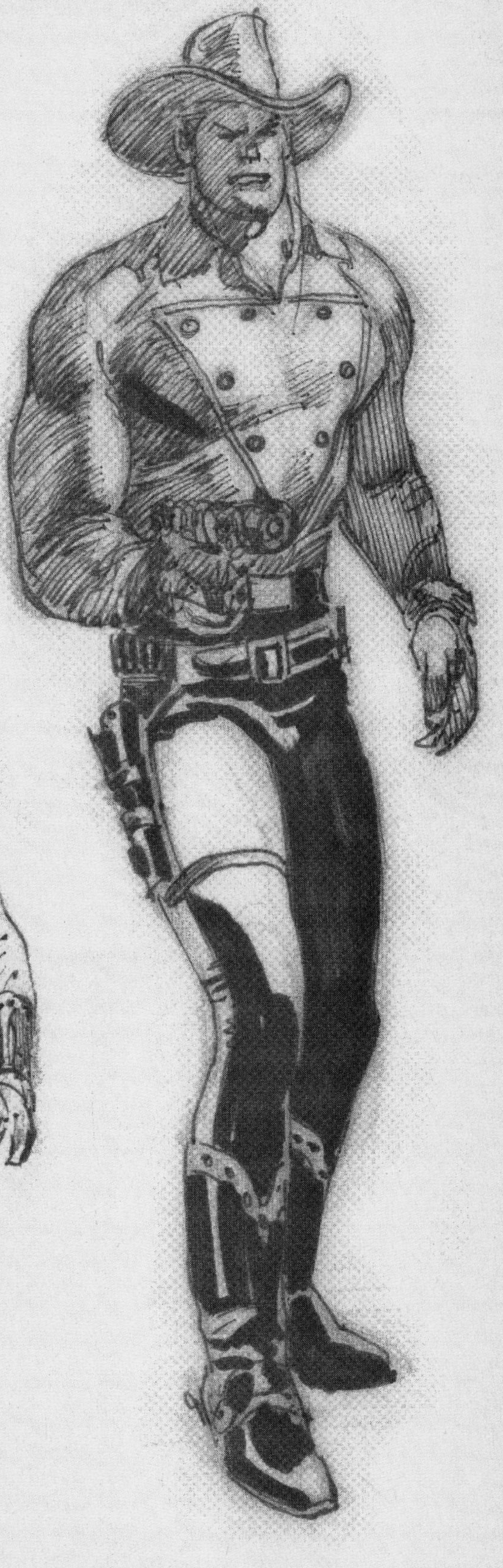

Alternate cover design
by ALAN WEISS for
Chapter One

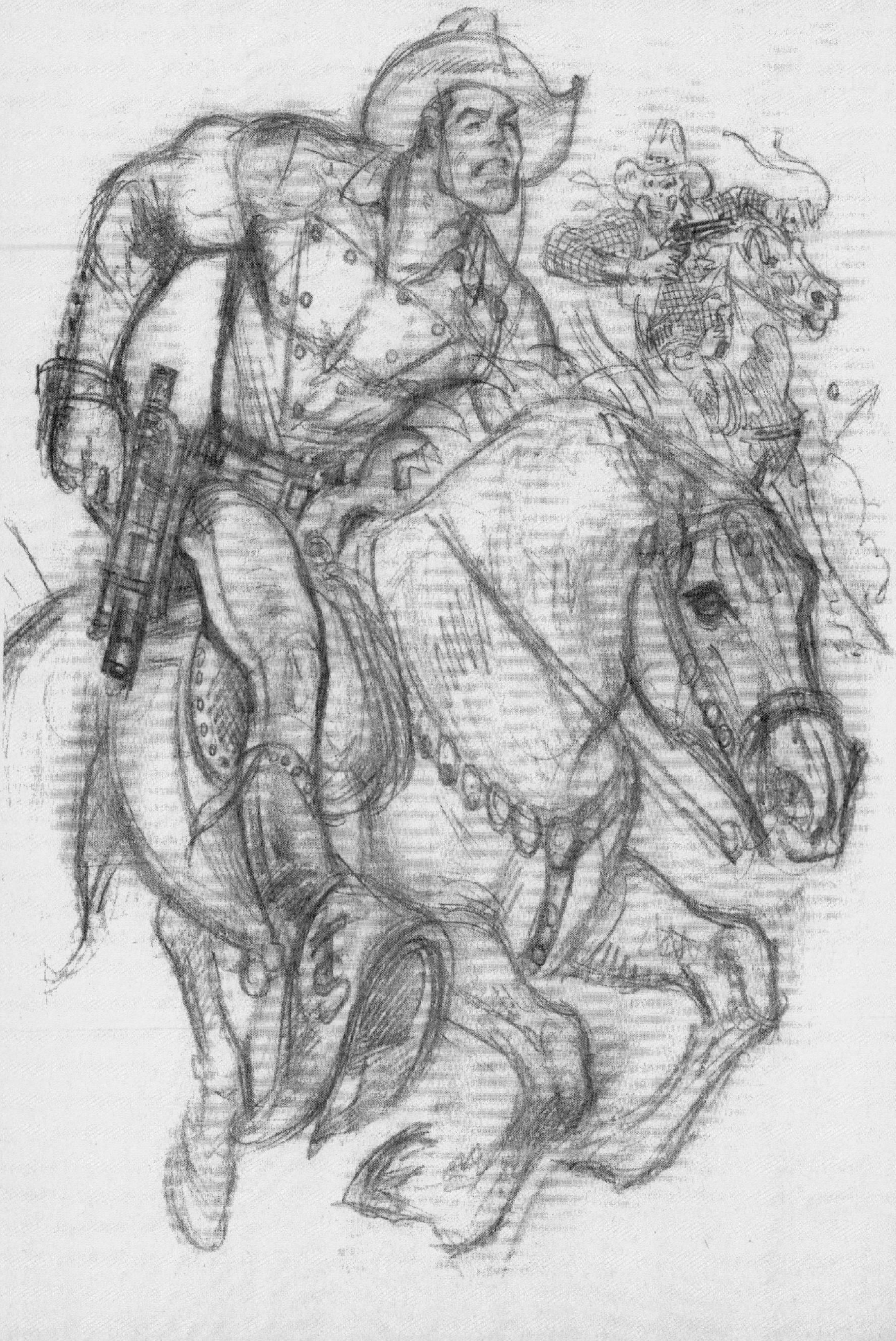

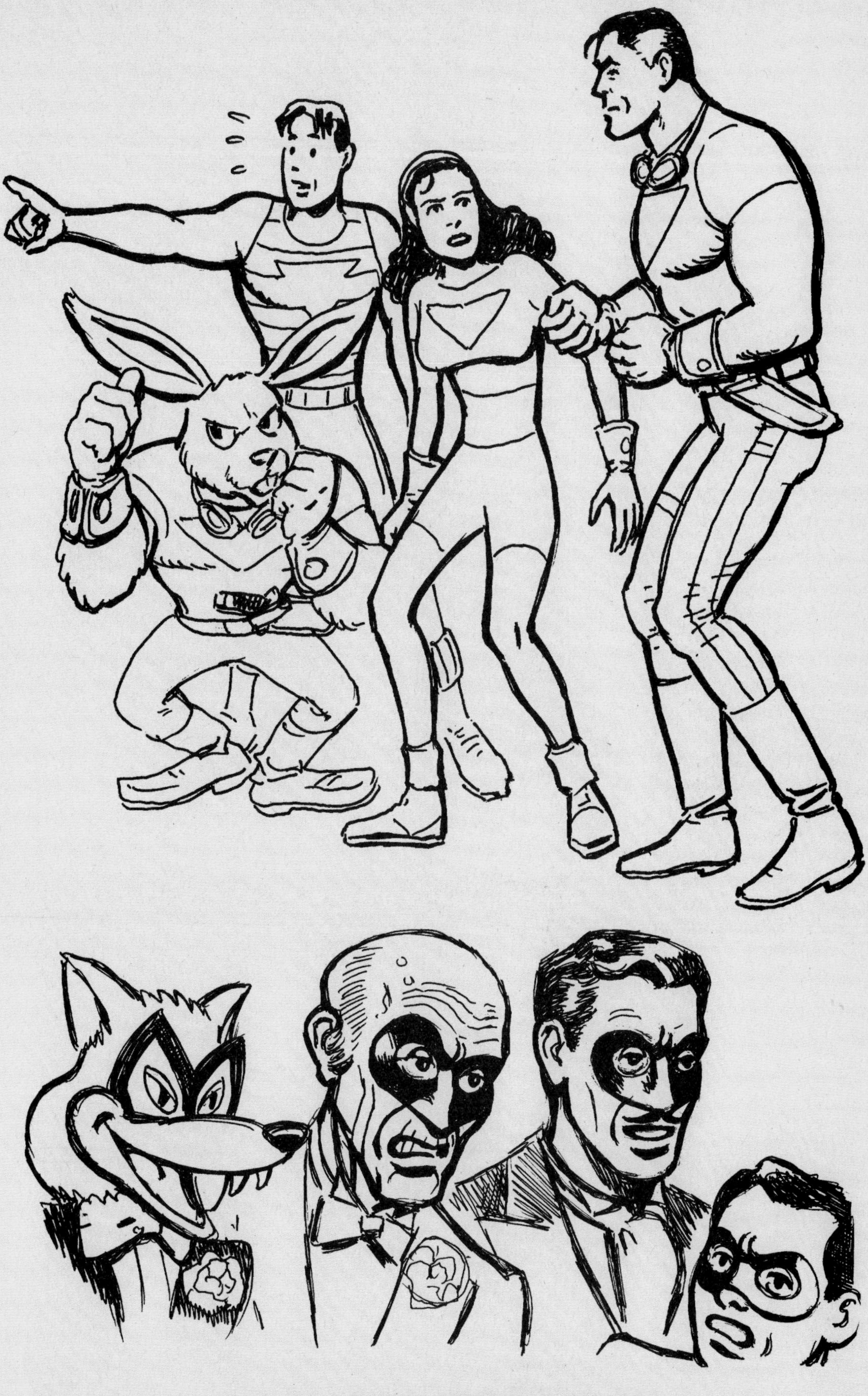

Character sketches by **PETE POPLASKI**
for his story in Chapter Six

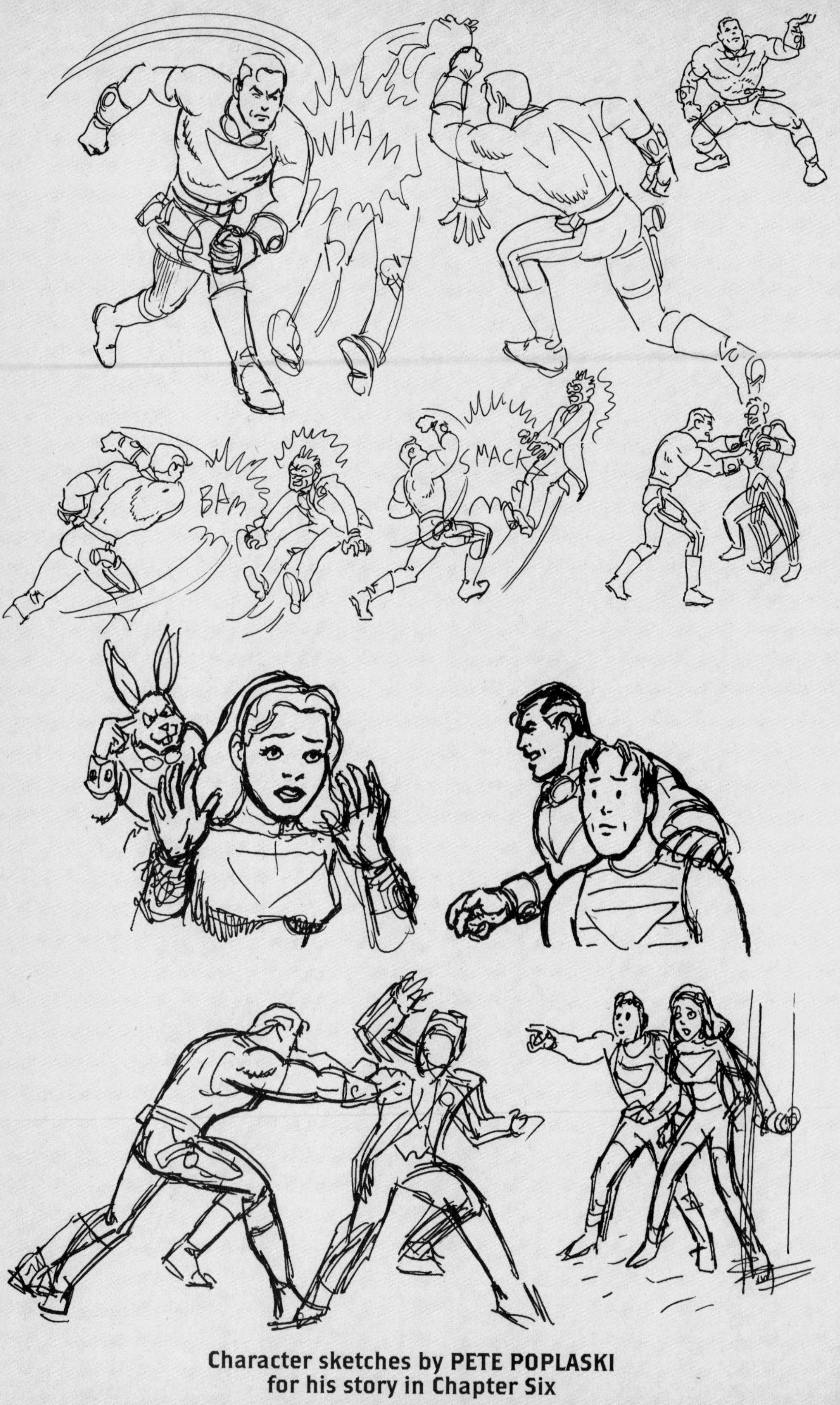
WHAM
BAM
SMACK

Character sketches by PETE POPLASKI for his story in Chapter Six

DEDICATIONS

To Leah, Amber, and Melinda;
To all my family, all my friends.

To Xan, my Doctor Zira,
my Penny Pretty, my
sanctuary.

ALAN MOORE is perhaps the most acclaimed writer in the graphic story medium, having garnered many awards for works such as **WATCHMEN, FROM HELL, MIRACLEMAN, SWAMP THING** and **SUPREME**, among others, along with the many fine artists he has collaborated with on those works. He is currently masterminding the entire America's Best Comics line, writing **PROMETHEA, TOP 10** and **TOMORROW STORIES** in addition to **TOM STRONG**, with more in the planning stages. He resides in central England.

CHRIS SPROUSE, the penciller and co-creator of **TOM STRONG**, began working in comics in 1989, gathering approval for his work on such books as **LEGIONNAIRES**. He previously worked with Alan Moore on **SUPREME**. Chris currently lives in Ohio.

Tom Strong is about a lot of things. If you were to judge from his name, you'd assume it's about strength...though, I think, not the physical kind.

To my Mom, my Dad, and my brother, who taught me about strength.

ALAN GORDON, teamed as inker with Chris on **TOM STRONG**, is a veteran of the comics business, having worked on many projects. Some of his favorites include **WILDSTAR** and **JUSTICE LEAGUE**. He began partnering with Chris on **LEGION OF SUPER-HEROES**, and joined Alan and Chris on **SUPREME**. Al lives in California.

AMERICA'S BEST COMICS COLLECTED EDITIONS

TOM STRONG BOOK 1, BOOK 2
Alan Moore, Chris Sprouse & Alan Gordon

PROMETHEA BOOK 1, BOOK 2
Alan Moore, J. H. Williams III & Mick Gray

TOP 10 BOOK 1, BOOK 2 (Forthcoming)
Alan Moore, Gene Ha & Zander Cannon

THE LEAGUE OF EXTRAORDINARY GENTLEMEN VOLUME 1
Alan Moore, Kevin O'Neill

TOMORROW STORIES BOOK 1
Alan Moore, Kevin Nowlan, Rick Veitch,
Jim Baikie, Melinda Gebbie, Hilary Barta

Look for our magazines each month
at fine comics retailers everywhere.

To locate a comics retailer near you,
call 1-888-COMIC BOOK

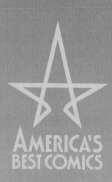

AMERICA'S
BEST COMICS